CELEBRITY CHEFS, FOOD MEDIA AND THE POLITICS OF EATING

Contemporary Food Studies: Economy, Culture and Politics

Series Editors: David Goodman and Michael K. Goodman
ISSN: 2058-1807

This interdisciplinary series represents a significant step toward unifying the study, teaching, and research of food studies across the social sciences. The series features authoritative appraisals of core themes, debates and emerging research, written by leading scholars in the field. Each title offers a jargon-free introduction to upper-level undergraduate and postgraduate students in the social sciences and humanities.

Emma-Jayne Abbots, *The Agency of Eating: Mediation, Food, and the Body*
Terry Marsden, *Agri-Food and Rural Development: Sustainable Place-Making*
Peter Jackson, *Anxious Appetites: Food and Consumer Culture*
Philip H. Howard, *Concentration and Power in the Food System*
Tania Lewis, *Digital Food: From Paddock to Platform*
Hugh Campbell, *Farming inside Invisible Worlds*
Henry Buller & Emma Roe, *Food and Animal Welfare*
Kate Cairns and Josée Johnston, *Food and Femininity*
Claire Lamine, *Sustainable Agri-food Systems: Case Studies in Transitions towards Sustainability from France and Brazil*
Eva Haifa Giraud, *Veganism: Politics, Practice and Theory*

CELEBRITY CHEFS, FOOD MEDIA AND THE POLITICS OF EATING

Joanne Hollows

BLOOMSBURY ACADEMIC
LONDON • NEW YORK • OXFORD • NEW DELHI • SYDNEY

BLOOMSBURY ACADEMIC
Bloomsbury Publishing Plc
50 Bedford Square, London, WC1B 3DP, UK
1385 Broadway, New York, NY 10018, USA
29 Earlsfort Terrace, Dublin 2, Ireland

BLOOMSBURY, BLOOMSBURY ACADEMIC and the Diana logo
are trademarks of Bloomsbury Publishing Plc

First published in Great Britain 2022

Copyright © Joanne Hollows, 2022

Joanne Hollows has asserted her right under the Copyright,
Designs and Patents Act, 1988, to be identified as Author of this work.

For legal purposes the Acknowledgements on p. ix constitute an
extension of this copyright page.

Cover design: Terry Woodley
Cover image © Louis Hansel/Unsplash

All rights reserved. No part of this publication may be reproduced or transmitted
in any form or by any means, electronic or mechanical, including photocopying,
recording, or any information storage or retrieval system, without prior
permission in writing from the publishers.

Bloomsbury Publishing Plc does not have any control over, or responsibility for, any
third-party websites referred to or in this book. All internet addresses given in this
book were correct at the time of going to press. The author and publisher regret
any inconvenience caused if addresses have changed or sites have ceased to
exist, but can accept no responsibility for any such changes.

A catalogue record for this book is available from the British Library.

Library of Congress Control Number: 2022932158

ISBN: HB: 978-1-3501-4572-6
       ePDF: 978-1-3501-4570-2
       eBook: 978-1-3501-4569-6

Series: Contemporary Food Studies: Economy, Culture and Politics

Typeset by Integra Software Services Pvt. Ltd.

To find out more about our authors and books visit www.bloomsbury.com
and sign up for our newsletters

For my mum and dad who raised me in the Church of Delia Smith.

CONTENTS

List of Figures	viii
Acknowledgements	ix
Introduction	1
Chapter 1 Celebrity Chefs, Restaurant Industries And The Culinary Field	13
Chapter 2 Celebrity Chefs And The Media Industries	33
Chapter 3 Food, Health And The Feminine Body	51
Chapter 4 Veganizing Masculinities	69
Chapter 5 Food Heroes, Food Politics And The Campaigning Culinary Documentary	85
Chapter 6 Eat Well For Less: Celebrity Chefs And Austerity Culture	105
Chapter 7 Celebrity Chefs, Food And Nation	125
Chapter 8 Celebrity Chefs And British Food Culture In The Times Of Brexit And Covid-19	147
Notes	170
Bibliography	177
Index	209

LIST OF FIGURES

4.1 Veganized Comfort Food: BOSH! with a finished dish of Pulled 'Pork' Baked Mac & Cheese on their YouTube channel. Author screenshot from: https://youtu.be/uRYU93njJF4   79

8.1 Celebrity chefs are part of political life: Clive Lewis MP carries a Delia Smith – inspired placard at the march for a People's Vote on the Brexit deal, 23 March 2019. (Credit: Emma Hampton)   150

ACKNOWLEDGEMENTS

Without the help of a lot of people, this book would never have got off the ground or been completed. It would also have been a lot worse. Lots of people shared ideas, tips and papers during the course of writing. With apologies to anyone I've forgotten, these include Karen Davis, Lorenzo Domaneschi, Kevin Geddes, Tania Lewis, Jess Martin, Michelle Phillipov, Alexandra Rodney, Estella Tincknell, Karen Throsby, Ana Tominc and Karen Wilkes.

Some people went above and beyond by giving up their scarce time and mental space during a pandemic to read through and give me generous and invaluable feedback on the book. Huge thanks to Jonatan Leer, Nick Piper, Elaine Swan and Ben Taylor and even bigger thanks to David Bell and Mark Jancovich who waded through the entire book. I wasn't up to answering all the issues you raised but I did my best and you've all hugely improved this book.

I would never have got my act together to write this book without the encouragement of Mike Goodman. I am grateful to both Mike and David Goodman for inviting me into their series, the helpful feedback on the proposal and the general sense of cheer, enthusiasm and positivity. I'm also grateful to the two anonymous readers who gave engaged and generous advice which I really valued. Thanks also to Miriam Cantwell at Bloomsbury for initially supporting the project and to Lily McMahon who was very, very patient with me when it was late and offered continued support.

This book would also never have existed without earlier collaborative research with Steve Jones and David Bell and I am incredibly grateful to both of them. Some of the chapters in the book draw on this collective work, particularly on campaigning culinary documentaries and culinary travelogues (Chapters 5, 6 and 7). However, both have contributed so much more by sharing ideas, arguments and resources that allowed me to think about things in ways I would never have done otherwise – and by enabling my addiction to Jamie Oliver's ever-evolving career. Steve's seemingly encyclopaedic knowledge of *Guardian* articles and political commentators was also invaluable in many places in this book.

Finally, thanks to Mark Jancovich for living with me through the lockdowns. I am sure I haven't been the easiest person to live with. I know I should have doomscrolled less and I may have asked you to check my temperature a few too many times! I can't imagine being cooped up for over a year with anyone else. An enormous thanks for the very *very* many kinds of support; the repetitive late afternoon walks round 1970s housing estates and to visit the emu; and the endless evenings spent watching Australian reality TV when we ran out of everything else.

INTRODUCTION

Most of this book was written during the Covid-19 pandemic. The world changed in ways I could never have predicted when I planned this project. During the UK's first lockdown in Spring 2020, it often felt frivolous or irrelevant to be writing a book on celebrity chefs. As a volunteer coordinator with Norwich FoodHub, a local organization that redistributes surplus food to people experiencing food poverty, the urgent and material aspects of food during a pandemic felt rather more pressing. When local restaurants and catering companies were forced to close, we were inundated by waves of high-end stock. At the same time, supermarket surplus became totally unpredictable as many people stockpiled food and retailers struggled to estimate supply and demand as shopping patterns changed. Meanwhile, many people who were already living in precarious conditions were going hungry as lockdown left them with little or no income.

As I wondered whether studying celebrity chefs had any relevance during a pandemic, they rapidly emerged at the centre of numerous lockdown narratives in the British media. Celebrity chefs appeared as representatives of a hospitality sector devastated by the lockdown who attempted to support their workers and take their case to the government. They were celebrated for their resourcefulness as they diversified into an expanding market for high-end meal kits and takeaways. They emerged as heroes feeding local communities and health workers. They used their social media profiles to offer advice on what to cook in unprecedented times. As trusted public figures, celebrity chefs were also put to work to help people get through the 'crisis'. Jamie Oliver, Jack Monroe and Matt Tebutt appeared on quickly thrown together cookery series which lifestyled the lockdown experience while, as the pandemic progressed, Nadiya Hussain and Asma Khan were drafted into the NHS's campaign to tackle alleged vaccine hesitancy among British Bangladeshi communities. Celebrity chefs also joined forces with footballer Marcus Rashford to force changes to government policy in order to address child food poverty, the extent of which had been further exposed and increased by the pandemic (see Chapter 8).

Celebrity chefs might seem frivolous but they are part of the fabric of contemporary life in the UK and elsewhere. Their high-profile media presence means they have a key role in shaping contemporary foodscapes, intervening in ideas about 'what kind of food is being sold, who controls the food system, who eats well (and who does not), as well as how resources are sustained (or deteriorated) through our food practices and engagements' (Johnston and Goodman 2015: 207). At the end of a tumultuous year in the United States, Adam Reiner (2020) claimed that 'the age of the politically agnostic chef is over'. This is perhaps unsurprising as food, the very substance of what celebrity chefs deal with, is political. What is more noteworthy, as Reiner observes, is that more celebrity chefs are explicitly politicizing food practices, whether by representing hospitality workers' interests to the government, campaigning for more environmentally sustainable practices or highlighting how sexism and racism pervade restaurant cultures. Events such as the high-profile MAD symposium in Denmark have called on chefs to take a more informed and explicit acknowledgement of their position, to 'become self-aware about the cultural shift in their activity and … to boost their positions of authority and advocate for better recognition of their alleged contributions to the world' (Matta 2019: 194).

This might seem a long way from someone on television demonstrating how to make a cake but, as I go on to show in this book, even seemingly mundane recipes can be infused with questions about production, provenance and consumption as well as issues about nation, migration and multiculturalism. Celebrity chefs act as 'cultural intermediaries' who practise and popularize particular dispositions towards food and help to shape public understanding of what is 'good' to eat (Bourdieu 1984). These questions about 'good' and 'bad' foods are not only ethical and moral but also deeply political: how food practices are ranked and evaluated creates and reproduces forms of privilege and distinction (Naccarato and Lebesco 2012). Political interventions by celebrity chefs have become more explicit as new formats focus on campaigns to transform government policy and the food industries as well as individual behaviour (Rousseau 2012b). As I show in Chapters 5 and 6, celebrity chefs have used campaigning culinary documentaries to address wide-ranging issues, from the fishing industry and chicken welfare to child obesity and food waste. This book demonstrates, therefore, how celebrity chefs are both implicitly and explicitly bound up with the politics of food and eating.

What is a celebrity chef?

The term 'celebrity chef' is widely used but also deeply problematic. Many people who are described as celebrity chefs claim not to be one. Some television stars like Nigella Lawson and Delia Smith refuse the term 'chef' because their expertise and appeal comes from their experience as home cooks rather than restaurant professionals. This shapes how they represent cooking practices. 'Cooking should not be exclusive or "cheffy". It's about sitting down around a table and having a nice meal', claims Delia (cited in Evening Standard 2012). Likewise, Nigella asserts 'I am not a chef; I am not even a trained cook … I cook in much the same way as my readers or viewers' (cited in Day 2013).

Many restaurant chefs who have found fame on TV also strenuously reject the label celebrity chef. However, their resistance is primarily to associations with celebrity. 'I never chased TV and I am not a celebrity chef', claims former *Masterchef: The Professionals* and *Food and Drink* presenter Michel Roux Jr (Myall 2014). Star of *The Chef's Brigade* and the British version of *My Kitchen Rules* Jason Atherton assures people that 'I'm a chef not a celebrity. I'm not interested in fame' (Thompson 2016). Back in 2001, Gordon Ramsay – who many people might consider epitomizes the celebrity chef – announced 'I am not a celebrity chef' and claimed that his TV appearances were 'about giving something back to the [hospitality] industry' (BBC News 2001). As I go on to explain in Chapter 1, these vehement refusals of the label need to be understood within the logic of the culinary field in which the pursuit of celebrity and economic success can threaten a chef's claims to legitimacy as a skilled and gifted professional. Nonetheless, it is not only high-profile restaurant chefs who resist associations with celebrity. Delia Smith and Jack Monroe refuse the term 'chef' but they also refuse the term 'celebrity' because it threatens the sense of being 'ordinary' that is, in different ways, central to their brands.

However, the label celebrity chef is widely used by the media to classify people with a public profile that is primarily associated with cooking. The use of the term may have little conceptual precision; it may unite people with significantly different levels of cooking expertise and fame. But it is also widely understood to refer to people who are famous for cooking and whose fame is the product of a significant media presence because, as Jessica Evans argues, 'celebrity *by definition* requires mediation' (cited in Driessens 2013: 548).

The forms of mediation through which people gain celebrity vary. Chapter 1 demonstrates how some big-name celebrity chefs whose standing is attached to their restaurant may make few television appearances but their reputation is shaped by newspaper restaurant reviews, food magazines and guides such as Michelin. However, television has played a key role in the development of the celebrity chef and, as I explain in Chapter 2, many well-known celebrity chefs are TV personalities as well as food experts. An on-screen presence in people's homes creates a sense of closeness between viewer and celebrity and the feeling that we 'know' them (Bennett 2010). Furthermore, while social media platforms afford established celebrities opportunities to develop their image and attain a seemingly more immediate relationship with their fans (Bennett 2010), new digital platforms such as blogs, Instagram and YouTube have also enabled the emergence of new celebrity chefs (see Lewis 2020). As I explore in Chapters 3 and 4, some of today's successful celebrity chef brands such as Deliciously Ella and BOSH! are the products of digital media.

Celebrity chefs are not the only public figures who shape ideas about what and how to eat. Josée Johnston and Mike Goodman (2015: 206, 210) refer to 'food celebrities' and 'food personalities' to capture the range of celebrities who have become 'voices of cultural and culinary authority', from Gwyneth Paltrow's association with 'healthy eating' to George Clooney's close associations with the Nespresso brand (see also Rodney et al. 2017). While celebrity chefs are included in the idea of the 'food celebrity', Johnston and Goodman highlight the multiple and diverse ways in which celebrity figures intervene in public debates about food, often taking on a campaigning role. Although most of this book concentrates on celebrity chefs, their interventions need to be understood within this wider landscape. For example, as I go on to demonstrate in my analysis of campaigns against food poverty during the pandemic (Chapter 8), celebrity chefs joined forces with footballer Marcus Rashford who has emerged as a highly influential new food celebrity.

This book, therefore, uses the term 'celebrity chef' in ways that mirror its popular usage. What distinguishes celebrity chefs from the more general categories of food personalities and food celebrities is their close association with the practice of cooking. Whether primarily known as a Michelin-starred restaurant chef, a TV chef or founder of a YouTube cookery channel, the key figures in this book are celebrities who are mainly known for cooking. However, as I go on to show, their influence extends way beyond the kitchen as they use the culinary capital obtained through their roles in restaurants and the media to become significant public and political actors.

Studying celebrity chefs

The study of celebrity chefs emerged out of a wider context. On the one hand, celebrities in general achieved a new visibility in popular culture and public life in the 1990s. Celebrity studies emerged as an academic sub-field that tried to make sense of the role of celebrities and to investigate the processes of celebritization that produced celebrity as, at least partly, a new phenomenon (see, for example, the journal *Celebrity Studies*; Cashmore 2006; Marshall 1997; Redmond and Holmes 2007; Rojek 2001; and Turner 2004). From the late 1990s, there was also a rapid expansion in food television which provoked academic interest in new forms of entertainment-led food programming which foregrounded a new type of celebrity chef (see Chapter 2). In the United States, this produced studies of the Food Network cable TV channel (for example, Adema 2000; Ketchum 2005, 2007; Naccarato and Lebesco 2012) and also spawned an interest in the history of cookery TV (for example, Collins 2009; Polan 2011). In the UK, the rise of lifestyle programming on broadcast TV from the late 1990s onwards provided the context for an increasing interest in new forms of cookery programme that represented cooking and eating as lifestyle practices (for example, Brunsdon 2003, 2006; Hollows 2003a, 2003b; Moseley 2000, 2001) with similar interests also emerging in Australia (for example, Bonner 2003; de Solier 2005; Lewis 2008a). The study of both celebrities and celebrity chefs also developed alongside a growing interest in the relationships between food, culture and society across a range of academic disciplines such as sociology and geography (for example, Beardsworth and Keil 1997; Bell and Valentine 1997; Warde 1997) which later also became more established in media and cultural studies (for example, Ashley et al. 2004) and other disciplines such as linguistics (for example, Matwick and Matwick 2019 and Tominc 2017).

Much research, my own included, has often been preoccupied with the contemporary and there has been far less interest in the history of celebrity chefs.

Research by Ferguson (2004) shows how, in the nineteenth century, chef Marie-Antoine Carême achieved a significant cultural impact and was a prototype of later celebrity chefs in his development of own-brand products and a media profile (see Chapter 1). However, most historical research has focused on TV chefs in the immediate pre-war and the post-war period: for example, Julia Child (Polan 2011), Marguerite Patten (Charlesworth 2022; Moseley 2009), Fanny Cradock (Geddes 2018), Marcel Boulestin (Geddes 2022) and Philip Harben (Geddes 2022). This research demonstrates the long-running influence of celebrity chefs on ideas about how and what to eat, a dynamic relationship between education and entertainment, a persistent gendering of ideas about cookery and some significant continuities between past and present. It also contributes to the history of factual programming on TV (see also Bonner 2009). While there is now a developing history of celebrity chefs on early European television (Tominc 2022a), historical research presents a particular challenge as copies of many old TV cookery shows no longer exist (Tominc 2022b).

While the role of the media in shaping how people eat is not a recent phenomenon, there has been an intensification in 'media interventions into how we think about what we put into our bodies' (Rousseau 2012b: xxxiii). Celebrity chefs, like the producers of food media in general, may not determine how people think about food but they are both a key source of information and knowledge about food and a 'resource' offering 'possibilities, guides and recommendations' about what and how to eat (Dickinson 1998: 267). However, the advice and information they offer is not neutral and is frequently highly normative: celebrity chefs shape ideas about 'what becomes "permissible" and "normal" as well as "desired" in everyday discourses, practices and institutional processes' (Boykoff et al. 2010: 5). Recommendations about how and what to eat, therefore, are shaped by assumptions about what are legitimate food practices and – often by implication or exclusion – which food practices are illegitimate or of little value. As I go on to show throughout this book, advice on eating healthily or ethically, for example, is bound up both with the politics of class, gender and race and with discourses that can naturalize political systems built on inequality.

Many of these issues emerge in a key theme of much research – the role of celebrity chefs as lifestyle experts. Many researchers were fascinated by new television series such as *The Naked Chef* and *Nigella Bites* which emerged in the late 1990s and early 2000s (for example, de Solier 2005; Hollows 2003a, 2003b; Lewis 2008a; and Moseley 2001). In these series, Jamie Oliver and Nigella Lawson did not simply educate and inform people about how to cook but demonstrated how food practices were part of a wider lifestyle. Images of Jamie Oliver zipping around London delis on his Vespa and making food to be consumed at his band's practice session demonstrated how cooking practices could be situated 'in the art and aesthetics of everyday living' (Lewis 2020: 8). These shows were seen to offer valuable advice on how to live at a time when there had been an alleged detraditionalization of established ways of life. As Rachel Moseley (2001: 39) argued, Jamie Oliver appeared to sell 'a whole lifestyle through a discourse of accessibility and achievability, of a way to be through clothes, looks, domestic space and ways of being a man'. From such a perspective, celebrity chefs could be seen to democratize knowledge and skills so everyone could use food to construct distinctive lifestyles. Acting as cultural intermediaries, celebrity chefs appeared to make 'available to almost everyone the distinctive poses, the distinctive games and other signs of inner riches' which were previously only associated with an intellectual elite (Bourdieu 1984: 371). However, as I explain in Chapter 2, while these celebrity chefs might have appeared to democratize food knowledges, their series represented particular types of lifestyles associated with the new middle classes as *the* legitimate way to live and, by implication, rendered other lifestyles as less legitimate.

Since this period, many researchers have examined how celebrity chefs represent particular kinds of food practices as the only legitimate food practices. As Peter Naccarato and Kathleen Lebesco (2012: 113) argue, celebrity chefs may offer access to particular forms of 'culinary capital' but this 'requires adherence to a set of privileged practices, thereby reinforcing specific cultural values and ideologies'. Many researchers, myself included, have studied how particular ways of cooking and eating are given value and held up as models of 'good' and 'appropriate' living. This is evident in the representations of food as a cool, pleasurable and youthful leisure activity in *The Naked Chef* but also in representations of the pleasures of ethical eating in the bucolic rural locations of Hugh Fearnley-Whittingstall's *River Cottage* series in the UK and Matthew Evans' *Gourmet Farmer* in Australia (see, for example, Bell and Hollows 2011; Parkins and Craig 2011; and Phillipov 2017). These themes are developed throughout much of this book: for example, in my analysis of how particular forms of 'healthy eating' are legitimated (Chapters 3 and 6), the mainstreaming of plant-based diets (Chapter 4), the representation of environmentally responsible food practices (Chapter 5) and ideas of 'national' foods (Chapter 7).

Given women's longstanding responsibility for feeding work in the domestic sphere, it is perhaps unsurprising that much research has also focused on how celebrity chefs mediate ideas about gender and food. This can again be found in studies of Jamie Oliver and Nigella Lawson that investigated how they represented cooking and eating as specifically gendered lifestyle practices (see, for example, Hollows 2003a, 2003b; Leer 2016b; Moseley 2001; Sanders 2008). When celebrity chefs such as Jamie Oliver took on responsibility for cooking in domestic space, it was sometimes seen as a sign of progress towards a more equal gendered division of domestic labour. However, *The Naked Chef* was among a number of series that represented domestic cookery as a pleasurable, masculine leisure practice rather than part of the work of caring for the family that was a longstanding feature of feminine domestic labour (Hollows 2003a; Leer 2016a, 2016b, 2017, 2018; Rodney et al. 2017). Furthermore, many male TV chefs occupy far more conventional gender roles – for example, as mobile adventurers in culinary travelogues as I show in Chapter 7 (see, for example, Bell and Hollows 2007; Leer and Kjaer 2015) or making political interventions in the public sphere as I demonstrate in Chapters 5, 6 and 8 (see also, for example, Bell et al. 2017; Gibson and Dempsey 2013; Hollows and Jones 2010b; Pike and Kelly

2014; Rich 2011; Rousseau 2012b; Warin 2011). Moreover, many male celebrity chefs are still firmly associated with professional roles in restaurant kitchens, reproducing the assumption that professional cooking is still a primarily masculine occupation and the idea that 'great chefs' are male (see, for example, Johnston et al. 2014).

Much of the research on celebrity chefs has largely been the product of textual analysis of TV shows. Textual analysis alone, however, tells us little about what people make of their advice and interventions or about the extent and nature of the influence that celebrity chefs have on everyday cooking practices. Audience research by scholars such as Nick Piper (2013, 2015) and Christine Barnes (2017) addresses some of these absences by demonstrating the complex ways in which people engage with, use and resist advice from celebrity chefs (see Chapter 2). Other researchers have explored how professional chefs understand 'celebrity' and media engagement and the impact it has on their career trajectories (see, for example, Lee 2014 and Curnutt 2015; see Chapter 1). Celebrity chefs do not simply appear from nowhere. Their brands are not only developed by specialist PR agents (see Chapter 2) but also through the work of TV producers and other media professionals who help to create cookery TV, cookbooks and social media content. Researchers such as Gilly Smith (2020), David Inglis and Ana-Mari Almila (2019) and Luke van Ryn (2018) offer insights into how media production practices shape food television and the careers of celebrity chefs.

As the discussion above suggests, many debates about celebrity chefs have centred around television – and, to a lesser extent, cookbooks – because these are the media spaces where many celebrity chefs established their profile. However, as the distinctions between 'older' and 'newer' media forms become less meaningful, digital media are fertile spaces for building celebrity chef brands. As Mike Goodman and Sylvia Jaworska (2020: 3) observe, while established 'TV-based food celebrities' migrate onto digital platforms, 'many have been eclipsed or are in competition with the likes of food vloggers, bloggers and other personalities who originated in these digital food landscapes and then move into "offline" spaces'. This is reflected in a range of recent publications that try to get to grips with the specificity, affordances and content of digital food media (Leer and Strøm Krogager 2021; Lewis 2020; Lupton and Feldman 2020; see also the earlier Rousseau 2012a). While many of the chapters in this book focus on TV texts and their associated intertexts, I also consider the new forms of 'celebrity chef' that emerge out of blogging platforms and YouTube and how they have shaped food knowledges (see Chapters 2, 3 and 4).

However, in order to understand the significance of celebrity chefs, one cannot stay for very long with one textual or media form. Their interventions and influence spill out in many directions across social media and newspaper commentary, into parliamentary committees and mass petitions, via supermarket endorsements and product advertising and into our kitchens through the recipes we cook, the chopping techniques we adopt or the celebrity-branded pans or sauces we use. In order to understand the significance of celebrity chefs in contemporary culture, this book attempts to follow them as they veer off in many directions.

About this book

This book examines food media to demonstrate how celebrity chefs have shaped the politics of eating in the UK in the twenty-first century. Adopting an interdisciplinary approach, I examine how celebrity chefs shape how we feed ourselves and how we think about food and its role in social and cultural life. The book demonstrates how celebrity chefs act as cultural intermediaries who not only play a role in defining what is 'good' and 'bad' food but also how we should shop, cook and eat. As I go on to show, their advice is entangled with wider questions about class, gender, race, health and the environment that extend beyond the culinary field. In food media, judgements about the value of food practices are also often judgements about the value – and values – of different groups of people. The book demonstrates how celebrity chefs impact on many aspects of contemporary life, from ideas about healthy eating and veganism through to food scares and fish sustainability. I highlight how some celebrity chefs have also become activists and campaigners who intervene in public policy and become caught up with contemporary politics around racism, Brexit and food poverty.

The early chapters of this book introduce the emergence and characteristics of different types of celebrity chef and their relationships to food media. While some restaurant-based chefs are dependent on media to promote their businesses, other celebrity chefs such as Jamie Oliver, Giada De Laurentiis and Guy Fieri are primarily TV stars. Others such as Andrew Rea – famed for his YouTube channel Binging with Babish – emerge as celebrities through digital media. Across the first four chapters, I demonstrate the power of celebrity chefs and how they shape the meaning of food and the ways in which this intersects with lived experience and the politics of everyday life. The second part of the book examines how celebrity chefs have adopted a more explicitly political role as they have become public figures who act as political intermediaries who seek to effect change.

While interdisciplinary in nature, the book's approach lies on the cusp between food studies and media and cultural studies. To understand contemporary food media, it is necessary to think about the significance of both media (the forms, practices and genres that shape how meaning is produced) and food (production, distribution, regulation and consumption) together. The conceptual framework and theoretical perspectives I engage with throughout are shaped by both fields as I think about issues ranging from taste and provenance to inequality and neoliberalism. Crucially, I think about how celebrity chefs are produced through the logics of two distinct but overlapping fields – the culinary field and the field of media.

Given the proliferation of both food media and celebrity chefs, I have narrowed down my field of study by largely focusing on celebrity chefs in the UK. However, many of the celebrity chefs I discuss – for example, Jamie Oliver and Gordon Ramsay – are well-established global brands whose output is sold across a range of territories and who also produce content tailored to different national and supranational markets. Even back in the early 2000s, I kept finding that Jamie Oliver followed me on holiday. In a Brittany bookshop, I discovered tables stacked high with French translations of his early cookbooks, recommending his accessible style with the description *'sans chichi ni tralala'* [without fuss or frills]. In Hamburg, I saw a large cut out of Jamie Oliver with the line 'Englands Junger Spitzenkoch' [England's young top chef] in the window of a kitchen shop. In Copenhagen, a restaurant casually displayed a copy of a Jamie Oliver cookbook on shelves while I ate my dinner. The global success of British celebrity chefs in the period is backed up by less anecdotal evidence. In 2002, Oliver's newly launched television company Fresh One produced the series *Oliver's Twist* to launch him in a global market. It was 'sold to over 200 territories' (Barraclough 2014). It was not only Oliver's cookbooks and cooking series that found audiences abroad. His campaigning documentaries aired in a range of international markets and also spawned localized versions such as *Jamie Oliver's Food Revolution* in the United States. Numerous British celebrity chefs, therefore, have a massive international reach. Alongside Jamie Oliver, celebrity chefs such as Gordon Ramsay and Nigella Lawson are global stars. On *Masterchef Australia* contestants swoon when British-based chefs such as Yotam Ottolenghi, Nigella Lawson or Heston Blumenthal make appearances, demonstrating the extent of their star power.

The influence of British food media cannot simply be understood in terms of these celebrity chefs alone and producers such as Pat Llewellyn played a key role in creating new forms of British cookery television that had a huge international influence (see Chapter 2). The development of lifestyle cookery programming in Britain in the late 1990s which enabled the emergence of new types of celebrity chefs such as Jamie and Nigella also impacted on the types of celebrity chefs that emerged elsewhere. Celebrity chefs such as Tim Mälzer in Germany and Bill Granger in Australia were hailed as the home-grown version of Jamie Oliver. British lifestyle cookery formats were adopted and adapted in different locations: for example, Ana Tominc (2017) documents how Luka and Valentina Smej Novak emerged as celebrity chefs in Slovenia by employing elements of these formats. Therefore, while the focus of this book is on British celebrity chefs, the global influence of the UK on food media means that the discussion has a much wider resonance.

Furthermore, as I go on to show, it is increasingly difficult to think of food media simply in national terms. While there is a well-established global trade in food television programmes and formats – especially after the rise of specialist cable and satellite channels devoted to food – the development of streaming services such as Netflix has made conventional national boundaries of transmission less important, although far from irrelevant. Furthermore, the emergence of new forms of food media and celebrity chefs on social media platforms such as YouTube also makes it increasingly difficult to think about celebrity chefs in strictly national terms. Therefore, while my focus is the UK, the themes, arguments and texts I discuss have purchase across a range of different national and supranational contexts, although how the politics of food media play out frequently has a specifically national flavour and resonance.

In Chapters 1 and 2, I explore how 'celebrity' can operate in different ways for those celebrity chefs primarily operating in the gastronomic realm of restaurants and those whose celebrity is primarily a product of their role as television personalities. Chapter 1 examines how celebrity operates in the culinary field that shapes the careers and standing of chefs. I demonstrate that, while celebrity status in the culinary field is primarily associated with qualities such as artistry and innovation, star chefs in the restaurant industry are nonetheless dependent on the media to achieve visibility and promote their brands. I investigate the role of food media in building chefs' profiles through an analysis of series such as Netflix's *Chef's Table* and *The Final Table*. Drawing on the work of Pierre Bourdieu, I show how celebrity in the culinary field involves a delicate balancing act between investing in the chef's art and pursuing economic success and fame. I also demonstrate how the culinary field, like other cultural fields, is based on exclusion and highlight how gender, race and ethnicity impact on a chef's ability to achieve success, visibility and celebrity.

Chapter 2 explores celebrity chefs in relation to the media industries. The chapter offers a brief history of celebrity chefs and cookery TV before going on to examine the significance of the new wave of celebrity chefs who emerged in lifestyle television formats from the late 1990s onwards. I highlight how the conventions of food television shape the ways in which different lifestyle choices, tastes and food practices are mediated and how this produces, and reproduces, classed and gendered distinctions. The chapter demonstrates how celebrity chefs' brands are negotiated across different sites and media and how established celebrity chefs have increasingly migrated across a range of digital platforms. I also show how these digital platforms have enabled the emergence of new forms of food celebrity and question whether this has led to the democratization of culinary expertise.

Chapters 3 and 4 largely focus on celebrity chefs who emerged via digital platforms and both explore the gendering of food practices. In Chapter 3, I examine how celebrity chefs mediate ideas about 'healthy eating'. Through an analysis of 'clean eating' practices associated with the Deliciously Ella blog, I demonstrate how women are encouraged to use food as a form of self-care and empowerment within a wider neoliberal context in which people are increasingly responsibilized for their own health while welfare provision is eroded. Blogs such as Deliciously Ella promise an end to diets while continuing to identify femininity with a slender and glowing (white) body. As a contrast, I examine the hugely successful Pinch of Nom, a multi-platform diet brand led by 'anti-celebrity' chefs, to demonstrate how diets can also be used as a mode of classed resistance to middle-class forms of 'healthism' (Crawford 2006). In Chapter 4, I focus on the rise of male celebrity chefs promoting vegan diets through an analysis of BOSH!, Avant-Garde Vegan and the Dirty Vegan. The chapter demonstrates how the potentially feminine associations of plant-based eating are displaced through a masculinization of veganism, partly achieved through a meatification of vegan foods. While these celebrity chefs have helped to mainstream vegan eating, I show how they also represent plant-based diets in terms of an aesthetics of lifestyle and consumer choice, downplaying many of the political dimensions of ethical veganism.

In Chapter 5, I turn to the more overtly political roles adopted by celebrity chefs that use the televisual format of the campaigning culinary documentary. The chapter introduces the key features of the format and identifies how it emerged as a key strand in British food TV, and as a key vehicle for building celebrity chefs' brands, which was also deployed in other national contexts – for example, in Matthew Evans *For the Love of Meat* (2016) in Australia (Phillipov 2017). Through a case study of Hugh Fearnley-Whittingstall's campaigning culinary documentaries which focus on the ethical and environmental aspects of food, I identify how the format enables celebrity chefs to emerge as public figures who not only seek to transform viewers' practices but also intervene in public policy, institutions and the food industry.

Campaigning culinary documentaries are also part of my focus in Chapter 6 which analyses how celebrity chefs mediated the virtues of frugality and thrift during a period of austerity policies implemented by the UK government. I demonstrate how celebrity chefs contributed to a range of austerity narratives, frequently using visual motifs and discourses associated with 'austerity chic'. The chapter shows how Jamie Oliver and Hugh Fearnley-Whittingstall used campaigning culinary documentaries that, while not uncritical of government actions, naturalized austerity policies by demonstrating how 'bad' and 'unhealthy' food practices – and the (working-class) people associated with them – were an unnecessary drain on the welfare state. The chapter also examines how the BBC 'makeover' series *Eat Well for Less* with celebrity chefs Gregg Wallace and Chris Bavin reinforced the values of thrift and frugality. However, the chapter also shows that celebrity chefs did not make uniform response to the austerity agenda and highlights the significance of Jack Monroe who used food media to construct an anti-austerity position that challenged government policy and its demonization of the poor.

The culinary travelogue is another TV format that has proved useful in building celebrity chefs' brands and, in Chapter 7, I explore how these shows mediate ideas about the nation and national cuisines. Although the chapter focuses on British examples, the culinary travelogue is a format that is put to work in many similar ways across a range of national and international contexts. I examine how celebrity chefs such as Rick Stein and the Hairy Bikers represent British food in limited and conservative ways and imagine Britishness in relation to a pre-modern past that can easily be traded in a global television market for 'heritage'. Using case studies focusing on Jamie Oliver and Nadiya Hussain, I explore how celebrity chefs have attempted to represent a more 'diverse' and 'multicultural' Britain and their impact on ideas about both Britishness and British food. Finally, I identify how Jamie Oliver's culinary travelogues around continental Europe use identifications with Europe to reflect on the problems with British food practices.

If food is caught up in wider political agendas (DeSoucey 2010), it is perhaps unsurprising that, as key public authorities on culinary matters, celebrity chefs respond to political currents. For examples, chefs' interventions in debates about #MeToo and Black Lives Matter have been important across a range of national contexts. In Chapter 8, I examine how celebrity chefs intervened in two of the major political events in early twenty-first-century Britain: Brexit and the Covid-19 pandemic. In the first half of the chapter, I chart Jamie Oliver's often contradictory position-taking within Brexit's discursive framework – from the pro-European identifications explored in Chapter 7, via anti-EU positions in debates about food regulation through to pro-EU identifications in the aftermath of the 2016 Referendum on membership of the EU. In the process, I demonstrate how national and supranational identities were mobilized in celebrity chefs' campaigns about food safety in relation to government negotiations on a new trade deal with the United States. The second part of the chapter examines the role of celebrity chefs in response to the pandemic. I focus on two particular examples – lockdown cookery shows and campaigns about food poverty associated with footballer Marcus Rashford – and identify two key meanings of austerity that emerged in response to the pandemic: austerity as the absence of consumer choice about food and austerity as the absence of food.

Much of this book highlights how celebrity chefs are contradictory figures. They act as moral entrepreneurs who help to form public opinion and feeling and shape the contemporary imagination about food matters. They recruit people to campaigns while also polarizing public opinion. While much of my argument demonstrates how the narratives, discourses and makeovers used by celebrity chefs help to reproduce unequal power relations, they also act as public figures that hold government and industry to account. And, as I demonstrate in Chapter 8, food celebrities also have the capacity to reshape the ways in which political issues are imagined and to empower people to engage in collective action.

Chapter 1

CELEBRITY CHEFS, RESTAURANT INDUSTRIES AND THE CULINARY FIELD

While most of this book focuses on celebrity chefs as media figures, this chapter focuses on how celebrity operates within the restaurant industry and the culinary field. Many star restaurant chefs do not become television chefs or other kinds of media celebrity yet they still use the media to build their profiles. Using the media to build a brand is now part of the job of many chefs who own or lead restaurants. For some chefs, this might involve TV appearances or columns in the press; for many more, posting on social media platforms like Twitter and Instagram has become part of their everyday labour (Giousmpasoglou et al. 2019; Lee 2014). While some chefs trade a career in the kitchen for one in TV (Curnutt 2015), even chefs with little desire for media attention often build social media profiles to promote their restaurants.

However, the pursuit of celebrity, fame and money poses risks for the professional reputation of chefs. Chefs may be keen to distance themselves from the label 'celebrity chef' because they want to be recognized for their culinary skills as chefs rather than their ability to entertain media audiences. In order to think through these issues, I distinguish between different forms of culinary celebrity. For some chefs, their celebrity comes from their position within the 'culinary field' (Ferguson 2001). Examples include chefs such as Ferran Adrià, the Roca brothers and Massimo Bottura whose position is primarily a result of their critical reception within the culinary field as they earn awards and rave reviews from influential restaurant critics. Other chefs use celebrity as a 'competitive resource' that enables them to move across a range of fields, building a wider media profile (Driessens 2013). The reputation of celebrity chefs such as Jamie Oliver, Ainsley Harriott, Manu Feidel and Anthony Bourdain is, in different ways, largely a result of their media exposure. As I go on to show, many chefs attempt to balance the quest for legitimacy and professional recognition with the desire for financial success and a public profile. The next two sections explore these issues by examining the role of branding and celebrity in the restaurant industries.

I then explore two case studies of how chefs are branded in different kinds of formats within cookery TV. The first focuses on competition formats featuring professional chefs such as *Top Chef* in the United States, the *Great British Menu* in the UK and Netflix's international battle of the chefs *The Final Table* and examines chefs' roles as contestants, judges and mentors within what is essentially a reality TV format. The second explores documentary formats such as Netflix's *Chef's Table* which create portraits of star chefs as gifted artists who are characterized by their unique vision and creativity. The discussion raises questions about how the operation of the culinary field produces and reproduces inequalities based on gender and race, themes which the final section of the chapter develops.

Branding, celebrity and the restaurant industry

As branding has become more important within the restaurant industry, many chefs have used the media to raise their public profile and build a brand identity. Some of the most widely known celebrity chefs have built brands that combine a high-profile media presence with extensive business interests, both within the restaurant industry and beyond. While Gordon Ramsay had already achieved professional recognition with two Michelin stars prior to achieving media fame, his TV career grew alongside his ownership of restaurants. The launch of his first restaurant as a chef-proprietor in 1998 gained huge levels of visibility as the subject of the Channel 4 documentary series *Boiling Point* (1998) which followed his mission to gain three Michelin stars. The series established key elements of Ramsay's brand image as a celebrity chef: expletive-ridden bursts of temper that expressed an overwhelming passion for the highest culinary standards (Higgens et al. 2012). This brand was cemented in many of his subsequent TV series in Britain and beyond such as *Ramsay's Kitchen Nightmares* (2004–7) and *Ramsay's Kitchen Nightmares USA* (2007–14), the UK and US versions of *Hell's Kitchen* (2004; 2005–) and in *The F-Word* (2005–10). Meanwhile, he built up an international restaurant empire that was branded by his passion for quality, set up his own TV production company, published numerous books, established partnerships for his own range of tableware and launched the gaming app Restaurant DASH (Gordon Ramsay n.d.). Although in many ways Ramsay is now as much a 'celebrity CEO' as a celebrity chef (Boyle and Kelly 2010; Littler 2007), careful branding has resulted in considerable financial success and four of his restaurants still have Michelin stars. Although Gordon Ramsay is far from typical, economic security in the restaurant industry is often dependent on a distinctive and recognizable brand and a well-developed social media profile.[1]

Although I go on to explain why branding became so important to contemporary chefs, it isn't an entirely new phenomenon. In nineteenth-century France, 'the first celebrity chef' Marie-Antoine Carême (Kelly 2003) was 'an extraordinarily gifted cultural entrepreneur … whose celebrity extended beyond the kitchen to the culture at large' (Ferguson 2003: 40). His culinary creations were discussed in the press and by famous novelists like Alexandre Dumas and Emile Zola, while his cookbooks reached huge readerships for the period (Ibid.: 42–6). Carême also understood the importance of branding the self: he invented a distinctive white chef's hat that gave him a signature visual style and lent his name to a range of 'time-saving stock concentrates' (Ferguson 2004: 170). Therefore, while the obligation to brand is a result of changes in late twentieth-century culinary culture, some of the branding techniques used are far from new.

The increased use of marketing, PR and branding, including more pressure on chefs to engage in self-branding, is not simply a result of changes in the restaurant industry: during the late twentieth century, promotional activity intensified and permeated 'all areas of society, at the organizational, social and individual levels' (Davis 2013: 5). However, the importance of branding to contemporary chefs also has its roots in changes in the culture of restaurants. With the rise of nouvelle cuisine in France from the late 1960s, many ambitious chefs who wanted to challenge the established conventions of gastronomy chose to become chef-proprietors to emphasize their economic and cultural 'autonomy' (Rao et al. 2003: 798), opening their own restaurants rather than working for a restaurant or hotel owner (Gillespie 1994; Mennell 1996). These new chef-proprietors didn't just cook but had to become 'cultural entrepreneurs' engaged in a wide range of activities (Ferguson 2004: 159); they had 'to juggle to resolve artistic, marketing (especially branding) and financial imperatives' (Gillespie 1994: 21). Given the costs of launching a restaurant, celebrity and publicity became increasingly necessary for gaining a profile in a highly competitive restaurant trade (Ashley et al. 2004).

Nouvelle cuisine not only transformed some chefs into entrepreneurs but was also associated with the idea of the chef as artist. Nouvelle cuisine chefs were characterized as a 'conceptualist avant-garde' (Ferguson and Zukin 1998: 94) and as creative artists who could become culinary stars rather than invisible artisans (Ferguson 2004; Hollows and Jones 2010a; Rao et al. 2003). As artists, celebrated chefs became associated with their own distinctive, signature style (Gillespie 1994). This creativity was not only associated with the taste and flavour of food but a new emphasis on the 'visual aesthetics' of dishes (Gillespie 1994: 21), a change that would also contribute to dishes becoming more *tele*visual and aid the development of new forms of television food programming (Ashley et al. 2004). Although the culinary styles associated with 'nouvelle cuisine calcified into a new orthodoxy' that would be challenged by trends such as comfort food and molecular gastronomy (Hollows and Jones 2010a: 525; Johnston and Baumann 2007; Rao et al. 2003; Svejanova et al. 2007), many of the changes that nouvelle cuisine introduced into restaurant cultures remained. Indeed, the aestheticization of chefs' practices has been heightened as the practices of some cutting-edge chefs have been conceptualized as art practices. For example, celebrated Catalan chef Ferran Adrià, who located his culinary practice within aesthetic practices of 'deconstruction', was invited to participate in the 2007 Dokumenta avant-garde art exhibition in Kassel (Svejenova et al. 2007). While the model of chef as artisan – associated with 'craftsmanship, independence, self-reliance, honesty, and a masculine appreciation of quality products' (Johnston et al. 2014: 13) – has undergone a renaissance and achieved increased visibility in recent years, the figure of the unique, artistic genius has not been entirely displaced.

One result of these changes was the increased visibility of chefs. As Priscilla Parkhurst Ferguson (2004: 150) argues, chefs in higher-end restaurants are no longer inconspicuous artisans: chefs and their cooking practices have been transformed into a 'culinary spectacle'. In many restaurants, cooking is no longer a back-stage activity: both the kitchen and the chef take 'centre stage' (Ibid.: 154). Celebrity chefs such as Wolfgang Puck used theatrical lighting in their restaurants to highlight the chefs' performance for diners and to generate publicity (Ray 2007). This can be seen in the trend for open kitchens where guests consume the view of their food being cooked as well as the final products. Many top restaurants offer a 'chef's table' where a small number of guests can get closer to the spectacle. For example, in London's two-Michelin star restaurant Dinner by Heston Blumenthal, the chef's table offers a 'behind the scenes dining experience' and 'an intimate insight into the energy and activity of the kitchen' with dinner 'served direct to your table by the head chef' (Dinner by Heston n.d.). As cooking becomes a spectacle, Ferguson (2004: 161) suggests, 'the practice of cooking trumps the experience of eating.' To achieve visibility, 'chefs simply can't afford to stay in the kitchen' (Ibid.: 167).

The status of chefs is not simply shaped by branding and marketing practices. Their reputation and identities are also shaped by awards and reviews. Although there are a wide range of restaurant awards – some judged by professionals and others by the public – Christel Lane's research on chefs in the UK and Germany demonstrates how the Michelin Guide is still the dominant 'taste maker'. The Michelin Guides create 'a hierarchy of chefs and restaurants' and the boundaries between one, two and three stars are 'translated by chefs into both reputational and economic value' (Lane 2013: 359). Lane (2010: 499) also shows the impact of the Michelin Guides on the financial fortunes of restaurants: 'they provide the most effective promotion of their businesses. An award of one star increases business by 20–30 per cent, and of two or three stars by even more.' Although many chefs in smaller restaurants enjoy the 'intrinsic satisfactions' of recognition for their culinary achievements, 'a small group of super chefs' have used this recognition to build high profiles and high incomes through television and publishing (Lane 2010: 503). Newspaper restaurant reviews also play a key role in producing stars within restaurant scenes (Lee 2014: 126-7), shaping reputations and, in the case of positive reviews, playing a key role in marketing practices (English and Fleischman 2019).

Many chefs have to 'actively cultivate publicity' so their restaurants gain a 'competitive advantage' (Ferguson and Zukin 1998: 93). While the increasing importance of branding 'changed the occupational culture and occupational identity of chefs' (Giousmpasoglou et al. 2019: 2), the labour involved in building brands has expanded with the increasing use of social media platforms. In her study of the 'lived experience of celebrity' for chefs in Sydney, Nancy Lee (2014: 8, 173) observes how using social media is 'folded into the everyday labour of cheffing'. Social media helps to create 'a (pseudo) intimacy and proximity between celebrity chefs and their followers' that create 'affective networks' that can enhance people's attachment to, and investment in, their brand (Abbots 2015: 226; Giousmpasoglou et al. 2019: 2; see also Rousseau 2012a). If changes in the restaurant industry have already put the chef centre stage, then a chef's use of Instagram can make visible some of the remaining back stage areas such as prep or recipe development (Lee

2014: 170). Social media platforms also offer opportunities for free advertising as followers retweet something from a favourite chef or post photos of their meals on Instagram (Lee 2014: 170). Of course, the social media profile of a celebrity chef such as Gordon Ramsay – who had 7.3 million followers on Twitter, 7.4 million followers on Instagram and 11.6 subscribers on YouTube in October 2019 – is very different to those of an up-and-coming ambitious local chef. Many chefs employ PR and marketing companies to create 'intimate' relationships for them on social media. Those with high television profiles may even have a talent manager to check that their social media accounts stay 'on brand' (Lee 2014). But there is a much more widespread obligation to use social media in order to keep restaurants afloat, bills paid and staff employed.

While many chefs use social media platforms, far fewer have the opportunity to promote themselves via more established media such as television, magazines and book publishing. As I go on to explain later in this chapter, televised culinary competitions offer professional chefs one route into broadcast media. Much of this book focuses on big name celebrity chefs but the wider celebritization of cooking has an impact on the restaurant industry as a whole. This has an impact on chefs' aspirations. American celebrity chef Wiley Dufresne notes how some young chefs now want to develop 'television-centric' rather than 'restaurant-centred' careers (cited in Curnutt 2015: 155). Chef and star of the Australian TV series *My Kitchen Rules* Colin Fassnidge puts it more bluntly: 'People's goals have changed; they don't want to be just a great chef, they want to be a fucking good chef and then go and sell fucking frypans somewhere on telly' (cited in Lee 2014: 197).

Frypans – alongside food processors, chopping boards and a whole range of household and kitchen equipment – offer another source of profit and some big-name celebrity chefs have their own ranges of branded goods, often in partnership with a name manufacturer. In her study of people's interactions with goods associated with celebrity chefs, Emma-Jayne Abbots (2015: 225) finds a range of celebrity-branded equipment lurking in her participants' kitchens. These items are not only a source of economic profit for chefs but help to cement their brand as they 'make their material presence felt' in people's everyday lives. The practice of using a celebrity-endorsed frying pan creates and strengthens 'intimate and affective relationships' between chefs and home cooks (Ibid.: 239). Some chefs also produce own-brand supermarket produce or endorse product ranges: for example, at the time of writing, Heston Blumenthal's range for high-end British supermarket Waitrose includes Cherry Bakewell Vodka, a Salt Beef Pretzel Sub and a Heston Top Hat Cake. In Australia, chef Curtis Stone has a long-running position as the face of Coles supermarket, increasing his presence in everyday life while also attaching his culinary credentials to the Coles brand. In this way, supermarkets and food producers try to attach the 'brand capital' of chefs, and people's emotional attachments to them, to their produce (Phillipov 2017: 12; see also Lewis and Huber 2015).

Changes within the restaurant industry, therefore, have created some of the conditions for the increased visibility of chefs and the increased importance of self-branding in a competitive restaurant marketplace. While these concerns may be irrelevant to many chefs quietly getting on with frying onions or making pasta dough in local restaurants, they have created an increased pressure on head chefs and chef-patrons to be visible. Brand extensions have created additional opportunities for some of the most famous celebrity chefs as they attach their name to a range of products. However, as I go on to explore in the next section, building well-known brands and pursuing economic profits can also be fraught with risk.

'That *Celebrity Chef*': Authenticity, selling out and the culinary field

For professional chefs in high-end restaurants, the pursuit of celebrity is a risky business. Visibility helps to promote restaurants so they can remain competitive and can produce additional income from sales of cookbooks or frying pans. But with visibility comes the risk of being branded a 'sell out', of being a media chef rather than a 'real' chef. Chefs who want to be seen as 'real' or as 'artists' need to work within the complexities of the culinary field in order to do celebrity in the right way. As Michel Roux Jr puts it:

> I don't consider myself a celebrity chef and I don't particularly like that title or moniker. Celebrity chefs are chefs who spend more time on television than they do in the restaurant and most don't have a restaurant. I'm very careful to pick and choose the television that I do because I don't want to fall into the trap of being *that* celebrity chef. First and foremost I am a chef and restauranteur and this is where I feel the most at ease and the happiest.
>
> (Bod Edit 2018)

Drawing on the work of French sociologist Pierre Bourdieu, this section explores celebrity in relation to the culinary field in order to understand how and why chefs position themselves in relation to what Michel Roux Jr calls '*that* celebrity chef'.

As James Farrer (2020: 3) argues, the culinary field can be thought of 'as a space of interactions among the actors who produce, sustain and also contest the "rules of the game" of modern restaurant cuisine – investors, owners, chefs, critics, regulators, consumers, guidebooks, food media, etc.' (see also Matta 2019). As I have already shown, since the 1960s, the culinary field was increasingly structured around the idea of cooking as an 'art' and the chef as an 'artist' (Ferguson and Zukin 1998). A chef's position in the culinary field is partly shaped by their 'culinary cultural capital' (Bell 2002) which shapes their degree of legitimacy and authority in matters of taste (Ashley et al. 2004: 179). The chefs with the most legitimacy in the culinary field tend to be those who appear driven by a single-minded pursuit of culinary perfection (which may include certain kinds of chef-artisans obsessed with perfecting their craft) or artistic innovation, but their legitimacy is a product of the judgements of those whose opinions count. In the culinary field, these tend to be the opinions of reviewers for major guides such as Michelin, key newspaper restaurant critics and other chefs who 'consecrate' particular chefs as having greater 'power and prestige' (Gualtieri 2021: 3).

Chefs such as Massimo Bottura in Italy, the Roca brothers and Adrià brothers in Spain and René Redzepi in Denmark all tend to be portrayed in these terms today. They are not mere chefs but portrayed in terms of their artistry and creativity, and their intellectual curiosity. For example, Bottura positions himself within both culinary and artistic fields and conceptualizes his practice in terms of avant-garde art. The Guide to the World's 50 Best Restaurants, in which his three Michelin star restaurant is a former number one, describes him as

> the most accomplished avant-garde chef of his generation … There is no food without poetry, deep thinking, and music for Massimo Bottura … Some of his dishes and menus are inspired by musicians and conceptual artists such as Thelonious Monk and Lucio Fontana … During his presentations at congresses, he cooks his dishes and quotes Joseph Beuys, as if food and art are both part of the same recipe.
>
> (Bianchi 2011)

Given these credentials, it is perhaps unsurprising that Bottura was selected as the subject of the first episode of *Chef's Table*. His aesthetic credentials are supplemented by his intellectual ones: the chef's philosophies are manifested in his not-for-profit organization Food For Soul which aims to fight for social inclusion by combatting food waste, orchestrated around the idea that 'a meal is a gesture of inclusion' (Food For Soul n.d.).

A chef's relationship to celebrity, therefore, is shaped by their relationship to the culinary field. This reminds us that not all forms of celebrity work in the same way. As Joe Moran (2000: 4) argues in his study of star authors, 'Literary celebrity in the US is not simply an adjunct of mainstream celebrity, but an elaborate system of representations in its own right, produced and circulated across a wide variety of media.' Chefs who gain their celebrity from within the culinary field rather than as TV personalities – those whose culinary capital is legitimated through awards and critics – cannot be simply compared to celebrity footballers or reality stars.

However, most chefs are not in a position to *just* be artists: they need to feed people who pay for food in order to keep their restaurants open.[2] The value of cultural capital is not as stable as economic capital (Bourdieu 1971, 1993) so most chefs experience a pressure to convert culinary prestige into economic wealth (Ashley et al. 2004: 179). Yet this is partly masked by the operation of the culinary field. Representing specific chefs as artists 'with special gifts or qualities (what Bourdieu calls the "charismatic illusion")' creates a 'separation of cultural and economic capital' (Moran 2000: 4–5). Coverage of chefs who are celebrities *within* the culinary field often focuses on their aesthetic rather than financial achievements. Therefore, Bottura tends to be represented as an artist rather than as a businessman who has expanded beyond his flagship restaurant in Modena to Florence and Dubai. Indeed, his economic investments *are* aestheticized – the walls of his restaurant Osteria Francescana exhibit his collection of avant-garde art (Sotherby's 2019).

There are some similarities between the positions of star chefs and literary authors. Both are 'ambiguous figures' who combine ideas of the 'charismatic, uniquely inspired creative artist' privileged within the culinary field with 'the notion of celebrity as supported by broad popularity and success in the marketplace' (Moran 2000: 7). However, this wider popularity and economic success has to have limits if it is not to threaten a chef's legitimacy as an artist. As Bourdieu argues:

> Producers and vendors of cultural goods who 'go commercial' condemn themselves, not only from an ethical or aesthetic point of view, because they deprive themselves of the opportunities open to those … who, by concealing from themselves and others the interests that are at stake in their practice, obtain the means of deriving profits from disinterestedness.
>
> (Bourdieu 1993: 75)

For example, Massimo Bottura's refuses to do much television – which he associates with shouting, screaming and mockery – and this distances him from chefs who 'go commercial' and pursue the profits attached to fame (Dirindin 2019).[3] High-profile celebrity chefs, therefore, often must walk a fine line between seeking culinary distinction and securing economic profits.

Wenche Ommundsen (2007: 249) draws on John Frow to distinguish between two types of literary celebrity that can be usefully applied to celebrity chefs. The first type is associated with 'the aesthetics of the signature' and an authenticity that rests on the idea of a 'unique creator' and 'romantic ideas of authorship'. Chefs such as Massimo Bottura and Ferran Adrià fall into this category and, as I go on to discuss below, these ideas shape the representation of chefs on Netflix's *Chef's Table*. The second type of celebrity is associated with 'the aesthetics of the brand [that] functions more like a trademark or corporate signature, associated with advertising and product differentiation'. Numerous media chefs could be argued to fall into this category. For example, despite early training as a professional chef, Jamie Oliver is a businessman whose brand became attached to restaurant chains rather than his role as a chef in a restaurant kitchen, business interests that developed alongside his high-profile presence as a media chef. 'Jamie Oliver' is now a brand that can be attached to various ventures and products, from frying pans to pasta sauces. In this way, Jamie Oliver operates as an example of '*that* celebrity chef' that those chefs who want to be understood as an artist rather than a media brand must distance themselves from. This can be seen in the case of Gordon Ramsay who, despite owning Michelin-starred restaurants, operates as a brand applied to a range of products and has a very high-profile media presence. Despite this, Ramsay is keen to be seen as an 'authentic' chef: 'I'm not a TV chef, I'm a real person who works on TV. I mastered my craft and continue to push boundaries' (Clarke 2017). His attempt to position himself as not '*that* celebrity chef' – not simply a brand – is reinforced by very public attempts to distance himself from branded chefs such as Jamie Oliver who he dismisses: 'Sadly, the only time he opens his mouth is when he's got something to promote' (McCahill 2017). Arguably, however, Ramsay *has* become '*that* celebrity chef': as I put together the final draft, his latest venture was as the host of a new, non-culinary, BBC primetime quiz show *Gordon Ramsay's Bank Balance* (2021).

Some chefs attempt to achieve visibility while maintaining their culinary credentials by seeking out TV formats which enable them to, in the words of Colin Fassnidge, 'play the chef on television' (cited in Lee 2014: 223). As I go on to show in the rest of this chapter, many of these chefs have appeared in formats such as television cooking competitions and documentaries which enable them to gain publicity for their restaurants while maintaining their culinary credentials. Other chefs seek to walk the fine line between celebrity within the culinary field and wider celebrity status. This can be seen in the case of Heston Blumenthal who runs, among other restaurants, the three-Michelin starred and former number one restaurant in the world The Fat Duck. Television series such as *In Search of Perfection* (2006–7) and *Heston's Feasts* (2009–10) broke with many of the conventions of cookery TV to emphasize the artistic, scientific and intellectual processes involved in Blumenthal's culinary practice. This highlighted 'the chef's aesthetic practices and tastes, helping to cement Blumenthal's image as an autonomous artist rather than a TV chef' (Hollows and Jones 2010a: 523). Yet this carefully constructed image was threatened when the chef signed a partnership with British supermarket Waitrose in 2010. While Waitrose clearly gained prestige from a special product range associated with an award-winning chef, Blumethal's credentials as a chef who produced unique avant-garde dishes to a small number of diners were threatened through his association with mass-produced supermarket goods.

However, not all high-end chefs accept the logic of the culinary field. On the one hand, there are well-publicized cases in which chefs 'hand back' their Michelin stars to rid themselves of stress, pursue more relaxed cooking styles, challenge the legitimacy of Michelin and/or spend more time with family.[4] On the other hand, in the British restaurant industry, there is a high 'degree of financialization' and some chefs have developed business empires based around restaurant and/or hotel groups. As Christel Lane (2010: 513) observes, respected Michelin-starred British chef Michael Caines 'has publicly declared that accumulating financial capital is preferable to preserving the cultural capital that the award of Michelin stars has bestowed upon him'.

In order to understand how restaurant chefs position themselves within the culinary field, it is necessary to understand the tensions between art and commerce. As Farrer (2020: 3) observes, 'Restaurants are simultaneously members of the fine dining "art world" and businesses that compete for diners' dollars in a market.' Chefs who gain prestige, legitimacy and celebrity for their art and skill within the culinary field can also threaten this position if they are seen as sell-outs who pursue fame and economic profits beyond it. Nonetheless, as this book explores, many celebrity chefs have expanded beyond the culinary field into arts, entertainment, media and politics (Matta 2019: 190). In some cases, these political interventions arise directly from the concerns of the restaurant industry.

During 2020, many star chefs in the UK such as Angela Hartnett, Asma Khan and Tom Kerridge campaigned on behalf of their sector in response to the economic impact of the pandemic on their industry and its workers, resulting in the 'A Seat at the Table' campaign for better representation within government. In other cases, celebrity chefs such as René Redzepi and Massimo Bottura make wide-ranging political and philosophical interventions (Matta 2019) while others engage in televised campaigns (see Chapters 5 and 6). However, it is also necessary to look more closely at the politics of the culinary field itself. As I explore later in this chapter, the operations of the culinary field are strongly marked by gender inequality and 'racial hierarchy' (Gualtieri 2021: 2).

Visibility, exposure and competitive cooking

While many chefs define their careers within restaurants and have little desire for celebrity (Nemeschansky et al. 2017), there is a pressure for head chefs and chef-patrons to be visible within a competitive restaurant industry. Since the 2000s, the development of TV cooking competitions for professionals has offered opportunities for chefs to gain exposure for their cooking and their restaurants without the risks of becoming '*that* celebrity chef'. TV appearances can have a significant impact on restaurant profits: for example, an appearance as a guest judge or mentor on a TV cooking competition can generate a huge increase in restaurant reservations (Lee 2014). In this section, I examine the rise of cooking competition formats on TV and explore how these shows represent chefs and their work.

Tasha Oren (2013: 20) charts the rise of a television format centred around 'restaurant-set competition' and 'professional, high-stakes performance, criticism, stress, and risk'.[5] This was part of a wider shift in food television from an emphasis on domestic cookery to an increasing preoccupation with restaurant cooking. The Japanese cooking competition *Iron Chef* (1993–9) – and the various international versions it spawned, including *Iron Chef America* (2004–) – was a key influence on the development of these formats.[6] However, non-food reality TV formats such as *America's Next Top Model* and *Project Runway* also shaped the development of cooking competitions such as the US's long-running *Top Chef* (2006–) and its over twenty international adaptations. The narrative of *Top Chef* uses a 'skilled-challenge-judgement-elimination' structure and shifts the focus from 'how to cook successfully?' to 'will he succeed?' (Oren 2013: 28–30). Oren's gendering of the chef as 'he' is not accidental as the majority of the chefs in cooking competition formats are male.

Series such as *Top Chef* emphasize the chef's professional role. While the competition format suggests fun and play, these shows demonstrate that professional cooking is not only creative but also *labour* that is often 'sweaty, anxious, painful and risky' (Oren 2013: 30). They also introduce benchmarks of excellence that are reproduced in some amateur cooking competitions on TV: series such as *Masterchef* (2005–) in the UK and *Masterchef Australia* (2009–) put home cooks to work in professional kitchens and reward contestants who produce 'restaurant-quality' dishes in the studio.[7] In this way, the emphasis on 'professionalism and competition' extends more widely into cookery TV: amateur cooks talk about 'plating' and 'elevating' dishes and contestants on the *Great British Bake Off* (2010–) are praised for cakes that look like they belong in the window of a French patisserie.[8]

In the UK, the *Great British Menu* (2006–) is a BBC annual televised cookery competition for high-level professional chefs. The first season saw chefs compete to cook a starter, fish course, main course and dessert at a birthday banquet for the Queen. Subsequent seasons have featured themed banquets for different groups, from D-Day veterans and NHS staff to Olympians and rock stars. While the first season featured many already high-profile and well-established Michelin-starred chefs such as Marcus Wareing, Gary Rhodes, Angela Hartnett and Michael Caines, later seasons have introduced some faces less familiar to TV viewers. Over four courses, the audience learns about each chef's style and their restaurant, providing valuable publicity for the chef's business. Selection for the banquet can have a more significant impact on a restaurant's fortunes. Richard Bainbridge jokes that his trifle that won the 2015 dessert category paid for his restaurant: 'Without that dish I genuinely don't know if I'd still be in business' (Lutrario 2017). The dessert winner in the subsequent year, Adam Reid, claims 'we opened a restaurant on the back of it!' (Stiritup 2019).

A connection with *Great British Menu* can bring other rewards. Some chefs establish a longstanding connection with the series and contestants are frequently classified as 'newcomers', 'returnees' and 'former winners'. Chefs can 'matriculate' into other roles within the series (Curnutt 2015: 161) – winners return to the show as judges, cementing their public profile and brand. Hugh Curnutt argues that *Top Chef* and its associated shows produce 'durable participants' which enables 'television producers to "grow their own" celebrities' and 'repurpose' them across a range of shows. Appearances on the *Great British Menu* can lead to guest slots on other BBC shows such as *Saturday Kitchen* (2001–) and, for some chefs, they have been the start of more substantial television careers. For example, after his launch on *Great British Menu* in 2010, Tom Kerridge is now one of the BBC's key television chefs and Tommy Banks, who first featured on the show in 2016, became a co-host on the BBC's *The Big Family Cooking Showdown* (2017–18), an amateur cooking competition that reinforced the importance of family in the brand of his Michelin-starred restaurant.

Great British Menu reinforces the legitimacy of the culinary field and the authority of chefs, restauranteurs and food critics as arbiters of culinary taste. Heats are judged by former winners and regional and grand finals by a panel of food experts. The panels are joined by a guest judge, usually an 'ordinary person' who represents the tastes of the guests of the banquet such as a nurse or D-Day veteran. These panellists are not treated as culinary experts who make 'objective' comments about what is good to eat but are treated as the 'subjective' voice of the group they represent. The format therefore comes with a whole lot of assumptions about who has the power to classify the 'best' food. While the show might democratize knowledge of high-level cuisine, like many other professional culinary competition formats, it reaffirms power relations by 'validating a relatively narrow range of foods that require considerable cultural and/or economic capital' (Johnston and Baumann 2007: 169).

Chef-participants can also gain legitimacy through association with the chefs they appear alongside in TV cooking competitions (Curnutt 2015: 157). While *Great British Menu* creates a stable of chefs who are branded through their association with the show and each other, this occurred on an international scale in Netflix's *The Final Table*.[9] The chef-participants, many of whom had high-level culinary accolades such as Michelin stars, competed to join an 'Avengers-like supergroup of titans' (Morabito 2018), a roster of superstar chefs who operated as judges, including chefs who had gained three Michelin stars such as Anne-Sophie Pic and Clare Smyth. The publicity for the series emphasized the culinary authority of the show and its participants – even judge Clare Smyth claimed 'being among this bunch of people is phenomenal. They're a huge inspiration to me' (Morabito 2018). Although the first round in most episodes included celebrity judges, the ultimate authority in each episode was a prestigious chef that participants felt honoured to cook for. *The Final Table* therefore offered chefs publicity and a way of enhancing their reputation through association with other culinary greats – as Michelin-starred contestant Graham Campbell put it in the first episode 'I am floored with the amount of talent in the room' and honoured 'to get my name out there with all these great chefs'. *The Final Table* operated as a shop window for the chefs' talents. In to-camera segments and in discussion with judges, chefs established their philosophies, passions, signature and brand. Although the show featured a studio audience, the viewer was frequently given an aerial perspective on chefs' hands at work as they cooked and plated food. Glossy aerial shots of completed dishes looked like they were 'designed to be uploaded on Instagram' (Aftab 2018), reinforcing the increasing emphasis on the visual in food media as a result of social media platforms (Lewis 2020).

In this way, the series reinforced a view of cooking as an aesthetic practice associated with the culinary field. Despite having contestants who represented a range of national cuisines – and even chefs whose credentials came from food trucks – the legitimacy of a French culinary tradition was ultimately reproduced when the final challenge centred around French cuisine with a winner selected who had trained in the French tradition (Martin 2018). TV cooking competitions featuring professional chefs not only provide publicity and career opportunities to chefs who conform to values of the culinary field, but they also reproduce the wider legitimacy of the field and the rights of chefs and food critics to act as arbiters of culinary taste.

Chef's Table: *Cooking, aesthetics and distinction*

In their work on celebrity, Su Holmes and Sean Redmond (2006: 13) argue that different fields, genres and formats produce 'their own ways of understanding fame, and its aesthetic, technological or ideological implications'. The discussion so far has demonstrated how different types of celebrity chefs achieve fame in different ways. Some are celebrities according to the aesthetic values of the culinary field, others conform to wider notions of celebrity achieved through widespread media exposure and others attempt to bridge both worlds in an attempt to win both cultural recognition and economic rewards. In this section, I look more closely at how aesthetic discourses associated with the culinary field are used in media representations of notable chefs, focusing on the Netflix documentary series *Chef's Table* (2015–). The series, which usually focuses on chefs in their workplace, offers the selected chefs huge international publicity while focusing on their culinary, aesthetic and intellectual credentials and portraying them as artists with a unique vision.

In its sixth season at the time of writing, Netflix's *Chef's Table* capitalized on the increased popularity of documentary formats in general which had enabled the rise of documentary film-making with a food focus. While many of these food documentaries focused on food politics and activism – for example, *King Corn* (2007) and *Supersize Me* (2004) – Fabio Parasecoli (2016) draws attention to a range of films that focus on celebrity chefs and 'engage with the Michelin star system', including *Jiro Dreams of Sushi* (2011), *Step Up to the Plate* (2012) and *Three Stars* (2010). Many of the themes and cinematic techniques used in these films were later employed in *Chef's Table*, from a focus on creative work of the chef to the use of 'extreme close-ups' of chefs and their kitchen practices (Parasecoli 2016: 325). This is unsurprising given that David Gelb who directed *Jiro Dreams of Sushi* created *Chef's Table*. To different degrees, these films also emphasized many of the values of the culinary field, drawing on a 'global discourse of *haute cuisine*' that privileges 'masculinity, professionalism dedication, tradition, individual skills, the relevance of the media, and the pressure of the restaurant business' as well as, in the case of *Step Up to the Plate*, the importance of terroir (Parasecoli 2016: 330). These values would be central to *Chef's Table*.

Chef's Table draws on some of the aesthetic strategies associated with these feature-length documentaries about star chefs, yet it is also partly a product of the Netflix documentary house style. This is informed by the principles of Slow Media which, like those of the Slow Food movement, 'are not about fast consumption but about choosing the ingredients mindfully and preparing them in a concentrated manner' (Köhler et al. cited in Binns 2018: 61).[10] The aesthetics of *Chef's Table* as a documentary, therefore, frequently mirror – and accentuate – the aesthetics of the food and the chefs featured. As Daniel Binns (2018: 64) argues, the show uses 'experimental techniques' such as 'smooth camera movements, super slow-motion shots, soft-focus or *bokeh* cinematography, the use of computer-controlled camera rigs, and a representation of food that is comparable to the arrangement of props for a still-life painting' in combination with 'ultra high-definition' and carefully designed sound. The ways 'the content is treated as prized' creates the sense of 'event streaming' that helps the Netflix brand and these qualities are also transferred on to chefs and their food (Ibid.: 65). The film-making techniques accentuate the sense that we are in the presence of something – and someone – special so that the viewer must be prepared to slow down and savour their work. The use of both experimental aesthetic technique and slow media principles, therefore, portrays chefs as celebrities within a seemingly 'less commercialized' media environment (Ommundsen 2007: 245), distancing the chefs involved from the types of celebrity chef who occupy 'more commercial' media spaces.

Sofia Ulver and Marcus Klasson's (2018) analysis of *Chef's Table* also demonstrates how the series reproduces the 'taste regime' associated with the culinary field. Focusing on the first two seasons, they identify how the narrative structure of many episodes share similar characteristics which construct elements in a 'hero's journey' that legitimates the chefs as culinary authorities (Ulver and Klasson 2018: 40). These elements include a sense of 'struggle' – becoming 'an avant-gardist chef' involves 'suffering and a lot of determination' (Ibid.: 34). The narratives feature a 'turning point', a moment when their mission became clear and/or their aesthetic recognized by a prestigious critic (Ibid.: 36–7). The chefs' stories also usually feature a moment when they achieve independence and find their voice, although many chefs are also shown to be on a continuous search for improvement (Ibid.: 38). For some chefs their aesthetic mission is articulated with intellectual endeavour and political activism. For example, in the first two episodes, we learn about Massimo Bottura's 'recipe for social justice' in the wake of the earthquakes that hit Modena in 2012 and about Dan Barber's research into ethical and sustainable food which makes him 'a chef who wants to change the world'. While the narratives portray chefs as 'independent rebels', Ulver and Klasson observe how their stories are often remarkably similar, reproducing the unwritten rules that structure the culinary field (Ibid.: 40–1).[11]

Once the struggle to establish their restaurant and achieve independence has been overcome, the chef's work is represented in aesthetic, intellectual and sometimes political terms, maintaining a 'charismatic illusion' which masks the relationship between their creative activity and economic profit (Moran 2000: 4–5). This view of chefs is reinforced by the show's creator David Gelb in interviews: 'And then they risk everything – they really risk it all. Chefs sell everything they have to keep their restaurants open. These are chefs that have an uncompromising vision ... They're not just pandering to increase business' (Nguyen n.d.). This distances these chefs from '*that* celebrity chef': as food critic Matt Preston says of New Zealand chef Ben Shewry in season one, 'He's not your celebrity chef – your supermodel-dating, Ferrari-driving, leather-jacket wearing celebrity chef.'

Chef's Table also frequently reproduces contemporary culinary discourses that emphasize *terroir*. 'Geographical specificity', as Johnston and Baumann (2007: 179) observe, is 'the most common discursive strategy for legitimating food'. It is not simply the food they serve but the chefs themselves who are represented as the product of place. The series frequently makes extensive use of lingering establishing shots that position the chef within a landscape. In series one, Massimo Bottura is represented as a product of Modena: 'in my blood is balsamic vinegar and my muscles are made by parmigiano'. Ben Shewry gains an appreciation for place in a childhood spent foraging and tasting the land around him and, Matt Preston tell us, 'there's a sense of place in his food'. Likewise Swedish Magnus

Nilsson is positioned in terms of the land he grew up in and the landscape that produces his cooking. Although we learn that Francis Mallmann enjoys being on the road, part of 'a band of gyspy chefs', his episode features lengthy shots of him living slowly, at one with nature and cooking over fire, at home in Patagonia. Just as foods that that have the specific flavour of a place are seen as more 'authentic' in culinary discourses, so 'authentic' chefs are also represented as formed through the tastes of a place.[12]

The rebellious 'outsider' status of creative chefs is often associated with a 'rock 'n' roll coolness'. This draws on wider representations of star chefs that emerged in the 1990s that built on (then) three Michelin-starred British chef Marco-Pierre White's image of rebellious, masculine cool that featured in his book *White Heat* (White 1990; see Johnston et al. 2014). This image of the chef was accentuated following the publication of US chef Anthony Bourdain's (2000) *Kitchen Confidential* which also portrayed the (masculine) chef as a rock 'n' roll outsider. Episode one of *Chef's Table* featured a series of photos of the young Massimo Bottura on the streets of New York, dressed in a leather jacket and quirky sunglasses, looking like – in the words of his future partner Lara – 'a very cool dude'. Two episodes later, in the episode featuring Francis Mallmann, this is taken much further. Styled like an older rocker, the guitar-playing Mallmann is continuously represented as a 'rolling stone', refusing to be contained by the domestic space of his partner and child and wanting 'the freedom of loving'. Intoxicated by the freedom of his nomadic lifestyle, movement 'is a drug' and he seeks encounters with the new that make him 'tremble', 'breathe' and 'live'. Even his cooking technique is infused with a romanticized vagabond masculinity – to build a fire 'is a bit like making love'. While Dan Barber is less rock, he also reproduces the sense that a great chef must have masculine attributes by emphasizing the physicality of the work as a form of 'abuse' and the feeling of being 'in the trenches' with a brigade of chefs. In contrast, Niki Nakayama – who bears the burden of being the only female chef, the only chef of colour and the only out non-heterosexual chef in season one of *Chef's Table* – is largely positioned in interior space. While later seasons of *Chef's Table* partly corrected the omissions of season one, the series helps to reproduce the masculinity and whiteness of notions of culinary greatness. It also reproduces the gendering found more widely in representations of chefs in cookery television. As Lee (2014: 102) observes about guest chefs on *Masterchef Australia*, 'tough, masculine chefs receive quiet reverent awe while gentle feminine chefs inspire joyful, giggly admiration'.

Chef's Table helps to reproduce the values of the culinary field based on the 'aesthetics of the signature' and to popularize the illusions that sustain it. Rather than business people, the show reproduces gastronomic discourses which portray great chefs as 'creative geniuses whose aesthetic innovations represent a personal charisma and personal expression' (Johnston and Baumann 2007: 199). While *Chef's Table* has attempted to increase the diversity of the chefs and cuisines featured in later seasons, its representations of great chefs as tough soldiers or badass outsiders reproduce the idea that professional kitchens are largely male spaces with a masculine culture and the characteristics of the 'great chef' are associated with heterosexual masculinity. As I explore in more detail below, this does more than reflect the existing inequalities within restaurant cultures and industries; it also helps to reproduce them.

Gender, race and the possibility of celebrity

These associations between culinary visionaries, the culture of 'great' restaurants and masculinity are not simply a product of *Chef's Table* but reproduce wider discourses which shape judgements and classifications within the culinary field. In this section, I explore these issues in more detail to examine how both gender and race impact on the possibilities of achieving 'greatness' and celebrity status within the world of restaurant cooking, rendering some types of chef as more visible and prestige-worthy than others. As political movements around Black Lives Matter and #MeToo have highlighted, gender and race impact on the working lives of kitchen staff – for example, through harassment and discrimination.[13] However, as I go on to show, the lower value given to cooking styles and practices frequently associated with women and particular ethnic groups can also shape the careers of chefs.

Women are underrepresented in the restaurant industry as a whole and at higher levels of prestige within it. Although home cooking is closely identified with feminine domestic labour, at a professional level only 17 per cent of chefs in the UK were women in 2018 (Morgan 2018). Gender inequalities were exacerbated at the highest levels of prestige: in 2017, only 10 out of 172 restaurants with Michelin stars in the UK had a female head chef (Henderson 2017). This is not a specifically British problem. In the same year, only 3 of the World's Best 50 Restaurants had a female head chef (Holland 2018). Female staff often face significant challenges in restaurant work cultures which emphasize masculinity and homo-social bonding, a cultural response that aims to create a distance from the feminine associations of cooking as a domestic practice (Harris and Giuffre 2015). The idea that masculinity is seen as a natural feature of top kitchens was evident when a tweet from Michelin praised Asma Khan's restaurant Darjeeling Express for having 'a female kitchen team coping effortlessly with the demand' (cited in Ward 2018). In the same year, two-Michelin Star Claude Bosi reportedly said that Khan 'should "take the risk" of working in a man's kitchen', suggesting that this was still the benchmark of culinary achievement (cited in Ward 2018). Many female restaurant staff recount experiences of discrimination and bullying, and allegations of sexual harassment against celebrity chefs such as Mario Batali in the United States and Dan Doherty in the UK operated as high-profile examples of the problem.

Deborah Harris and Patti Giuffre's study of representations of chefs in US food media finds significant differences between how male and female chefs are portrayed. As was evident in my analysis of *Chef's Table*, great male chefs are repeatedly represented as dedicated, creative and highly trained professionals and often depicted as 'iconoclastic' rule breakers with a unique vision or style (Harris and Giuffre 2015: 48–58). In contrast, female professional chefs are often judged in terms of homestyle cooking which 'devalues the training and skill required' and, by representing their food as 'amateur and homely', links them to a domestic tradition rather than the professional standards which are crucial to recognition in the culinary field (Ibid.: 66–7). In this way, the operations of the culinary field reproduce gender inequalities by valuing qualities associated with a masculine tradition more highly and excluding women from criteria used to classify 'great chefs'. This limits a female chef's ability to gain recognition and to accrue the economic, cultural and symbolic rewards that recognition generates.

The culinary field is not only structured by classed and gendered inequality but also racial hierarchies that shape the career of chefs and the ways in which their work is classified and evaluated (Gualtieri 2021: 2). In 2018, only 6 per cent of head chefs at Michelin-starred restaurants in the UK came from a Black or south Asian background, and only two Black head chefs had Michelin stars (Mohdin 2018). These issues gained heightened visibility following the impact of Black Lives Matter on 2020's cultural landscape. Leading Black chefs such as Michael Caines (2020) – holder of two Michelin stars for eighteen consecutive years – and *Eater* Chef of the Year 2018 James Cochran (2020) spoke out against racial discrimination in the industry which hindered Black chefs' progression and left them over-represented in the lowest level kitchen positions. Caines (2020) highlighted how his achievements were the exception rather than the norm as 'the first black chef at a three-Michelin-star restaurant; the first to work for Joël Robuchon; the first to receive two Michelin stars'. In a poignant call for change, Caines (2020) observed: 'I'm descended from slaves, but now I run the Michelin-starred Lympstone Manor in Devon, which was built from the profits of slavery. If Lympstone can be liberated from its past, so can society.'

While Caines achieved success within the 'classic' tradition rewarded within the culinary field and guides such as Michelin, the standing of many chefs of colour is shaped by the ways in which they are classified and positioned as specialists in 'ethnic' cuisines. While mobile, middle-class chefs may do stages across the globe to gain exposure to different ethnic and national cuisines (Farrer 2020), chefs from particular ethnic minorities may face 'the assumption that they will be more experienced or more comfortable with the cuisine of their "homeland"' (Finney 2020). Ainsley Harriott, who has carved out a successful career as celebrity chef and television personality, recalls that, when he started cooking French food in restaurants, people 'would ask: "Shouldn't you be cooking jerk chicken?"' (cited in Mohdin 2018).

As Gillian Gualtieri (2021: 4) explains, the culinary field is distinct from many other cultural fields because it is organized 'according to "ethnic" categories' that 'describe the cuisine served' and 'signify the kinds of dishes and practices that actors recognize as matching (or not) their expectations of that category'. These categories are 'implicitly and explicitly racialized' so an Indian restaurant is thought of as non-white while 'modern British' or 'new Nordic' are marked as white. For Gualtieri (2021: 4–5), 'cuisine is a unique case, as the *cultural product* itself ... is racialized, sometimes distinctly from the racial identity of the producer'. Her analysis identifies how the 'classic' and 'flexible' styles valued by Michelin in the United States have an 'explicit association with whiteness' while 'ethnic restaurants' 'are categorized using labels of non-whiteness' (Ibid.: 14). She concludes that this 'differential system of evaluation produces a system of ethnoracial inequality that consecrates products categorically associated with whiteness and devalues products associated with non-whiteness' (Ibid.). This has consequences for both the economic and reputational success of ethnic minority chefs and their restaurants. As Michael Caines (2020) observes, 'There are loads of brilliant restaurants out there owned by minorities: Indian, Chinese, Caribbean, African, Lebanese. The point is, we don't celebrate it [...] Caribbean food, for example, has struggled to reach outside its community.'

It is not only how restaurants are evaluated that shapes their position in the culinary field but whether they are evaluated at all. As I noted earlier, newspaper restaurant reviews are a key mechanism shaping a chef's standing in the culinary field and this highlights the importance of *which* restaurants are selected for review and *who* is doing the reviewing. Melissa Thompson (2020) recently reported that major British national newspapers have featured 'only two reviews of a restaurant serving African or Caribbean cuisine in the last 10 years'. Reflecting on the gatekeeping role of restaurant reviewers, Jimi Famuwera (2020), the only Black food critic on a major British newspaper, observes that the dominance of a singular perspective of 'the white and powerful' means that 'entire culinary traditions awaiting a benevolent cheerleader can be wholly ignored ... and coverage generally snaps back to a modern European or broadly Western culinary default'. Like the Michelin guides, reviewing practices help to produce and sustain racial hierarchies in the culinary field and who has the opportunity for success and visibility.

Chefs who are female and/or associated with specific ethnoracial culinary styles have less opportunities for achieving prestige, visibility and recognition and this shapes who can become a 'celebrity chef'. As Johnston et al. (2014: 13) observe, 'the exclusion of women from professional status is reproduced, and ideologically bolstered, by the masculine tendencies of professional food personas available for celebrity chefs'. Male celebrity chefs are often celebrated as artists, rulebreakers or adventurers – or through their mastery of 'classic' professional technique. In contrast, chefs who are women and/or associated with a particular 'ethnic' cuisine are frequently evaluated in terms of the 'authenticity' of their flavours within a home-cooking tradition: for example, 'ethnic' foods often have a 'comparatively lower position of symbolic value in the Michelin star system' (Gualtieri 2021: 20). While these chefs may be praised, they are also denied the rewards associated with the values of creativity and professional accomplishment that underpin the culinary field.

While there have been many calls to end discrimination so that all chefs are evaluated as skilled and creative professionals, some chefs have offered a more profound challenge to the values of the culinary field. The first (and, to date, only) British-based chef to feature on *Chef's Table*, Asma Khan specializes in an Indian domestic culinary tradition which consciously celebrates the values of 'authenticity' and 'home'. Rather than demanding the right to be judged equally within professional Western culinary values derived from the public sphere, she suggests that the logic of the culinary field needs a more fundamental reformulation so the authentic taste of home is valued in the same way as innovation or classic French technique (Sarkar 2020). Furthermore, Khan argues:

> I don't want restaurants to be ranked by Michelin stars for the fluff and edible flowers they put on a plate. I want to know how they treat their people, they should be ranked on that. Where there is bullying and racism, where there is sexual harassment, where staff don't seem safe, people should boycott those restaurants.
>
> (Asma Khan cited in Iqbal 2020)

This suggests that the professional standards of chefs and their restaurants could be evaluated in radically different ways.

Conclusion

The label 'celebrity chef' is not a homogeneous category and this chapter has demonstrated how celebrity functions within the culinary field that shapes the reputations and careers of chefs. Celebrity status in the culinary field is associated with attributes such as artistry, innovation, creativity and technical mastery. Legitimacy, prestige and celebrity within the field offers opportunities to accrue further cultural, economic and symbolic profits, although top chefs must ensure their pursuit of economic profit or fame does not render them a 'sell out' and threaten their culinary credentials and reputation as an artist. However, like other cultural fields, the culinary field is built on systematic forms of inequality and exclusion. As Johnston et al. (2014: 2) argue, 'certain cultural producers continue to be disadvantaged by the fact that critics, peers and other key agents evaluate work based on race and gender characteristics'.

As this chapter also makes clear, chefs who wish to build reputations cannot exist outside the wider mediatization of society (Couldry 2015; Driessens 2012). Even chefs in neighbourhood restaurants may feel obliged to build social media profiles to promote their businesses. The food critics and guidebooks whose judgements shape hierarchies within the culinary field are part of the media industries. Food television such as *Chef's Table* and *The Great British Menu* and publishing can play a key role in building the professional reputations of chefs. This means that 'celebrity chefs' are not only produced by the logics of the culinary field but also by the media industries. However, as the next chapter goes on to explore, the careers of celebrity chefs such as Jamie Oliver, Nigella Lawson and Nadıya Hussain are shaped far more by their relationship to the media than the culinary field.

Chapter 2

CELEBRITY CHEFS AND THE MEDIA INDUSTRIES

This chapter shifts from a focus on chefs whose celebrity is a product of the culinary field to consider celebrity chefs whose fame and influence is primarily associated with their roles as media personalities. Culinary figures who have achieved celebrity on television come from a range of backgrounds: while some such as Gordon Ramsay, Heston Blumenthal, Jock Zonfrillo and David Chang have already achieved celebrity in the culinary field, many others have been home economists, food writers, enthusiastic home cooks or relatively unknown chefs. The backgrounds of celebrity chefs have further diversified as blogs, YouTube and Instagram have given alternative routes into culinary celebrity. This clearly problematizes the term 'celebrity chef' as many people to whom it is applied are not chefs yet the label is widely applied to people who achieved celebrity as media cooks (see Introduction).

While some post-war cookery writers achieved a degree of celebrity through food writing,[1] the rise of the celebrity chef is closely related to the development of food television. This chapter examines how changing practices and conventions within the television industry impacted on both food programming and the types of celebrity chefs that came out of cookery TV. However, celebrity chefs are also cross-media 'entertainment packages' (Negus 1992: 5). Most straddle television and publishing and increasingly operate across a range of digital platforms. The latter part of the chapter explores how these platforms have created spaces for the emergence of new types of food celebrity and assesses whether they differ from the celebrity chefs associated with more established media.

This chapter, therefore, focuses on celebrity chefs as media products and brands and how they operate across media forms, platforms and products. In the process, I examine how the logics of the media industries shape which food knowledges are privileged and how they are mediated. While my focus is on the UK, as I explained in the Introduction, the formats and production techniques used to represent celebrity chefs and their food has a much wider international influence. I also consider the forms of authority and expertise that are associated with celebrity chefs. If the previous chapter looked at how chefs achieve legitimacy through their position in the culinary field, this chapter explores how different media forms also legitimate modes of 'ordinary' and 'amateur' expertise (Lewis 2008a, 2020).

Television cookery in the UK: A very brief history

Cookery was part of the history of British television broadcasting from its birth in 1936. Already established as an element of BBC radio programming in the interwar period, BBC TV included some cookery in its launch year and the first regular cookery series, *Cook's Night Out* starring Marcel Boulestin, was broadcast in 1937 (Geddes 2022). Following a pause in transmissions during the Second World War, television cookery became an established part of the BBC's output from the mid-1940s. Although television ownership was still relatively low during the early post-war period, celebrity chefs such as Philip Harben, Marguerite Patten and Fanny Cradock became household names. While there is not space here to do justice to this early history of celebrity chefs, this section highlights how the principles of public service broadcasting and the gendered distinctions between daytime and evening broadcasting shaped the development of cookery programming in the UK and the emergence of celebrity chefs with distinctive performance styles.[2]

Advertising and sponsorship helped to shape the form and content of early US cookery programming within a system of commercial television. However, the early history of British food television was shaped by the BBC, the UK's sole television broadcaster until 1955. The BBC was a publicly funded institution oriented around public service principles that broadcasting should inform, educate and entertain. From the outset, cookery programming was shaped by the tensions between informing and educating the audience and entertaining them. While the divisions between information and entertainment were never entirely clear cut, daytime cookery programming was more closely associated with informational shows for female viewers that sought to enhance their domestic skills while evening programmes had a greater entertainment element (Geddes 2022).

The articulation of information and education with entertainment can be seen in two male cooking stars of early British television who appeared in primetime slots, Marcel Boulestin in the pre-war period and Philip Harben in the post-war period. Research into the reception of these figures demonstrates that both were represented as authorities who could convey information about how to cook in an entertaining style and had distinctive performance styles that created a sense of familiarity with audiences (Bennett 2010; Geddes 2022). Both had 'recognisable on-screen styles and personas', with distinctive trademark looks – the slick suited look of the Maître D in the case of Boulestin and a striped butcher's apron in the case of Harben – that helped to develop their brands (Geddes 2022). These visual styles helped to underline their role as '*vocationally skilled* performers', their associations with a (masculine) world of food lending 'credibility to their vocational skill' and 'the authenticity of their image' (Bennett 2010: 130). Indeed, even in these early years of television, both men were cross-media entertainment packages, operating across platforms such as radio, television and publishing (Ashley et al. 2004; Bonner 2009; Geddes 2022). Both men also embarked on national tours, and Harben profited from his celebrity by creating his own branded range of cooking equipment, Harbenware, which boasted a £100,000 annual turnover by the 1960s (Geddes 2022). Even at this early stage, many elements of the contemporary television chef were in place. Although the shift to 'infotainment' is associated with changes in cookery television in the 1990s (Brunsdon 2003), cookery shows that blend instruction with entertainment had a much longer history, especially in primetime slots.

In its afternoon programming for women from 1948, the BBC took a much more educational and informational approach to cooking (Charlesworth 2022). The figure most closely associated with daytime cookery in the post-war period is Marguerite Patten, an established radio broadcaster and cookery writer who was closely involved in the Ministry of Food during the Second World War (Charlesworth 2022). Patten aimed to 'help the wife at home cook properly' by offering 'cheap, filling and exciting meals to make with what was available' (Moseley 2009: 18–19). Rather than being associated with leisure and entertainment, these daytime cookery slots used instruction to help women with their labour in the home. The producers assumed an audience of housewives who were prepared to devote time to watching a slow and careful demonstration of how to cook a dish (Ibid.: 22). Although there was less daytime cooking on the BBC by the early 1960s, instructional programmes continued to be featured as part of the daytime offering for women on commercial television.[3]

While these gendered distinctions between educational daytime cookery programming and more entertaining evening shows partly structured the development of food television in the UK, these distinctions were not always clear cut. Harben appeared on daytime TV and Patten would later appear in the evenings. Food programming was often viewed within the BBC's remit to inform and educate and some very successful evening cookery series emphasized education over entertainment. For example, in the 1990s, the restaurant chef Gary Rhodes star vehicle *Rhodes around Britain* (1994) was produced by the BBC Education Department and cookery writer Madhur Jaffrey's *Flavours of India* (1995) by the BBC Multicultural Programmes Unit, both departments with strong public service remits (Strange 1998). From the 1970s to the early 2000s, Delia Smith was one of the UK's best-known TV chefs and cookery writers, operating as 'the nation's official domestic science teacher' (Lane 1999). Similar figures have appeared in other national contexts such as Alison Holst in New Zealand. Primetime cookery series such as *Delia Smith's Cookery Course* (1978–82) and *How to Cook* (1998–2002) featured painstaking explanations of how to prepare dishes, her careful demonstration of a cook's skills adding to the 'authenticity' of her image as a celebrity chef (Bennett 2010). While Smith was not associated with the world of light entertainment, she achieved sufficient celebrity for 'Delia' to enter into the Collins English Dictionary as a distinct term to describe her cooking style (Gray 2001) and, although relatively low profile, she has used her celebrity to support Norwich City Football Club and to campaign for the Labour Party and against Brexit (see also Chapter 8).

However, more entertainment-oriented cookery series also featured throughout the long post-war period and these were not exclusively associated with men. Fanny Cradock, a theatrical and flamboyant celebrity chef from the 1950s to 1970s on both BBC and ITV, is frequently remembered for both spectacular clothing and ornamental dishes, although this arguably underplays her significance as both a television chef and cookery writer (Geddes 2018; Humble 2005). However, her affinities with light entertainment programming can be seen in events such as the televised spectacular of her performance at the Royal Albert Hall in 1956 in which Cradock gave an 'iconic performance' dressed in 'ball-gown and furs, creating extravagant soufflés and surrounded by ice sculptures of swans' (Geddes 2018). Information and entertainment were also blurred in the popular Canadian series *The Galloping Gourmet* starring flamboyant celebrity chef Graham Kerr, first broadcast on the BBC in 1969 (see Bonner 2005, 2011).

This brief and, by necessity, incomplete exploration of the development of cookery programming and celebrity chefs on British television raises a series of key issues that help to understand patterns of development from the 1990s onwards. First, it is worth noting that, while a variety of people have retrospectively been dubbed the 'first celebrity chef', the term was not in widespread currency until the 1990s. The term does not appear in descriptions of BBC food programmes until 1996.[4] Second, food programming on British television developed within public service principles but the inflection and emphasis given to information, education and entertainment varied across series, personalities and times of day. Third, despite notable exceptions, female celebrity chefs have been more closely associated with instruction and education while male celebrity chefs were more likely to be entertaining and flamboyant characters. While the distinction between daytime and primetime became much less important from the 1990s, these gendered associations would continue to shape the later development of TV cookery and the opportunities afforded to male and female celebrity chefs.

Finally, as I suggested above, celebrity chefs have operated across multiple platforms from the outset, creating spin-off products across a range of media and beyond (Ashley et al. 2004; Bonner 2009; Geddes 2018, 2022). This has also been a valuable source of profit for the media industries: for example, in the 1990s, the BBC's publishing ventures enabled them to generate profits from the books that accompanied Delia Smith's TV series (Barrie 1999). 'Multiplatforming' has, therefore, become important for both television cookery and celebrity chefs (Bonner 2009). By the early twenty-first century, the ability to exploit content across multiple platforms was increasingly built into the economics of food programming, enabling media production companies to create 'multiple revenue streams from essentially fixed production costs' (Murray cited in Bonner 2009: 345). As I go on to show later in this chapter, digital media platforms have increased opportunities to extend celebrity chef's brands across a wider range of texts. However, these intertexts also offer 'sites for the extension, disruption or transformation of the discourses within the original text', adding both complexity and potential contradictions within celebrity chef's brands (Strange 1998: 312).

Lifestyle television and the pleasure of cooking

The term 'celebrity chef' became more widespread in the UK – and elsewhere – from the mid-1990s. Although there were already well-established television cooks such as Delia Smith and Madhur Jaffrey, and celebrated restaurant chefs who had forged successful television careers such as Gary Rhodes, a number of changes occurred in the late 1990s and early 2000s that helped to foreground the 'celebrity chef' as a recognizable public figure. As I demonstrated in Chapter 1, some of these developments were a result of changes within the restaurant industry that gave increased prominence to PR and branding. While wider processes of celebritization discussed later in this chapter contributed to the rise of the celebrity chef, more specific transformations in the media industries also played a role. This section examines how changes in the media industries during the 1990s and early 2000s created the conditions for both new types of celebrity chefs and new types of food programming. In particular, I explore how celebrity chefs became cultural intermediaries who did not simply teach viewers how to cook but also how to live and, in the process, legitimated cooking as a new middle-class lifestyle practice.

Press commentary from the time suggests that the UK witnessed an explosion of cookery programming in the late 1990s. Some journalists criticized the ways in which television had transformed food into mere entertainment. Nigella Lawson (1998), who would launch her first TV series in 2000, claimed that by transforming cooking into 'the new rock 'n' roll', food television had reduced it to a 'spectator sport'. Likewise, the *Guardian*'s food critic Matthew Fort (1999) associated TV cookery with the much-maligned ready meal: 'We watch the TV series. We buy the book of the series. And to sustain us while we watch or read, we go to the freezer, take out a frozen pizza, bung it in the microwave and make do.' Critics such as Fort echoed wider critiques of mass culture, associating the boom in cookery programming with the passive consumption of both television and food.

The expansion of television cookery during the 1990s and early 2000s did not just happen on broadcast television but also through a wide range of new satellite, cable and digital channels. The significance of these developments first became evident in the United States following the 1993 launch of the Food Network which, by 2005, had an 'estimated reach of 85.6 million' viewers (Ketchum 2007: 167).[5] From 1999, the impact of the Food Network in the United States was to make food television more '*personality*-driven, rather than *cuisine*-driven, as this would establish a more intimate connection to the audience' (Ibid.: 167; see also Hyman 2008). The Food Network created chefs with distinctive personalities who operated as both brands and assets owned by the channel. This had an impact on the types of celebrity chefs the network created: in a competitive multi-channel context, they selected personalities and cuisines that fitted with the particular demographics and consumer markets they wanted to reach (Ketchum 2007: 161). One result was an attempt to woo under thirty-five and male audiences with 'cool' new types of masculine television chefs such as Anthony Bourdain.

The Food Network UK was launched in 2009. Initially on Sky, it subsequently became a widely available freeview channel. However, it was preceded on cable and satellite by a range of food channels including Carlton Food Network, which ran from 1996 until 2001 and was based around archive ITV cookery programmes, and UK Food, first launched in 2001. The latter went through a series of identities and rebranding exercises but was primarily a vehicle for re-runs of BBC cookery series, unsurprisingly given the BBC had a stake in the channel for much of its history. Its final incarnation, Good Food, would finally merge with the Food Network. These new channels opened up opportunities for existing cookery series to be re-purposed and reshown, expanding the potential to extract profit from them and increasing the importance of international markets for food television.

Cookery TV also boomed as a result of wider changes in UK television in the 1990s. The BBC grappled with changing industry pressures in which they were forced to outsource more production to independents,[6] and to produce cheaper programming that responded to the increasing fragmentation of audiences in a multi-channel context (Brunsdon 2003; Brunsdon et al. 2001). One result was the increasing 'daytime-ization' of primetime television schedules in which 'feminine' topics associated with domestic life that had been mainly confined within daytime schedules migrated to primetime within new formats and reworked or hybridized genres (Brunsdon 2003; Moseley 2000, 2001). Some of this output was produced by independents such as Bazal, who abandoned the educational tone of much earlier cookery TV in favour of infotainment that could deliver audience ratings (Brunsdon 2003, Moseley 2000), and Optomen whose shows included Jamie Oliver's debut series *The Naked Chef* (1999–2001). (For more on Optomen, see G. Smith 2020.) However, the boom in cookery was not restricted to primetime: Bazal hybridized cookery and game show formats in daytime series such as *Ready, Steady, Cook* (1994–2010; 2019–) and *Can't Cook, Won't Cook* (1995–2000). The emphasis on performance in these infotainment formats enabled the development of a number of celebrity chef careers, including Ainsley Harriott and James Martin (Bennett 2010: 134–5). These hybridized formats were also another way in which developments in British cookery television shaped trends elsewhere. For example, the *Ready, Steady Cook* format was replicated in a number of European countries, as well as Australia, New Zealand and on the Food Network in the United States (in which Ainsley Harriott would also star).

The daytime-ization of primetime 'opened up to men' what had formerly been seen as largely feminine interests (Moseley 2001: 32).[7] This took place in the context of an expanding 'gourmet culture' in the 1980s and a booming number of, largely white and middle-class, 'foodies' who invested heavily in 'eating and learning about good food' (Johnston and Baumann 2015: x). Both trends helped to create the sense of cooking as a legitimate masculine pastime.[8] While there was nothing novel about male celebrity chefs on television, some of the emerging celebrity chefs developed new televisual modes of culinary masculinity. For example, in *The Naked Chef*, Jamie Oliver developed a form of domestic masculinity in which the home was represented as a space for masculine leisure and lifestyles rather than female labour (Ashley et al. 2004; Hollows 2003a; Moseley 2001). In this way, Jamie played a role in the transformation of cooking into a youthful and masculine practice.[9]

Daytime-ization was also associated with the opening up of discourses associated with domesticity and everyday life (Moseley 2001). Series such as *The Naked Chef* and Nigella Lawson's *Nigella Bites* (1999–2001) made their stars seem more accessible, approachable and ordinary by taking us into the everyday world of their home, their family and friends. This was accompanied by 'the democratization of an old public service discourse, dominated by experts and a very official kind of talk, and the creation of a new mixed public sphere where common knowledge and everyday experience play a much larger role' (Bondbjerg cited in Moseley 2001: 37). Viewers were encouraged to establish a relationship with the chefs through their conversational tone which made their expertise appear 'ordinary', a point developed further later in the chapter (Bonner 2003; Tominc 2017). Rather than instruction, these new celebrity chefs offered advice using 'a much gentler approach' that suggested 'if you choose to do this, here's how you should go about it' (Bonner 2011: 135). In *The Naked Chef*, Jamie's conversations with the unseen producer strengthened the sense that he was just offering friendly advice about how to cook.[10]

These series are frequently cited examples of lifestyle television. *The Naked Chef* marked a break from earlier cookery shows by incorporating cooking sequences in Jamie's home within wider footage of Jamie's lifestyle in which he was shown zipping around London on his trademark Vespa scooter, shopping, socializing with friends and engaging in a range of leisure pursuits (Hollows 2003a). Rather than simply educating the viewer about how to cook, Jamie demonstrated how to use food as one element 'in an expressive display of lifestyle' (Lury 1996: 65). As Moseley (2001: 38) observes, this was accentuated by the use of a 'grainy realist aesthetic' which gave the audience the sense they were viewing a 'docu-soap' about Jamie's life. This stylized appearance was also injected with an additional sense of cool by borrowing visual strategies from Guy Ritchie's *Lock, Stock and Two Smoking Barrels* (1998), a cult movie set in London's gangland East End (Wilkinson 2019). This highlights the importance of production teams as cultural intermediaries who create the look, feel and dispositions found in cookery television (Piper 2015: 248; G. Smith 2020). Rather than offering the precise instructions on how to cook associated with both Delia Smith and restaurant chefs such as Gary Rhodes, Jamie's more casual style and directions demonstrated how culinary practice could be a source of pleasure and entertainment for the cook as an 'aestheticized leisure practice' centred around the 'care of self' (Hollows 2003a; Lupton 1996: 146). Descriptions of recipes as 'pukka', 'funky' and 'wicked' made cooking appear as a fun, youthful and masculine activity (Hollows 2003a; Moseley 2001; Tominc 2017).

Lifestyle television educated viewers on how to 'makeover' their everyday lives through the use of food in the art of lifestyle. For Moseley (2001: 39), *The Naked Chef* emphasized 'a discourse of accessibility and achievability' and offered viewers the opportunity to transform both their cooking and their 'self'. On the one hand, these shows can be read in terms of a wider social and cultural context in which, some theorists argued, processes of detraditionalization had made 'lifestyle concerns the very core of self-identity' (Giddens 1991: 81). As Mike Featherstone (1991: 86) put it, people no longer inherited lifestyles but were forced to construct them, to 'make lifestyle a life project' through which they 'display their individuality and sense of style'. This was said to provoke a sense of anxiety – in a world of proliferating consumer choices, how were people to construct the 'correct' lifestyles? Lifestyle shows such as *The Naked Chef* addressed these concerns by offering guidance and advice about how to live and by democratizing knowledge and skills so that everyone could participate in lifestyle culture (see Bell and Hollows 2005).

However, on the other hand, the rise of lifestyle did not necessarily indicate the declining importance of class but instead transformations within the class structure. Drawing on the work of Pierre Bourdieu (1984), many critics argued that cookery shows such as *The Naked Chef* and *Nigella Bites* legitimated the tastes and lifestyle practices of the new middle classes and, implicitly or explicitly, rendered other classed lifestyle practices as illegitimate (see, for example, de Solier 2005; Hollows 2003a, 2003b; Lewis 2008a). Food practices in these series were divorced from the economic and temporal pressures of putting a meal on the table faced by many people in their everyday lives, particularly by women. Cultural intermediaries such as Jamie Oliver represented cooking and eating as an 'aestheticized leisure practice', 'a source of entertainment, of enhanced sensory and social enjoyment, pleasure rather than work' (Lupton 1996: 146). *The Naked Chef* appeared to democratize knowledge through fun and friendly recipes with stylish ingredients. However, the ability to engage in cooking as a pleasurable leisure practice required both an investment in culinary cultural capital and an ability to invest in the 'leisure-work' needed to produce and maintain new middle-class lifestyles (Bell 2002; Hollows 2003a). For Bourdieu (1984: 376), the key factor shaping differences in lifestyle 'and, even more, "the stylization of life", lies in objective and subjective distance from the world, with its material constraints and temporal urgencies'. The ability to view cooking as a pleasurable and aestheticized leisure practice is, therefore, both classed and gendered, requiring forms of economic and cultural capital – and a relative lack of temporal constraints – that are not available to all. This raises significant questions about the extent to which celebrity chefs on lifestyle cooking shows democratize food tastes, skills and knowledge.

As I go on to explore in more detail later in the book, the lifestylization of cooking and eating practices by celebrity chefs has further ramifications. By presenting the tastes and competences associated with the new middle classes as desirable and achievable, they produce not only 'aesthetic norms' in relation to cooking and eating but also forms of 'ethical conduct'. Celebrity chefs define modes of 'good' citizenship and 'mark a convergence between questions of lifestyle choice and a broader model of selfhood' which demands we think of lifestyle in terms of both 'pleasure *and* responsibility' (Lewis 2008a: 11–13). These themes are important, not only in identifying which lifestyle practices are legitimated as desirable and responsible but also, which are designated undesirable, irresponsible, and in need of transformation.

Of course, audiences do not necessarily accept the authority of celebrity chefs to legislate on how we should cook and eat or the legitimacy of lifestyled cooking practices seen on TV. While most studies of celebrity chefs use textual analysis to examine how meaning is constructed in media texts, Nick Piper and Christine Barnes explore how audiences both embrace and resist advice from celebrity chefs. Their research suggests that the meaning of food programming, and of celebrity chefs themselves, is negotiated in different ways by audiences in different contexts, 'structured by pre-existing notions of value, gender and social class' (Piper 2015: 260). While some people may consider the lifestyles of celebrity chefs to be 'inspirational, showing them a path to better eating in manageable and delicious ways', others may resist their authority (Barnes 2017: 177). However, this research also demonstrates the extent to which celebrity chefs have become part of everyday life and an important cultural resource: as Piper (2015: 262) argues, 'the ease with which people talk about Jamie Oliver demonstrates how far food media and celebrity chefs are an embedded part of the social fabric'. Audience research highlights how the meaning of celebrity chefs extends beyond texts such as television shows and cookery books – and beyond commentary in the press and across social media platforms – into everyday practices and conversations. As chef's brands are extended, they can also be reinflected, resisted or disrupted (Strange 1998).

Lifestyle cookery series also enabled television channels to build branded personalities who are part of the channel's identity (particularly important for the development of the Food Network in the United States and elsewhere). Like other TV personalities, celebrity chefs can 'act as intermediaries' for, and as the face of, a channel or network (Bonner 2011: 10). Although much cookery television continues to be produced by independents, Channel 4 in particular has used its celebrity chefs – alongside other television personalities – to brand the channel. For example, first runs of Jamie Oliver's output for British audiences have been exclusively on Channel 4 since 2002 and he currently enjoys a multi-million pound 'golden handcuffs' deal with the channel (Sweney 2017). While much of this output is fairly conventional 'chop and chat' cookery television, Oliver's televised public campaigns (see Chapters 5 and 6) became an additional asset for a commercial TV channel with a public service remit (Bell et al. 2017). For the celebrity chefs themselves, lifestyle television offered opportunities to build brands that could be extended into a range of other profitable products. If the images in their cooking shows often resembled lifestyle advertising (Ashley et al. 2004), then products such as cookware and supermarket sauces offered audiences a synergistic connection to the chef's lifestyled brand (Lewis 2008a; Phillipov 2017). However, as I go on to explain in later chapters, the values attached to their brands – for example, authenticity, honesty, passion or caring – were also mobilized to enable celebrity chefs to emerge as campaigners and activists whose significance as public figures extended beyond the kitchen.

The rise of the celebrity chef

As I have shown so far, transformations in both the culinary field and media industries created the conditions for the rise of the celebrity chef. In this section, I want to pause my analysis to reflect on two other reasons why television chefs became celebrities. First, I examine how their roles as television personalities helped to create the conditions for their celebrification. Second, I explore how the rise of the celebrity chefs was shaped by more widespread processes of celebritization in the 1990s and 2000s.

Although not all celebrity chefs owe their success to television, many are known as TV personalities as well as food experts. Bonner (2011) identifies how TV chefs frequently use the sense of familiarity and intimacy enabled by television's established role as a domestic medium to build relationships with their audience. Like the audience at home, celebrity chefs such as Jamie Oliver and Nadiya Hussain in the UK – and Ree Drummond and Ina Garten in the United States – appear on screen in 'ordinary' domestic situations where they engage in everyday activities such as cooking, even if their cooking and kitchens appear are highly aspirational and some of 'their' kitchens are sets. Their ability to perform 'seeming spontaneity and relaxed naturalness' helps to create a sense of intimacy with the audience and to convey a sense of ordinariness (Scannell cited in Bonner 2011: 15; Bennett 2010). Because successful celebrity chefs are important assets for TV channels, their 'televisual image' is created over time and across performances, emphasizing the sense that the audience 'knows' them (Bennett 2010: 124–5). This is exemplified by Nadiya Hussain who has starred in a number of cookery series following her success as a contestant on the *Great British Bake Off* (2010–). Although her cooking skills were validated by her competition win, Nadiya's graduation from 'ordinary person' to 'celebrity chef' enabled audiences to relate to her as 'one of us'. Nadiya's expressive face, conversational skills and disarming candour all worked to cement her sense of ordinariness and authenticity – qualities which, by association, were transferred on to her recipes (see Chapter 7). However, the idea that TV personalities are simply 'being themselves' masks the 'talent, skilled performance or hard work that goes into their on-screen persona' (Bennett 2010: 117).

Audiences' sense that they 'know' a celebrity chef can also be increased by media coverage of their private lives. Graeme Turner suggests that 'a public figure becomes a celebrity' when 'media interest in their activities is transferred from reporting on their public role … to investigating the detail of their private life' (cited in Holmes and Redmond 2006: 12). While not all celebrity chefs generate this kind of coverage, a significant number do. This means that their ability to 'perform' sincerity and authenticity demands 'congruence' between their public and private selves (Bonner 2011: 24, 57). For example, in 2013, aspirational images of Nigella's warm and hospitable screen 'home' were punctured by photographs and stories of domestic abuse by her then husband Charles Saatchi. Johnston and Goodman (2015: 212) have argued that media chefs often appear as both 'authentic and aspirational'; they appear to be 'real people' but 'present idealized lifestyles'. The press reports of Nigella as a victim, and survivor, of what she called 'intimate terrorism' called into question the idealized lifestyles portrayed in her cookery shows (cited in Booth 2013). However, they also accentuated her sincerity and authenticity as she rebuilt her career and remained 'Nigella' despite extensive and intrusive press coverage of her private life. If, in many ways, the aspirational lifestyles represented in Nigella's cookery programmes already were self-consciously modelled as fantasies of domestic life (Hollows 2003b), her post-2013 career was able to draw on this, presenting images of how cooking might enhance domestic life and be a source of comfort with the reassurance of recipes associated with the authenticity of the Nigella brand.

However, it is not only food experts' roles as television personalities that helped to create the conditions for their celebrification. The 'structural shifts' associated with 'mediatization' which saw 'the increasing involvement of media in all spheres of life' also played a role in the rise of celebrity chefs (Couldry 2015: chapter 6; Driessens 2012). As Jessica Evans explains, 'if celebrities are the few, known by the many, then people can only become celebrities through the transmission of their image: celebrity *by definition* requires mediation' (cited in Driessens 2013: 548).

One aspect of these wider processes of celebritization has been the diversification of celebrity into new fields such as cooking (Driessens 2012: 647). This is often driven by a 'profit dynamic' in which celebrity status equates with more financial success and leads to the use of marketing and PR to increase visibility across a range of fields. As I highlighted in Chapter 1, these strategies became important for financial success in the restaurant industry. PR agents like Borra Garson emerged who developed a roster of celebrity chefs. For example, after working with Michelin-starred television chef Gary Rhodes, Garson helped to transform a then unknown Jamie Oliver into a household name.[11] Her agency Deborah McKenna Limited currently represents a significant number of celebrity chefs including Michelin-starred Simon Rogan, Daniel Clifford and Tom Kerridge; culinary entrepreneurs such as Levi Roots; former *Masterchef* winners such as Irini Tzortzoglou; and YouTube cooking star Ben Ebbrell from SORTEDFood.

Accompanying the diversification of celebrity, Driessens (2012) argues, is the increased migration of celebrities, as they move within or beyond their original position within a field. As I suggested in Chapter 1, this can be risky: for example, the credibility and reputation of Gordon Ramsay as a restaurant chef within the culinary field where he first made his name has been threatened by his increasing pursuit of economic profit and his diversification into entertainment and media fields. But some celebrity chefs who achieved fame through cookery television have become well-established television personalities beyond food programming. For example, Gino D'Acampo has starred in a range of light entertainment formats alongside his cooking shows.[12] Numerous celebrity chefs have starred in celebrity reality formats: for example, D'Acampo and Antony Worrall Thompson appeared on ITV's *I'm a Celebrity, Get Me out of Here* while James Martin, Gary Rhodes, Ainsley Harriott and Hairy Biker Dave Myers have all appeared on BBC1's *Strictly Come Dancing*. Another crucial form of celebrity migration is into political life. Some celebrity chefs such as Jamie Oliver and Hugh Fearnley-Whittingstall have launched high-profile public campaigns (see Chapters 5, 6 and 8). Many more use their position to comment on a range of political issues as the discussion of responses to Black Lives Matter demonstrated in Chapter 1. If celebrity chefs migrate into other fields, then non-culinary celebrities have also migrated into food media: for example, *Top Gear* presenter James May's *Oh Cook* (2020) on Amazon, Gwyneth Paltrow's culinary offerings as part of her goop brand and Valerie Bertinelli's cookery shows on the Food Network.

Bourdieu's concept of field can be applied to celebrity as well as gastronomy. Driessens (2013: 549) argues that celebrity is 'a kind of power' that can generate economic profits (for example, when attached to a branded range of pans or sauces), can help generate social connections (meeting people who can further influence your opportunities) and 'possibilities to enter new domains', whether this is new business ventures in television production such as Studio Ramsay or the opportunities to shape political life documented in *Jamie's School Dinners* (2005). Celebrity chefs can use their 'celebrity capital' as a 'kind of reputational capital' that helps them in new ventures, enabling them to migrate and 'work across social fields' (Ibid.: 549, 551). Media appearances enhance their opportunities to do this by increasing their visibility (Ibid.: 552). Therefore, although celebritization can pose a risk to a chef's professional credibility, the culinary field has become at least partly 'celebritized' so that 'celebrity capital becomes a competitive resource' within it (Ibid.: 553). However, because celebrity is a limited resource, celebrity chefs are in competition to acquire it, and this partly explains the increased use of agents. Like other celebrities, chefs who want to 'gain celebrity capital have to be prepared to play the game of the celebrity industry' (Ibid.: 557), often prioritizing economic ends in ways that contrast with the emphasis on aesthetic value within the culinary field (see also Couldry 2015).

Digital media and new forms of celebrity chef

Social media platforms have created a massive expansion in the 'promotional space' in which celebrities operate (Couldry 2015). As I demonstrated in Chapter 1, using social media has become part of the job description of many neighbourhood chefs who need to attract diners to their restaurants. However, most celebrity chefs maintain high-profile social media accounts as part of the labour of modern celebrity, even if that labour is performed by media professionals on their behalf. As Mike Goodman and Sylvia Jaworska (2020: 2) observe, 'Digital foodscapes … are material semiotic "places of curation" designed for rolling performances of identities, brands, personalities and, of course, value generation.' This enables established and emerging celebrity chefs to increase the 'intertextual circulation' of their image and offer audiences what appear to be more immediate and unmediated access to their 'authentic' self (Bennett 2010: 170). Celebrity chefs' social media accounts appear 'unedited', not only 'creating and curating "real" and "authentic" chronicles of their lives' but also offering opportunities to more carefully manage public perception of their image (Goodman and Jaworska 2020: 9).

Digital media platforms have become increasingly important in shaping food knowledges (see, for example, Goodman and Jaworska 2020; Lewis 2020; Leer and Strøm Krogager 2021; Lupton and Feldman 2020: Presswood 2020; see Rousseau 2012a for earlier work). While it is easy to downplay the significance of social media for food knowledges, just over 50 per cent of adults in the United States watch YouTube food videos (Lewis 2020: 47). An established celebrity chef such as Jamie Oliver has 7.6 million followers on Facebook, 8.2 million followers on Instagram,

6.6 million followers on Twitter and over 5 million subscribers to his YouTube channel.[13] However, in digital spaces like YouTube, established celebrity chefs compete for visibility with other established players, with well-resourced digital enterprises such as Buzzfeed's Tasty, and with popular YouTube channels such as Emily Kim's Maangchi and Andrew Rea's Binging with Babish. YouTube, blogs and other digital platforms can operate as 'a source of new talent' for television and publishing industries (Deller and Murphy 2019: 2). High-profile celebrity chef Ree Drummond, 'The Pioneer Woman', first established her brand on a blog as did Ella Woodward with 'Deliciously Ella' (see Chapter 3). Likewise, the highly successful YouTube vegan cooking channel BOSH! also enabled its creators to move into publishing and broadcast TV (see Chapter 4). However, as I go on to show, the division between established and social media celebrity is not straightforward: the routes to becoming a 'digital food influencer' and a celebrity chef 'are multiple and bi-directional' (Goodman and Jaworska 2020: 9).

While people may share food ideas and knowledge on social media for a range of reasons, many also engage in self-branding activities through which they construct 'DIY celebrity personas' (Bennett 2010: 171). These strategies are often discussed in terms of 'microcelebrity', a 'practice of constructing and preserving an online identity, managing it like a commercial product or brand' (Deller and Murphy 2019: 3). Through these practices, 'the audience is constructed as a fan base, popularity is maintained through ongoing fan management, and self-presentation is carefully assembled to be consumed by others' (Marwick 2015; see also Banet-Weiser 2017). Hits, likes and comments are crucial to these branded selves, not only because they contribute to metrics that can enhance commercial success but, crucially, because they increase visibility (Banet-Weiser 2012: 68). As Baker and Walsh (2020: 56) suggest, 'online metrics operate as a means of symbolic exchange, signifying behaviours that both affirm validation and status'. YouTubers use a range of strategies to enlist the support of their followers in their metric-enhancing endeavours: for example, Avant-Garde Vegan Gaz Oakley promised fans he would open a restaurant as their reward once he hit 1 million subscribers. However, it is debatable just how 'micro' these celebrities are. The social media presence of celebrity chefs with an established 'offline' profile can be 'eclipsed' by digital food influencers (some of whom also expand 'offline') (Goodman and Jaworska 2020: 3).

While many would-be celebrity chefs use platforms such as YouTube to construct a 'subjectivity comprised of distinct sets of self-referential, attention-seeking, market-aware practices' (Hearn and Schoenhoff 2015, ch. 11), the appearance of authenticity is crucial to their brands (Marwick 2015). Many draw on strategies used in lifestyle cookery television to create a sense of familiarity that gives 'followers access to their intimate, ordinary, authentic selves' (Bennett 2010: 171). However, social media platforms also extend the possibility to invite followers into celebrity chefs' everyday lives through repeated, and often highly aspirational, images of routine and everyday activities with family and friends (Goodman and Jaworska 2020: 6). Although radically different and creative uses can be made of food videos on YouTube (see, for example, Lewis 2020), one heavily used vlogger style uses personal stories to create a sense that what they are doing is 'real' and 'unmediated' (Braun and Carruthers 2020: 85). The delivery is highly conversational, drawing on lifestyle television conventions, but can be rambling or unfocused, with minimal editing, to suggest a lack of professional polish that conveys authenticity. YouTubers often focus on their everyday life to highlight their ordinariness and relatability, accentuated by performances of 'amateur-ness' or 'spontaneity' familiar from lifestyle television (Deller and Murphy 2019: 4). For example, while popular YouTuber Rachel Ama carefully demonstrates how to cook vegan dishes shaped by her British, Caribbean and African roots, these demonstrations are framed by conversational pieces to camera and sequences in which she sings and dances like an 'ordinary girl' around her home. These are complemented by some staple YouTube food formats which invite the viewer into her everyday life: for example, 'what I eat in day' videos and 'vegan grocery hauls'.

However, many successful digital food influencers use a limited range of predictable techniques to signify 'authenticity' (Banet-Weiser 2012: 81). Branded selves are constructed by enhancing the 'most appealing or lucrative aspects' of the self and 'underplay[ing] those that do not further their branding objectives' or convey a marketable form of 'authenticity' (Khamis et al. 2017: 199). Although 'authenticity' is often associated with emotional 'truth' and transparency, this can take various forms: Deliciously Ella's self is branded around affective message of 'self-empowerment and positivity' (Goodman and Jaworska 2020: 7) while Jack Monroe's 'truth' often conveys raw anger at injustice (see Chapters 3 and 6 for more on these celebrity chefs). The ability to perform 'keeping it real' is key to monetizing content so that, in digital spaces such as YouTube, authenticity and monetization cannot simply be thought of 'in oppositional terms' (Lewis 2020: 50).

While very few food YouTubers and bloggers earn significant amounts of money from their online activities, some brands such as SORTEDfood outperform many celebrity chefs' own channels (de Solier 2018: 56). While it might be assumed that digital media stars wish to graduate to established media forms, it is questionable whether successful YouTubers need television deals (Deller and Murphy 2019: 16). Furthermore, the divisions between social and established media are not straightforward: as Tania Lewis (2020: 50) notes, 'it is increasingly difficult to draw a clear line between the professionalized realm of the commercial institutions such as broadcast TV and that of video sharing platforms'. SORTEDfood provides a useful illustration of this. Ben Ebbrell, the culinary brains in the original team of four friends who founded the channel, is represented by Borra Garson, the PR and management agent for celebrity chefs. While the channel – and associated social media accounts, cookbooks, app and club – is represented as the creation of an enthusiastic team of ordinary lads straight from university, Ebbrell won cable channel Good Food's *Market Kitchen*'s (2007–10) search for the next celebrity chef and co-presented the children's show *Munch Box* (2013–14) on ITV, among other broadcast TV appearances (DML 2021). Many successful YouTubers use a number of 'content producers' for their brand (Usher 2020: 178); SORTEDfood had sixteen staff members by 2019 (Dropbox 2019). In this way, as Lewis (2020: 56) argues, while the channel uses 'the rhetoric, aesthetics, and practices of friendship and participation' that is viewed as embodying the spirit of videosharing, it 'inscribes such practices within a normative, neoliberal logic of entrepreneurialism'.

While some commentators have stressed the utopian or democratizing potential of platforms such as YouTube as a community project for building and sharing collective knowledge, Lewis (2020: 55) argues that the 'YouTube food space' is 'a complex digital economy … in which ordinary expertise bears a range of types of exchange value: social, informational, communitarian, and monetary'. Although advice might be shared, it is also an entrepreneurial space for constructing 'personal branding' (Lewis 2020: 55). As I go on to explore in more detail in the following chapters, this emphasis on self-branding means that many bloggers and YouTubers do not just promote activities such as cooking and eating as a means of constructing the self through lifestyle practices; they also model the forms of identity and selfhood demanded by neoliberal economies. Furthermore, while these platforms have the potential to produce creative and diverse ways of representing food practices, the pursuit of a fan base – and potential economic profits – often results in the visibility of a narrow range of generic conventions and branded identities which shape the meaning of food in particular ways.

YouTube channels such as SORTEDfood – and the healthy eating bloggers and vegan YouTubers I discuss in Chapters 3 and 4 – also exemplify Lewis's (2020: 50) argument that 'we need to rethink how we map out and categorize the relationship between DIY and professional, monetized media practices'. For Lewis, 'the sharing, participatory ethos of YouTube – with its emphasis on "authenticity" and "community" – is also central to the logics of the entrepreneurial practices enabled by and through the platform'. The conversational style of many lifestyle cookery shows encourages a form of intimate 'para-social' relationship between presenters such as Jamie Oliver and Nadiya Hussein and their audience (Moores 2000: 20–2), a relationship extended through social media platforms such as Twitter and Instagram. YouTube stars frequently take this further by creating 'at least "the illusion" … of a two-way relationship' (Usher 2020: 173). In the voiceover that introduces most videos on SORTEDfood, viewers are invited to 'Join our community where everything we do starts with you', accompanied by visuals which demonstrate how new content directly responds to viewer comments.

Although digital media have the potential to be more democratic than established media forms with high costs of entry, the reality is less optimistic. Alane L. Presswood (2020: 8) suggests that food blogging tends to reinforce 'gender, race and class-based hierarchies' while Goodman and Jaworska (2020: 9) conclude that the vast majority of high-profile food influencers are either white, male celebrity chefs' or white, middle-to-upper class female wellness influencers. As Sarah Banet-Weiser (2012: 85) observes, there are 'limits to what kind of self is brandable' – and commercially viable. The representation of 'microcelebrity as a "bottom up" practice' giving a voice to groups who have been marginalized by established media forms and industries ignores the extent to which not everyone has 'the same access to professional production technologies or support' (Usher 2020: 178).

The ways in which consumption practices are used to construct lifestyles to create social media brands impact on how food is given meaning on digital platforms. In part, these are shaped by established conventions for representing food practices in lifestyle television. Just as Jamie Oliver makes domestic cookery appear to be a leisured lifestyle practice rather than a form of labour, so 'through discourses of passion, bloggers create a notion of work that *doesn't seem like work* as leisure and labour blend seamlessly together' (Duffy and Hund 2015: 9). New forms of food media on digital platforms, like more established forms of food media, curate particular ways of understanding 'how and what we should be buying, cooking and eating – and looking at and "knowing"' (Goodman and Jaworska 2020: 2). As I go on to explore in later chapters, the emphasis on the entrepreneurial and brandable self within social media networks shapes how food practices are given meaning. This is not to suggest that platforms such as YouTube and Instagram are only used in one way: there are many channels and accounts that challenge these tendencies. However, in order to gain visibility and get your voice heard, there is a pressure to present the self – and food – in a limited range of ways.

Conclusion

This chapter has explored how celebrity chefs operate within the media industries and the generic and technological transformations that have enabled new types of celebrity chef and food influencer to emerge. The boom in cookery TV foregrounded the importance of food practices in everyday life and shaped what kind of food knowledges are available. Lifestyle cookery programming is often associated with new forms of 'ordinary' expertise that focuses on 'skills and knowledges associated with everyday life' (Lewis 2008a: 2). However, just because this expertise is 'ordinary' does not mean that it doesn't produce or reproduce wider power relations and inequalities based on a range of structural differences such as class, gender and race. As I go on to explore in the rest of the book, these issues are important because celebrity chefs help to shape public discourses about food and impact on people's everyday practices and experience.

The distinctions between celebrity chefs operating within established media industries such as television and celebrity chefs or food influencers associated with digital media platforms are often far from clear cut. As Jean Burgess and Joshua Green comment, 'it is not helpful to draw sharp distinctions between professional and amateur production, or between commercial and community practices' (cited in Banet-Weiser 2017: 277). The forms of 'ordinary expertise' that Lewis (2020: 48) identifies with the emergence of lifestyle television have some continuities with the 'amateur advice culture' enabled by social media platforms. Influencers, she argues, 'are close relatives' of Bourdieu's professional cultural intermediaries, 'guiding people again through a morass of lifestyle choices though they also represent something of a shift in the culture of lifestyle media and advice' (Ibid.: 32). Despite the inequalities that structure whose voices are amplified on social media and whose images get seen, there has been some 'democratization' of expertise: 'online culinary advice today … in many ways represents the ultimate triumph of ordinary expertise' (Ibid.: 49). This has led some academic and media commentators to question the legitimacy of advice offered online (Baker and Rojek 2020): for example, the healthy eating bloggers discussed in the next chapter are often accuses of 'promoting ignorance and encouraging harmful activities without recourse to experts' (Deller and Murphy 2019: 11). However, at the same time, amateur expertise – with its admissions of mistakes and mishaps – can sometimes appear more trustworthy because it is accompanied by a sense of 'ordinariness' and 'authenticity' from people who might appear more 'like us'.

As this chapter makes clear, content creators on digital platforms further complicate who we understand to be a celebrity chef. While many celebrity chefs are also food influencers on platforms such as Instagram and Twitter, some influencers whose careers started on digital media such as Jack Monroe and Ella Woodward are now also referred to as celebrity chefs. It is for this reason that the discussion in this book moves across these conventional boundaries between 'old' and 'new' media, working within the more expansive and widely used understanding of the term 'celebrity chef'. The following two chapters both look more closely at some of the ways in which celebrity chefs have influenced contemporary food culture across media forms, focusing on celebrity chefs and healthy eating advice in Chapter 3 and how celebrity chefs mediate gender and veganism in Chapter 4.

Chapter 3

FOOD, HEALTH AND THE FEMININE BODY

The trend for 'clean eating' had achieved a huge international presence on digital media by the mid-late 2010s. Many millions of Instagram posts featured 'eatclean' and 'cleaneating' hashtags (Walsh and Baker 2020). In the UK, 90 per cent of Amazon's bestselling food and drink books in the UK focused 'on healthy eating and diet' in 2016 (Wilson 2017). Publishers eager to capitalize on trends like 'clean eating' signed up predominantly female bloggers and Instagram influencers who offered new ways of cooking and eating that promised health, beauty and vitality. The most recognizable face of this trend in the UK was Ella Woodward, a slim and youthful blogger-turned 'wellness entrepreneur' (O'Neill 2020: 3). Her cookbook *Deliciously Ella* recorded the highest-ever sales of a debut cookbook in 2015. She epitomized many features of the new wave of celebrity chefs who emerged more widely on digital platforms (see Chapter 2) and the Ella brand continued to be anchored around her Instagram-friendly image as her media power and business interests grew.

By 2019, a very different diet cookbook was breaking publishing records. Kate Allinson and Kay Featherstone's *A Pinch of Nom* recorded the highest-ever first-week sales for a non-fiction book in the UK and had sold over half a million copies within its first month (Collins 2019; Flood 2019). Its authors were also a social media phenomenon who, by 2020, boasted a Pinch of Nom Facebook community of 1.5 million users (Allinson and Featherstone 2020b). However, *Pinch of Nom* was very different to *Deliciously Ella*. Its creators preferred to be 'in the shadows' and had a 'dislike of publicity' and were frequently described as '"jolly", "middle-aged", "fat"' (Lytton 2020). Rather than promising new superfoods and dietary revelations, their books and social media output focused on more well-worn ideas of calorie counting. Rather than promoting clean eating, they became well-known for their low-calorie versions of 'dirty' convenience foods, from 'Loaded Potato Skins' to 'fakeaway' dishes such as 'Cheeseburger Pizza' (Allinson and Featherstone 2020b, 2020d).

In both this and the following chapter, I develop arguments about how social media food influencers and celebrity chefs shaped ideas about how and what to eat in the 2010s. While this chapter focuses on questions about diet in relationship to health and the body, Chapter 4 explores the developing interest in vegan food practices during the period. These chapters share a number of themes. First, the chapters provide case studies of digital food influencers, their relationships to more established media and to a wider community of fans and readers. Second, they examine how the authority of these food influencers is often based on forms of what Tania Lewis (2008a, 2020) calls 'ordinary expertise' which has been linked to both a democratization of food knowledge and the declining authority of expert knowledge. Third, these chapters explore how ideas about 'clean' and 'dirty' food shape contemporary eating practices and reproduce more longstanding oppositions between 'pure' and 'impure' foods that structure ideas about what it is both 'safe' and 'good' to eat (Ashley et al. 2004; Douglas 1966; Mudry 2018). These oppositions are mobilized to classify and rank gendered, classed and racial identities (see, for example, Perrier and Swan 2020 and also Chapter 6).

However, both chapters are primarily concerned with the gendered politics of cooking and eating. As I have already discussed, there is a well-established body of research that highlights how celebrity chefs mediate not only ideas about how to cook and eat but also about gendered practices, tastes, dispositions and identities. This chapter focuses on a largely feminine space within a new media landscape that is often dominated by male celebrity chefs. It analyses how 'healthy eating' discourses are linked to the production of appropriately feminine bodies. In particular, I identify how women are 'empowered' to use food not only to take responsibility for their own health but also to produce themselves as desirable and attractive post-feminist subjects. The following chapter explores how the entry of veganism into mainstream food media has involved a masculinization of veganism that, paradoxically, works to reaffirm the importance of meat to masculine identities while championing plant-based alternatives.

Neoliberalism, well-being and the healthy body

Concerns about the impact of food on the body and health are far from new. As well as longstanding religious influences that categorize some foods as 'impure' or 'dirty' and therefore bad to eat (Douglas 1966), more specific ideas about the relationships between hygiene, nutrition and health had emerged by the mid-1800s and these formed the foundations for twentieth-century health foods movements (Biltekoff 2013; Dubisch 2017; Mudry 2018). Although slimming diets that emerged in the interwar period were shaped by scientific thought about calorific consumption, many maintained a theological dimension through ideas of 'confession', 'conversion' and 'sacrifice' and the promise of 'transcendent physical transformation and renewal' (Contois 2015: 120–2, 117). While scientific ideas about nutrition now compete with religious proscriptions about what is good or bad to eat, much dietary advice continues to have a strong moral dimension. Furthermore, ideas about nutrition, diet and the body have always been entangled with ideas about classed, gendered and racialized identities. In particular, women have frequently been both the objects and subjects of dietary advice because of both the role of female domestic feeding work in producing healthy families and the influence of idealized notions of the feminine body on women's eating practices (Cairns and Johnston 2015).

The meanings of the relationships between health, food and the body are reshaped in different cultural and historical contexts. Since the 1970s, 'health' has become an increasingly 'central way to "define the self"' (Crawford 2006: 402). By the twenty-first century, health had morphed into 'healthism', the term used by Robert Crawford (2006: 411) to capture how health became both a matter of lifestyle and a 'super-value' informing many aspects of everyday life. The rise of healthism was accompanied by holistic ideas of 'well-being' which promised people access to a new and improved self. New forms of eating advice emerged that 'evoke[d] an ideal of optimal health, achievable through the correct diet' with many focusing on the benefits accruing from enhanced control of the body and 'psychological and emotional control over eating' (Braun and Carruthers 2020: 83; Kjaer 2019: 708).

Healthism also transformed health into a personal responsibility. As this idea became 'hegemonic', it helped to legitimate and naturalize wider neoliberal ideologies which see the individual, rather than the state, as responsible for their own well-being (Crawford 2006: 409). Food media operated as crucial sites for producing and circulating 'biopedagogies', those 'knowledge practices concerned with the "*bios*" – how people should live, including how and how much to eat and move, to be healthy' (Rodney 2019: [4]). These biopedagogies 'define the value of bodies and produce subjectivities, particularly in relation to the ideal-typical healthy body' (Rodney 2019: [4]), distinguishing between 'healthy' and 'unhealthy' practices and types of people. For example, the 'choice' to practise detoxing, clean eating, superfood diets or healthy eating is often linked to the 'choice' to have increased health – and associated benefits such as increased energy and productivity. These discourses position people as responsible for the 'choice' to maximize their health and, in the process, become effective and productive neoliberal consumer-citizens who are not a burden on the state or other people (see, for example, Baker and Walsh 2020; Harjunen 2016; Kjaer 2019; Lupton 2018c; Rodney 2019; Sikka 2019). As a result, 'the healthy body has come to signify the morally worthy citizen' (Lebesco 2011: [2]).

Wellness culture needs to be understood, therefore, as 'part of the apparatus of neoliberal state power that seeks to regulate, normalize and discipline its citizens to render them more productive' (Lupton 2018c: 33). Healthism legitimates the idea that the visual appearance of the body acts as an indicator of a person's health, and hence wider economic and moral value: slimness is equated with health, an idea reinforced across countless Instagram images and healthy eating blogs that promise the benefits of 'feeling lighter' (Kjaer 2019: 705). In this context, fatness becomes 'stigmatized as an indicator of an individual's poor health' (Cairns and Johnston 2015: 103). Fatness is represented as a choice, as 'self-inflicted' and the result of 'faulty agency' rather than the result of a whole range of factors including the various forms of inequality that structure access to healthy food (Harjunen 2016: 73; Raisborough 2016: 17). In this way, distinctions between 'healthy' and 'unhealthy' bodies are frequently both classed and racialized (see Chapter 6).

However, the meaning of food practices in women's healthy eating blogs cannot be explained with reference to neoliberalism alone. Feminine identities are also produced within a post-feminist context that works in tandem with neoliberalism. Post-feminism promotes a 'relentless individualism' which 'renders the intense surveillance of women's bodies normal or even desirable, that calls for endless work on the self and that centres on notions of empowerment and choice while enrolling women in ever more intense regimes of "the perfect"' (Gill 2017: 609). In this context, clean eating gurus encourage women to discard restrictive slimming plans which once promised the route to a perfect body and instead 'experience the pleasures of healthy eating – and the svelte physique that is an assumed embodiment of health' (Cairns and Johnston 2015: 88). Women are empowered to 'choose' the pleasures of health which also conforming to the obligation to be slim and beautiful: in wellness discourses, health is conflated with both slimness and beauty (Harjunen 2016: 75). Therefore, while the opportunities to engage in DIY media production via blogs or Instagram might offer women a sense of empowerment, food bloggers and influencers often do 'little to challenge the overwhelmingly rigid standards to which women's bodies continue to be held' (Dejmanee 2016: 433).

Women's healthy eating blogs tend to represent foodwork as a pleasurable choice rather than obligatory domestic labour (Rodney et al. 2017: 701). This marks a shift from long-established ideas of feeding work as a way of caring for, and giving pleasure to, family members, neatly encapsulated in the title of Anne Murcott's (1995) article 'It's a pleasure to cook for him' (see also Charles and Kerr 1988; DeVault 1991). Instead, these bloggers often suggest that food can be used as a form of 'self-care, pleasure and satisfaction', enabling women to please – and look after – the self rather than only caring for other people (Rodney et al. 2017: 690; see also Hollows 2003b). Yet this emphasis on caring for the self is often tied back into the values of healthism in which self-care is obligatory in order to be a responsible, productive consumer-citizen.

These debates, which demonstrate how contemporary ideas about health, eating and the body are deeply political, provide a context for making sense of the recent wave of female food bloggers who have established lucrative careers by offering dietary advice. The rest of this chapter explores how two digital media brands shaped by women – Deliciously Ella and A Pinch of Nom – configure the gendered relationships between food, health and the body in different ways. While advice on diet and health in women's media is far from new, my analysis examines how these issues are reimagined and mediated in digital media.

Clean eating

Clean eating diets – associated with the consumption of 'health-giving' foods that are 'pure' and 'unprocessed' – were popularized across a range of media sites in the 2010s. However, the rise of clean eating is often associated with new digital media food influencers, food gurus who established their brands on blogs, Instagram and

YouTube. The cultural intermediaries who promoted clean eating were primarily female, youthful, white and attractive, their visual image a representation of the health- (and beauty-) giving powers of their dietary practices. Despite later attempts to distance themselves from the phrase, 'clean eating' in the UK became associated with blogging sisters Hemsley + Hemsley – who would also publish cookbooks and feature in the Channel 4 series *Eating Well with Hemsley + Hemsley* – and Ella Woodward (later Mills), the blogger behind the Deliciously Ella brand that I explore in more detail below.[1] More generally they can be seen as part of a wave of digital media influencers discussed in Chapter 2, whose 'ordinary expertise' began to replace more conventional forms of expert knowledge (Baker and Walsh 2020: 53; Lewis 2020: 48–9). Alexandra Rodney (2019: [2]) uses the term 'blogspert' to 'describe this phenomenon of online health "experts" …. cultivating knowledge of (lay) experience and anecdotal evidence that they have applied this knowledge to achieve thinness'. In retrospect, this can be seen as part of a wider trend in which the value of more established forms of expertise was increasingly questioned in political life, in conflicts over Brexit in the UK and the rise of Donald Trump in the United States (see Mangan 2018a).

While clean eating bloggers were not the only advocates of 'superfoods' associated with amazing health benefits, they certainly helped boost their sales and normalize their presence in UK diets. In the month following the publication of Ella Woodward's first cookbook, sales of psyllium husk powder – an ingredient in her 'Superfood bread' – rose by 1311 per cent (Daily Telegraph 2015). More generally, ingredients such as spirulina and chia seeds which had gained a 'halo effect' (Eriksson and Machin 2020) became sufficiently mainstream to be sold in discount supermarkets such as Aldi.[2] As Angela Smith (2020) notes, clean eating foods became so embedded in UK food culture that celebrity chef Nigella Lawson, an outspoken critic of clean eating, began to incorporate aspects of the trend in her TV series *Simply Nigella*. Both in the UK and elsewhere, consuming superfoods became a way of building identities and lifestyles based on 'dietary selection and display' (Sikka 2019: 356). Because it was thought of as a 'lifestyle rather than a diet', its practitioners viewed clean eating as 'central to identity with the term used to express the moral ethos of the consumer' (Baker and Walsh 2020: 54). Furthermore, despite the diffusion of some superfoods in the mass market, the use of these products has 'become a way of expressing cultural capital as knowledge and difference' and a means of practising class distinction (Wilkes 2021: 6).

As cookery writer Ruby Tandoh (2017) observed in the *Guardian*, 'while the machinery of these fads is constructed largely by a small group of men' selling questionable 'science', the public face of clean eating – and the target for the backlash against it – was the pretty, 'unfailingly young and thin, overwhelmingly white' woman. In the UK, the most recognizable face of clean eating was Ella Woodward. Her brand Deliciously Ella started out in 2012 as a blog that charted her attempt to cure her Postural Tachycardia Syndrome (PoTS) by learning to cook and care for herself through her food practices. By the release of her first cookbook *Deliciously Ella* in January 2015, Woodward was a significant enough brand to record the highest-ever first-week sales of a debut cookbook in the UK (a figure since surpassed by other digital food influencers) (Swanson 2015) and went on to sell over a quarter of a million copies by 2017 (Onwuemezi 2017). While publishing further cookbooks and writing for newspapers such as the *Daily Telegraph*, she has continued to build her digital brand, primarily through her blog and Instagram (with 1.7 million followers in March 2020) as well as other social media channels such as YouTube and Facebook. She has also extended her brand to a range of widely available plant-based frozen meals, breakfast products such as muesli and granola, and snacks such as Nut Butter Balls as well as a small chain of delis. She has achieved sufficiently widespread celebrity for her wedding and baby photos to feature in celebrity magazines such as *Hello!* and in national newspapers.

The Deliciously Ella blog centred around Woodward's developing role as an 'expert patient' (Braun and Carruthers 2020: 85) as her eating practices facilitated her 'journey' from illness to health. In her writing, 'the Hippocratic conception of "food as medicine" comes to function not so much as proverbial wisdom but as a literal statement of fact' (O'Neill 2020: 9). Indeed, the very practice of blogging and sharing becomes part of her narrative of recovery. As she notes in an early post, 'I'm really starting to find blogging a very empowering adventure … It's making me feel so positive' (Woodward 2012a). This confessional tone associated with diaries is also articulated with the confessional aspects of religious practices, a staging post in the process of 'conversion' to new eating practices and a new identity (Contois 2015: 120). On her blog and in interview, there are frequent references to her previous identity as a 'sugar monster': As she put it in the 'About Me' page of her blog: 'I know how hard changing your diet in such a radical way can be … I was a total sugar monster … Knowing the love and health I'm giving my body makes me so happy' (Woodward n.d.). In this way, Ella contributed to a wider 'gendered "confessional culture" that compels the private worlds of young women into the public sphere' (Duffy and Hund 2015: 7).

The confessional tone of the diary creates a sense of authenticity and intimacy between Ella and her readers. Indeed, the earlier entries often sound naive and innocent; she is frequently 'obsessed' by her latest food crush. This helps to create the sense that the benefits of clean eating are as much emotional as physical; for example, a vegan pesto pasta 'makes me really happy' and 'will do wonders for your body and mind' (Woodward 2012c). As with some of the female food bloggers discussed by Alexandra Rodney et al. (2017: 698), the pleasures of eating are the pleasures of consuming health, reproducing wider clean eating trends on Instagram where aestheticized images of 'bowl food' promise to make 'people happy and relaxed as well as healthy' (A. Smith 2020: 2). Indeed, Ella suggests, we can literally consume happiness: 'it really feels like you're eating a bowl of healthy happiness' she says of a dish of 'Wild rice with avocado, cherry tomatoes, broccoli and pomegranates' (Woodward 2012e). Through consuming the correct foods, women can help to achieve the 'positive mental attitude' demanded of the successful post-feminist subject (Gill 2017: 619). The increased sense of energy Ella's recipes promise seems to be as much a feeling as a physical property. If we have the choice to eat in ways that boost energy, then, by implication, 'lack of energy … is a punishment' experienced by those who choose to eat the 'wrong' foods (Kjaer 2019: 710). This helps to link the practice of eating responsibly to the consumption practices demanded of the productive neoliberal consumer-citizen.

In her study of detox diets, Katrine Meldgaard Kjaer (2019: 707–8) argues that they are often represented as an emotional project in which a sense of well-being is associated with 'psychological and emotional control over eating'. While not represented as a detox per se, these same processes are evident in Deliciously Ella. There are frequent references to her need to control and overcome bad 'cravings', often the product of the internal 'sugar monster': kale chips 'satisfy that crunch I'm always craving' (Woodward 2012g). Recipes for afternoon high tea in her *Telegraph* column use natural ingredients 'to sate sweet cravings' (Woodward 2015c) while, on her blog, eating 'raw brownies' means 'every craving I've ever had is sated, it's perfect. You'll never want refined sugar again' (Woodward 2012d). In this way Ella, like many other female healthy eating bloggers, suggests that 'cravings, which often have naughty connotations' are instead 'urges for nutritious foods' (Rodney 2019: [9]).

It is easy to get the sense that this control implies restriction. The blog's 'About Me' page states 'I hope you enjoy the recipes as much as I do: every one is gluten, dairy, sugar and meat free with nothing processed or chemical based' (Woodward n.d.). While the 'halo effect' of veganism became, in time, part of Ella's 'free from' brand, at times this seems more like an accidental result of restriction and a means of seeking nutritional purity rather than a central identification. Restriction becomes a selling point in early recipes that are subtitled in terms of the ingredients they lack: being 'free from' becomes a key 'principle of recommendation' (Warde 1997): 'Triple stuffed butternut squash: vegan, gluten and dairy free' and 'raw brownies: gluten, dairy and sugar free' (Woodward 2012a; 2012d). But restriction is redefined as 'a positive *choice*' (Cairns and Johnston 2015: 93). Ingredients that are present often are represented in instrumental terms so that the whole purpose of eating can appear primarily geared around health. In a recipe for 'Sweet Potato Brownies', Ella tells readers, 'Don't forget raw cacao is also a superfood as it is such a rich source of antioxidants, as well as being packed with a number of other beneficial nutrients: manganese, which helps oxygenate the blood; magnesium, which helps maintain healthy nerves, muscles and bones; and sulphur which builds strong nails and hair, and promotes beautiful skin' (Salter 2014). However, this doesn't just instrumentalize food but suggests that preparing and eating food can be a practice of 'virtuous self-care' (Sikka 2019: 361). The combination of restraining 'bad' foods and consuming 'superfoods' presents 'the body as fixable and correctable through dietary practice and perceives measures of constraint as a sign of moral strength' (Sikka 2019: 366). This is written into Ella's journey as she heals herself through her eating practices and her recovery prompts doctors to further investigate the medical possibilities of her eating practices.

Deliciously Ella's approach to food, therefore, epitomizes many aspects of 'healthism' as her healthy practices become a way of 'remaking' and 'defining' the self. There is a holistic emphasis on body and mind, on 'self-love, self-confidence, a sense of happiness and purpose' (Crawford 2006: 410–11). This emphasis on the self encourages her readers to see health as an individual responsibility – and even a choice – contributing to a neoliberalism that absolves the state of responsibility for citizens' welfare. By responsibilizing people for working to improve their health, Deliciously Ella implies, but doesn't make explicit, that ill-health is a matter of personal choice. While she shows sympathy for her former 'sugar monster' self that consumed Haribo sweets, this is the self that must be reformed and rejected if health is to be achieved. The choice between Haribo and 'sweet potato brownies' – or indeed own-brand Deliciously Ella Nut Butter Balls – is about whether to choose to be healthy.

The tension between health and indulgence is one of the key ways in which foods are given meaning in contemporary British culture (Warde 1997). Therefore, it is perhaps unsurprising that Ella makes frequent use of ideas of abundance and deliciousness to counteract the potentially negative associations of restricted and instrumental eating (Sikka 2019), a play on the 'dialectic between pleasures of consumption and the ethic of asceticism as a means of constructing the self' in contemporary consumer culture (Lupton 1996: 153; see also Crawford 2006; Featherstone 1991). Her dietary advice echoes wider dispositions towards food that are familiar in healthy eating advice in which, Cairns and Johnston (2015: 88) argue, 'healthy' femininity involves a process of 'calibration' through which women must balance the competing pressures to consume both the nutritious and delicious, the healthy and indulgent. Although there is a well-established literature on representations of the asceticized pleasures of fasting associated with eating disorders and diets frequently celebrate restraint in ways that echo theological discourses (Baker and Walsh 2020; Bordo 2003; Contois 2015), Deliciously Ella relentlessly represents restraint as indulgent and delicious, celebrating the 'abundance' of what she can eat (see Braun and Carruthers 2020: 90).

For Ella, the sweet pleasures of 'free from sugar' dishes not only far exceed the ordinary pleasures of sugary ones but they also can be enjoyed in excess. Indeed, natural foods are 'nature's candy' (Woodward n.d.). By taking responsibility for consuming the 'right' kind of non-sugary sweetness, she is free to enjoy indulgent greed: 'you may end up eating half the cookies before they even go into the oven – that always seems to happen to me … I know I'll eat at least half of them' (Woodward 2015a). As the title of her blog suggests, Ella relentlessly tells us just how 'delicious' and 'amazing' her 'free from' recipes are. Instead of being about deprivation, recipes exceed the originals. 'Courgette Noodles with Minted Avocado Sauce […] honestly tastes like there is a pot of cream in the sauce' (Salter 2014). 'Strawberry, banana and cinnamon muffins' are 'the best muffins ever, even better than any normal muffin' (Woodward 2012b). Her 'great vegan, gluten free mayonnaise substitute', Ella tells us, 'tastes much better, much more authentic and more nutritious than any real mayonnaise or sour cream I've eaten' (Woodward 2012h). This, of course, works with an interesting definition of authenticity in which the 'substitute' tastes more 'authentic' than the 'real'.

While Ella partly represents foods in functional terms in relation to their health-generating and healing properties, like other dietary practices associated with 'clean eating', the food practices are used as elements 'in an expressive display of lifestyle' (Lury 1996: 65), contributing to the wider process of the lifestylization of health (Crawford 2006). By eating food that is both better for you and expressly 'better', followers are offered the opportunity to transform themselves into both healthy and better subjects through their consumption practices. In Deliciously Ella's world, eating healthily as a route to becoming healthy is represented not only as 'the condition of possibility for the good life' but also as 'the good life itself' (Crawford 2006: 404). However, as I go on to discuss in the next section, not only have these practices been widely criticized, they are also gendered in problematic ways.

Gendering clean eating

The public face of clean eating was usually attractive, young, white and middle-class and Ella Woodward epitomized these features. An ex-model and art history student from a privileged and well-connected background, Ella was not simply 'any' girl who popped up on the internet with some healthy recipes. Despite her naive and girlish writing style, Deliciously Ella was quickly infused with an entrepreneurial spirit in a highly successful exercise in self-branding also found among superfood gurus. (Sikka 2019; see also Lewis 2020: 50). In these endeavours Ella emerged as part of a growing number of female influencers engaged in the 'professionalization of social media' (Braun and Carruthers 2020: 86). As Rachel O'Neill (2020: 3) argues, figures such as Ella offer 'wellness work … as a route to financial as well as physical empowerment, with culinary labour recast a creative labour through new media technologies'.

As I noted above, the Deliciously Ella brand centres around Ella herself. Her use of her blog to narrate her journey in the confessional and expressive style of a personal journal helped to create an 'authentic' and 'relatable' image of an 'ordinary' girl engaged in an amateur activity (Deller and Murphy 2019: 4; see also de Solier 2018). This echoes the wider ways in which many successful female food bloggers' identities combine the 'ordinary' and the 'aspirational' (Rodney et al. 2017: 687). Despite criticisms of the expense and obscurity of some of her recommended ingredients, Ella continued to stress the ease and accessibility of her recipes. As Woodward shared her recipes, echoing the wider cultural practice of sharing food, she also gave readers the sense that they were involved in a shared and interactive 'digital participatory culture' (Lupton 2018a: 68) in which 'emotion and effect' are used to create 'a strong sense of community' (Rodney et al. 2017: 688). This authenticity and relatability created a sense of trust between Ella and her followers that gave her advice on healthy eating a sense of credibility despite – or perhaps because of – the amateurism of her expertise (Rowe and Grady 2020). In this way, Ella worked as a cultural intermediary operating 'in line with a postfeminist ethos that privileged neoliberal forms of self-reliance, self-branding and innovation as the way to achieve one's authentic self' (Sikka 2019: 357; see also Dejmanee 2016). The considerable amount of social and cultural capital associated with her class position also enabled her to 'propertize' her identity and 'market a culturally legitimate, high-status version' of the self (Johnston et al. 2014: 20).

Furthermore, while Ella's blog entries read as a seemingly unmediated account of her everyday life, this apparent amateurism and accessibility distracts from the amount of labour involved in doing the 'Deliciously Ella' brand, 'the disciplines and investments that go into this mode of self-production' (Duffy and Hund 2015: 4; see also Banet-Weiser 2017).

The visual image of a healthy glowing Ella helps to anchor the meaning of her brand. Although many images on her Instagram feed – and her blog – use beautiful images of food to signify the desirability of clean eating (Baker and Walsh 2020: 58), these are peppered with images of Ella: smiling, kooky (signified by a hat), often alone but increasingly with husband Matt. More recently, Ella features pregnant, or with baby, reproducing romanticized images of 'perfect' – and attractive – pregnancy found more widely on Instagram (see Mayoh 2019). Press commentary on Deliciously Ella reproduces a causal link between clean eating and Ella's attractive appearance. Olivia Parker (2015) in the *Daily Telegraph* observed 'Ella is now a picture of health, with glowing skin, a slim and toned body' while, in the same paper, Elizabeth Grice (2016) took this further

> Floaty and poised with a waterfall of glossy hair, think a size eight venus rising from the waves, with a bottle of green juice in her hand. The most obvious thing about Deliciously Ella, clear-skinned, grey-eyed, fresh as almond milk, is what a persuasive argument she is for healthy eating – and the growth of her food empire reflects that.

Numerous other journalists reinforced this same picture: Ella's hair, eyes, skin and slim body acted as a visual manifestation of the benefits of clean eating. These images of 'glow' represent health 'not simply as freedom from disease, but a kind of preternatural exuberance and luminous vitality' (O'Neill 2020: 3).

These images clearly gender clean eating as a practice. While diets aimed at men may emphasize improved skin and hair (see Chapter 4) – and while Instagram clean eating imagery suggests these diets 'as a rational choice for men when framed in terms of individual's health and protection of the environment' (Baker and Walsh 2020: 61) – the language used in relation to Ella reproduces dominant images of desirable feminine appearance. Hair should be glossy, skin glowing, bodies toned and slim (or even ethereal and 'floaty') and eyes bright. However, as Karen Wilkes (2021: 10) argues, these images of 'glowing' skin and 'glossy' hair are well-established signifiers of white beauty in which lighting strategies produce the sense that these white clean eating advocates are 'lit from within' (see also O'Neill 2020: 16). The benefits of clean eating are associated with whiteness, undercutting the seemingly inclusive mode of address (Wilkes 2021: 17).

Ella embodies a form of post-feminist subjectivity in which 'the body is recognized as the object of women's labour: it is her asset, her product, her brand and her gateway to freedom and empowerment in a neoliberal market economy' (Alison Winch cited in Gill 2017: 616). Eating practices are accentuated as part of the aesthetic labour that goes into producing a recognizably attractive feminine self in an on-going process of what Angela McRobbie (2009: 63) calls 'self-perfectability' (see also O'Neill 2020). If, in the twenty-first century, female success is equated with '(hetero)sexual attractiveness' then there is a 'beauty imperative' in which, whatever else she achieves, a woman 'must also be beautiful and normatively strive for perfection' (Elias et al. 2017: 25–6). Clean eating offers thinness and beauty as the reward for self-discipline (Cairns and Johnston 2015: 102). If clean eating becomes part of the work of looking good that defines contemporary (white) femininity, then a failure to eat clean appears as a failure by women to maximize not only their physical and mental health but also their appearance. Numerous studies highlight how some female followers of clean eating developed 'orthorexia', a form of disordered eating in which 'goodness, control, purity and restriction are positively correlated with idealized femininity' (Sikka 2019: 362).

Foods, and their functions, are also gendered by Deliciously Ella in other ways. Bowl food, salads and sweet treats are often seen as feminine foods and do not conform to traditional ideas of the 'proper meal' anchored around meat that are associated with masculine tastes (Devault 1991; Rogers 2008; Ruby and Hein 2011; Sobal 2005; see Chapter 4). As noted above, the pursuit of sweetness is a recurring theme. There are long-established cultural connections between women and the taste for sweet food – and in the ways in which this is embodied in claims about 'naturally' sweet dispositions and the sweetness of women's bodies, images which are often racialized. Women are also more likely to be portrayed as powerless to resist sugar (Throsby 2020), an image continually repeated in Woodward's portrait of her former self as a 'sugar monster'. By associating clean eating practices with conventionally feminine food tastes, Deliciously Ella strengthens the sense of clean eating as feminine practice. This is also reinforced by the ways in which natural foods are claimed to engender feelings of lightness. In relation to a dish based on spiralized courgette 'noodles', Ella tells *Telegraph* readers 'I cannot even begin to explain how much lighter and more energised a bowl of this makes you feel compared with conventional creamy pastas' (Salter 2014). In this way, consuming the 'light' foods conventionally associated with women (McPhail et al. 2012) becomes a way of producing the 'light' feminine body. Therefore, while Woodward frequently rejects the idea that her form of healthy eating is a diet for weight loss, the end result is the same.

By 2017, there was a substantial media backlash against clean eating with increasing scepticism about the truth claims and 'science' upon which it was founded (Tandoh 2017; Wilson 2017; Yeo 2017). Woodward quickly distanced herself from clean eating:

> My problem with the word 'clean' is that it's become too complicated, become too loaded ... Clean now implies dirty and that's negative ... I haven't used it, but as far as I understood it when I first read the term, it meant natural, kind of unprocessed, and now it doesn't mean that at all. It means diet; it means fad.
> (cited in Yeo 2017)

However, whether Ella used the phrase clean eating or not, she and other bloggers such as Hemsley + Hemsley were symbols of the trend and used 'approaches that fell in line with its core beliefs: slimness is health, health is everything and – crucially – diets are bad' (Tandoh 2017). On the one hand, clean eating was easily discredited precisely through its association with young, female social media food influencers: their age and gender, and the media platforms they employed, were all used to render these women's advice as inherently illegitimate, despite wider feminist critiques of the treatment of women's health within conventional medicine (O'Neill 2020; Rowe and Grady 2020). On the other hand, media-savvy youthful femininity was central to the success of their brands and ensured the continued success of Deliciously Ella. The brand, and range of free-from products, has survived, partly because 'free-from' eating was a lifestyled practice that was 'deeply aspirational' (Wilson 2017).

While Deliciously Ella offers women a vision of how to use food for their own pleasure, to care for themselves and prioritize their own well-being, these practices are not quite as empowering as they might first seem and are 'incorporated into normative ideals of femininity' (O'Neill 2020: 3). Although women are not encouraged to see feeding work simply as something done on behalf of others, they are encouraged to 'choose' to invest in their health as a way of improving themselves and their appearance and maximizing who they can be. As a result, it is difficult to understand Ella outside wider neoliberal and post-feminist structures of feeling in which people's life chances are their own responsibility.

Anti-celebrity chefs: Pinch of Nom, branding and community

While Deliciously Ella can be understood as an exercise in self-branding, Kate Allinson and Kay Featherstone are relatively unknown names and their visual image rarely appears in the media. Unlike most digital media stars who share healthy eating diets and recipes, they are not youthful and slim and do not conform to typical images of post-feminist social media celebrities. However, the pair created Pinch of Nom which, they claim, is the 'UK's most visited food blog' (Allinson and Featherstone 2019c: front cover) and has a Facebook community of over 1.5 million members. Their 2019 debut cookbook sold over 200,000 copies in its first three days on sale, the fastest selling non-fiction book in the UK on record at that time (BBC News 2019). This section examines how Pinch of Nom operates as an 'anti-celebrity' brand and social media phenomenon. In the following section, I explore how Allinson and Featherstone negotiate the relationship between food, health and the body in ways that are very different from healthy eating advocates such as Deliciously Ella.

Pinch of Nom's 'origin myth' begins with a Facebook group and blog, which partners Allinson and Featherstone started after their own experience of attending a local slimming group (Tandoh 2019). From the outset, they were positioned as people who wanted to lose a considerable amount of weight (thirty stone collectively) and as being among a community of fellow slimmers facing similar struggles. Both had experience in the restaurant industry – Allinson's 'classical training' as a chef backs up their culinary credentials – and they wanted to help fellow slimmers who struggled to make tasty and varied low-calorie meals (Allinson and Featherstone 2020b; Tweedy 2020a). Their online community grew – at first slowly, then very rapidly – helped by an unofficial relationship with Slimming World (which ended very officially in 2019). By 2019, they had published their bestselling cookbook *Pinch of Nom* and written widely for national newspapers. By early 2020, their second book had been published – *Pinch of Nom: Everyday Light* (Allinson and Featherstone 2020e) – and the Pinch of Nom community included a considerable number of staff who feature on their website.

Unlike many successful food influencers, Allinson and Featherstone have tried to avoid celebrity status. Features on the duo repeatedly make reference to their 'dislike of publicity' (Lytton 2020): they are 'shy and private people' (Collins 2019), a 'delightfully low-profile couple' (Hale 2019b) who prefer being 'in the shadows' and 'incognito' (Lytton 2020). The pair deflect attention away from themselves onto the community that is an essential element of their brand: as Allinson puts it, 'It's not about us ... It's about the community and the people we're helping' (cited in Lytton 2020). While an emphasis on the importance of community is common in social media brands, the desire for invisibility marks them as very different to celebrity chefs such as Deliciously Ella. As Ruby Tandoh (2019) put it in the *Guardian*, the authors 'aren't visible. There are no aspirational photos of slim women in summer dresses or aspirational lifestyle shots'. Allinson and Featherstone avoid the forms of self-disclosure that give access to the '"authentic" self' that are frequently seen as a crucial element of women's self-branding on social media platforms and are exemplified by Deliciously Ella (Banet-Weiser 2012: 60).

However, while the pair remain relatively invisible, they use tone of voice to create the sense of a friendly community. This tone is frequently casual, conversational and friendly rather than aspirational: 'sometimes you just need a tasty brekkie in a flash' (Allinson and Featherstone 2020a). The authenticity of the brand is built within the restricted (if huge) community of their closed Facebook group in which members can be transparent because it is 'private and respectful' and away from 'fatphobic bigotry' (Angry Chef 2019). Within this community, members have the opportunity to use 'self-disclosure' to build a sense of 'shared identity' based on a common sense of struggle over weight (Rodney 2020). At the same time, the size and engagement of this community gives Pinch of Nom its visibility, demonstrating they are a brand 'that other users are "buying"' (Banet-Weiser 2012: 68).

While Allinson and Featherstone may adopt different strategies from image-conscious and lifestyled food influencers, their success is based on strategically deployed social media marketing techniques. Their writing style is tightly written and focused, resembling bright and upbeat women's magazine journalism and advertising copy rather than confessional forms of personal expression. This can be seen in clear and straightforward principles of recommendation: 'Everyday Light recipes are those you can have at any time: they're easy on the calories, filling and perfect for every day' (Allinson and Featherstone 2019c: 13). Furthermore, as Tandoh (2019) observes, they are 'forthright about the brand, its traffic and revenue, and a careful and constant monitoring of community feedback': 'Pinch of

Nom was a targeted, keenly reactive business from the start' in which the Facebook group is used to learn 'crowdsourced appetites'. This community involvement also acts as a principle of recommendation: the usability and success of 'tried and tested' recipes is represented as a product of Pinch of Nom's collective endeavour. As Allinson and Featherstone (2019c: 8) put it in the introduction to their first cookbook

> This book wouldn't have existed without every single member of our Facebook group, every visitor to the website and every person who contributed to Pinch of Nom: team members, volunteers, taste testers and commenters that have provided constructive criticism to improve the recipes and content on the site.

In the publicity for the launch of the follow-up book, the veracity of the recipes is secured because they have been tested by fans in a 'secret Facebook group ... to ensure we're not the only ones who love the food in our books' (Allinson and Featherstone 2020a). In this way, *Pinch of Nom* is sold to members of the community as *their* cookbook, although the ability to profit economically from user-generated content is not shared equally and the community is sustained through the unpaid labour of its members.

Allinson and Featherstone are unusual because they have built a successful social media diet brand while remaining relatively invisible. Their avoidance of celebrity is perhaps understandable in a context in which 'fat' bodies are stigmatized, rendering some selves as more brandable than others (Banet-Weiser 2012). Although their decision not to pursue the profits of celebrity might be the result of the chefs' natural reserve and shyness, it could also be a calculated decision about the opportunities that exist to brand the white, middle-aged, lesbian self in the world of healthy eating. However, as I go on to show in the next section, Allinson and Featherstone also challenge some of the classed, gendered and racialized assumptions about healthy eating associated with 'healthism'.

Gender, class and the comforts of food

The success of Pinch of Nom has been interpreted as a refreshing response to the popularity of clean eating (Hale 2019b; Lytton 2020; Steafel 2019). Their first recipe to go viral was the avowedly 'unclean' Cajun Dirty Rice (Allinson and Featherstone 2019a). Although the embrace of dirty foods is more commonly associated with metropolitan hipster masculinity (see Chapter 4), dirtiness in Pinch of Nom could be seen as both a refusal of the privilege, purity and healthism associated with clean eating and an identification with the comforting aspects of eating. While Pinch of Nom is a brand thoroughly intertwined with the weight loss industries that exploit body insecurities, this section explores how it nonetheless refuses the legitimacy of lifestyled modes of healthy eating associated with healthism.

Food has very different meanings in Pinch of Nom to those found in Deliciously Ella. Allinson and Featherstone's brand is based around the word 'nom' which is an expression of deep-seated bodily enjoyment of food. In contrast, Ella's 'injunction to "love your food" … is … less about gustatory delight' and more about its 'health benefits' (O'Neill 2020: 11). While clean eating gurus frequently promise the feeling of 'lightness', Pinch of Nom emphasizes the pleasures of 'hearty food' – 'We all love a good, comforting, home-cooked meal' (Allinson and Featherstone 2020a). The emphasis on comfort, frequently identified with the meanings of home (Czikszentmihalyi and Rochberg-Halton 1981; Gullestad 1995; Rybczynski 1987), locates food practices within households and families rather than within the individualized feminine body. Pinch of Nom frequently emphasizes both the practical necessity and pleasures of eating together, demonstrating how weight loss recipes are something 'the whole family can enjoy' (Allinson and Featherstone 2020a). The ability of the idealized family meal to nourish emotional health is associated with the physical benefits of healthy eating: 'you're not just eating together, you're eating healthy too' (Allinson and Featherstone 2020a).

Therefore, while Deliciously Ella tends to reproduce the individualism that characterizes contemporary post-feminism, Pinch of Nom positions its readers within the collective life of households and 'cooking for all the family' (Allinson and Featherstone 2020a). The Pinch of Nom reader is not explicitly gendered. However, the brand acknowledges the difficulties and demands of feeding work, labour that is typically performed by women (Cairns and Johnston 2015; DeVault 1991). The brand acknowledges the difficulties and demands of the feminine labour involved in feeding the family (DeVault 1991). For example, the problems of time management and time scarcity are acknowledged in recipes for food that whole households can eat at the same time and in 'fakeaway' dishes such as Beef Kofta Curry that 'takes the same amount of time' as collecting a takeaway (Allinson and Featherstone 2020a). While Deliciously Ella encourages women as neoliberal, post-feminist subjects to engage in self-care to realize their value, Pinch of Nom acknowledges that these are not the only values against which parents, and particularly mothers, are judged. As Deborah Lupton (2018c: 98) suggests, while nutrition and body management are viewed as important in neoliberal societies, so are 'the values of family togetherness and enjoyment, the emotional dimensions of love, nurturing and shared pleasure'. In this way, Pinch of Nom recognizes how women – and, in particular white working-class women and women of colour – have been judged by their ability to care for their families through food practices and acknowledges that these demands can be at odds with the emphasis on individualized body management in neoliberal culture.

While Deliciously Ella demonstrates how healthy eating can be experienced as indulgent, Pinch of Nom favours 'healthy indulgences' (Allinson and Featherstone 2020b). If clean eating is associated with forms of purity built on classed and racialized exclusions of both 'pollutants' and 'the polluted', Pinch of Nom refuses its terms and the taste for 'bland white meat with a side salad' (Allinson and Featherstone 2020a). Some of their most popular dishes are based on fast and 'dirty' foods with 'loaded' dishes, spicy barbeque flavours and 'fakeaway' recipes such as Sausage and Egg McMuffin and a Cheeseburger Pizza (Allinson and Featherstone 2019a, 2020a). In this way, Pinch of Nom refuses the validity of middle-class tastes based on ascetic and aestheticized forms of pleasure (Bourdieu 1984). The brand attempts to negotiate an alternative response to the 'continuing dialectic between the ascetic imperatives of disciplining consumption to ensure a healthy body and the pleasures of consumption as part of the hedonistic enjoyment of life' (Lupton 2018c: 103). However, this opposition is ultimately inescapable so Pinch of Nom remains trapped within it. While Allinson and Featherstone attempt to validate the right to indulgent, comforting and 'dirty' tastes, the brand reproduces associations between the overweight body and the taste for the products of 'a degraded food system' and, ultimately, proposes that these tastes must be reformed (Farrell 2011: 151).

However, Pinch of Nom resists the makeover narratives that structure lifestyled, healthy eating media. Ella transforms her eating practice to makeover both her health and her 'self', moving from a prior state of illness into a healthy, glowing and successful young woman, brimming with energy and entrepreneurial zeal. Makeovers are also a staple of health and body coverage in women's magazines in which beautiful and toned selves are revealed through the process of shedding pounds. As Hannele Harjunen (2016: 92) observes, the 'makeover paradigm … ties the fat body to consumer culture and the dutiful subject who is forever dieting, exercising and beautifying herself, to achieve the unattainable body ideal'. While Pinch of Nom is a diet brand, Allinson and Featherstone's claims to still be on the weight loss 'journey' partially resist the terms of the makeover narrative (Lytton 2020), refusing to offer 'reveals' of happy-ever afters enjoyed by newly slender bodies. While makeover narratives suggest that slimness and health are the reward for anyone willing to put in the effort, Pinch of Nom acknowledges the cultural obligation to achieve a 'healthy' body but refuses the moral judgements frequently made against those who 'fail' to achieve it.

Pinch of Nom focuses more on the continual struggle of trying to lose weight than narratives of transformation with a happy ending. This marks a significant difference to both reality TV shows such as *The Biggest Loser* and healthy eating blogs and Instagram accounts. In these lifestyled media formats, the makeover 'propels its participants from the public shame and humiliation of the "before" (polluted state), through diet and exercise regimes of "extreme self-control" (purification) to the "reveal" – the new "cleansed" and thinner self (redemption)' (Raisborough 2016: 20). By refusing to the obligation to transform into 'improved' selves, Allinson and Featherstone may not displace the validity of healthism, an alleged 'obesity epidemic' or makeover narratives, but they create a community in which weight loss can be represented as an 'ongoing challenge' to be achieved 'at our own pace' (cited in Collins 2019). In this way, Pinch of Nom contributes to wider commentary that 'can provide a counter-institutional space for re-framing and learning about weight (loss), fat and health in ways that challenge, circumvent and resist dominant narratives and metaphors' (Monaghan et al. 2019: 9).

Although Allinson and Featherstone are rarely overtly political, they refuse the right of other people to define them as fat and embrace body positivity (Lytton 2020; Tweedy 2020a). This contributes to a wider social media landscape in which Instagram hashtags such as #obeselifestyle and #notyourgoodfatty seek to disrupt the ways that #eatclean Instagrammers normalize the connection between health and slimness and to challenge how ideas of health and well-being produce fat stigma (Lupton 2018a: 71–2; see also Lupton 2017 and 2018b). However, while Pinch of Nom dissolves the connection between health and beauty that characterizes wellness culture (Harjunen 2016) – and refuses the values of healthism – the brand ultimately promotes the health benefits of weight loss, even if these are claimed to be reducing symptoms of arthritis rather than achieving glowing skin.

Celebrity chefs frequently demonstrate how food practices can be used within distinctive and distinguished lifestyles (see Chapter 2). However, Pinch of Nom is characterized as 'resolutely unmetropolitan' and 'thoroughly untrendy' (Steafel 2019) and as offering 'normal food for normal people' in contrast to the elitism of clean eating (Angry Chef 2019). This does not mean that Pinch of Nom should be understood as outside of classed, gendered and racialized inequalities – and the emphasis on the 'normal' excludes those who lack the economic, social or cultural resources to occupy the category. Instead, Allinson and Featherstone use 'ordinariness' as a 'defensive' strategy 'to try to evade social fixing' (Savage et al. 2001: 889). In neoliberal societies in which fat denigration is linked to race and class (Farrell 2011: 51) – and is likely to be experienced more acutely by women – Pinch of Nom uses the values of home as a defence against judgements enacted in the public sphere and defends the right to guilty pleasures as a way of coping with daily life (Lupton 2018c).

Conclusion

Celebrity chefs have a significant influence on what and how people eat and this includes approaches to diet, health and the body. Longstanding ideas about 'clean' and 'dirty' foods, and bodily purity and impurity, have been reworked in new ways in twenty-first-century neoliberal societies as cleanliness became attached to ideas of healthism and wellness. New celebrity chefs such as Deliciously Ella linked clean eating with ideas of self-care and empowerment as part of a wider cultural shift in which people were responsibilized for their own well-being in neoliberal societies and notions of restrictive diets were replaced with the 'choice' – and obligation – to be healthy (O'Neill 2020: 10–11). Deliciously Ella represents food in instrumental terms while promising the female reader that she can 'be in control without denying herself pleasure' (Cairns and Johnston 2015: 92). As I go on to show in Chapter 6, this emphasis on making the 'choice' to be responsible for your own health exemplified by Deliciously Ella is part of a wider economic, social and cultural context in which 'a logic of personal responsibility' is used to justify the shrinking of the welfare state (O'Neill 2020: 14).

Weight loss eating plans associated with Pinch of Nom can be partly understood within a longer-standing tradition of restrictive diets in which women in particular were encouraged to reduce intake to maintain ideal body shapes. Like many other diet programmes, Pinch of Nom encourages readers to 'calibrate' their practices and balance factors such as health and indulgence (Cairns and Johnston

2015). Nonetheless, Pinch of Nom values the ordinary and undistinguished and understands the appeals of invisibility and anonymity in a world in which visibility (and celebrity) runs the risk of judgement and censure. Pinch of Nom also (at least partially) resists makeover narratives that suggest that health, beauty and slimness can be simply achieved if people are prepared to put in the effort to value, and work on, the self. However, in a digital media landscape saturated with images that equate 'healthy eating' with attractive and slim feminine bodies – and in which discourses of 'healthism' are pervasive – Pinch of Nom can only puncture rather than displace more widespread meanings of food, gender and the body.

Chapter 4

VEGANIZING MASCULINITIES

Veganism was a key food trend in the 2010s across many countries traditionally associated with meat-based or omnivorous diets. A study of Google Trends in 2020 suggested that interest in veganism continued to rise despite the pandemic (Chef's Pencil 2020). According to this evidence, interest in veganism is highest in the UK, Australia, Israel, Austria and New Zealand although this potentially marginalizes nations where plant-based diets have a much longer history.

Between 2014 and 2019, the number of British vegans quadrupled: by 2019, 600,000 people identified as vegan in the UK, 1.16 per cent of the population, a figure that had risen to an estimated 1.5 million people and approximately 3 per cent of the population by 2021 (Chiorando 2021; Vegan Society n.d.). This was accompanied by a wider shift towards vegetarian and flexitarian diets: for example, a 2018 study found that a quarter of evening meals in the UK were vegan or vegetarian (BBC News 2018).[1] Initiatives such as Meat Free Week and Meat Free Monday used social media campaigns and celebrity chefs such as Jamie Oliver to promote the reduction of meat consumption (Friedlander and Riedy 2018; Jallinoja et al. 2019) while the annual Veganuary campaign, launched in 2014, encouraged people to try a plant-based diet for a month, attracting 400,000 participants in 2020 (Smithers 2020).

A booming market for vegan products capitalized on, and further developed, these trends. In 2018, there were more vegan product launches in the UK than in any other country and 16 per cent of new product launches were vegan (Mintel 2019). Some of these products such as tofu were already naturally vegan; many others such as non-dairy milks had already gained popularity in response to the growing market for free-from food and drink. However, other new vegan foods generated a significant amount of media attention. These included the 'bleeding burger', a much-publicized US plant-based burger, distinguished from other veggie burgers through an ability to ooze beetroot-based 'blood'. The mass market national bakery chain Greggs used Veganuary to launch highly publicized and commercially successful vegan versions of some of their most popular products with a vegan sausage roll in January 2019 and a vegan steak bake in the following year. These product launches, seemingly paradoxically, linked the search for meat substitutes with 'the idea of meat-eating as the centrepiece' of eating practices (Malte Rödl cited in Hunt 2020). Alongside the rise of vegan fast food, some middle-class foodies have embraced vegan tasting menus at high-end restaurants and, in France, ONA was the first vegan restaurant to receive a Michelin star. Plant-based eating practices also gained exposure through association with a range of celebrity vegans such as Beyoncé, Venus Williams, Ariana Grande, Joaquin Phoenix and Forest Whitaker. Like many of the new products, these celebrity advocates rendered veganism more accessible but also 'more marketable and thus more consumable' (Doyle 2016: 787–8).

Social media platforms have played a key role in expanding interest in veg* diets in the UK.[2] As Piia Jallinoja et al. (2019: 10) observe, since 2013, platforms such as Instagram and YouTube have played important roles in 'changing the images of both animal-derived and vegan foods, increasing competences in vegan cooking and shopping, and building and strengthening communities and connectivity'. While established high-profile celebrity chefs such as Jamie Oliver, Hugh Fearnley-Whittlingstall and Nadiya Hussein have all been involved in promoting veg* eating, this chapter focuses primarily on a new wave of celebrity chefs for whom vegan identity is central to their diet. Clearly these celebrity influencers cannot be understood alone: there are a huge number of people posting vegan recipes, hacks and shopping tips on blogs, Instagram, YouTube and Facebook, alongside other online spaces that enable discussion of vegan politics and activism.

This chapter focuses on a new wave of male vegan celebrity chefs in the UK who have had significant success over the past few years, with TV series, cookbooks and/or influential YouTube channels: 'Dirty Vegan' Matt Pritchard; Henry Firth and Ian Theasby who form the duo BOSH!; and Avant-Garde Vegan Gaz Oakley. Pritchard – who has a background as a chef, skateboarder and hard-living TV daredevil – is the star of the BBC's first vegan cooking show *Dirty Vegan*. The show was launched by BBC Wales to coincide with Veganuary 2019 with a second season during Veganuary 2020 and is more widely available via the BBC's i-player.[3] BOSH! are a well-established social media brand who had a popular YouTube channel and a bestselling vegan cookbook prior to their first television series *Living on the Veg* which was broadcast by ITV during Veganuary 2020. Gaz Oakley's Avant-Garde Vegan YouTube channel has over 1 million subscribers. He has published three vegan cookbooks and featured at number eighteen on the *Sunday Times* Influencer List 2019.

One of the most striking things about the success of these celebrity chefs is that both BBC and ITV used white, male cooks to anchor their new vegan cookery shows. There was certainly no shortage of female vegan influencers on blogs or YouTube – largely, if not exclusively, white – and some of the brands associated with clean eating such as Deliciously Ella were predominantly vegan. There are still significantly more female than male vegans in the UK, and an estimated 89 per cent of participants in Veganuary 2019 were women (Jones 2020). Not only are women more likely to be vegans but, as I go on to explore further in this chapter, veganism is frequently associated with attributes that are coded as feminine. Press coverage often represents vegans as 'over-sensitive', 'irrational' and 'sentimental' and 'explicitly or implicitly associated meat-eating with toughness and realism in comparison' (Cole and Morgan 2011: 145; see also Doyle 2016). In this way, the male vegan appears initially as a case of what Emily Contois (2020) calls 'gender contamination' in which male consumption of 'feminine' foods appears unnatural.

This chapter explores how these celebrity chefs contribute to a masculinization of vegan food practices. I analyse the types of representational strategies that are used to render vegan food and vegan identities as masculine. While these celebrity chefs acknowledge animal welfare and environmental concerns in their discussion of their vegan 'journey', my discussion demonstrates how veganism is articulated with neoliberal forms of healthism that focus on individual responsibility for the self. However, this is achieved in rather different ways to feminized modes of clean eating discussed in the previous chapter so that the health benefits of veganism become identified with fitness and performance. The chapter also demonstrates how the masculinization of vegan food is achieved through a preoccupation with 'meatiness' that distances the male vegan from the feminine associations of plant-based eating. This involves a return to the opposition between 'clean' and 'dirty' eating introduced in the last chapter and I demonstrate how vegan food practices are rendered masculine through 'dirtying' them up and creating a distance from feminized clean eating. My analysis demonstrates how this wave of male vegan cooks, therefore, constructs both the benefits of veganism and the contents of a vegan diet as consistent with (white) masculinity.

Gender, meat and veg*

Veganism is well-established as a '*counter*cuisine' and political philosophy, practice and identity that is opposed to the exploitation of non-human animals (Wrenn 2019). The radicalism of the movement is frequently associated with anti-speciesism or, more loosely, a general discourse of animal rights (Cole and Morgan 2011: 135). Yet there are 'many *veganisms*': 'Vegan protest may be anti-speciesist, anti-racist, environmental or health-centric' (Wrenn 2019: 190). While my interest in this chapter as a whole is the ways in which male celebrity chefs mediate the politics of eating, this section provides a context for the later analysis by exploring how the politics of meat and veg* are gendered and by considering how celebrity veganism inflects the meaning of vegan practices in particular ways.

In many Western societies, eating meat has often been associated with the powerful and the privileged (Ruby and Heine 2011). If the ability to consume meat has, at many times, been seen as a class privilege, then who gets to eat meat within the home has often been structured by gendered power relations. However, some forms of ecofeminism do not simply see this as a symbol of men's economic power within the home, but also a way in which men 'do' dominance over women. Indeed, feminists such as Carol Adams (1990) connect men's dominance over women with dominance over nature in a patriarchal society based on violence against both women and animals, and in which both women and animals are rendered as 'flesh' to be consumed by men.[4] In this way, veg* practices can be seen as resistance to male dominance.

Consuming meat continues to be associated with masculine characteristics and dispositions in many Western countries, although many of the sociological studies of the relationship between masculinity and meat come from the United States. As Jessica Greenebaum and Brandon Dexter (2018: 637) argue, eating meat is associated with '"masculine traits" of emotional stoicism, strength and virility'. Eating meat is not only a way of performing masculinity but also a way 'by which men are able to assert their dominance as hegemonic men in patriarchal culture' (Ibid.). It is therefore unsurprising that a range of studies demonstrate that people, especially men, view 'vegetarians as less masculine than omnivores' (Ruby and Heine 2011: 450). This is neatly illustrated by Richard A. Rogers' (2008) analysis of how the relationships between meat, veg* and masculinity were represented in a series of US adverts in the 2000s. For example, an ad for Hummer cars positioned tofu as a feminizing force and men's enemy – 'not just *nonmeat*, it is *antimeat*' – while, in an ad for Burger King, men were encouraged to eat red meat as an act of resistance that was necessary to restore 'men's "authentic" masculinity' (Rogers 2008: 291, 296). As Rogers (2008: 282) concludes, 'These advertisements articulate the oppositions of men's versus women's food, meat versus vegetables, and meat versus tofu to trivialize and oppose contemporary movements towards less meat-centred diets.' This not only begins to explain attempts by the food industry to sell meatified plant-based products such as the 'bleeding' veggie burger, but also proves crucial to understanding the vegan cuisine popularized by male vegan media stars I discuss later in this chapter.

Despite evidence to suggest an increasing openness to meat-free dishes and diets in UK newspapers (Morris 2017), press representations have often been 'derogatory', representing veganism as ridiculous, ascetic and faddish (Cole and Morgan 2011). Segments of the British media continue to represent vegans as 'over-sensitive and irrational' (Cole and Morgan 2011; Doyle 2016: 780), linking vegan identities with dispositions conventionally coded as feminine. If the plant-based diet associated with Deliciously Ella's healthy eating practices foregrounds feminine characteristics such as lightness and purity, some of the other key celebrity advocates for vegan lifestyles also gender veganism as feminine. For example, actor Alicia Silverstone's 'The Kind Diet' uses an explicitly gendered mode of address: she talks to readers as 'us womanfolk' (cited in Johnston et al. 2018: 294) and encourages them to 'treat yourself like a total goddess' (cited in Doyle 2016: 782). Veganism is associated with feminine characteristics such as caring and kindness – she represents her diet as a way of caring for the self, others and the planet (Johnston et al. 2018: 295). Silverstone characterizes her vegan practices through a feminized 'language of positivity, emotion and love' (Doyle 2016: 783), in many ways reminiscent of healthy eating gurus such as Ella Woodward. Indeed, Julie Doyle (2016: 783) notes how Silverstone, despite her clear position against animal cruelty, represents veganism in terms familiar from lifestyle and makeover media: 'Her body signifies as a slim, healthy, kind, vegan body that fits with the idealized and commodified body in celebrity consumer culture.' 'The Kind Diet' not only provides a recent example of the continued gendering of veganism in terms of (white) femininity, but also contributes to making veganism more media friendly. While her emphasis on care and compassion 'is consistent with ethical veganism', Doyle (2016: 788) argues that Silverstone's vegan lifestyle is also infused with 'the commodity logic of celebrity culture to make it more marketable and thus consumable'.

The association between meat consumption and masculinity, and veg* diets and femininity, means that the position of the male vegan is rendered problematic. Mari Mycek (2018)'s study of veg* men found that men avoided discussing their practices in terms of care and compassion towards animals because these qualities are viewed as feminine. Greenebaum and Dexter (2018: 638) argue that veganism is often promoted to men through an emphasis on 'health benefits, more specifically sexual virility and physical fitness'. Masculine vegan role models are often hypermasculine sports stars, examples of what Justine Johnson (2011) dubs 'hegans' whose excessive masculinity overwhelms the feminine associations of veganism. These meanings come through in Greenebaum and Dexter's study of male vegans. Although their respondents embraced compassion as a valuable quality, they also viewed being a vegan man as rebellious and heroic as they fought for animal rights. However, their respondents also legitimated veganism as a masculine practice by stressing how their diet enhanced their energy and stamina. As a result, 'by focusing on strength, power and athleticism, they remain complicit to the hegemonic notion of men, masculinity and muscles' (Greenebaum and Dexter 2018: 345).

In the rest of this chapter, I build on this research to demonstrate how these factors influence the ways in which a new wave of vegan celebrity chefs popularize plant-based diets in the UK. These male celebrity chefs transform the consumption of plants into a masculine practice through an emphasis on masculine health and fitness. Furthermore, as I go on to show, they also transform 'feminine' plants into 'masculine' meat by veganizing meaty comfort foods.

Living on the veg: Masculinity, veganism and health

Bloggers and vloggers have played a key role in creating images of veganism as a 'desirable lifestyle' (Jallinoja et al. 2019: 12). The emergence of vegan cookery shows on network television not only contributed to this process but brought, predominantly white, vegan lifestyles to mainstream audiences. This section explores how veganism was inflected in particular ways as it was represented as a healthy, accessible and masculine lifestyle practice in three key British vegan media brands: BOSH!, Dirty Vegan and Avant-Garde Vegan. That these media cooks are known by their brand names rather than given names is telling and suggests a shifting food media landscape in which the high-level branding associated with social media success is becoming more widespread (as Pinch of Nom also demonstrates). These brands also exemplify the difficulty of clearly distinguishing between 'old' and 'new' media food stars. BOSH! emerged on social media as YouTube stars attracting '26 million video views per month' by 2019 (Hurst 2019) and had achieved the UK's bestselling vegan cookbook and a considerable presence in the press before the launch of their ITV series *Living on the Veg* in 2020. Dirty Vegan Matt Pritchard had an established television career prior to remaking himself as a TV chef and cookbook writer and, while he has a less high-profile social media presence, he also has a YouTube channel. Avant-Garde Vegan Gaz Oakley has over a million YouTube subscribers but has also published cookbooks and made guest appearances on broadcast TV. Despite these different profiles, all operate within a common media ecology.

Culinary masculinities, like masculinities in general, are not uniform but discursively produced and structured by forms of difference (Johnston et al. 2014; Leer 2016a). Each of these culinary brands negotiates different 'formulations of masculinity', performing and practising masculine identities in different ways (Gill 2003: 38). However, as I go on to show, they also share similar approaches in the ways in which they resist the potentially feminizing associations of cooking, plant-based eating and a preoccupation with health and the body to maintain widely understood forms of 'normative masculinity' (Gill et al. 2005).

It is unsurprising that *The Times* dubbed BOSH! 'the vegan Jamie Olivers' (Rose 2018) as their laddish image and use of language is reminiscent of the Oliver brand. The duo's construction as normal lads – 'the kind of guys you might meet on an unremarkable Bumble date' (Hurst 2019) – suggests that veganism can be easily articulated within 'ordinary' – white and middle-class – British masculinity. As one half of BOSH! Henry Firth puts it, being a vegan 'is perfectly normal and blokey … Vegans can drink a pint of beer and get wasted with their mates on a night out. Vegans can do all that stuff and it can just as masculine or feminine – or neither – to be vegan. You don't have to be a boring dude wearing a jumper' (cited in Hurst 2019). This construction of veganism as compatible with modern, mainstream and youthful gender roles is repeatedly constructed against stereotypes of the vegan. If they are not the jumper-wearing 'boring dude', they are also not the ascetic 'joylessly earnest vegans of old' (Woods 2018) who eat 'something awful like braised mung bean salad' (Ian Theasby cited in Francis 2018). Despite Firth's attempt to refuse the gendering of veganism, BOSH! are nonetheless keen to distance themselves from feminine 'clean eating' versions of veganism found on Instagram: they're not going to 'pop a little bit of quinoa on a strawberry … it's just a badass lasagne' (Henry Firth in Francis 2018). If lasagne is 'badass', this kind of laddish language fills their TV series in a style adapted from Jamie Oliver: recipes are 'banging', avocado toast gets 'pimped' and there is incessant wordplay accompanying their cooking: 'I'm a bit of a champion tosser' quips one of them in *Living on the Veg*.

BOSH! also masculinize veganism by associating it with strength and athleticism, echoing wider representations of the masculine vegan. As Firth puts it, 'Some of the strongest animals in the world eat greens – gorillas, rhinos, elephants. And some of the best athletes in the world are vegan' (cited in Francis 2018). As Greenebaum and Dexter (2018: 243–4) demonstrate, the vegan sports star is frequently invoked as a symbol of desirable vegan masculinity and works to 'validate and reinstate hegemonic masculinity for other vegan men'. Obviously, the link between veganism and physical strength isn't specifically gendered. While

Avant-Garde Vegan offers advice on high protein vegan meals for body building and training in a video that attracted over 5 million views – and, on occasion, uses his own well-defined body to display the successful results of his diet (Avant-Garde Vegan 2017a, 2019a) – his address tends to be relatively inclusive.[5] However, the association between veganism and masculine strength and sporting performance is accentuated by Dirty Vegan Matt Pritchard. 'I started looking into veganism because a lot of endurance athletes were vegan', he says. 'On a vegan diet, I did the Decker, which is 10 full Iron Men in 10 days' (cited in Draper 2020).

Indeed, high-performance masculine physicality, combined with irreverent, rebellious 'wild man' credentials, is central to Pritchard's celebrity image.[6] He previously found fame on the long-running MTV show *Dirty Sanchez* in which a self-styled maverick group of risk-taking men carried out dangerous and outrageous pranks and stunts. As the TV chef introduces himself in the voiceover on the opening credits of *Dirty Vegan*: 'I'm Matt Pritchard. Skateboarder. TV daredevil. Ultra athlete. And chef. And a proper vegan to boot. I'm on a mission to prove that a vegan diet can make you stronger, fitter and healthier.' This is reinforced by a title sequence that features him skateboarding, chopping with a cleaver, doing stunts, participating in Ironman events, juggling food, clowning around and cooking using his frequently featured muscular and heavily tattooed arms. Pritchard is surrounded with so many signifiers of masculinity that they quickly overwhelm any potentially feminine associations of veganism. This might explain why, although animal rights are largely absent from the TV series, Pritchard can speak openly about anti-speciesism in interview. 'I love animals. I've got a dog and I wouldn't eat him. What's the difference between a dog and a pig?' (Pritchard cited in Draper 2020). While such a position is often trivialized as sentimental and feminine (Cole and Morgan 2011), Pritchard's physicality and athletic prowess associates him with a 'hegan' masculinity which appears as a heroic identity 'different from veganism practised by women or certain other men – Birkenstock-wearing anaemic hippies' (Wright 2015: 149). As Pritchard notes, 'I think a lot of people think that vegans are hippies, but soon they realise that someone like me has gone plant-based, and they're like "hang on a minute, I might look into this"' (cited in Sweeney 2019). In this way, he suggests that people will embrace veganism once they see it articulated with a legitimate masculinity rather than its others. The Dirty Vegan positions himself as 'something other than merely vegan … so ultramasculine as to be able to make that dietary choice manly as well' (Wright 2015: 149).[7]

Within the TV series *Dirty Vegan*, however, the focus is not on animal rights but on debunking myths about the nutritional and culinary value of vegan food. The first episode sets Pritchard the challenge of meeting the nutritional needs of a high-level women's rugby team before an important match. These women are shown to largely view vegan dishes as 'rabbit food' and 'for wimps'. Supported by nutritional science – Pritchard makes regular visits to nutritionists at a local university throughout the series – the episode focuses on seitan as a source of plant-based protein and the importance of vegetables like kale that are 'high in iron and make our muscles work properly'. While cooking sequences emphasize flavour and taste in similar ways to many cookery shows, the series frequently uses a form of 'nutritionism' which 'functionalizes' foodstuffs that is also a feature of discourses about superfoods (Sikka 2019: 363). In another episode, Pritchard prepares breakfast for teenagers in a school in a 'brain bashing vegan food challenge' which aims to 'kickstart their brains and bodies for the day'. This functional approach is echoed in some of Gaz Oakley's videos. Ingredients such as quinoa and beans are included as they are good for muscle repair in a training regime. Although recommendations for functional energy foods are common in female healthy eating blogs and vlogs, Avant-Garde Vegan masculinizes the functional capacities of chia seeds by observing that they used to be munched on by ancient warriors to give them energy in battle (Avant-Garde Vegan 2017a). While this approach to food as a means to maximize how the mind and body function fits within a wider emphasis on 'healthism' discussed in the last chapter, it is also reminiscent of dispositions towards the masculine body found in men's lifestyle magazines, where men's bodies are represented as machines that need the correct tuning and fuelling to retain their invincibility (Jackson et al. 2001).

Although the BOSH! team stress the importance of environmental issues in their 'vegan journey', they also privilege health in promoting the benefits of a vegan diet. This reproduces wider ways in which many vegans use health to frame and discuss their practices in order to sidestep 'contentious aspects of veganism' such as the politics of climate change and animal rights (Scott 2020: 69–70). BOSH! link a plant-based diet to a sense of vitality and health. As Ian Theasby put it in an interview with the *Sun* (2020a) newspaper, 'We feel an awful lot healthier now … When we first went vegan, all the weight we'd been carrying dropped off, our skin got clearer, our hair got thicker, we slept soundly and woke up fresher. It's remarkable how much good comes from eating only plants.' In this way, BOSH! appear to echo some of the concerns of female celebrity vegans and clean eating gurus who promote veganism as a lifestyle choice based on ideas of individual self-improvement and self-care (Fegitz and Pirani 2018; Johnston et al. 2018; Kjaer 2019; Sikka 2019). The emphasis on weight, hair and skin suggests that adopting a vegan diet is a route to desirability and attractiveness for men as well as women, reproducing narratives of transformation found in makeover narratives in lifestyle media (Doyle 2016: 783; see also Moseley 2000). However, these practices are masculinized through the association of plant-based eating with virility and sexual prowess. As Henry Firth puts it in an interview, 'our sex drives have massively improved. You can last much longer in bed' (Francis 2018). In this way, BOSH! use 'masculine-coded discourses' to make veg* practices consistent with conventional performances of masculinity (Mycek 2018: 240).

Foods are also 'functionalized' by BOSH!. Although, as I go on to show, they emphasize indulgent comfort foods, *Living on the Veg* demonstrates a constant preoccupation with health. In the first episode we learn how to make a 'healthy Sunday roast' centred around Mushroom Wellington parcels encased in filo pastry because it is healthier than other doughs. We learn that seeds are an important source of Omega 3 and 6 that people need on a plant-based diet. Alfalfa and other sprouts are 'nutrient dense'. In later episodes we learn about the functional benefits of ingredients such as black beans, nuts, chickpeas and sweet potatoes. Like the veg* men studied by Mycek (2018: 231), 'expert research' in the form of nutritional science is used to legitimate a plant-based diet as a masculinized 'rational choice' rather than a feminized sentimental response to animal cruelty.

While the health benefits of a plant-based diet are foregrounded by these vegan celebrity chefs, this is not to suggest that their motivations for becoming vegan are exclusively concerned with health. As we have already seen, Matt Pritchard was also motivated by concerns about animal welfare. Avant-Garde Vegan Gaz Oakley was inspired by vegan UK rapper Jme to watch a speech by Gary Yourofsky which made him 'become vegan overnight', motivated by concerns about animal cruelty, the environment and the impact of animal products on the body (Avant-Garde Vegan 2019b). Like many vegans, watching films such as *Cowspiracy* were 'turning points' in the 'vegan journeys' of Matt Pritchard and Henry Firth (Jallinoja et al. 2019: 11). The tone in the BOSH! books is more politicized and polemical than in their TV shows. In *BOSH! How to Live Vegan* (2019), the emphasis is both on health and on the power of plant-based eating to fight climate change and to care for the planet neatly encapsulated in the book's subtitle 'Save the Planet and Feel Amazing'. Individual readers are responsibilized to fight their feelings of 'helplessness'. 'The best way to make a change is to start with yourself' we are told: 'Let's spend our time on Earth trying to fix what we've broken … YOUR MONEY IS YOUR VOTE' (Firth and Theasby 2019). In this way, BOSH!'s vegan environmental politics draw on elements of neoliberalism with an emphasis on 'self-improvement' and 'consumer choice', elements increasingly incorporated into social media campaigns by animal rights activist groups (Jallinoja et al. 2019: 15).

However, these issues are largely absent on television. BOSH! make only occasional references to the environmental issues that underpin their veganism in *Living on the Veg*. For example, in episode two, they explain to TV weatherman Alex Beresford how they were 'proper meat eaters but then we just found out about climate change and … the impact that the food we eat can have on the climate and we both went vegan, felt fantastic'. Even this fleeting reference to climate change is quickly brought back to the theme of veganism's health-giving properties. Furthermore, despite their activist sympathies, both BOSH! and Pritchard are keen to distance themselves from the figure of the 'militant vegan' that frequently haunts press coverage of veganism (Cole and Morgan 2011). As Firth puts it, 'we're not out to convert anyone and we are certainly not in the least bit militant' (cited in Woods 2018) while Theasby claims 'people don't want veganism shoved down their throats … a softly-softly approach is always best' (cited in Francis 2020). Likewise Pritchard doesn't want to be 'one of those activist vegans' (*Western Mail* 2020). A wider philosophical discussion is also largely absent from Gaz Oakley's output as he realized his skills lay in cooking and 'food could be my activism' (Avant-Garde Vegan 2019b).

These celebrity vegan cooks, therefore, largely promote veganism within the mainstream by focusing on veganism as a consumer choice rather than political practice. All of them emphasize the varied and wonderful flavours of plant-based cooking and the pleasures that come from eating their recipes. In this way, the functional aspects of eating for health are combined with a more hedonistic pursuit of food as pleasure in a form of 'calculated hedonism' (Featherstone 1991). By demonstrating that a vegan diet is flavourful rather than flavourless, pleasurable rather than ascetic, easy to achieve rather than difficult, ordinary rather than faddish, and masculine rather than just feminine, these vegan cooks counter some of the key forms of 'vegaphobia' that previously dominated in the British media (Cole and Morgan 2011).

However, when vegan food practices are abstracted from the wider political motivations that underpin many people's decisions to go vegan, a vegan diet can appear as just another way of constructing lifestyles through food practices (Fegitz and Pirani 2018). Being a vegan risks becoming just another way to manage 'self-identity and lifestyle performance through consumption [and] … dietary selection and display' (Sikka 2019: 356). In *Living on the Veg*, the BOSH! duo suggest that change can come from mass participation in small acts – 'Even if you just have one veggie burger every month, we'll be happy.' However, they offer an individualized approach to consumer activism that shows the political potential of everyday food practices while also working to 'individualize responsibility for structural problems and food systems' (Johnston et al. 2018: 289). Furthermore, the emphasis on taking responsibility for your own health by changing your diet echoes wider neoliberal discourses in which welfare is seen as an individual rather than state responsibility (see Chapters 3 and 6). This also reflects wider discourses of 'healthism' in vegan communities which work 'within a highly individualized framework of risk and responsibility' (Scott 2020: 76) that can 'elide the socio-political context of food and eating' (Braun and Carruthers 2020: 84).

The discussion so far demonstrates how these mainstream representations of veganism attempt to render a plant-based diet ordinary; to open it up to more people, especially men who may be put off by the feminine associations of plant-based diets; and to offer a food politics based on care and compassion. If this demonstrates how the relationships between food, lifestyle and healthism can be gendered in different ways, the masculinization of veganism has further consequences, as I go on to demonstrate in the next section.

Masculinity, veganizing and the meatification of plant-based eating

Despite the emphasis on the health-giving properties of vegan food, these celebrity chefs frequently cook indulgent comfort dishes. In some ways this echoes wider representations of food identified by Alan Warde (1997: 96) in which the opposition between health and indulgence is one of the key antinomies that structure food consumption in the UK, between dishes that 'promise good health' and ones that 'indulge physical and emotional cravings'. These vegan chefs attempt to resolve this tension by transforming functionalized nutrient-rich foodstuffs that promise health into indulgent and comforting dishes. As I go on to show, the feminine associations of health foods are erased through the production of manly and (meat-free) meaty dishes.

4. Veganizing Masculinities

While all the cooks under discussion create some 'naturally vegan' dishes, many of their recipes are for 'veganized' animal-based meals. The Avant-Garde Vegan channel is full of dishes such as 'The Meatiest Vegan Meatballs Ever', 'Vegan Streaky Bacon', 'Sticky BBQ "Ribs" Vegan' and '"Chorizo" Vegan Hot Dogs'. As Gaz Oakley puts it, 'I constantly get requests to veganize things and often find they taste better than the original' (Bryant 2018). Ian from BOSH! claims 'When we cut out meat, we didn't want to change our diet from eating a burger … We wanted to eat the same sort of food as we'd been eating before, just made from plants' (cited in Francis 2018). It is worth noting that both BOSH! and Gaz Oakley describe a 'vegan journey' that moves straight from having a heavily meat-based diet to veganism without a detour via vegetarianism. While Matt Pritchard places less emphasis on 'veganizing', many of the dishes on *Dirty Vegan* are assessed in terms of their 'meatiness'.

This emphasis on meaty comfort foods echoes wider food trends. The veganized dishes often resemble the staples of meaty and greasy 'dude food', conventionally associated with masculine resistance to both culinary elitism and healthy eating advice (Contois 2020: 21). However, these vegan influencers have more specific roots in the masculine culinary persona that Tania Lewis (2020: 79) identifies as the 'Meatrosexual'. These are 'softly masculine foodies who pedal meat in a non-aggressive, non-confrontational style via such hipsterisms as "street food", "authentic eats" and "comfort food"'. This is exactly the terrain that both BOSH! and Avant-Garde Vegan inhabit with their emphasis on comfort foods – from the Sunday roast and Shepherd's Pie to Pad Thai and Carbonara – and US fast foods such as Buttermilk Fried 'Chicken' and Pulled 'Pork'. As Henry Firth puts it in an interview, 'it's all appropriated from meat' (Hurst 2019). Seemingly paradoxically, these vegan cooks target the same market as meatrosexual influencers, 'hipster foodies and millennial males unashamedly wanting to eat meat' (Lewis 2020: 81).

Figure 4.1 Veganized Comfort Food: BOSH! with a finished dish of Pulled 'Pork' Baked Mac & Cheese on their YouTube channel.

The virtue of 'meatiness' is a frequent feature in product and recipe descriptions. In *Dirty Vegan*, tempeh is 'very meaty' and seitan has 'the textures and flavours of meat'. In *Living on the Veg*, BOSH! add layers of meatiness to a lasagne: mushrooms 'will start to look like mince', sun-dried tomatoes do 'the same job as bacon' and miso has an 'umami richness' that gets frequently associated with meatiness. Even when guest Prue Leith challenges the 'desire to make things look like meat … or taste like meat', she judges that BOSH!'s Mushroom Wellington 'tastes really meaty. Not like meat, but hefty'. Despite being a considerable leap from comfort foods, the BOSH! duo admire guest chef Alexis Gaultier's 'Faux Gras': 'it looks real', 'it's like rich and fatty and smooth' and 'it's really hard to believe you're eating plant'.

Meaty, umami flavours are also a frequent principle of recommendation in Avant-Garde Vegan. Meat substitution becomes naturalized as part of modern vegan cooking practices as a base seitan recipe is adapted into a range of different meaty forms.[8] For example, it can be 'adapted to make it into that fillet steak look. It's really meaty' (Avant-Garde Vegan 2017b). The *look* of fillet steak is not only used as a way to recommend the dish in image-rich social media worlds, but also constitutes part of its meaty qualities. As Gaz Oakley says of the finished dish: 'This is going to look amazing on the plate. You could definitely fool someone by showing them and they taste amazing. No animals were harmed.' In this way, while Oakley rejects meat-based diets based on animal cruelty, he nonetheless reproduces ideas of the 'proper meal' in which meat is naturalized as central to meals and, in particular, masculine eating practices (Charles and Kerr 1988; Murcott 1995; Sobal 2005).

Meat is not the only foodstuff that requires a plant-based alternative. However, the vast majority of savoury dishes that seek to replicate the flavours or textures of fish, dairy or eggs are drawn from the repertoire of comfort foods. In *Living on the Veg*, even plant-based fish dishes can be 'meaty'. In a recipe for Thai Jackfruit Fishcakes, BOSH! praise jackfruit for having a 'meat-like or fish-like consistency' and being a 'fantastic meat replacement': 'it really really really does look like kind of meat … or fish in this case.' 'There's a lot of meatiness', they declare as they form the fishcakes although the taste of the final dish is 'remarkably fishy'. Gaz Oakley veganizes fish-based fast food with dishes such as '"Fish" and Chips' and 'Filet-O-"Fish" Burger (GF)'. Aquafaba is used by all the cooks as a substitute for some of the functional qualities of eggs in baking processes and tofu is regularly used as the base for vegan scrambled eggs in dishes like Pritchard's 'Vegan Brekkie'. Oakley has devised a vegan 'egg' in partnership with the casual dining chain Wagamama, a version of which appears on his YouTube channel in 'Ramen with Vegan Egg!?' Unlike the 'meatiness', 'fishiness' or 'cheesiness' associated with many of these vegan comfort foods, the vegan egg is valued for its appearance and texture rather than an 'eggy' taste (Barrie 2019).

This emphasis on veganized, and frequently 'meaty', comfort foods raises a series of issues. First, potential anxieties caused by 'neophobic' responses to seemingly alien vegan food practices and foodstuffs are countered by producing veganized versions of familiar and 'safe' dishes (Fischler 1980). Just as the 'average lad' personas of BOSH! make veganism ordinary, the choice of dishes ordinari-izes vegan food. For example, BOSH! dishes frequently reproduce meal categories and structures that are familiar to British viewers such as English breakfasts, roast dinners, curries, puddings and 'snack hacks'. The sense that a vegan diet is familiar rather than strange is reinforced by BOSH!'s claim that they simply want to 're-imagine our favourite meals' (Firth in Francis 2018): 'the recipes in our book are all meals you will recognise' (Theasby in Francis 2020) and 'Our food is incredible results with basic ingredients from Tesco [supermarket]' (Firth in Hurst 2019). Therefore, they balance the tension that Warde (1997) identifies between novelty and tradition, disavowing the unfamiliarity of vegan food by making it resemble staples of the (globalized) British diet. While this overcomes potential barriers to becoming vegan by demonstrating that people do not need to radically change their diet, it also naturalizes meat-based dishes and cooking styles as a 'normal' way to eat. Rather than focusing on potentially unfamiliar 'naturally vegan' dishes from other cuisines, these media cooks use unfamiliar ingredients – seitan, 'facon', 'nooch' – within familiar dishes. The emphasis on 'meatiness' normalizes the omnivorousness that veganism might be seen to challenge and inscribes plant-based eating within a normatively masculine diet.

Second, the emphasis on indulgent comfort foods distances these male cooks from long-established associations between femininity and health foods. Although functionalized, nutritious foodstuffs are required to build the desirable male body – particularly in an era in which the male body is something to be 'worked upon' (Jackson et al. 2001: 95) and 'read as an indicator of self-control and self-discipline' (Gill et al. 2005: 55) – risk-taking behaviours are also read as a sign of men's innate strength (Courtenay 2000: 1397). However, the emphasis on indulgence also asserts the right to pleasure and fun associated with laddish masculinities. Therefore, although men are encouraged to take a rational and instrumental approach to their bodies in order to keep them 'running smoothly' (Jackson et al. 2001), they also engage in forms of 'calculated hedonism' (Featherstone 1991) that differentiates them from what is seen as a feminized concern with the health of the self and others. The potentially feminine associations with plants and health are offset by the emphasis on indulgence and meat.

In particular, vegan media cooks such as BOSH! use indulgent, comfort foods to distance themselves from ideas about 'clean eating' associated with plant-based diets. As Henry Firth puts it, 'we aren't clean eating, we are the opposite. Our brownies are filled with sugar and fat' (in Myall 2018). They also celebrate fast food and its naughty and indulgent associations – although the plant-based and home-cooked 'fast food' dishes they feature are often time consuming to prepare. In opposition to a clean eating movement associated with women which associates fast food with impurity, these vegan media stars make plant-based home-cooked fast food dishes. For example, the BOSH! YouTube channel features videos celebrating 'dirty' 'dude foods' such as '4 Way Loaded Fries' and 'Pulled "Pork" Baked Mac & Cheese'. If, as Tina Sikka (2019: 362) argues, 'goodness, control, purity and restriction are positively correlated with idealized femininity' in clean eating, the celebration of 'dirty' foods as manly suggests 'that a man's body is invulnerable and can withstand the effects of unhealthy food' (Steim and Nemeroff cited in Sikka

2019: 362). This is also in contrast with the ways in which 'conversion to veganism' is often 'framed as a process of purification' (Scott 2020: 75). In this way, comfort food is not simply about veganizing the familiar but also about masculinizing the plant-based.

Finally, the preoccupation with 'meaty' comfort foods often results in the quest to veganize the most masculine of meaty foods such as barbeque. Therefore we see rather more attempts to produce veganized BBQ ribs or steak and chips than veganized skinless grilled chicken breast or steamed fish! A range of dishes are flavoured with liquid smoke or paprika to get a smoked bacon or barbeque flavour. In this way, vegan cooking becomes associated with what is often seen as the highly masculinized cooking practices of the barbeque, practices located outside of the domestic space of the kitchen which associate cooking with playful masculine leisure rather than feminized domestic labour (Neuhaus 2012). In dishes such as Avant-Garde Vegan's 'Sticky BBQ Ribs' and 'Easy BBQ Sausages', or BOSH!'s '3 Vegan BBQ Meat Dishes', vegan food appears in its most manly form: as a masculine meat product produced through the most masculine of cooking practices.

One key aspect of the mainstreaming of veganism, therefore, is the meatification of plant-based food through a process of veganizing meat-based meals. This not only reaffirms the centrality of meat in Western eating practices, it also associates veganism with the most masculine of foods. While this may render plant-based eating more accessible, it does so by affirming the legitimacy of masculine tastes and cooking practices in contrast to the forms of feminine healthy eating discussed in the previous chapter. The emphasis on comfort foods, particularly in their use by BOSH!, may create ways to imagine vegan versions of popular family dishes. However, they also 'dirty' up the image of veganism to make it consistent with masculine toughness and tastes for 'dude food' that resist the feminine associations of plant-based, healthy eating (Contois 2020).

Conclusions

Like many female plant-based healthy eating advocates, these male celebrity chefs represent veganism as an individualized lifestyle choice which promises health and vitality for those who are prepared to make the choice to go vegan and take responsibility for their body. Although masculinized, their representation of the health benefits of veganism reproduces wider discourses of healthism which organize thinking about health, welfare and the self in neoliberal societies. By representing vegan food practices in terms of the aesthetics of lifestyle, it could be argued that these celebrity chefs evacuate veganism of its politics and make a vegan diet appear as just another consumer choice. This is in contrast to ethical veganism which, as Jessica Greenebaum (2017: 356) argues, 'rejects food consumption as "personal choice", and rejects the ideologies of speciesism and carnism'.

Nonetheless, it is also important to remember that these chefs have had an impact on food practices as part of a wider shift towards decreased meat and dairy consumption that can benefit the treatment of non-human animals and have positive environmental impacts. By popularizing vegan cooking techniques and eating practices and demonstrating how veganism is compatible with pleasure rather than asceticism, these chefs have played a role in mainstreaming vegan food practices. Like other social media influencers, there may be a focus on 'lifestyle and self-image' but at the same time this helps to promote veganism in terms of 'hedonism, self-care and consciousness of the adverse effects of the meat and dairy industries' (Jallinoja et al. 2019: 17). As I have demonstrated, the ways in which these chefs render vegan cooking and eating as pleasurable rather than ascetic practices involve masculinizing plant-based food practices which, paradoxically, reaffirm the pleasures of meatiness, meat products and meat-based diets. Indeed, one of the key pleasures of their veganism appears to be the ability to enjoy the benefits of veganism *and* omnivorousness, representing a plant-based diet in terms of a wealth of consumer choices rather than restriction. This image of vegan practice, therefore, aligns political consumption with unrestrained pleasure, proposing a form of 'alternative hedonism' in which ethical practices can be about indulgence rather than ascetic forms of restraint (Soper 2008).

TV shows such as *Dirty Vegan* and *Living on the Veg* also attempt to demonstrate the ease with which veganism can be incorporated into mainstream British food practices and meal events, from barbeques and Sunday lunch to wedding banquets and Christmas dinner. This promotes a sense of inclusion and seeks to counter ideas that vegans are inherently 'difficult' or 'killjoys' (Greenebaum 2018). However, if these vegan food practices are shaped by gender differences, they are also promoted with scant regard to other forms of difference and constraint. The recipes are often expensive – especially for anyone who lacks an already diverse and well-stocked pantry – and time consuming. For example, although it serves '20+', Gaz Oakley's seitan 'Streaky Bacon' requires over twenty ingredients, a substantial amount of kitchen gadgetry and three hours preparation before it is ready to cook and combine with other ingredients to make a meal (Avant-Garde Vegan 2018). While the investment in time and expense to engage in lifestyled culinary practices is certainly not unique to vegan celebrity chefs, it places limits on the ability to mainstream plant-based eating, a gap in the market which supermarkets have been quick to exploit with vegan fast foods and ready meals. Tesco appointed Derek Sarno as Executive Chef Director of plant-based innovation in 2017. Sarno, who had already established a profile through his association with the Whole Foods Market chain in the United States, very much embodies the modes of heavily tattooed and muscular masculinity associated with some of the male vegan celebrity chefs discussed in this chapter. The title of his plant-based range for Tesco – Wicked Kitchen – plays on the double-meaning of wicked as both good and naughty, creating the sense that vegan food is about indulgence and taste rather than restraint and denial. BOSH! have also launched their own mass-market range of plant-based cakes and cake mixes.

The importance of budget eating is recognized in YouTube videos such as BOSH!'s '21 Tips for Eating Vegan on a Budget' and Avant-Garde Vegan's 'Budget Vegan Meal Prep'. Yet both these videos emphasize more familiar vegan or healthy eating dishes based on vegetables, pulses and seeds rather than a celebration of indulgent 'meaty' comfort foods which are central to the BOSH! and Avant-Garde Vegan brands. The masculinized pleasures of meatiness are reserved for those who can afford it, and like carnivorous diets are associated with power and privilege. This is not to suggest that veganism as a movement is inherently based on privilege but to identify the ways in which the popularization of vegan diets in particular ways – whether in the form of feminine clean eating or the masculine meatification of veganism – is entangled with and extends other forms of inequality, rendering veganism increasingly inaccessible for particular groups. While the use of these male celebrity chefs to present the UK's first vegan cooking shows on broadcast television challenges images of vegans as killjoys, hippies or female clean eaters, it does little to challenge the overwhelming whiteness of images of veganism in the mass media (Greenebaum 2018), marginalizing how Black vegans have used their food practices to resist racism (Harper 2010: xv).[9] These mainstream representations of veganism on British television – like other forms of ethical consumption – may have the potential to effect meaningful change but they also risk becoming part of white, middle-class lifestyle practices that reproduce cultural distinctions and wider inequalities.

Chapter 5

FOOD HEROES, FOOD POLITICS AND THE CAMPAIGNING CULINARY DOCUMENTARY

If headlines are to be believed, celebrity chefs have had a huge impact on public life. Jamie Oliver's televised fight to improve school dinners provoked a range of hyperbolic headlines. 'Jamie's School Dinners Boosts School Exam Results' claimed the *Evening Standard* (Evening Standard 2010) and 'Govt Caves in Over Jamie's School Dinner Demands' declared *Broadcast* (2005). For the *Independent*, Hugh Fearnley-Whittingstall and Jamie Oliver's TV-led campaign on chicken welfare 'Changed the Eating Habits of a Nation' (Hickman 2008). While not all headlines are as positive, they attest to the significance of celebrity chefs in national life (Rousseau 2012b).

While my early chapters largely focused on how celebrity chefs implicitly politicize a range of food practices, this chapter shifts attention to the more explicit ways in which they have intervened in the politics of food. I examine how celebrity chefs have launched campaigns to tackle 'food crises' which produce particular ways of imagining the politics of food and the relationships between consumers, food producers and distributors, and the state (Bell et al. 2017). While some chefs' campaigning activities largely take place off camera, other chefs such as Jamie Oliver and Hugh Fearnley-Whittingstall have produced distinctive television formats which position them as heroes, fighting on our behalf to solve a range of problems.

This chapter focuses on how a particular TV format – the campaigning culinary documentary (hereafter CCD) – has been used to brand chefs as compassionate and caring heroes who move beyond their positions in the culinary and media fields to intervene in the political life of the nation (and beyond). I begin by introducing this format, its characteristics and how it has been used to brand both chefs and television channels in the UK. The chapter then examines British television chef and food writer Hugh Fearnley-Whittingstall's CCDs that focus on ethical and environmental issues in relation to food production, distribution and consumption. This discussion draws on earlier collaborative work with David Bell and Steve Jones that explored CCDs and the responsibilization of food crises (Bell et al. 2017; Bell and Hollows 2011; Hollows and Jones 2010b).

Many celebrity chefs' interventions need to be understood within broader changes during the early twenty-first century in which ethical food production and consumption became more mainstream concerns. This period was also characterized by an increasing interest in the environment and sustainability, including questions about corporate responsibility for adopting more ethical and sustainable practices, the role of the state and global agencies in devising and regulating environmental agendas to combat climate change, and the need for more ethical and sustainable forms of consumption in order to safeguard both the planet and its inhabitants. Popular culture became a key site of struggle over the meanings of the environment and the significance of issues such as climate change. Examples include 'green' lifestyle programming, the CCDs discussed below and high-profile documentaries such as *An Inconvenient Truth* (2006) and *Cowspiracy* (2014) as well as global protest movements (Lewis 2008b: 230). The '*contemporary cultural politics of the environment*' were played out and 'contested' across these spaces. As Goodman et al. (2016: 677–8) argue, 'environmental meanings are constructed and negotiated across spaces, place and at various scales which … involve assemblages of science, media, culture, environment and politics'. However, the ways in which these politics play out happen in uneven and often contradictory ways.

Celebrities have also played a key role in giving environmental issues increased visibility. By working for good causes, celebrities can attach qualities such as care and compassion to their brand (Littler 2008) and caring for the environment is a major form of celebrity advocacy (Craig 2019). Therefore, celebrity chefs' campaigns on environmental issues need to be understood within a wider 'celebrification' of the environment which spawns new forms of 'envirotainment' (Goodman and Littler 2013: 271; see also Brockington 2013). This celebrity campaigning helps to shape public understanding of – and engagement with – ethical and environmental issues and 'frame[s] how the public should think about, feel and relate' to them (Abidin et al. 2020: [1.17]). For example, as Abidin et al. suggest, part of the power of figures such as Greta Thunberg lies in her unedited displays of sad or angry emotions, situating 'her concerns about climate change within affective and performative registers … that attempt to frame our own affective responses' (Ibid.). As I explore below, celebrity chefs frequently communicate their responses to complex questions about food ethics and sustainability through emotion, encouraging us to share their pain as they respond to damage to the Earth and its residents. The capacity to feel, and the ability to communicate the intensity of this feeling, becomes not only part of the celebrity brand but also part of the strategies through which celebrity chefs seek to mobilize change.

However, 'unlike entertainment celebrities, celebrity chefs are also food system actors' (Phillipov and Gale 2020). This chapter examines how Hugh Fearnley-Whittingstall's political interventions can be understood as brand extensions that built on his existing image and also enabled him to acquire a sense of gravitas and moral authority as he traded on compassion as an asset (Goodman 2013). In the process, Fearnley-Whittingstall, like Jamie Oliver and others, has become a moral entrepreneur and a 'political intermediary', as well as a cultural intermediary, within lifestyle formats (Hollows and Jones 2010b; Matta 2019: 186; see also Powell and Prasad 2010). Drawing on debates about neoliberalism introduced earlier, this chapter examines how the narratives of CCDs responsibilize consumers to solve social and economic problems by transforming their own behaviour (Bell et al. 2017). However, celebrity chefs' campaigns cannot only be seen as an expression of neoliberal ideologies. CCDs also feature celebrity chefs as heroes battling corporate power and demanding state solutions to food problems.

The campaigning culinary documentary

The campaigning culinary documentary (CCD) emerged as a recognizable new format within British food programming following the success of *Jamie's School Dinners* in 2005. The celebrity associated with this series – Jamie Oliver – and the channel on which it was broadcast – Channel 4 – became closely associated with the format. This section, which draws on earlier collaborative research (Bell et al. 2017), charts the development and characteristics of the CCD. Its key narrative conventions were informed by reality TV and lifestyle makeovers as well as aspects of campaigning documentary formats.

Although the blueprint for the CCD was *Jamie's School Dinners* (2005), it was the earlier Channel 4 series *Jamie's Kitchen* (2002) that established the potential of problem-solving documentary formats for managing the identities of both TV chefs and TV channels. The series followed Jamie Oliver's attempt to makeover a group of unemployed young people, transforming them into chefs who would staff his new restaurant venture Fifteen which was established with a charitable status. *Jamie's Kitchen* enabled Oliver to move away from the recipe-led lifestyle formats in which he had forged his television career towards a more explicitly public service role (Lewis 2008a).[1] Broadcast soon after his move from the BBC, Jamie helped to bolster Channel 4's roster of lifestyle experts which were becoming increasingly central to the channel's identity (Barnes 2017). However, his deployment in a format that introduced issues such as social exclusion and youth unemployment not only helped to recast him as both a lifestyle expert and moral entrepreneur but also enabled Channel 4 to combine entertainment programming with their public service remit. The future development of the CCD was enabled by the show's success in audience ratings. It was one of Channel 4's top two shows of 2002 and screened in over thirty other countries (Kelly and Harrison 2009).[2] It is also worth noting that, like many later CCDs, the show was aired in the '8-9' primetime slot that was already associated with lifestyle programming (Brunsdon 2003).

This blend of elements from lifestyle and reality TV with more 'legitimate' documentary formats was used in the four-part series *Jamie's School Dinners* (2005).[3] Generating a significant amount of press coverage and debate that extended the cross-media reach and impact of the series, the show helped to reposition Jamie Oliver as a caring and compassionate public figure after a period in which there had been a public backlash against him. The series also laid down a blueprint for a format that could be used and adapted across later CCDs. First, the narrative of *Jamie's School Dinners* was structured around a perceived 'crisis' (substandard school meals) which Jamie attempted to resolve through a crusading campaign (by transforming practices in school kitchens and government policy on funding school lunches). Later CCDs would be motivated by a range of other crises such as poor animal welfare (*Hugh's Chicken Run*), obesity (*Jamie's Ministry of Food*, *Britain's Fat Fight*), the excessive power of supermarkets over food consumption and production (*The People's Supermarket*) and food waste (*Hugh's War on Waste*). The identification of a crisis and a campaign in *Jamie's School Dinners* provided a framework for a problem-solving narrative in which Jamie intervened, heroically overcame a series of obstacles and transformed food practices for the better. This narrative format, replicated across many CCDs, provides some of the excitement and tension within the format.

Second, *Jamie's School Dinners* presented positive change as the result of a special and inspirational figure. Jamie was represented as the only person capable of effecting change, a viewpoint replicated in often approving press commentary (Hollows and Jones 2010b). This worked to individualize social change and led to the widespread sanctification of Oliver in the British press where he was called a saint (Heathcote Amory 2005) and 'a latter-day prophet' (Shilling 2005: 2). The CCD, therefore, became an exceptional vehicle for a branding exercise. While only Hugh Fearnley-Whittingstall has approached the same level of acclaim for his campaigning as Jamie Oliver in the UK, less well-known celebrity chefs such as Jimmy Doherty and Arthur Potts-Dawson have used the CCD to both strengthen and nuance their brand.

Third, chefs' interventions in CCDs frequently rely on makeovers of 'ordinary people' as well as transformations of institutions and industries. These attempts to makeover 'ordinary people' often provide much of the dramatic conflict. In many series, the drama centres on a male chef's attempts to transform the practices of a working-class woman (Hollows 2016). While *Jamie's School Dinners* documented Oliver's transformation of school dinner lady Nora from an adversary into an ally (Fox and Smith 2011), characters who refuse to change can act as dramatic foils throughout a series. In this and the following chapter, I explore the classed and gendered politics of this relationship in more detail.

Finally, *Jamie's School Dinners* and subsequent CCDs shifted celebrity chefs away from their association solely with lifestyle, enabling them to address wider social problems. Nonetheless, their expertise as a food personality and their role as a cultural intermediary are usually central to the format. Although some celebrity chefs have expanded into campaigns that move beyond food, some aspect of their established expertise tends to be utilized.[4]

The use of food television to intervene in crises in national life has, therefore, extended the brand images of celebrity chefs. Jamie Oliver's various campaigns have enabled him to trade on the celebrity produced by his investment in lifestyle in order to recast it as a more serious and symbolically rich asset (Hollows and Jones 2010b). CCDs also enabled Channel 4, who had invested heavily in lifestyle programming, to attach some of these associations to its channel identity and its roster of lifestyle stars.[5]

Many of the CCDs associated with issues around ethical food production, distribution and consumption were broadcast as part of the annual Channel 4 Food

Fight season that ran from 2008 until 2011. Food Fight established both celebrity chefs and the channel as campaigning and caring but they were also crucial in branding Channel 4 as the home of the UK's leading celebrity chefs. The trailer for the first Food Fight season in 2008 was a branding exercise that focused on the star images of its line-up of celebrity chefs – Jamie Oliver, Hugh Fearnley-Whittingstall and Gordon Ramsay. Set in a spoof team-building camp, each chef moans about their fellow supergroup members, reinforcing their celebrity images while creating space for the viewer's own potential reservations about them: Jamie 'is not the sharpest tool in the box'; Hugh is a 'hippy' who cooks chicken 'stuffed in a badger's backside'; and Gordon is a hyper-competitive yuppie ('on your BlackBerry all the time') associated with fancy food 'cooked in a jus' (Channel 4 2008). The following year's trailer used a similar format. This time the celebrity chefs were represented as members of a Great Britain sports team with Channel 4's latest acquisition, Heston Blumenthal, added to the mix. Heston was characterized in terms of gadgetry and scientific wizardry – established elements of his star image from his earlier BBC series (Hollows and Jones 2010a). While the trailer was constructed for comedic effect, Heston's comment that 'the moment I stepped into this team, I felt like I'd been here all my life' cemented his place in the Channel 4 team of celebrity chefs (Channel 4 2009). These trailers highlighted Channel 4's identity as the home of lifestyle experts rather than focusing on the food politics that provided the focus for much of the content of the Food Fight seasons.

As they acquired new food personalities, the CCD proved an adaptable formula to articulate their talent with Channel 4's brand identity. Variations on the CCD format have also been used by the BBC – for example, one of their key celebrity chefs James Martin applied Jamie's format to improve school dinners in *Operation Hospital Food* (2011–14). Moreover, the BBC's associations with the CCD were accentuated once they acquired Hugh Fearnley-Whittingstall, starting with his *War on Waste* (2016). The CCD has also proved to be a successful export. As well as sales of British CCDs to foreign markets, celebrity chefs such as Jamie Oliver have used the CCD to develop their brand elsewhere – for example, *Jamie's Kitchen Australia* and *Jamie's Food Revolution* in the United States. Variations of the CCD have also been used internationally to develop the brands of celebrity chefs.

The CCD has also provided celebrity chefs with a public platform to intervene in the politics of food production, distribution and consumption. These shows frequently demonstrate how food cannot be abstracted from wider questions of power and politics, from the organization of economic life and the role of the state in healthcare provision and tackling poverty. This chapter focuses on Hugh Fearnley-Whittingstall as a case study to examine how celebrity chefs have used the CCD to address ethical issues about food production, retail and consumption. I explore how his celebrity image and the constraints of the CCD impact on how three ethical issues around food are framed and mediated: animal welfare, sustainable fishing practices and food waste. In Chapter 6, I return to the CCD as part of a wider discussion of how celebrity chefs have shaped public understanding of the relationships between food, health and the body within a wider politics of austerity.

Hugh Fearnley-Whittingstall as ethical brand

By the time Hugh Fearnley-Whittingstall starred in his first CCD, he was a well-established Channel 4 television chef and cookery writer.[6] After a short career as a restaurant chef, his early television series used innovative formats to establish him as a different kind of celebrity chef. In *A Cook on the Wild Side* (1997) he learned about foraging from local people. In *TV Dinners* (1997) he assisted members of the public in their homes as they prepared memorable meals. This established him as a learner more than an instructor and, through continual encounters with the public, as an affable, familiar and relatively ordinary person. If the ability 'to be "just-as-they-are" with ordinary members of the public' is often part of the television personality's image (Bennett 2008: 41), then these early series established Hugh as a comforting, 'authentic' and trustworthy presence on screen. Hugh's ability to relate to, and learn from, ordinary people also helped to build his legitimacy in later speaking *for* ordinary people and to play down his poshness and associations with elites afforded by his Eton and Oxbridge education. As Tania Lewis (2010: 582) observes, in lifestyle media, 'the expert and the celebrity are ... characterized by a ... tension between a claim to exceptional or elite status and a kind of public representativeness'. By smoothing out some of his posh associations, these series helped to pave the way for Hugh to lead, and act on behalf of, the public in later CCDs.[7]

Hugh's association with 'green lifestyle' programming and 'a personal ethics around food choice' was cemented through the *River Cottage* television shows and cookbooks that became synonymous with his name and his approach to food and cooking (Lewis 2008a: 59; see also Parkins and Craig 2011).[8] Early seasons of *River Cottage* were structured around what has become a familiar downshifting narrative in which Hugh traded a hectic urban lifestyle for a change of pace in a 'rural idyll'. As Hugh explained in the introductory voiceover to the first series: 'Like many city dwellers, it's long been my dream to escape the urban sprawl, find a little place in the country and live off the fat of the land, thriving off whatever I can grow, gather or catch.'

These comments not only established continuity with the earlier foraging stories in *Cook on the Wild Side* but also linked Hugh to approaches to ethical consumption associated with 'consuming less through the capitalist marketplace' and eschewing 'unnecessary' consumerism (Binkley and Littler 2008).[9] As Michelle Phillipov (2017: 56) observes, '*River Cottage* presents rural self-sufficiency as the "solution" to the problems and anxieties of contemporary food production'. By associating ethical consumption with abundance and indulgence rather than asceticism, the series imagined a form of what Kate Soper (2008: 572) calls 'alternative hedonism', 'the sensual pleasures of consuming differently'. The early series represented Hugh as an enthusiastic amateur, in which the audience learned alongside him about how to run a small holding and live a more simple, rural life. Like many other green lifestyle programmes, the *River Cottage* series took 'a softly softly approach to providing lessons in "good" modes of consumption ... [o]ffering viewers rather romanticized, escapist images of slow living' (Lewis 2008b: 233). The invitation to share in Hugh's ethical practices was divested of its potentially smug or preachy associations by his own 'amateur' status and by representing ethical consumption as fun.

Nonetheless, despite being positioned as an often hapless novice in rural living, Hugh still acted as a cultural intermediary, legitimating particular dispositions towards ethical consumption centred around an image of rural life that emphasized community, caring and common goals. As the series progressed, Hugh began to share his skills and took a more explicit educational and campaigning role in relation to ethical living. For example, *River Cottage Spring* (2008) made an overt connection between ethical consumption and production by initiating a Landshare scheme. Hugh secured a patch of disused land from the local council in Bristol and helped a group of 'locals' to develop a smallholding with vegetable beds, an orchard and some livestock. In each episode, Hugh returned to the 'Bristol gang' as they (re)connected to the processes and practices of growing, preparing and cooking their own food, adding a 'reality TV' element to the *River Cottage* franchise.

River Cottage Spring launched Hugh's attempt to roll out the Landshare scheme at a national level, aiming to match would-be food growers with unused land. By 2013, 80,000 people had signed up to the scheme which translated the fantasy of 'consuming differently' into active involvement in food production (Bramall 2013).[10]

River Cottage Autumn (2008) and *River Cottage Summer's Here* (2009) reported back on the Bristol gang's progress and Hugh's success in getting institutions such as the Church of England and the National Trust to share some of their land. While Hugh's scheme veered 'towards a model of feudalistic patronage' and was limited in its critique of globalized food systems, it nonetheless offered 'an intelligible figuration of the environmental and social impacts of food production and consumption' (Bramall 2013: 80–1). These series not only strengthened Hugh's associations with ethical food practices but also reconstructed him as a 'people's champion', using his celebrity status to galvanize ordinary people and to affect institutional change.

Developments within the *River Cottage* franchise echoed Hugh's shift to the role of moral entrepreneur within the CCD format. However, the representation of the moral and ethical dimensions of consumption validates performative dispositions towards consumption associated with the new middle classes (Barnett et al. 2005; Bonner 2010; Bourdieu 1984). More specifically, Hugh privileged both white and new middle-class dispositions towards consumption. As Julie Guthman observes, 'getting your hands dirty' celebrates 'an agrarian past that is more easily romanticized by whites than others' (cited in Probyn 2019: 248). It is also difficult to ignore how Fearnley-Whittingstall used his investment in ethical food practices to establish a highly successful River Cottage brand that generated economic profits not only from the sales of cookbooks and DVDs but also, at various points, a range of courses, dining ventures, shops, wedding and event services and retreats.[11] While this success might validate 'the viability and achievability of sustainable business practice' (Parkins and Craig 2011: 195), it also highlights how ethical production and consumption are used to sell brands and how entrepreneurialism was central to Hugh's celebrity image.

Ethical and 'unethical' consumers in Hugh's Chicken Run

Channel 4's first Food Fight season in January 2008 focused on animal welfare. As well as a Jamie Oliver fronted special – *Jamie's Fowl Dinners* – concerned with chicken welfare in egg production, *Hugh's Chicken Run*, which screened over three consecutive nights, formed the centrepiece of the season.[12] Based on the CCD format established in *Jamie's School Dinners*,[13] Hugh's campaign focused on the problem of the unethical production of cheap supermarket chicken by highlighting the plight of intensively farmed birds. The series – and 2009's follow-up *Chickens, Hugh ... and Tesco Too* – aimed to transform the producers, retailers and consumers of 'cheap', low-welfare chicken. This section focuses on how *Hugh's Chicken Run* used the CCD format to attempt ethical makeovers of 'ordinary' chicken consumers.

While the *River Cottage* series highlighted the pleasures of green lifestyles, Hugh's chicken campaign takes a much more didactic approach by demonstrating the consequences of 'unethical' consumption practices. Industrial food production had been largely 'invisible' in the *River Cottage* series (Phillipov 2017: 56–7). Here it took centre stage as Hugh tried to raise viewers' awareness of how 'two-for-a-fiver' cheap chickens depended on a system of deeply unethical production in which birds are raised in cramped, unhealthy and 'unhappy' conditions. The series documents his attempts to transform the residents of the Devon market town of Axminster into ethical consumers of free-range chicken, climaxing in a 'free-range week' in which residents were asked to only buy free-range chicken. A relative success, this set piece emphasizes consumers' capacity to make a change through their purchasing power and highlights how consumption can be a form of citizenship (Littler 2009). In this way, consumers on screen and at home are responsibilized to use their practices to end the horrors of cheap chicken production.

Much of the drama and conflict in the show comes from a specific group of largely working-class residents of Axminster's Millway council estate. This, Hugh explains, 'is the tough end of town', an image reinforced through repeated shots of graffiti-covered signage. 'This is life, this is real life', he informs viewers, where people are 'struggling with their food budget' and know little of the 'grim life of cheap chickens'. Geographically close to (but a world away from) the rural idyll of River Cottage, the programme suggests that if Hugh's campaign can work here, then it can work anywhere, including in the viewers' own lives. The series follows the residents as they learn about the pleasures of ethical chicken production by raising their own birds on a local allotment. It documents their shocked reactions when confronted with the realities of industrial chicken production. In the process, the group – like the 'Bristol gang' before them – act as 'ordinary people' with whom the audience might identify as both Hugh's celebrity and expert status became harder to disguise.

While the narratives of lifestyle cookery programmes tend to legitimate the celebrity chef's dispositions, the CCD produces narrative conflict by introducing the voices of ordinary people who question their authority. Although Hugh's experiment with the Millway residents starts well, one resident increasingly casts doubt on the assumption that ethical consumption practices are 'middle-class virtues to which we should all aspire' (Lewis 2008b: 238). The dissenting voice belongs to Hayley, a single mother who adopts a 'mother hen' role by organizing her neighbours on the allotment. Hayley remains adamant that – as a working-class single mother – she cannot afford the ethical luxury of free-range chicken. Like many other CCDs which depend on the transformation of an initially resistant and aberrant working-class woman, the series offers the promise of Hayley's transformation into a 'good', moral and ethical consumer.

The series documents how Hayley, despite working tirelessly on the allotment, refuses to demonstrate the 'appropriate' emotional dispositions when Hugh confronts her – and the viewer – with the grim reality of intensive chicken production. As Goodman et al. (2016: 681) argue, these types of shocking scenes aim to work not only through 'the transmission of facts, words and "rational" knowledge' but also by 'fostering emotion and ecologies of feeling', produced to 'get our attention and pique our environmental imaginaries in ways that work to get us to feel, to connect and to "do"'. However, Hayley refuses to be the object of a makeover narrative in which she is expected to be transformed through education. Industrial chicken production is, she says, exactly what she expected. This contrasts starkly with a scene which lingers on Hugh in tears over the chickens' plight, demonstrating his empathy with their situation and his willingness to fight to change it. In this way, the show not only educates viewers about what they should know about chicken production but also frames how they should *feel* about it (Abidin et al. 2020). This also attaches qualities of care and compassion to Hugh's brand, valuable assets in the celebrity economy (Littler 2008).

In contrast, Hayley's refusal to feel for chickens – and to make the ethical choice to buy free-range birds – marks her out as self-centred and lacking moral worth. She refuses the validity of these judgements by drawing on a different ethical system in which working-class mothers are evaluated by their ability to care for their families. Hayley tells Hugh that cheap chickens are 'for people's pockets like mine' and reiterates that her primary ethical responsibility is to care for her family through budgeting wisely. Here the 'ethics' of ethical consumption conflict with the 'ordinarily ethical' dimensions of everyday domestic practices, oriented around values such as thrift, that enable Hayley to be recognized as a 'good' and responsible mother (Barnett et al. 2005: 28; DeVault 1991; Miller 1998). Despite Hayley's protestations, the series devalues this everyday feminine labour in which consumption is a way of 'caring for' others in favour of displaying Hugh's ability to 'care about', a more typically masculine disposition oriented towards the public sphere (Tronto 1989: 74; see also Silva 2007: 143).[14] Therefore, *Hugh's Chicken Run* privileges the '*performative* practice associated with being an ethical consumer' (Barnett et al. 2005: 41), a practice more easily capitalized on by both Hugh and the viewers who choose to adopt his dispositions. Furthermore, as ethical food practices have become increasingly part of the dispositions associated with middle-class standards of 'good' mothering, women who cannot afford to take part are positioned in terms of 'personal deficiency, rather than structural inequality' (Cairns et al. 2013: 111). The show rests on a discourse of choice in which a refusal to make the 'right' choice and a refusal to change are taken as signs of moral failure, a failure that the series largely identifies with the working class.

Hugh's Chicken Run, therefore, acknowledges resistance to Hugh's mission to transform people's shopping practices. The men in the pub who remain unmoved by a film about chicken production. A woman who accuses him of being a 'guilt-tripping' 'elitist'. And Hayley, who is filmed buying cheap chickens during Hugh's 'free-range week'. This demonstrates the limits of Hugh's celebrity as a tradable asset and his lifestyled approach to ethical production and consumption. However, overall, the viewer is left with an image of Hugh as a caring and compassionate hero devoting himself to improving the lives of chickens while those who resist him are rendered as obstacles that our hero must overcome in his battle for the good.

Like other CCDs, the series provided a useful vehicle for branding a celebrity chef. If compassion is 'part of the contemporary celebrity job description' (Littler 2008: 238), the show branded Hugh in terms of his capacity to care, enabling him to use his moral and ethical investments to generate profits in distinction and to enhance his brand image as a moral entrepreneur. Nonetheless, while the show acknowledged the question of whether all people can afford to care, it also privileged those people who were prepared to become more like Hugh and prioritize ethical consumption practices, whatever the costs. In this way, the series remained caught within the parameters of the lifestyle formats that spawned both it and Hugh's celebrity.

Responsibilizing retail

The lifestyle television heritage of both celebrity chefs and CCDs means that consumers are frequently given responsibility for effecting social change by transforming their own practices. However, while this remains central to the format, the CCD cannot be read as simply a straightforward example of neoliberal forms of individual responsibilization and self-governance in action. CCDs also draw on a wide range of food media formats – for example, campaigning feature-length documentaries and TV 'commodity-chain exposés' – that seek to produce more ethical food consumers, critically engage with the food industry and act as a medium for 'food pedagogies' (Flowers and Swan 2011; Friedberg 2004). The close entanglements between celebrity chefs and the food industry – for example, supermarkets such as Sainsbury's and Waitrose – suggest that celebrity chefs might be reluctant to bite the hand that feeds them. However, although problematic, these relationships have also been used to ethicalize supermarket practices, demonstrated by Jamie Oliver's relationship with Woolworths in Australia (Lewis and Huber 2015; Phillipov 2017). In this section, I examine how CCDs do not only responsibilize consumers to change their practices but also attempt to makeover the food industry.[15]

Beyond its focus on ethical consumption, *Hugh's Chicken Run* also demonstrated how the major supermarkets, as both chicken producers and retailers, were responsible for perpetuating cheap, intensively reared chicken. This, as the title suggests, became the main focus of the follow-up programme, *Chickens, Hugh … and Tesco Too*, broadcast as part of 2009's Food Fight season. The show shifts the focus from free-range chicken to the 'qualitative difference' between the conditions of chickens raised under the 'standard system' of intensive farming and the lower density RSPCA-approved 'Freedom Foods' system of intensive chicken production.[16] The difference between the methods is established visually through visits to farms which illustrate how different levels of intensiveness impact on chicken's lives and welfare, a difference that is shown to have only a limited impact on price. Hayley reappears to back up Hugh's case, prepared to pay a little more and eat chicken less if she knows the chickens she buys have had better lives. 'Even hard-bitten Hayley is now a Freedom Foods fan', enthuses Hugh while getting in a last insult.

With Hayley no longer an adversary, the series focuses on Hugh's battle with the corporate might of the UK's largest supermarket, Tesco. His mission is to make Tesco 'upgrade its basic chicken offering to Freedom Foods', to make their practices fit their ethical statements on their website and to achieve greater transparency in Tesco labelling so that consumers can make informed decisions about their purchases. In a series of sequences that would become familiar in other CCDs, Tesco repeatedly dodge Hugh's requests to meet with senior decision-makers for an on-camera interview. In response, the programme follows Hugh's attempt to fight Tesco from within: because Tesco is 'answerable to its shareholders', he becomes one. His single share in the company enables him to table a resolution at the company's AGM that demands that Tesco 'upgrade[s] its basic chicken welfare' or abandons its claims to uphold animal freedoms.

This initiative is thwarted at every turn. In order to table a resolution, Hugh needs the support of 100 shareholders and, despite dire warnings that shareholders are only interested in profit, Hugh finds likeminded 'activist shareholders' to join *his* fight. The programme repeatedly features press coverage of *his* campaign, emphasizing his star power and his role as a heroic and remarkable individual bravely fighting for change. As Hugh's resolution is tabled, Tesco finally offer an on-camera meeting but their media representative simply portrays Tesco as powerless in the face of their customers' demands and offers 'an onslaught of corporate welfare wash'. In the process, the show highlights how corporate practices do not necessarily match with public responsibility statements and simply act as 'a form of reputation management in the face of criticism' (Littler 2009: 61). Meanwhile, Tesco again try to combat Hugh's resolution at the AGM, asking him to pay over £86,000 in postage costs to send it to shareholders, an obstacle overcome by Hugh as he raises the costs in just 24 hours via a fundraising website because 'people care enough to put their hands in their pockets'. The combat metaphors continue as Hugh comments that this is no longer 'just a postal bill – it feels more like a fighting fund'.

Following Tesco's announcement that Hugh needs to get 75 per cent of shareholders onside if his resolution is to pass, we get ready for his 'showdown with the shareholders'. While the meeting is not televised, we see Hugh's arrival and the subsequent result announced via BBC news footage, accentuating again the celebrity chef's role as a newsmaker and public figure. Despite gaining 'unprecedented' support, his resolution fails but, as the programme closes, we are told that Tesco has finally agreed to meet him, farmers and welfare groups to discuss how 'to improve the lot of the humble chicken'. We are left with the sense that, off-camera, Hugh's struggle continues, enabling us to choose to consume chicken ethically. The show, therefore, reasserts Hugh's position as a moral entrepreneur who frames issues as moral problems that demand both attention and action.

The focus on corporate practices in *Chickens, Hugh ... and Tesco Too* suggests that CCDs are not always simply expressions of neoliberal logic. While the programme never calls for government intervention on chicken welfare, Tesco's resistance to Hugh's campaign demonstrates the limits of corporate self-regulation. The show highlights how corporate social responsibility statements rarely go far enough and that supermarkets need to also be accountable to society (Littler 2011). Major shareholders are shown only to be interested in profit, responding to ethical issues only when they pose a reputational risk that also poses a financial risk. While this privileges a model in which consumers must take responsibility and influence corporations through their shopping practices, it also suggests that responsibilized consumers may use forms of political consumerism and opt not to shop at Tesco.

Battles against the corporate power of supermarkets over food production, distribution and consumption are a popular narrative in CCDs. As I go on to demonstrate, supermarkets remain a potential adversary in many of Fearnley-Whittingstall's CCDs, as they do for other celebrity chefs. Arthur Potts-Dawson's *The People's Supermarket* (2011) examined cooperative-based alternatives to the dominance of supermarkets over production and retail while Jimmy Doherty took on Tesco in *Jimmy and the Giant Supermarket* (2012).[17] The latter demonstrated supermarkets' increasing awareness of the potential reputational damage that could be caused by campaigning chefs. A potentially adversarial relationship developed into more of a partnership, enabling some of Doherty's established animal welfare credentials to rub off on Tesco. This allowed the supermarket to drive home their message that retail's ability to self-regulate is dependent on consumers' willingness to take responsibility through their buying power. This demonstrates how celebrity chefs can also be used to rehabilitate brand images, a lesson learned by Australian supermarket Coles who, in response to a series of scandals, brought together an 'ethical agenda with strategies designed to tap into the popularity of food media, the appeal of its high-profile celebrity chefs and its politics of food provenance' (Phillipov 2017: 171).

Fish fights and people power

> There's a problem in our seas, a problem created by our unstoppable appetite for fish. I've been on a journey to discover just how bad that problem is ... and what I've found is that it's not just bad, it's mad ... At times, it will be a struggle to watch. It'll be an even bigger struggle to solve.
>
> (*Hugh's Fish Fight*)

Hugh Fearnley-Whittingstall's voiceover at the opening of *Hugh's Fish Fight* quickly established a number of features of the series. We do not know what the problem is but the consumer is implicated (with 'our unstoppable appetite'). The stakes are simple and we must take Hugh's side in a moral and rational battle ('it's not just bad, it's mad'). It's going to be an emotional 'struggle to watch' and, by implication, only one man – Hugh – is able to lead the 'even bigger struggle to solve' it. In this way, both chef and public are united in a common quest. The series – which ranges across a range of issues including sustainable fishing practices, ethical fish consumption, responsible labelling and government regulation – was first broadcast in January 2011 as part of the Food Fight season. It was accompanied by one-off programmes – *Jamie's Fish Supper, Gordon Ramsay: Shark Bait* and *Heston's Fishy Feast* – with a follow-up programme *Hugh's Fish Fight: The Battle Continues* aired later in the year. While not the focus of my discussion, a further series *Hugh's Fish Fight: Save Our Seas* aired in 2013 (see Probyn 2019 for a detailed analysis). This section examines how *Hugh's Fish Fight* built on Fearnley-Whittingstall's now established reputation as a trusted figure who can achieve transformations by responsibilizing consumers to change their ways and by encouraging viewers to act collectively to create a form of people power that demands that the government takes action. In the process, the series helped to strengthen Hugh's position as a public figure and built his image as an 'environment celebrity' in what was already a 'crowded' field (Craig 2019: 780).

One strand of the series centres on Hugh's attempts to get the British public to eat a greater range of more sustainable fish to help both the environment and fishermen (people involved in catching fish are always fisher*men* in the show). Through a series of set pieces, the public and viewers are introduced to alternative 'fishy delights' that are economical and plentiful.[18] In another strand of the narrative, Hugh takes on 'old adversary' Tesco, revealing how their misleading labelling on cans of tuna prevents consumers from making informed and ethical choices about which tuna to buy. However, instead of facing resistance, the show demonstrates that Hugh now wields such power that Tesco not only change their labelling but announce a wholesale shift to sustainable (pole and line caught) tuna in their own-brand products.

However, the main narrative thrust of the series focuses on the dramatically unpromising topic of EU policy regarding fish discards. Across a range of scenes, fishermen tell Hugh about the problems of EU fish quota policies that compel them to throw dead fish back into the sea because they have already reached the quotas limiting what they are allowed to catch. Hugh acknowledges that this is a complicated issue because the EU must factor in a range of complex issues – not least, the sustainability of fish species. In the face of these complex ideas, he instead offers 'a really simple one – let's end fish discards'. Because complexity is inconsistent with the action that motivates the series, 'Hugh's legitimacy allows him to filter [it] out …, channel anger and provide simple action' (Hopkinson and Cronin 2015: 1393; see also Probyn 2019). This becomes the focus for his campaign and is dramatized through a series of set pieces, including a flotilla of fishing vessels advancing down the Thames to Westminster. These aim to create a 'public voice' and 'stir it up' while also spectacularizing environmentalism through a series of branding and entertainment opportunities (Goodman et al. 2016: 680).

The representations of the EU, especially in earlier parts of the series, make for particularly uneasy viewing in hindsight. If they echo well-rehearsed British representations of the EU 'as a foreign-dominated forum for fish wars and sausage spats' (Anderson and Weymouth 1999: 23), *Fish Fight*'s representation of the EU and its 'crazy rules' also makes liberal use of discourses that would be used to inform the Brexit campaign (see Chapter 8 for more on Brexit). Hugh wants to 'stop the madness' of EU regulations, challenge how 'EU laws leave us no choice' and influence 'whatever they're now cooking up in Brussels'. This is backed up by a chorus of fishermen saying 'It's beyond our control' and using their own experience to question the expert scientific knowledge that says North Sea cod is endangered. These rejections of both governmental and scientific legitimacy are part of a wider story in British politics where, as Will Davies (2019) argues, 'the crisis of democracy and of truth are one and the same: individuals are increasingly suspicious of the "official" stories they are being told, and expect to witness things for themselves'. Although the series features a lone dissenting scientific voice to explain how maritime sustainability is a complex issue, this complexity is lost as the series develops. However, while Hugh wants to take back control and drums up some anti-EU sentiment as he vows to make the public 'as angry as I am', he sets out to solve the problem by influencing the European parliament rather than rejecting it.

Hugh's key battle in *Fish Fight* is, therefore, not with consumers or the food industry but with (EU) government. The British state offers little resistance to his proposals. Tory politicians Richard Benyon and Zac Goldsmith enthusiastically back his campaign in both the UK and Europe. The British parliament passes a motion to put pressure on the EU to change its policy on discards which, the series suggests, is a direct result of Hugh's intervention.

Instead the major battle is set up between Hugh – backed by 'the people' – and the European Union using populist language. As Hugh tells viewers early in the follow-up show 'When the public expresses its outrage, politicians have to listen … and things are changing'. This mirrors strategies already used by Jamie Oliver in *Jamie's Ministry of Food* in which forms of government are represented as too calcified or bureaucratic to achieve change without the intervention of an exceptional and inspirational figure backed by the will of 'the people' (Hollows and Jones 2010b). In the follow-up programme, Hugh frequently returns to Brussels armed with visual displays and set pieces to dramatize escalating public support for his campaign to ban discards, a campaign he increasingly attempts to roll out across Europe. With the support of the EU Commissioner for Maritime Affairs and Fisheries, Maria Damanaki, Hugh takes his battle into the EU policy-making machine. The programme charts Hugh's initial struggle to persuade MEPs of the validity of his campaign and his later success as an increasing number of MEPs champion his cause, seeking to acquire a little of Hugh's stardust by posing for photos with him. The complexities of the issues surrounding discards, quotas and sustainability – and the wider policy context and campaigns of which Hugh's initiative is just a part – are largely ignored. Hugh appears to heroically succeed in making the EU listen on 'a day that promises the possibility for real change'. While his 'claim that its campaign produced the EU ban on fish discarding is arguable' (Probyn 2019: 252), the show gives the impression that Hugh – backed by the 'people power' he has generated and unleashed – has achieved real change.

Hugh's Fish Fight, therefore, uses the CCD format to position the celebrity chef as a public figure who can effect political change and mobilize people power. Yet despite asking the public to 'emulate' Hugh's heroism, as Gill Hopkinson and James Cronin (2015: 1390) observe, we are constantly reminded that 'this battle is *his*'. 'While the purpose of his campaign is to gain social support, to popularize malcontent and to ultimate rally the troops to effect change', Hugh is represented as a solitary 'campaigner … single-handedly taking on a personal mission'. As Elspeth Probyn (2019: 253) points out, Hugh's later series *Save Our Seas* cements this view, reminding the viewer how the Fish Fight mobilized 'people power' and of Hugh's 'courage in braving it "through the maze of EU government bureaucracy"'.

Fish Fight dramatizes how Hugh's influence expands out beyond his cosy corner of cookery television on to social media and into national government before finally mobilizing the public and political actors at a supranational level. While the series invites viewers to try lesser-known fish, they are not responsibilized to change their behaviour but to use social media to 'voice their outrage from the comfort of their sofas' to demand that their state representatives take action (Hopkinson and Cronin 2015: 1396). This form of clicktivism requires little in the way of sustained political connection with these issues, and state bureaucracy – particularly within the EU – is often represented as unresponsive and stifling. Using this 'easy means to express moral indignation to relevant organizations, the responsibility to develop legislation and institutional forms which enable a clearly articulated end point is thrown entirely on others' (Hopkinson and Cronin 2015: 1393–4). Nonetheless, while clicktivism can appear to be a relatively passive and individualized form of politics, CCDs such as *Fish Fight* also have 'a democratic potential, engaging people in places and ways that conventional politics cannot reach' (Littler 2011: 32). Furthermore, by demanding the state takes responsibility for solving food crises, *Fish Fight* cannot be seen as a straightforward reflection of neoliberal agendas. Nonetheless, this gets a neoliberal twist: the state, like the consumer, is open to correction by the entrepreneurial and heroic celebrity chef (Bell et al. 2017). While Abidin et al. (2020: [1.17]) argue that celebrity environmentalism generally tends to 'encourage individual consumer action over state-supported structural change', *Fish Fight* suggests that both forms of action can work in tandem.

'The rubbish revolution starts here'

Hugh's War on Waste (2016) marked Fearnley-Whittingstall's move from Channel 4 to BBC1 and he took his well-established formula for celebrity environmentalism and campaigning documentaries with him. The series was closely modelled on his previous CCDs with Hugh adopting the role of investigative journalist across an initial exposé of the scale of waste and the inevitable follow-up programme later in the year (Craig 2019; Hopkinson and Cronin 2015). While the series also took on domestic waste of clothing and electrical goods, the campaign against food waste took a by now well-worn path, ranging over waste in agricultural, retailing and catering industries and everyday consumption practices. As Geoffrey Craig (2019: 781) argues, the series is 'an explicit exercise in televisual environmental activism': Hugh traces 'networks and power relations … and a case for change provides the narrative drive'. After years of austerity policies in the UK, poverty lurks uneasily in the background as Hugh lays out the moral terms of his latest struggle: 'Millions of people are struggling to pay their food bills yet a third of all the food we produce never gets eaten. That has to be wrong.' Yet the 'wrong' he sets out to tackle is food waste rather than food poverty (a theme I return to in more detail in Chapters 6 and 8).

One strand of the series focuses on wasteful domestic consumption practices, taking on both the reduction of food waste and the responsible disposal of waste products through appropriate recycling practices. The series demonstrates that ethical consumption practices do not finish with purchase and use but also involve responsible 'divestment' and 'disposal' as items go through a process of 'devaluation' (Evans 2018: 118). Early in the first episode, Hugh rummages through residents' bins unearthing discarded food on the Manchester street that becomes the focus of his experiment. 'I didn't come to Prestwich to find Britain's worst food wasters', he tells us, 'I came because they're no different to the rest of us, which means most of the households are binning on average £15 of food a week'. But, of course, the logic of the series means that although they might not be different to 'us', they are certainly different to *him* and, using a series of set pieces and interventions, Hugh provides both locals and viewers with tips to reduce their food waste. In the process he meets local couple Joanne and Peter, positioned as middle class through lingering shots of their tastefully decorated Victorian house, a point of view validated by Hugh when he comments on their 'lovely home'. Although Peter does most of the cooking, 'lovely Joanne' is tasked with reducing their food waste. She is a willing pupil, learning how to make resourceful use of things past their best and sharing tips on a local 'Waste Not' Facebook page that Hugh has started as part of his 'recipe for change'. This is part of Hugh's attempt to roll out a nationwide programme through social media that responsibilizes the public both to transform themselves through 'processes of self-governance' (Craig 2019: 785) and to take responsibility for food waste as a national issue. Joanne is also used to model the 'pleasures of sustainability' that echo those found in *River Cottage* as she demonstrates pride in her new practices and dispositions (Craig 2019: 780).

The series also features two working-class women whom Hugh singles out to be reformed, reproducing the gender and class dynamics of *Chicken Run* in which 'a conjunction of signs, bodies and landscape … compose a familiar assemblage of classed and gendered values' (Tyler 2011: 210). In episode one, Hugh meets Kelly who works in a local 'caff' where she refuses to sort waste for recycling. She is positioned by her workplace, her tattoos and a strong Manchester accent as working class and, in Hugh's words, as 'the toughest nut to crack' (echoing his description of 'hard-bitten Hayley' and in contrast to 'lovely Joanne'). Kelly refuses to take responsibility for waste because she believes it is the local council's responsibility.

As part of his attempt to reform Kelly, Hugh brings her together with a group of fellow 'recycling deniers' in a local pub (his choice of phrase suggesting they are on the wrong side of environmental politics with its allusions to climate change deniers). With echoes of the scepticism of officialdom and science demonstrated by the fishermen of *Food Fight*, the group distrust the council's claims about recycling and believe everything ends up in one place because it is all 'rubbish'. On a mission to rehabilitate them, Hugh takes the group on a tour of a materials recovery facility to demonstrate how sorting recyclables produces a valuable commodity that the council uses to generate money for services. The group initially remain sceptical because the material still appears to them as 'rubbish'. However, Hugh triumphantly demonstrates the range of everyday items made from recycled materials (while simplifying the incredibly complex politics, economies and geographies of waste management, which might have partly validated the residents' initial scepticism). On discovering a jacket and jeans made from recycled materials, Kelly declares herself a convert: 'this last bit impressed me because they do clothes.' Hugh classifies the trip as a success: 'my band of rubbish recyclers have promised to change their ways and I'm hoping they'll spread the word.'

Because Hugh does not trust Kelly to take responsibility and engage in self-surveillance, she is secretly filmed before his return. The footage reveals that Kelly has been reformed into a competent recycler. 'I'm impressed with myself' she tells Hugh, who affirms her judgement, telling her that he too is 'incredibly impressed'. This strategy of shaming followed by redemption is replayed in episode two with Michelle, a painter and decorator who 'has the most notorious bins in the neighbourhood' because she refuses to sort her rubbish appropriately. By the end of the episode, her bins are immaculate and Michelle too has been reformed. Despite their redemption, these sequences 'incite negative moral judgement' (Tyler 2011: 215) by drawing on wider techniques from lifestyle programming which identify and reform 'cases of "ignorance" and self-neglect, ... allowing the viewer at home to identify as normal in comparison' (Ouellette and Hay 2008: 476). Yet while part of Hayley's narrative in *Chicken Run* questioned who can afford to be an ethical consumer, there are no similar issues here: the audience is simply left with the sense that working-class women can't be bothered despite evidence to suggest that disadvantaged groups have historically been more interested in reducing waste through forms of careful and thrifty consumption (Miller 1998). Likewise, the emphasis on educating Kelly, Michelle and Joanne suggests that kitchen waste management is ultimately women's work.

However, the real villains of the series are once again corporations. Although other sub-plots are concerned with the waste reduction practices of supermarkets, takeaways and café chains – from surplus food to recyclable cups – the central campaign features an emotionally charged narrative about 'wonky veg' that is designated as unfit for sale before it even reaches supermarket shelves. Again, the series offers a critique of corporate power, focusing on the power supermarkets wield over producers. Across numerous visits to a Norfolk farm, Hugh 'uncovers' shocking levels of waste as farmers are forced to discard veg they have carefully grown because it fails to meet the aesthetic standards that Morrisons supermarket claim their customers' demand. By episode two, the farm owners are visibly emotional as they tell Hugh that, due to supermarket practices, this is their last harvest as they can no longer make a living from their farm. The series reveals how supermarkets not only impose narrowly defined cosmetic standards on crops but also unlawfully cancel orders. 'Who do we need more', asks Hugh rhetorically, 'people who produce our food or the people who sell it us?' Taking a stand against both the exploitation of farm owners and the levels of waste produced by supermarket policies, Hugh tells viewers 'I'm spoiling for a fight now'.

If Hugh acts as an 'advocate' on viewers' behalf, using his status to tackle corporations (Craig 2019: 782, 786), he also uses spectacular set pieces with wonky veg to provide entertaining teaching moments about environmental issues and to responsibilize consumers to use their power to take on the supermarkets (Goodman et al. 2016: 679). Like Tesco before them, Morrisons claim their stock simply reflects consumers' desires and prove resistant to meaningful change. Hugh tells viewers: 'The customer is king and that's you.' Replicating the model used to great effect in *Fish Fight*, Hugh directs viewers to the Waste Not website to pledge to join the fight against waste and to use their voice to 'show the supermarkets we mean business in our war on waste'.

Hugh's War on Waste articulates many of the features of his earlier CCDs – a campaigning message that seeks to effect change; distinctions between responsible and irresponsible consumers; education through entertainment; and a call to use political consumerism to transform bad corporate practices. In this way, the series, like many other CCDs, uses 'mediated spectacle to distort and de-politicize' while raising awareness and containing some 'conditions for more radical critique' (Goodman et al. 2016: 680). However, the show ultimately depends on a similar logic to that espoused by supermarkets – that the customer is king and supermarkets their servants – that mitigates against a wider need to regulate their practices.

Conclusion

CCDs fuse elements of lifestyle and reality TV with a documentary format shaped by a political agenda. The CCD has enabled celebrity chefs to take a much more explicit role in shaping the politics of food and helped some of them to emerge as public figures who attempt to transform not only individual behaviour but also public policy, institutions and industries. Therefore, while many of their initiatives responsibilize consumers (the consequences of which I discuss in more detail in the next chapter), the CCD cannot simply be understood as a straightforward manifestation of neoliberal logic (Bell et al. 2017). CCDs focusing on the ethical or environmental consequences of food production, distribution and consumption highlight the power of corporations, even if this is usually achieved by identifying particular 'villains' who need rehabilitation while ignoring the wider capitalist food system. State agencies are also given responsibility for solving food crises, although they too need to be improved through intervention by a heroic celebrity chef.

Despite the limitations of celebrity advocacy, celebrity chefs raise awareness of environmental, ethical and political dimensions of food and render them comprehensible and meaningful (Craig 2019: 781). While the CCD format is often repetitive and formulaic, and often built on an oversimplification of complex politics (Hopkinson and Cronin 2015; Probyn 2019), the consequences of these forms of celebrity advocacy 'are not wholly predictable' (Abidin et al. 2020: [1.3]). Of course, the ultimate beneficiaries of these campaigns are the celebrity chefs themselves, as they add value and increasing moral authority to their brand (Bell et al. 2017). As with other forms of celebrity politics, the CCD tends to ignore issues and people who are 'less celebrifiable' (Goodman and Littler 2013: 271). For example, Hugh Fearnley-Whittingstall's rural landscapes and agricultural industries are populated by farmers and largely cheery country dwellers, rendering farm labourers, the conditions in which they work, and the politics of migrant labour invisible. These issues seem even more stark in a Britain where migrant farm labourers have played a prominent role in the political imagination around issues such as Brexit and the spread of Covid-19 in rural food processing industries.

One of the striking features of the CCD remains the ways in which relationships between celebrity chefs and 'ordinary people' are gendered and classed. Their culinary protagonists are almost entirely male and the emphasis on heroism, battles and fights masculinizes the format. As I explore further in the next chapter, the narratives of CCDs are often predicated on an unequal relationship between male food personalities and working-class women in which the women's narrative redemption is dependent on their willingness to be madeover (Hollows 2016). While working-class women like Hayley are left to their everyday caring roles, male celebrity chefs are distinguished by their exceptional ability to 'care about' the bigger issues. This extraordinary ability to care is evidenced through repeated scenes of emotional responses as celebrity chefs like Hugh display anger and distress at wrong and injustice. These emotional displays are part of the wider work of celebrity: as Jo Littler (2008: 248) argues, 'the *performance* of celebrity soul, or the performance of the internalization of social anguish, becomes a necessary part of contemporary celebrity'. These displays of emotion add value to chefs' brands and act as a form of capital. However, they also help to assemble and mobilize the individualized acts of people power that helps to validate the success of their campaigns (see Ahmed 2004).

Chapter 6

EAT WELL FOR LESS: CELEBRITY CHEFS AND AUSTERITY CULTURE

In 2012, William Hague MP – a senior figure in the Conservative-led coalition – summed up the British government's austerity policies: 'There's only one growth strategy – work hard! And do more with less – that's the 21st Century' (cited in Biressi and Nunn 2013: 183). In many ways he could have been doing a pitch for a new lifestyle TV series. This chapter explores how a range of celebrity chefs demonstrated the virtues of doing more with less as they championed the values of thrift and frugality across a range of food media. However, as I go on to demonstrate, doing more with less did not only involve making food go further and adopting less wasteful practices. Food media also produced, reproduced and resisted wider austerity narratives that represented huge cuts in public spending on services as both inevitable and legitimate (Bramall 2015). My analysis shows how celebrity chefs intervened in 'austerity culture', 'the historically informed practices, discourses, values, ideological elements and representational strategies' that emerged from, and helped to construct, a new 'age of austerity' in early twenty-first-century Britain (Bramall 2013: 4). While many nations were implementing austerity measures after the global financial crisis of 2007–8, this chapter focuses on how austerity was given meaning and used to justify particular political choices in a British context.

'Austerity chic' emerged in British lifestyle media in the aftermath of the global financial crisis.[1] A 'culture of thrift' was manifested in a celebration of craft projects encouraging people to 'make do and mend' and to engage in 'upcycling' projects (Bramall 2013; Potter and Westall 2013). These often had a nostalgic edge, drawing on themes and iconography from the 'austerity Britain' of 1939–54 in which people allegedly 'submitted willingly to restriction with a sense that everyone was combined in a united effort in the national interest' (Bramall 2015: 187). These themes were evident in forms of 'foodie austerity' (Wincott 2016). Upmarket restaurants such as Fergus Henderson's St John in London championed thrifty 'nose to tail' eating and offered gastronomic versions of nostalgic and 'humble' dishes such as Eccles cakes and tripe at not at all humble prices (Wincott 2016). Hugh Fearnley-Whittingstall encouraged people to grow their own veg and cookery writer Nigel Slater advised on how to make frugal use of (extremely high-quality) leftovers (Potter and Westall 2013). In this form, austere food was represented as 'pleasurable, even indulgent' and often expensive (Wincott 2016: 30).

The Labour government's bailout of the banking sector in response to the 2007–8 financial crisis increased national debt. However, Conservative Party campaigns in the run-up to the 2010 election instead claimed that this debt was a result of overspending on the public sector in an 'age of irresponsibility' (May et al. 2020: 210). Tory leader – and soon to be British prime minister – David Cameron promised a new 'age of austerity' in which 'we're all in this together' in an attempt to reduce the national debt by cutting public spending. As the Tories gained power, 'austerity chic' provided a handy vocabulary that helped to justify austerity policies and savage spending cuts and operated as a pretext for dismantling the welfare state (May et al. 2020).

The government constructed a 'legitimising narrative of austerity as financial or even moral compensation for the preceding debt-based bubble' that 'intensified political demands for austere lifestyles marked by spending cuts, hard graft, individual "responsibility" and a new "culture of thrift"' (Potter and Westall 2013: 155). Lifestyle and reality TV helped to naturalize these ideas not only by offering desirable images of frugal living but also by distinguishing between 'good' responsible lifestyles and 'bad' lifestyles associated with people who are portrayed as a burden on the welfare state because of irresponsible consumption or 'unhealthy' practices. This was reinforced through widespread 'welfare myths' that created a stigmatized and 'abject cast of figures of dependency' (Tyler 2020: 191, 194) and a sense of a 'Broken Britain' created by 'personal failure and "bad behaviour"' (McKenzie 2015: Introduction). These helped to back up David Cameron's claim in 2011 that welfare culture 'doesn't just allow people to act irresponsibly but often actively encourages them to do so', a claim used to justify escalating cuts to public spending (cited in Tyler 2020: 193). However, alongside these austerity narratives that legitimated swingeing cuts to welfare provision, alternative narratives emerged that demonstrated the impact of austerity. There was increasing newspaper coverage of the shocking growth of food banks, food poverty, food insecurity and malnutrition in the UK during the 2010s (for more on food banks and their users, see also Chapter 8).

This chapter examines how celebrity chefs shaped ideas about 'eating well' in austerity culture. It starts with an exploration of how celebrity chefs' campaigns employed austerity narratives. The first section focuses on Jamie Oliver's 2008 campaigning culinary documentary (CCD) *Jamie's Ministry of Food* and analyses how the series combined elements of 'austerity chic' found in wider responses to the financial crisis with emerging austerity narratives that would help sustain Conservative policies. The second section maintains this focus on CCDs but shifts attention to the ways in which public debates about healthy eating – and, in particular, about 'obesity' – were refracted through austerity narratives. However, CCDs are not the only format through which celebrity chefs have attempted to intervene in the politics of eating. In the third section, I examine how makeover formats were used in the long-running BBC TV series *Eat Well for Less*. Although austerity is never explicitly mentioned, the series – as the title suggests – privileges the values of thrift and frugality as it shows 'food offenders' how to improve both their finances and their health. The final part of chapter examines how food media can also operate as a site of struggle over the legitimacy and desirability of austerity culture. This focuses on Jack Monroe, a former food bank user and blogger and now a celebrity chef, who offers cheap and simple recipes for people on low incomes. However, rather than championing the rewards of austerity, Monroe has become a key public figure in anti-austerity movements, acting as the voice of the food bank user and criticizing government policies.

Through these case studies, the chapter examines how celebrity chefs have intervened in the politics of austerity. This illustrates how austerity cannot be reduced to a single meaning but is 'a site of intense discursive struggle' in which different people and groups 'have mobilized ideas about austerity for different purposes' (Bramall 2013: 10, 13). In the process, the discussion also demonstrates how 'the economy enters everyday life and cultures' as abstract political and economic policies are rendered intelligible and made into commonsense through everyday food practices (Bhattacharyya 2016).

'The Poverty Shows in the Way They Feed Themselves'

In the 2008 Channel 4 CCD *Jamie's Ministry of Food JMoF*, Oliver carried forward his anti-obesity mission from *Jamie's School Dinners*. The book accompanying the series spelled out the problem: 'we have a ... war on our hands ... over the epidemic of bad health and the rise of obesity' (Oliver 2008: 4). This was a battle to transform people whose allegedly unhealthy and careless food practices were making them ill. This section draws on research with Steve Jones and David Bell to examine how representations of 'healthy' and 'unhealthy' food practices in *JMoF* contributed to emergent discourses and representations of austerity (Bell et al. 2017; Hollows and Jones 2010b). *JMoF* was broadcast in the wake of the global financial crisis of 2007–8 but before the implementation of wide-reaching austerity policies after David Cameron became prime minister in 2010. Nonetheless, the series resonated with the developing themes of a resurgent Conservatism in its combination of elements of populist anti-statism with representations of dysfunctional working-class communities associated with welfare dependency (Hollows and Jones 2010b). As I go on to demonstrate, the series combined nostalgic imagery of wartime austerity with an emphasis on reskilling as a form of self-improvement that enabled people to reduce their dependence on the state (for more on reskilling in austerity culture, see Wincott 2016).

Set in the Yorkshire town of Rotherham, *JMoF* follows Oliver's attempts to improve the health of its residents and to wean them off a diet of snacks, convenience foods and takeaways by teaching them to cook. The series assumes that healthy eating practices are an automatic consequence of learning how to cook (and, by extension, poor health is simply the product of a lack of cooking skills).[2] Jamie plans to get people to 'pass on' cooking skills within the community. These skills, he suggests, were once passed on between generations of women in the home and have declined because 'our girls have been sent out to work for the last 40 years', rendering women as partly culpable for the problem (cited in Fox and Smith 2011: 405). This emphasis on the 'normative', health-giving power of home cooking reproduces wider health discourses which link childhood obesity to women's lack of culinary skills and their dependence on convenience foods (Coveney et al. 2012; Halkier 2010).

Despite claims that an alleged 'obesity crisis' produced by 'poor' food choices is a national problem, the representational strategies used in the series suggest that 'poor' cooking and eating practices are a specifically working-class problem. *JMoF*'s visual and ideological conventions draw on earlier forms of social exploration that sought to investigate, explain and reform the working class (Colls and Dodd 1985; see Hollows and Jones 2010b for more detail). Shots of cooling towers on the outside of town and the council estates where much of the action takes place anchor the sense that this is a working-class problem, an interpretation backed up by audience responses to the series (Piper 2013).

In *Jamie's Return to School Dinners* (2006), Oliver declared that he'd had enough of 'being PC about parents'.

> If you're giving your very young kids bottles and bottles of fizzy drink, you're a fucking arsehole, you're a tosser. If you're giving them bags of fucking shitty sweets at that very young age, you're an idiot … If you never cook a hot meal, sort it out, do it once a week please … I'm here because I truly care … If they truly care … they've got to take control.

Jamie's outburst reinforced the authenticity, passion and capacity to care that were central to his celebrity image. However, he also created a narrative bridge to *JMoF* where, in episode one, Jamie meets the personification of this 'idiot' parent, single mum Natasha Whiteman whose daughter Kaya 'has never had a home-cooked meal' and who reveals a fridge packed with sweets and fizzy drinks.

Natasha acts a 'representative' figure who stands in for 'the collective experience of working-class life' in general (Hill 1986: 138), and working-class mothers in particular. As she confesses she can't cook, the camera lingers on an unused eight-ring cooker. Her two children are sitting on the floor of her living room, eating kebab and chips with their fingers out of Styrofoam containers. The voiceover discloses that 'dinner is nearly always a kebab'. Natasha recounts her struggle to make ends meet on benefits, a claim visually undercut by shots of a supersized television set in the corner. The significance of these objects is constructed through 'shots and sequences that incite negative moral judgement' and are used to justify distinctions between the 'deserving' and 'undeserving' poor (Tyler 2011: 215). Indeed, some commentators on the *Daily Mail* newspaper's website were more concerned with Natasha's cigarette consumption and the size of her TV than her successful acquisition of cooking skills across the series (Hollows and Jones 2010b).

This representation of working-class people in terms of 'aesthetically impoverished' consumption practices was reinforced by Jamie in a *Paris Match* interview (Hayward and Yar 2006: 14): 'They have state-of-the-art mobile phones, cars and get drunk in pubs at the weekend. The poverty shows in the way they feed themselves' (*Daily Mail* Reporter 2008). This comment reproduced a reading of unhealthy eating as a matter of cultural poverty rather than class inequality, economic poverty or other forms of food insecurity. *JMoF*'s representation of 'bad' working-class consumers contributed to wider processes through which class and moral value were being realigned (Skeggs 2005). By blaming the victims of widespread structural inequalities for their own ill health, the series contributed to a wider process through which stigma is used 'as a policy mechanism for reducing welfare costs and entitlements' (Tyler 2020: 190). While *JMoF* did acknowledge resistance to Jamie's plans and opposing viewpoints (Hollows and Jones 2010b; Warin 2011), there remained 'a certain inescapability to his influence ... even when he is resisted' (Piper 2015: 255).

The resonance of Natasha as a figure within austerity culture meant that she continued to be used to distil and refract qualities associated with the 'irresponsible' working class. In a 2013 interview, Jamie reinforced the idea that Rotherham's health problems might be understood as a result of cultural poverty rather than economic inequality.

> I'm not judgemental but I have spent a lot of time in poor communities, and I find it quite hard to talk about modern day poverty. You might remember that scene ... with the mum and the kid eating chips and cheese out of Styrofoam containers, and behind them is a massive fucking TV. It just didn't weigh up.
> (Deans 2013)

In his condemnation of how the working class allegedly spend their money on 'massive' televisions rather than more 'worthy' forms of consumption, Jamie neatly dodges his own position as a TV chef whose celebrity is not only dependent on the technology but whose educational campaigns are also mediated through it. In his seemingly throwaway 'it just didn't add up', Jamie suggests that 'modern day poverty' is not *real* poverty; that's it's the product of poor choices rather than lack of choice; and that it can be eradicated by reforming working-class consumption practices. On one level, this simply drew on well-established conventions from reality TV which teach people how to take responsibility by making better choices 'by diagnosing and rehabilitating cases of "ignorance" and self-neglect, and allowing the viewer at home to identify as normal in comparison' (Ouellette and Hay 2008: 476). Like its US counterpart *Jamie's Food Revolution*, *JMoF* reflected 'a long tradition of lifestyle make-over programs promoting themes of choice and responsibility' which normalize neoliberal ideologies and undermine the case for the welfare state (Gibson and Dempsey 2013: 50).

However, these comments cannot simply be understood within a generalized notion of neoliberalism. They also normalized the pathologization of benefits claimants and provided a justification for benefit cuts that were central elements of a specific austerity agenda. *JMoF* switched between images of benefit-dependent Natasha – struggling with finances yet with a large TV, feeding her kids takeaways that put them at risk of becoming 'obese' – to scenes of an over-stretched NHS, struggling with the effects of the 'obesity epidemic'. The 'burden' on the NHS is made visible through repeated shots of a hospital winch for the clinically obese. In the process, like many other aspects of austerity culture, the series helped to legitimate the idea that austerity is 'the punishment we must submit to for serving as a burden on the welfare state' (Bramall 2013: 98).

Natasha was not only used to represent irresponsible feeding work associated with a benefit-dependent working class, but to single out working-class mothers as those in particular need of responsibilization. This reflects the narratives in other CCDs which chart a male celebrity chef's battle to rehabilitate a working-class woman (see Chapter 5). Feeding work is frequently viewed as one of the primary signifiers of a mother's ability to care properly for their families and, to do femininity 'appropriately' (Cairns and Johnston 2015; DeVault 1991; Parsons 2015). In *JMoF*, Natasha's dependence on takeaways – associated with convenience rather than care – marks her out as both a bad mother and 'inappropriately' feminine.[3] In this way the series contributes to a wider climate in which working-class mothers are singled out for reform in order to secure the future health of the nation.

As *JMoF*'s narrative unfolds, Natasha recognizes her failure. By the end of the series, through Jamie's intervention and her willingness to work hard, she has acquired enough culinary skills not only to cook for her family and keep them healthy but also to qualify for a place at catering college which promises to move her away from a dependence on state benefits. In a similar way to participants in the US series *Jamie's Food Revolution*, she is constructed as 'ignorant' but amenable to 'correction' (Rich 2011; see also Gibson and Dempsey 2013; Slocum et al. 2011; Warin 2011).

JMoF also contributed to the motifs and values of austerity culture in other ways. Peter Jackson (2016: 755) locates the series 'within a wider cultural politics of food where wartime rationing, the values of thrift and the virtues of recycling ... have become the subject of nostalgic longing' within 'austerity chic' (see also Bramall 2013; Martin 2020a; Potter and Westall 2013; Wincott 2016). Jamie conceives of his project as following in the footsteps of the British government's Ministry of Food (1939–54), the two linked by notions of a national food crisis. This lineage is cemented through the dedication in the accompanying cookbook to Marguerite Patten, a fondly remembered figure from the original Ministry of Food; through Patten's appearance in the show; and through original footage from wartime and post-war newsreels. It is also suggested through the show's visual style – from typography through to flickering newsreel effects – which uses a retro aesthetic reproduced across other examples of austerity chic (Bramall 2013; Hollows and Jones 2010b). While the use of signifiers of the wartime state indicates 'a certain element of nostalgia for the historical moment ... when States, governments and communities could realistically expect to act decisively and together' (Jeremy Gilbert cited in Bramall 2013: 91), as Rebecca Bramall (2013: 91) argues, the programme did not call for the revival of the 'big' state. Whereas the original Ministry of Food was a state initiative, Jamie's ministry is a private enterprise initiated and partly funded by Jamie, which he hopes Rotherham will pass on to other councils. While past British governments are represented as providing solutions to crises, the need for Jamie's intervention suggests that the government is no longer able to initiate successful change. Therefore, while *JMoF* cannot be simply read as an expression of a neoliberal agenda that seeks to entirely eradicate the state, the series represents the state as reactive to ideas for change that can only come from those outside it (Hollows and Jones 2010b).

By focusing on Jamie's ability to create change and his willingness to 'do something' about national 'crises' such as obesity, *JMoF* enabled Oliver to trade on moral concern as a form of capital, strengthening his position as a moral entrepreneur, able to give to focus and leadership to debates about the place of food in national life (Hollows and Jones 2010b). However, despite his criticisms of the state and his invocation of people power ('They don't run us, we run the government' he quips at one point in *JMoF*), Jamie himself is sometimes associated with the 'nannying' and 'interfering' qualities that many Conservatives identify as the problems with the big state (for more on this, see Bell et al. 2017; see also Rousseau (2012b) on ideas about 'interference'). Indeed, in a response to public criticisms of working-class women in *Jamie's School Dinners*, Boris Johnson – then Mayor of London and, at the time of writing, British prime minister – argued that 'the poor and ignorant should be as free to spend their money as they choose as everyone else' (cited in Warin 2011: 36). In austerity culture, the proviso was they should also expect to be pathologized and not count on support from the welfare state.

'Obesity' in austerity Britain

In 2014, the UK's best-known medical journal *The Lancet* published an 'Open Letter to Prime Minister David Cameron on food poverty in the UK'. A number of key figures specializing in food and public health highlighted the impact of the austerity agenda on food bank use, nutrition and health among lower-income people. One factor was the dependence of poorer people on the 'cheap, sweet, fatty, salty, or processed foods that need very little cooking' which contributed to a 'worrying rise in obesity, diabetes, and other dietary related diseases' (Ashton et al. 2014: 1631). However, the impact of austerity was largely ignored in the representation of 'obesity' and its associated health problems in two CCDs from the same period – Jamie Oliver's one-part *Jamie's Sugar Rush* (Channel 4, 2015; hereafter *Sugar Rush*) and the four-part *Britain's Fat Fight with Hugh Fearnley-Whittingstall* (BBC1, 2018; hereafter *Fat Fight*). Developing ideas raised in Chapter 3 about the body under neoliberalism, this section examines how these TV shows represent the (alleged) 'obesity crisis' and who or what is shown to be responsible for it. As I go on to demonstrate, during a period of austerity in which services had been subjected to a series of swingeing cuts, the *cost* of 'obesity' is calculated not only in terms of the health and well-being of those deemed obese but also in terms of a burden on the state.

Both *Fat Fight* and *Sugar Rush* use the CCD's narrative conventions to make 'urgent demands that "something must be done"' that, more generally, 'are a hallmark of anti-obesity rhetoric and practices' in which sugar has become the key enemy (Throsby 2020: 19). Although both celebrities continued their roles as moral entrepreneurs, taking on the fights that government had failed to address, their focus was different. *Sugar Rush*, as the name implies, focuses on the health problems caused by the high-sugar content of the nation's diet and continued Jamie's campaigning role around the importance of healthy eating for children that dates back to *Jamie's School Dinners* and his anti-obesity mission in *JMoF*. *Fat Fight* shared this interest in the effects of sugary drinks, snacks and sweets but had a more wide-ranging interest in fighting the fat that had colonized British bodies. 'Two-thirds of us are overweight' and 'we are on our way to being the fattest country in Europe', Hugh announces at the start of the first episode and adds: 'Obesity is one of the leading causes of premature death.' However, although their emphasis was different, both chefs aimed to responsibilize individuals, food producers, food retailers and government to solve the 'crisis' they had identified.

Like many other CCDs, *Fat Fight* and *Sugar Rush* cannot be understood as monolithically neoliberal texts. Both Hugh and Jamie want the state and, in particular, the food industry and retailers to acknowledge their culpability in enabling overconsumption of unhealthy foods and to act to remedy the situation. *Fat Fight* sets out to reveal how people are manipulated to buy sweet treats by retailing strategies, are misled by food and drink that masquerades as healthy, are bombarded by advertising for unhealthy goods and misinformed because of opaque information on labelling. Both shows represent children as key targets for unhealthy foods, from the strategic placement of confectionary at children's eye level in supermarkets and advertising aimed at children for fizzy drinks to the calorie-laden puddings and 'bottomless' sugary drinks in family-friendly restaurants. These images moralize fatness by suggesting that (what is problematically often referred to as) 'the obesogenic environment' is responsible for the 'obesity crisis', leaving particular types of bodies and social groups 'at risk' of irresponsible behaviour.[4] Both celebrity chefs call on the food industry to change their practices. For example, Hugh sends a sequence of emails to food manufacturers and retailers asking them to act more responsibly while Jamie calls for restaurants to adopt a self-imposed tax on sugary drinks to fund food education programmes in schools.

Although both TV shows blame food producers and retailers for their role in the 'obesity crisis', they also pathologize the people who consume their products. Early in episode one, Hugh sends a group of children into a supermarket to select their own food and they return with largely unhealthy, and frequently high in sugar, choices. Children are represented as possessing 'fake agency in selecting food', powerless in the face of food marketing (Gibson and Dempsey 2013: 55) and this contributes to wider constructions of 'children as innately unable to resist sweet foods' (Throsby 2020: 22). Jamie connects the 'uncivilized' child consumer and sugar in his characterization of sugar as an unruly child: sugar 'needs to go on the naughty step', he tells a food industry representative, but the industry wants it to go 'feral'.

However, in *Fat Fight*, adults are also represented as unable to resist the sweet treats that surround retailers' checkouts. This suggests that *some* adults act like children, part of a wider process through which overweight people are represented in terms of 'an abdication of agency' (Raisborough 2016: 17). Despite its focus on changing education and industry practices, *Sugar Rush* features predictable images of headless large bodies which use 'the motif of the fat person as the symbol of a degraded food system' (Farrell 2011: 15). Furthermore, this focus on changing the 'obesogenic environment' to enable people to make 'good choices' pathologizes fatness (Lebesco 2011: [7]). It suggests that the non-fat are more 'immune' to the manipulation of the food industry and mount an active resistance to the mistakes that 'others' make in their lifestyle choices (Raisborough 2016: 75). Moreover, like these shows in general, it suggests that body shape is a direct indication of health.

While Jamie and Hugh have some success in getting food producers and retailers to change their practices, both series call for increased government regulation to tackle how the industry is fuelling the 'obesity crisis'. In a seeming critique of neoliberal ideologies, Jamie calls for state intervention. He argues that public health has to come before business: 'self-regulation and personal responsibility isn't working … kids are getting sicker. That's why I think now is the time for the British government to step up and just get tougher on the industry's ass.' A potential obstacle to reform is observed in *Fat Fight* when Hugh arrives at the Conservative Party Conference in pursuit of Health Minister Jeremy Hunt to talk about the need to tackle obesity. The conference sponsor, he notes, is major sugar producer Tate & Lyle. Nonetheless, by the end of the series, Hugh secures a face-to-face on-camera meeting with Hunt and also a commitment that the government is launching a formal consultation process on a range of measures, aimed at industry and retailers, to 'halve childhood obesity by 2030'.

Both TV series call on the audience to put pressure on the government to achieve change. Their narratives intertwine when Jamie joins Hugh in *Fat Fight* to give evidence to a cross-party committee of MPs looking into 'obesity' and both celebrity chefs highlight how industry practices are causing rising rates. When one MP suggests to Jamie that his ideas for regulation would lead to a 'nanny state' which reduces people's choice to eat what they want, Jamie replies, 'We keep talking about the concept of choice when largely we haven't got choice'. In this way, the State is responsibilized with the task of using legislation not only to improve public health but also to enable consumer freedoms.

However, Hugh reminds viewers after attending the committee, 'It's not just the government who have to act. We all need to take back control of our own bodies'. In this way, calls for government action are countered by a neoliberal discourse which articulates autonomy and freedom with personal responsibility. The need for responsibility is constructed through a series of biopolitical, disciplinary techniques as medical experts draw distinctions between healthy and unhealthy practices and body types: techniques which 'focus on observation, classification and production of normality/abnormality around statistical norms, individualising and standardisation' (Warin 2011: 29; see also Rich 2011). Although *Fat Fight* features a series of individuals whom Hugh helps on their weight loss journeys, the series reveals how he too must take back control over his slightly overweight body. After a visit to a doctor, he confesses 'I'm in the stats': 'I've got to sort things out too … If I don't get my weight on track, I could be joining the millions of people across the UK whose health is suffering because of their size and that's a huge pressure to the already over-stretched NHS.' In order not to become one of the overweight 'others' who are a burden on the state, Hugh models the values of 'self-control', 'self-discipline', 'self denial' and 'will power' associated with 'healthism' (Crawford 2006; see Chapter 3). Using some of the conventions from makeover reality TV, *Fat Fight* also documents a number of people's weight loss journeys – from an initial shaming, through their faltering steps to final 'redemption' as a slimmer self (Raisborough 2016: 120). This reaffirms wider representations of the body in which thinness has become 'a corporeal expression of individual responsibility and self-control' and fatness is 'perceived as a moral failure to fulfil the responsibilities of healthy eating' (Cairns and Johnston 2015: 89, 100).

Fat Fight suggests that everybody needs to take responsibility for the 'obesity crisis'. Hugh rallies his audience: it's a 'crisis we can all do something about – so let's do something about it … It's a fight that might just save your life'. Viewers are encouraged to be clicktivists who put pressure on industry and the government but also engage in self-surveillance and take action in their own lives (see Warin 2011). This collective endeavour is modelled in 'an ambitious social experiment', 'Newcastle Can' in which the Northern city is invited to unite in a quest to lose weight. Attempting to recruit volunteers in the city centre, Hugh is approached by Julie who offers him some 'home truths': his project doesn't speak to a working-class city where people are 'on a budget'. Eager to help, she takes Hugh to the working-class Walker neighbourhood where local shops have either shut down or been replaced with fast food outlets and where there is a 'dependency on takeaways', suggesting both passivity and addiction. The sequences set in Walker have the potential to develop into a serious discussion about food insecurity in terms of both food poverty and food deserts where affordable, healthy foods are largely unavailable. While Hugh attempts to bring fresh fruit and vegetables to the area for a day, it is a problem he seems disinclined to tackle. On discovering that the local convenience store is selling fresh veg that few people buy, Hugh simply concludes that younger people (in working-class areas) don't want to cook because 'it looks like work'. While there is widespread evidence to suggest that eating healthily costs more, such ideas are dismissed: 'If you've got money to spend on takeaway … You've got money to eat well and you can save a fortune.' *Fat Fight* leaves the impression that eating healthily is open to anyone prepared to put in the work, invoking austerity discourses that it is an absence of work ethic rather than resources that maintains inequality.

Sugar Rush and *Fat Fight* also naturalized austerity discourses in far more overt ways. 'Obesity' is repeatedly represented as an intolerable burden on the NHS, reproducing wider media representations of fat bodies as 'uncontained, destined for ill-health and an early death, and a burden on the public purse' (Lupton 2017: 20). 'We've seen all the headlines', Jamie says in *Sugar Rush*: 'unhealthy diets are putting incredible pressure on the NHS.' Hospitals are performing 'completely avoidable' surgery on children's tooth decay caused by sugar which 'costs the NHS around £30 million per year'. For Jamie, this is unacceptable: 'we're taking the piss' out of hospitals and putting them under 'extraordinary pressure' and 'it's getting absolutely ridiculous'. Furthermore, 'lifestyle factors such as diet', he claims, have caused an 'alarming' rise in Type II diabetes, 'costing the NHS almost £9 billion a year'. His diagnosis is backed up by a doctor who claims this is a 'huge burden on the health service'. This legitimates claims that the NHS are having to 'do more with less' because of irresponsible food practices and parenting rather than cuts to public funding.

Likewise, Hugh observes, the 'millions of people across the UK whose health is suffering because of their size and that's a huge pressure on the already overstretched NHS. We now spend more each year on the treatment of obesity than we do on the police, fire service and judicial service combined.' This suggests that 'obese' people are to be blame for an 'over-stretched' NHS which is 'left to pick up the pieces' of unhealthy practices and that, without these burdens, there might be more money available for other services. This focus on personal responsibility as the solution to adequate health funding ignores how the NHS had been required to do more with less during a period of sustained cuts and had to 'pick up the pieces' following cuts to public health initiatives, social care and welfare. It also ignores how austerity had contributed to 'worsening public health through stress, deprivation, precarity and hunger' (Foster 2018).

Fat Fight and *Sugar Rush* responsibilize industry and government to do something about the 'obesity crisis'. However, in the face of still relatively weak industry regulation and a government whose party conference is funded by sugar, responsibility is ultimately left to individuals. These shows, like many wider representations of obesity, demonstrate an 'attachment to the "wrongness" of obesity' which normalizes 'neoliberal ideologies of self-management and individual responsibility for healthy, productive citizenship' (Throsby 2020: 14). By representing obesity as ultimately a 'choice' – and, the manipulative practices of the food industry aside, largely minimizing constraints on choice – fat people are represented as 'unproductive' and a drain on the economy and healthcare systems (Harjunen 2016: 5). With austerity policies insisting people 'do more with less', those who expect state services to 'pick up the pieces' are represented as the problem that must be fixed in order for public services to be no longer 'overstretched'.

'The Nation's Worst Food Offenders'

BBC1's primetime series *Eat Well for Less* (*EWFL*; 2015–) aims to improve the health and spending practices of households that are 'the nation's worst food offenders'. Presented by former greengrocers turned celebrity chefs Gregg Wallace and Chris Bavin, each episode attempts to makeover a particular overspending and/or not sufficiently healthy household. Episodes are interspersed with taste tests, food education, recipes and nutritional tips. The presenters advise 'offending' households who are responsibilized to improve their health and their finances by transforming their behaviour. Viewers are offered the opportunity to improve themselves through accompanying media. Like many other reality and lifestyle television formats, the series draws distinctions between good and bad consumer-citizens (see, for example, Couldry 2010; Ouellette and Hay 2008; Sender and Sullivan 2008; Silk et al. 2011). The title *Eat Well for Less* clearly articulates the values of health and economy, applying ideas about how to 'do more with less' to everyday food practices in ways that normalize the values of austerity. While some featured households clearly struggle to make ends meet, *EWFL* appears to take place in a land without foodbanks and food poverty, where even the most challenging circumstances can be improved by better food practices. This section explores how the series mediates ideas about eating well on a budget within a discourse of austerity that articulates frugality and productivity (Biressi and Nunn 2013).

Unlike most food TV, *EWFL* doesn't abstract cooking from the wide range of practices involved in 'feeding' work – from planning meals and food shopping to storing food, scheduling meals and washing up (DeVault 1991). While celebrity chefs such as Jamie and Nigella represent food practices as leisured lifestyle practices for the middle classes, DeVault locates feeding work within the unequal sexual division of labour: feeding the family is part of the work of 'caring for' others which is central to 'doing' femininity (see also Bahr Bugge and Almås 2006; Cairns and Johnston 2015; Giard 1998; Parsons 2015). *EWFL* demonstrates the extent of this labour: people are shown juggling the food needs of household members with health conditions and struggling to schedule collective mealtimes where people can experience a sense of family. The series teaches people to plan more effectively to save work and money; to produce interesting and creative meals that encourage their families to eat better for less; to avoid convenience in order to care for the family; and to be environmentally conscious citizens with minimal food waste.

Despite recognizing that eating well for less involves considerable amounts of hard work, the series highlights a vast array of deviant food practices. This includes disorganized food shopping and poor storage; dependence on convenient or predictable meals; demotivated, lazy or unskilled cooking practices; and eating practices characterized by neophobia, fussiness and 'addiction'. While everyone is required to reform their food habits in the series, mothers are subject to more insistent pathologization. Women are much more likely to be portrayed as 'out of control' when they shop, reproducing longstanding images of pathological and irrational female consumers (see, for example, Bowlby 1992; Nava 1987). For example, the series introduces 'brand mad Mandy', 'impulsive Lisa' and 'shopaholic Lindsey' amid a cast of largely female characters 'easily swayed' and 'seduced' by marketing strategies. Although households are usually portrayed as 'hard-working families' with 'busy' lives, women's 'laziness' is represented as an obstacle to economy. There is persistent criticism of women who can't be bothered to chop and grate – 'we could halve Angela's hoping bill if we gave her a knife'. Even passive and unreflexive consumption is represented as a form of laziness. While Gregg and Chris encourage most family members to cook, mothers who lack cooking skills are portrayed as a particular problem. This sense that women have ultimate responsibility for feeding the family is reproduced by the female participants when confronted with the extent of their 'excessive' and 'deviant' spending. While most participants register shock, many mothers feel shame and embarrassment. 'It feels so shameful', says Lisa about her use of convenience foods. On hearing how much money she spends on food, she responds, 'I feel like crying … [starts crying] … Oh that's awful … I feel awful … God, that's terrible … God, that's awful'. Women are damned because they conform to negative stereotypes of passive feminine consumers or because they fail to exhibit 'positive' feminine attributes such as appropriate caring. Furthermore, these gendered images of dysfunctional foodwork position women as ultimately responsible for a household's economic, physical and mental well-being.

The series consistently sets normative standards for food which enable deviants to be identified, educated and reformed. In most episodes, the contents of participants' deviant food trolleys are laid out before them, provoking a moment of realization that they must change (Slocum et al. 2011). Deviance from the norm is often established by comparing their spend to the 'average' household of a similar size. Whether this average is a desirable amount to spend on food is never questioned; the emphasis is on what is 'normal'.[5] In marked contrast to many British cookery shows which demonstrate how food practices can be a source of distinction, *EWFL* uses averages as a disciplinary technique that encourages viewers to also survey and evaluate their own practices.

In order to reform their practices, participants are encouraged to adhere to a series of foodwork norms. First, they must become educated, active and rational consumers who take responsibility for budgeting wisely and eating healthily. 'Teach us how to choose', say the Warner household. There is little space for routine or habit in *EWFL*, nor for comforts or time benefits associated with tradition. Instead consumers must be constantly reflexive and active as they assess what represents value for money; plan interesting, creative and varied meals; avoid food waste; evaluate the nutritional content of their diet; and teach their children valuable life skills. In this way, despite the jolly tone of the series, even non-quantifiable aspects of foodwork and food consumption such as pleasure, care and community are largely reduced to this emphasis on assessment, measurement and evaluation against normative standards.

Second, ideas about *eating well* conform closely to middle-class ideas of healthy eating that privilege 'expert knowledge and promotes an ethos of continual improvement and risk management' (Cairns and Johnston 2015: 107). This is not only achieved by educating families about 'good' nutrition through varied and interesting meals but also by pathologizing certain foods. Giant packs of snacks act as symbols of unhealthy foods and of flawed consumers who are victims of the manipulative tricks of the food industry (Cairns and Johnston 2015: 104). For example, the series portrays 'convenience addicts' John and Lisa as irrational by infantalizing them: 'I think this is what children would buy if you let them do the shopping', quips Gregg and Chris adds, 'They're shopping like a couple of students'.

Third, while *EWFL* may promote the use of 'convenient' food as a form of effective time management and rationalized caring – for example, with time-saving recipes or batch cooking for the freezer – 'convenience' food and its users are stigmatized in terms of an absence of care, health and rational foodwork (Halkier 2017). This ignores how convenience can used as way of practising care – for example, by enabling people to cater for specialist diets or creating respite from the demands of domestic labour (Halkier 2017; Jackson and Viehoff 2016; Meah and Jackson 2017; Warde 1997). While the series acknowledges how the demands of both paid and unpaid work may result in a lack of time, the solution is often a speedy home-cooked meal. Alternatively, the time devoted to the labour of cooking is 'reduced' by recasting it as leisure. 'Cooking doesn't have to be a chore. It can be *your* time', Gregg tells mum Hannah while Angela is encouraged to forego eating out as a family on a Sunday in favour of the pleasures of slowly cooking an Indian meal. By portraying the investment of time, labour and skill as a pleasure, the series reproduces forms of lifestyled frugality found in the *River Cottage* series. However, this implies that 'if it is so easy and pleasurable to learn your way to a simpler, better life, then the poor must logically be lacking the will or the discipline to change or ignorant and in need of education' (Wincott 2016: 38).

Finally, the normative framework in *EWFL* privileges the values of both thrift and frugality. As David Evans (2011) explains, these values are not interchangeable. Frugality is associated with moderation and consuming less, with being 'sparing in the use of money, goods and resources' and is often geared to avoiding waste and environmental consciousness (Evans 2011: 552). *EWFL* represents frugality as an admirable value. For example, some episodes exhibit a sense of austerity as eco-consciousness in a critique of 'excessive consumption', demonstrating how avoiding food waste by more careful planning can result in reduced costs and a lighter environmental footprint (Bramall 2015). However, the series is far more preoccupied with thrift, 'the art of doing more (consumption) with less (money)', often taken as the mark of a 'savvy' consumer (Evans 2011: 551). Thrift is less concerned with the environmental concern to reduce consumption and more about the ability to consume more with less money. Most episodes of *EWFL* are geared around the use of thrifty food practices to release money from the food budget to be spent elsewhere – on a family holiday, a house extension or new home. Furthermore, all members of the household are mobilized in this collective endeavour: for example, children contribute by overcoming neophobia and 'fussy' tastes and by accepting own-brand substitutions for their favourite branded foods. In this way, the series represents thrifty practices as 'all about thriving as a family' (Cappellini and Parsons 2013: 132). Of course, economizing by 'trading down' only has a finite amount of elasticity. The show largely excludes the worlds of people on low incomes who cannot trade down because they are 'already on the most basic of diets' (Dowler cited in O'Connell and Hamilton 2017: 95).

This emphasis on doing more with less is one of the key themes in austerity culture. By bringing together affluent households spending £22,000 a year on food with a single mum of five who makes do with porridge so she can feed her children, *EWFL* suggests not only that we all have something to learn but also that we're all in this together, contributing to a wider 'romanticisation of austerity' which celebrates the 'collective experience' and 'solidarity politics of doing without' (Ibrahim 2018: 366). This sense of collectivity is reinforced through the inclusion of a diverse range of households although the vast majority live in families with children. However, people dependent on foodbanks are notably absent from the show. Instead, *EWFL* fits within a political narrative of austerity that seeks to naturalize the need for cuts, thrift, hard work and individual responsibility (Potter and Westall 2013).

Wallace and Bavin do demonstrate sympathy for the often difficult lives of participants. But the sense that 'we are in this together' is undercut both by the shaming and ridicule of participants as their deviant food practices are put on display and by the demands that the participants submit to a regime of self-improvement. All participants try to eat more healthy and varied diets on a budget. This suggests that, with work and determination, everyone should be able to do the same. The series legitimates the sense that we could all 'do more with less' – by breaking bad habits, consciously changing our practices and being willing to work hard and be flexible. This reflects the government-enforced agenda of 'short-term sacrifice' that consists of 'working hard, enduring discomfort and making do' (Biressi and Nunn 2013: 184). Taking responsibility for health and finances become part of the same ethos that demands that people are responsibilized for their own well-being.

Tin Can Cook

In the early mid-2010s, the UK government attempted to portray an anti-welfare position as 'commonsense' (Jensen and Tyler 2015). Foodbank use soared during this period. The UK's largest network of foodbanks, the Trussell Trust, served 26,000 people in 2008–9; during 2018–19, they gave out over 1.6 million emergency food parcels (Trussell Trust 2019; Wells and Caraher 2014). The government's response was 'symbolic violence' against the socially and economically excluded, 'blaming the poor for lacking budgeting skills, making poor food "choices" and being unable to cook' (O'Connell and Hamilton 2017: 95–8). At the launch of a report on food poverty in 2014, Tory peer Baroness Jenkin claimed 'Poor people do not know how to cook': 'I had a large bowl of porridge today, which cost 4p. A large bowl of sugary cereals will cost you 25p' (cited in Butler 2014). While both Jamie Oliver and *EWFL* showed considerably more sympathy to people in hardship, the narratives they constructed helped to legitimate this position. However, the government's austerity agenda was not without critics. Many commentators highlighted how austerity hit women and low-income families the hardest (Lambie-Mumford and Green 2017) and demonstrated how hunger and foodbank use was most prevalent in 'areas with greater unemployment and welfare sanctions' as well as 'reductions in local and central government spending' (O'Connell and Hamilton 2017: 96). In 2018, when United Nations poverty envoy Philip Alston visited the UK, he reported that a fifth of the UK population were living in poverty in the world's fifth largest economy. He judged it to be 'not just a disgrace, but a social calamity and an economic disaster' created by austerity policies that were a political choice rather than a necessity and exhibited 'a punitive, mean-spirited and often callous approach' (cited in Booth and Butler 2018).

It was within this context that Jack Monroe developed a profile as a celebrity chef. She emerged as part of a wave of austerity bloggers who documented the daily grind of living in poverty and who aimed to 'talk back' to the discourses of austerity and the celebration of virtuous frugality demonstrated in 'austerity chic' (Ibrahim 2018: 373–4). A single mother with a small child, Jack was a foodbank user who started her blog in 2012, initially under the name *A Girl Called Jack* and then later known as *Cooking on a Bootstrap*. Her blog offered recipes and a range of practical tips for cooking on a very limited budget. Monroe emerged as a public figure when her blog post 'Hunger Hurts' went viral. It painted a very different picture of 'doing more with less' than the tips on thrift associated with *EWFL* and the cultural poverty imagined by Jamie.

> Poverty isn't just having no heating, or not quite enough food, or unplugging your fridge and turning your hot water off. Poverty is the sinking feeling when your small boy finishes his one Weetabix and says, 'More Mummy? Bread and jam please, Mummy', as you're wondering whether to take the TV or the guitar to the pawn shop first, and how to tell him that there is no bread and jam.
> (Monroe 2014)

In posts such as this, Monroe 'positioned herself as an anti-austerity activist' and used 'emotive, personal testimony' to hold the government to account (Martin 2020a: 183–4).

Monroe may not be a typical celebrity chef but she has become a well-established cookery writer across cookbooks, newspapers and magazines and has a developing TV presence (see Chapter 8). She has achieved sufficient celebrity to be the subject of stories in the press about her identity (for example, she publicly came out as non-binary in 2015), her personal problems (for example, opening up about alcohol addiction) and her relationships (for example, with another celebrity chef Allegra McEvedy). However, by continuing to blog and through extensive use of Twitter, Monroe has branded herself as an 'authentic' and emotionally transparent figure in distinction to what she calls the 'aspirational celebrity chef kind of thing' (cited in Martin 2020a: 195). As Jessica Martin (2020a: 196) observes, this 'authenticity is crucial to her political legitimacy'. If this is central to blog posts that convey the experience of hunger and the shame and trauma it produces, it is also evident in unfiltered (and frequently deleted) tweets that also convey authenticity through rawness and immediacy. One example can be seen in Monroe's response to a further wave of claims that it is 'easy' to eat on a budget in autumn 2020:

> fuck off using select pieces of my work to try to 'prove' it's possible to eat on a budget. Don't share the recipes without sharing the very real PTSD seven years on, the multiple suicide attempts, the trauma, the pile of 100+ unopened bills,

the paranoia, the lasting [...] impact of living in a world of nothing, the long term chronic health problems I have from living in a freezing, uncarpeted, damp, completely unheated flat, the early onset arthritis, the lungs of a heavy smoker, the fear and loathing that multiple therapies can't assuage [...] the tremble when I put my PIN in at a checkout, 100+ unopened bills in my hall [...] don't you DARE take my work, my recipes built from desperation, thin air, a food bank box and use them to sanctimoniously declare it's EASY to cook while poor because 7 YEARS LATER I'M TELLING YOU THIS SHIT NEVER EVER STOPS STRANGLING YOU IN YOUR SLEEP. The fucking AUDACITY.

(Monroe 2020a)

While lifestyle cookery formats frequently focus on choices about how and what to cook and eat, people 'experiencing food poverty may be forced to procure foods in socially unacceptable ways (such as from foodbanks) and be unable to participate in ordinary social activities involving food, like eating out or offering and receiving hospitality' (O'Connell and Hamilton 2017: 197). By focusing on these issues, Monroe offers, therefore, very different meanings of austere eating to the forms of middle-class 'foodie austerity' found in lifestyle media that celebrate the *choice* to adopt the virtues of frugality (Wincott 2016). While Hugh's *River Cottage* exemplifies the trend towards the simple and home-grown pleasures of frugality, cookery writer and TV chef Nigel Slater is another commonly used example. As Lucy Potter and Claire Westall (2013: 165–6) observe, Slater promises a mode of 'frugal living' that celebrates 'the "homely smell(s)" of thrifty grain-based meals' and '"humble pleasures" based on carefully selected specialist ingredients'. In Slater's work, austerity becomes a 'culinary choice', what Bourdieu (1984) calls a 'self-imposed austerity' in which 'restraint .... bestows a form of distinction on its middle-class practitioners' (Wincott 2016: 34). For example, Slater's Boxing Day 'Celebration of Frugality' in his cookbook *Kitchen Diaries* offers a 'gesture of thrift as compensation for over-consumption' at Christmas that 'invites direct comparison with government spending cutbacks' (Potter and Westall 2013: 166). The aestheticized frugality of foodie austerity masks the harsh realities of sourcing, preparing and eating for people living in poverty (Wincott 2016). In contrast, Jack Monroe starts from the assumption that thrift and frugality are a necessary response to economic hardship rather than a lifestyle choice (Martin 2020a).

Monroe's political interventions also counter claims that the poor *choose* to eat unhealthily (Howarth 2015; Ibrahim 2018). In response to Jamie's comments about how poor diets are a product of cultural poverty, she argued:

Many of today's 13 million people living in poverty in the UK are the 'hard-working', the 'strivers', underemployed and underpaid. But there is a common fantasy among the self-appointed poverty experts such as Oliver that all struggling families are eating chips with cheese on top, reclining in front of their massive television sets.

(cited in Martin 2020a: 187)

Whereas the photo of 'essential' store cupboard ingredients in the *JMoF* cookbook (Oliver 2008) is stuffed with mid- to high-end brands, Monroe costs recipes based on supermarket 'value' ranges to produce simple and quick dishes designed for people who lack time, equipment and the money to cover fuel costs (Howarth 2015). Her book *Tin Can Cook* focuses on ingredients commonly found by foodbank users in their food parcels but, like many of her books, demonstrates how canned goods can also be nutritious and healthy. In this way, Monroe demonstrates that, while cooking healthy meals can be extremely challenging on little to no income, the poor can't simply be defined by the choice of unhealthy foods.

Monroe's writing demonstrates that, unlike the pleasures of foodie austerity, feeding work is complex and painful for the poor. Shopping becomes 'a carefully planned operation of stocktaking, online pricing of the cheapest and healthiest products' where small margins make a huge difference to one's chance of survival. This conveys 'the grinding banality of decision-making when a rise of 6p in the price of a jar of jam makes it unaffordable' (Howarth 2015: 19).

Series such as *JMoF* display a voyeuristic fascination with working-class otherness based on 'a separation between spectator and subjects' that offers the 'sensation of class difference' (Hill 1986: 136). In contrast to this external gaze, austerity bloggers such as Jack Monroe engage in forms of self-representation about the struggle to live in poverty (Ibrahim 2018). In a situation in which austerity has become so naturalized that 'the depth and scale of impoverishment' has become '*unseeable*' (Tyler 2020: 173), Monroe claims 'the right to speak' and attempts to take ownership of how the poor are represented (Ibrahim 2018: 366). While right-wing newspapers and poverty porn reality shows offered portraits of benefits claimants living indulgent lifestyles at the taxpayer's expense, austerity bloggers portray the impact of delayed benefit payments on people in highly precarious economic situations. This disrupts the government's 'narratives of skivers and strivers' and shifts blame for rising foodbank use away from the poor and back onto government policy (Ibrahim 2018; Martin 2020a: 186). However, as Monroe gained increasing celebrity, her voice was increasingly used by journalists to represent all foodbank users in the UK (Wells and Caraher 2014). While this gave the poor a (limited) voice, it also meant that her experience frequently stood in for all experiences of poverty.

Despite her campaigning anti-austerity role, Monroe has been partially recuperated within more dominant austerity discourses and narratives. Her retro-influenced visual image enabled her to be incorporated within a range of celebrity figures of 'austere femininity' – for example, Kirstie Allsopp – who celebrate the 'make do and mend' thriftiness associated with post-war femininity (Bramall 2013). As Martin (2020a: 204, 191) argues, although Monroe refuses gender binaries, press commentary has situated her within images of the 'happy, thrifty housewife' and her first cookbook, *A Girl Called Jack*, features her in gingham and floral aprons (see also Chapter 8). Photos accompanying her recipes often reaffirm this: although she advocates using charity shops as a source of cheap cookware and tableware, the use of old pots and pans in photoshoots conveys a vintage style associated with austerity chic.[6]

Therefore, as a figure in austerity culture, Jack Monroe's image is unstable. While she might be a vociferous critic of austerity, she has also been resignified as an image of 'resourceful' and 'cheerful' austerity (Martin 2020a: 190). Despite challenging the morality associated with austere practices in series such as *EWFL*, Monroe has also been recuperated within discourses of austerity that use her to embody these virtues (Martin 2020a: 201). In this way, she has been used to justify a 'new "normal" of austerity cooking where we can, and specifically *should*, all get along on limited food budgets' (Johnston and Goodman 2015: 212). Indeed, Baroness Jenkin used her as a role model who showed what the poor could achieve on a budget if they learned to cook (Elgot 2014). In order to resist this appropriation of her anti-austerity recipes to support austerity policies which demand the poor 'do more with less', Monroe now adds a disclaimer to her budget recipes on Twitter.

> (Customary postscript) This recipe isn't a simple answer to food poverty, so please don't try to use my work to belittle those it's intended to help. I write cheap recipes as a sticking plaster, and campaign for change because nobody should need to feed themselves for a pittance.
> (Monroe 2020b)

Despite attempts to reposition Monroe within austerity narratives of 'blame and responsibility' (Bramall 2013: 2), she demonstrates how celebrity chefs have intervened to inflect the meaning of austerity in different ways. This works to denaturalize the government's austerity narratives and uses food media to construct a campaigning anti-austerity position. In spite of their recuperation within forms of 'austerity chic', there is a clear fit between her straightforward recipes featuring genuinely cheap and everyday ingredients and her political message. This contrasts with the disjuncture between Jamie Oliver's often expensive and complex dishes that fit with his television persona and his campaigning role which aims to educate people about healthy eating on a smaller budget. This demonstrates how generic conventions also shape how celebrity chefs represent food politics, a theme to which I return in Chapter 8.

Conclusion

Food media have played a role in legitimating the UK's new age of austerity. This first emerged with the forms of 'foodie austerity' associated with *River Cottage* (see Chapter 5) and food writers such as Nigel Slater. Their forms of 'austerity chic' suggest that 'if it is so easy and pleasurable to learn your way to a simpler, better life then the poor must logically be lacking the will or self-discipline to change or be ignorant and in need of education' (Wincott 2016: 38). Series such as *JMoF* and *Eat Well for Less* went to work on this terrain, demonstrating how a willingness to work hard to learn and employ good foodwork skills could enable people to 'do more with less' and become responsible selves who spent wisely. Series such as *Sugar Rush* and *Fat Fight* also demonstrated the dangers of irresponsible eating practices, suggesting that 'obese' bodies put an intolerable burden on over-stretched services. By taking responsibility for health, these series suggested, the NHS would also be able to 'do more with less'. The need to restrain consumption runs through all these series, whether it is spending less on food or reducing people's intake of food. While this is, on occasion, linked to more environmental concerns about reducing waste, these series all legitimate the value of austere practices in ways that echo wider governmental policies that people must 'do more with less' to reduce public spending and pay off the national debt. Indeed, *JMoF* combines two key ways in which the need for austerity has been normalized in popular culture, merging elements of 'austerity chic' in its use of wartime imagery with some of the tropes of 'poverty porn' in the portrayal of Natasha. Through these devices, the series establishes 'a picture of both the need but also the virtues of frugality and thrift, and …. [also] those who most obviously threaten these values' (May et al 2020: 211).

However, while celebrity chefs played a role in legitimating the value of austerity, they also reinflected and resisted dominant narratives. Although series such as *Sugar Rush* and *Fat Fight* might legitimate neoliberal discourses which responsibilize citizens for their own well-being, they also call for governments to take action, to implement health initiatives and to regulate industry. Celebrity chefs such as Jack Monroe have offered a more overt challenge to government austerity narratives by demonstrating the experience of living with the impact of austerity policies and challenging images of the 'irresponsible poor'. This has begun to shift the focus of debate from restraint and austerity to the 'right to food'. As I go on to explore in Chapter 8, this has enabled a diverse range of celebrity chefs – including Oliver and Monroe – to combine forces to explicity campaign against food poverty.

Chapter 7

CELEBRITY CHEFS, FOOD AND NATION

National identifications are a key mechanism through which foods are classified and made meaningful. A supermarket promises 'A Taste of India' in its ready meals, a food manufacturer offers 'Great British Pork Sausage Rolls' and restaurant chains like Bella Italia are identified with particular national cuisines. Consumers may use national identifications to classify food choices by 'going for an Indian' or 'craving Thai'. The association between particular foods, national identities and values is also a central way in which foods are represented and rendered meaningful across a wide range of discourses and images, from claims about the 'French paradox' in newspaper articles about healthy eating to celebrations of 'iconic' national dishes in television food programming.

Despite the 'problematic obviousness' of ideas about the national diet (Ashley et al. 2004: 76), food is not 'a straightforward maker of national identity' (James 1997: 74). Many celebrated national dishes such as British fish and chips are frequently the product of global flows of produce, ideas, media and people (Appadurai 1988). Differences within nations also problematize ideas of a collective culinary identity: the restricted diet of the nineteenth-century British working class was very different from the French influenced diet of the British bourgeoisie (James 1997; Mennell 1996). Cookbooks and restaurants introducing 'Italian' or 'Indian' dishes to international audiences frequently render key regional differences invisible (Makalintal 2020), although the very idea of 'regional' cuisines is itself a modern invention (Ichijo and Ranta 2016). Furthermore, in the UK, 'British food' is often imagined as an amalgamation of 'regional' dishes such as Lancashire hot pot and Cornish pasties.

Much recent scholarship on food and nation draws on Michaela DeSoucey's (2010: 447) pioneering work on gastronationalism, a term she uses to refer to 'patterns of, and claims for, exceptionalism based on notions of tradition and patrimony'. This has proved to be a valuable concept to make sense of the role of food in explicitly nationalist projects – particularly those with 'coercive and regulatory powers' (Ichijo 2020: 222). While there are examples of jingoistic and anti-foreign nationalism in some TV food programming – for example, in the highly staged national food battles in Channel 4's *Jamie and Jimmy's Food Fight Club* (2012) – food writing and television frequently employs less intense forms of 'banal nationalism' (Billig 1995: 6). This is a sense of national identity generated by 'the mundane attachment, the gentle, comfortable sense of belonging, which is low key, taken for granted but immensely sustaining' (Ashley et al. 2004: 82) that creates 'a familiar sense of time, space and being' (Ichijo and Ranta 2016: 7).

In many countries, culinary travelogues are a popular sub-genre of food programming that map the culinary cultures of the nation or elsewhere. Through international sales or via streaming services such as Netflix, these series have made some celebrity chefs such as Anthony Bourdain into international stars. This chapter focuses on how British-based celebrity chefs mediate ideas about nation and belonging in culinary travelogues produced for a British audience, although many of these series have been broadcast elsewhere. (There is an alternative history to be written of how celebrity chefs from elsewhere represent British culinary culture.)[1] As I go on to show, the ways in which these series imagine a national cuisine can be partly understood in relation to transformations in the restaurant sector and the emergence of Modern British Cooking as a culinary style adopted by many leading chefs (Warde 2009). These series not only brand and promote 'British food' and encourage both real and imagined forms of tourism (Phillipov 2017) but they also offer useful branding opportunities for celebrity chefs as they become associated with particular landscapes, places and spaces.

As well as championing Britain and its produce, these shows generate forms of national belonging and can be understood within a much longer history of TV cookery series that helped to construct a sense of nation in post-war Europe (Buscemi 2022; Tominc 2022b). My analysis identifies how culinary tours of Britain frequently imagine British food culture in highly restricted ways through associations with folk traditions, rural locations and specific types of local characters. In the process, the chapter shows how these representations of nation are classed, gendered and racialized. Later sections explore *Jamie's Great Britain* (2011) and *Nadiya's British Food Adventure* (2017), culinary travelogues which, in very different ways, represent a 'multicultural' Britain shaped by colonialism and global flows of products and people. While seemingly offering a more inclusive image of Britishness and British food, these series also demonstrate the limits of who can speak on – and for – the nation and its food.

While the chapter may depart from my arguments about campaigning and activism by celebrity chefs that are covered in Chapters 5, 6 and 8, it engages with overlapping themes. The discussion that follows demonstrates how the seemingly escapist and pleasurable images of food and location in culinary travelogues are caught up with the wider politics of 'race', ethnicity and nation. In the context of Brexit Britain – in which questions about national identity and sovereignty are central and racist and anti-migrant rhetoric is widespread – representations of national cuisines are profoundly political and, as I go on to discuss in Chapter 8, can be articulated within wider political debate and campaigning.

In the final part of the chapter, I move beyond food tours of Britain to focus on culinary travelogues that explore regional, national and supranational food cultures elsewhere. While there is insufficient space to do justice to the sheer range and diversity of these series, I follow Bell and Hollows (2007) and Leer and Kjær (2015) in demonstrating how these series not only explore the food cultures of the 'other' but use travel to reflect on the meaning of food at home. In particular, I examine how Jamie Oliver's culinary travels in continental Europe are used to forge identifications with Europe and to reproduce class distinctions back home.

Culinary travelogues and the branding of celebrity chefs

In one of the foundational texts on food television, Niki Strange (1998) identifies the 'Tour-Educational' format – or 'Tour-Ed.' for short – as one of its key sub-genres. These culinary travelogues typically feature a form of staged gastro-tourism in which a travelling celebrity chef meets people, attempts to understand how their culinary practices express a landscape and culture, and often learns (or re-learns) how to cook the cuisine of their host destination (Bell and Hollows 2007). The 'Tour-Ed.' format has endured across a range of national televisions, whether focusing on the food of home or abroad (see, for example, Bell and Hollows 2007; de Solier 2019; Gunders 2008; Inglis and Almila 2019; Kong 2019; Leer and Kjær 2015; Phillipov 2017). These series frequently travel well and, as Linda Rossato (2015: 272) notes, through international television sales, British celebrity chefs act as 'the promoters and interpreters of foreign national cuisines on a global scale'. Indeed, the ability of the format to travel may partly explain the extensive presence of culinary travelogues on streaming platforms aimed at international audiences such as Netflix.

The origins of the 'Tour-Ed.' format are usually located in the mid-1980s and associated with Keith Floyd's popular culinary travelogues in the UK and abroad. These series broke with the 'chop and chat' format of many studio-based cookery series and featured outdoor shoots, a travelling chef and cooking sequences in a range of unusual or distinctive indoor and outdoor locations (Inglis and Almila 2019). While these shows enabled 'armchair tourism', allowing viewers to make 'imaginative journeys' while staying home (Dunn 2005; Moores 1993), they also encouraged people to experience first-hand what they had seen on screen (Phillipov 2017).

Culinary travelogues are not, of course, the only TV food formats to make use of location shoots. Location sequences feature, for instance, in magazine programmes (for example, *Food and Drink*, 1982–2002; 2013–15); primarily studio-based series focusing on national cuisines (for example, *Ken Hom's Chinese Cookery*, 1984); competition formats demonstrating how particular chefs or foodstuffs are the product of place (for example, *Great British Menu*); and lifestyled cookery series that situate their stars in particular locations (for example, *The Naked Chef* and *Nigella Bites* in London). For celebrity chefs such as Hugh Fearnley-Whittingstall and Rick Stein, the distinctive rural and coastal locations of South West England are particularly important to many of their TV series and to their brand identity (Phillipov 2017; Randall 2000).[2] This helps to boost their business interests: for example, Stein's programmes invite viewers to make 'pilgrimages' to his Padstow restaurants (Busby et al. 2013; Phillipov 2017).

Starting with *Floyd on Britain and Ireland* (1988), Keith Floyd pioneered the 'Tour-Ed.' format (Inglis and Almila 2019). His early series were shot on a tiny budget, frequently using 'only one camera and a minimal crew', and locations were found on an 'ad hoc basis' with filming taking place in unpredictable spaces. These conditions helped to produce the 'apparent spontaneity and authenticity' that contributed to the unexpected popularity of Floyd's early series before they calcified into a more predictable formula (Inglis and Almila 2019: 222). Later culinary travelogues – usually filmed on much larger budgets and now with a clear series of generic conventions – often tried to recapture the features of these early Floyd series, searching out the apparently unpredictable and performing spontaneity in a search for 'the real'.

While Inglis and Almila (2019) reject the characterization of Floyd as a macho adventurer, the culinary travelogue has been primarily associated with male celebrity chefs. As Rick Stein has observed, Floyd and many of the chefs who followed in his footsteps used the format to distinguish themselves from a female tradition of television cooks such as Zena Skinner and Delia Smith who were confined to the safe and quasi-domestic space of the studio set.[3] Many culinary travelogues feature their heroes cooking in outdoor spaces – on BBQs and campfires – and on the move, highlighting their mobility in contrast to the stasis of the female domestic cook (Bell and Hollows 2007; Phillipov 2017), a trend epitomized in the recent ITV series *Gordon, Gino and Fred: Road Trip* (2018–). *Two Fat Ladies* (1996–9) provided one of few exceptions to the gendering of the genre (see below). Outdoor locations offer a sense of unpredictability and opportunities to perform adventures through (now predictable) diving, fishing and hunting sequences that are among the pleasures of the series (Leer and Kjær 2015; Randall 1999: 45). For example, the descriptions in the *Radio Times* listings magazine for Gary Rhodes series *Rhodes around Britain* (1994) promise Gary 'in a survival suit to visit an oil platform', donning 'thigh-high waders to try to catch salmon' and going on 'a wild mushroom chase'.[4]

Culinary travelogues around Britain offer a 'romanticized view of nature' (Randall 1999: 45) in a landscape populated by recognizable icons of rural Britain – the village pub and church, sheep on rolling hills, cows in grassy fields, deserted beaches. While many series may make a brief venture into urban spaces – for example to visit the curry houses of Bradford (*Rick Stein's Food Heroes*) or to sample traditional working-class dishes in Birmingham (*Floyd on Britain and Ireland*) – the majority of the action takes place in rural or coastal settings. As I go on to show, in these 'pleasurable, leisurely and unhurried' environments (Phillipov 2017: 62), Britishness is associated with the rustic and pre-modern.

Mapping 'British' food

These kinds of idyllic landscapes flood the screen during the opening credits for *Rick Stein's Food Heroes* (2002). A series of words appear on screen: local, regional, traditional, flavour, British, discover, taste. If the final three words operate as an invitation to sample national foods along with the celebrity chef, the others operate as key values that underpin many television culinary travelogues around the UK. This section examines how these values not only work to privilege particular kinds of Britishness and British food but also reflect and refract wider culinary trends in UK restaurants. While the locations and foods that feature in these culinary tours of Britain are far removed from where and how the vast majority of people live in the UK, they contribute to how the nation is imagined 'by projecting a particular image of what the nation eats and what its food-related boundaries are' (Ichijo and Ranta 2016: 9).

Representations of nation in culinary travelogues need to be understood in the context of wider shifts in the British restaurant and tourism industries where there have been attempts to build recognizable and marketable forms of 'British cuisine'. In his analysis of the annual *Good Food Guide*, Alan Warde (2009) identifies a shift from the veneration of French cuisine in the 1950s (see also James 1997; Mennell 1996; Panayi 2008) towards increasing attempts to identify a distinctive and marketable form of 'British cooking' from the 1960s onwards that aimed to improve the image of British food (Warde 2009: 167–8).[5] This aim was only fully realized in the 1980s with 'the emergence of modern British cooking'. This restaurant cooking style became associated with 'regionality' (with location being key to the meaning of food); 'the market' and particularly ideas of seasonality; 'the relishes and spices' which gave British food a gutsy flavour; 'the garden'; and 'the tradition', most commonly associated with baking – especially puddings – and cheesemaking (Warde 2009: 158–9). As Modern British Cooking developed and diffused, the emphasis was increasingly on 'perfect, and often simply prepared, locally sourced, fresh ingredients' (Warde 2009: 160).

Although Warde (2009: 161–3) also identifies the emergence of two further culinary styles, it is Modern British Cooking that provided a key culinary reference point for many celebrity chefs' food tours around the UK. This can be seen, for example, in an emphasis on 'spatial provenance' and the construction of the nation through the local and regional (Warde 2009: 166). Modern British Cooking, however, was more of an improvisation on the past than a slavish dedication to it. For example, Gary Rhodes, one of the early stars of Modern British Cooking, often used gastronomic culinary techniques associated with haute cuisine to 'modernize' traditional British dishes, capturing the flavours of a steak and kidney pie in a French boudin-style sausage (Michelin 2019). In his TV series *Rhodes around Britain*, he demonstrated how to make new interpretations of traditional dishes such as piccalilli pickle, beef stew and dumplings, and Welsh rarebit.[6] This was echoed in other culinary travelogues in which celebrity chefs learned from locals before offering recipes for their own distinctive uses of traditional produce or twists on traditional dishes. As celebrity chef Antony Worrall Thompson put it in the 1990s, 'the public is ready for food their mothers have forgotten how to cook – gutsy, unpretentious food' (cited in James 1997: 79). In this way, dishes associated with a feminine, domestic food tradition were 'improved' and 'elevated' by largely male celebrity chefs in order to assert a distinctively British culinary tradition.

Although few British culinary travelogues featured celebrity chefs who had stellar restaurant careers like Gary Rhodes, the format frequently reproduced values associated with Modern British Cooking. These series featured British food associated with a living tradition of domestic cookery or artisanal production, primarily located in rural locations. This sense of tradition is captured in the image of a worn vintage-style atlas in the title sequence of *The Hairy Bikers Food Tour of Britain* (2009) and reproduced through a focus on small-scale producers who use traditional regional techniques and the use of people who enthusiastically extol the virtues of their local dishes and produce.[7] The emphasis on tradition is bound up with a sense of place. In *River Cottage Road Trip* (2005), Hugh Fearnley-Whittingstall's search for the 'authentic' taste of Yorkshire's baking traditions first takes him to a shop in the market town of Helmsley where he samples Yorkshire curd tarts. But, in a hunt for greater authenticity that is the product of place, he heads to a farm kitchen where a woman prepares it in 'the good old-fashioned way' using milk produced on the farm.

This search for authenticity in the 'geographic specificity' of terroir is not unique to British food culture: for example Johnston and Baumann (2015: 65–850) highlight how contemporary US foodie discourse privileges the 'simplicity' of artisanal, small-scale production, and a sense of both 'personal connection' with producers and 'history and tradition'.[8] In culinary travelogues, these values are given a British inflection through their association with landscapes, produce and dishes that are recognisable signifiers of nation. In *Rick Stein's Food Heroes*, the celebrity chef champions producers whose 'authentic' produce reflects British values but also demonstrates how these values are under threat from a homogeneous and creolized food culture. His visits to specialist oatmeal millers, fish smokeries and sheep breeders are interspersed with complaints about the 'inauthentic' and placeless food on offer in hotels as he travels the UK. He underscores the importance of 'natural' food produced by 'local characters' (Randall 2000: 126). Using a 'pastoral nostalgia' for a pre-modern nation (Leer 2019: 825), these series venerate places where it seems as if 'traditional, "slow food" practices have been preserved amid an increasingly globalized "fast food" world' (Phillipov 2017: 99). The opening episode of *The Hairy Bikes Food Tour of Britain* follows the show's stars as they arrive in Suffolk, 'a really rural county', where pigs are free range and game is caught with ferrets. In this way, most culinary tours around the UK rest on conservative views of white Britishness located in a rural past.

This inevitably has an impact on who is included in British food culture, with an overwhelmingly white and rural population representing the meaning of Britishness. However, while Leer (2019: 822) finds only a rural and 'white France' in Cyril Lygnac's similar culinary tour of his native country in *Le Chef en France* (2011–12), most of the culinary travelogues in the UK at least nod towards a more urban, industrial and/or multicultural Britain. This is often achieved through a trip to an urban Indian restaurant – the curry houses of Bradford in *Rick Stein's Food Heroes* or the Balti restaurants of Birmingham in *James Martin's Great British Adventure* (2019). In *River Cottage Road Trip*, Hugh Fearnley-Whittingstall, marked by his country gear, goes to the African-Caribbean area of Handsworth in Birmingham in search of the best 'goat curry' (which he is repeatedly told is called 'curried goat'). However, recurring shots of a non-white and very urban Handsworth are relocated within a more pastoral English tradition as Hugh visits the quasi-rural landscape of the local allotment to find people growing Caribbean vegetables. The Black British residents of Handsworth and its distinctly unpastoral streets are legitimated by relocating them within an agricultural tradition. Although *The Hairy Bikers Food Tour of Britain* takes in some industrial towns in Lancashire, these towns are also characterized in terms of a community with a shared culinary culture based on traditional dishes such as tripe and black pudding. While their tour takes in Leicester, their description of it as 'a wonderfully eclectic, cosmopolitan kind of city' is not reflected in their decision to cook pork pies in the marketplace of a city where roughly a third of the population is Muslim or Hindu.

While these culinary tours of Britain are rooted in tradition and the local, most celebrity chefs are represented as modern and on the move (Bell and Hollows 2007; Leer 2019). The Hairy Bikers image centres around the motorbike, James Martin cultivates an image as a petrolhead, Floyd and Stein are best known on TV as travelling chefs. While I discuss the gendered relationships between chefs in motion and static locals in more detail below, the dynamic between movement and stasis, global and local, modern and traditional is played out on the plates created by celebrity chefs. Unlike the local cooks and producers they visit, celebrity chefs distinguish themselves – and enhance their gastronomic image – by creating sophisticated dishes from simple ingredients they pick up en route. As Randall (2000: 127) observes, the 'juxtaposition of the source of raw ingredients with the final art form ... points up the significance of the presenter's auteurial role' (see also Leer 2019).

There are strong similarities between the locations, producers, products and dishes that feature in these culinary tours of Britain. However, it is the chefs themselves – through their movement, their judgements of taste and their construction of a culinary canon – who create 'British food' through an assemblage of local and regional dishes. This, in turn, brands these celebrity chefs in terms of their Britishness, whether to sell restaurants characterized by Modern British Cooking or to sell a 'British' brand in a global television marketplace.

'It's Ours Now': Jamie's Great Britain

The puddings and pies found in conventional culinary travelogues might offer easily exportable images of 'heritage' Britishness but they fail to capture a Britain where '"multicultural" food is the norm' (Panayi 2008: 216).[9] Contemporary British food culture has been strongly marked both by the activities of global food giants such as McDonalds and KFC and by waves of migration that have shaped British restaurants, takeaways, high streets and supermarket shelves.[10] While food is a long-established site for practising racism – for example, through refusal of 'foreign' flavours as 'dirty' or unpalatable (Humble 2005; Murcott 2019) – contemporary

British food is often characterized as a 'melting pot', in which culinary practices from elsewhere have undergone processes of hybridization and enculturation. However, as I go on to explore in this chapter, although the embrace of 'diverse' flavours might be seen as politically progressive, the celebration of 'ethnic' or 'exotic' foods can also 'produce cultural difference' (Ray cited in Murcott 2019: 116) and reproduce ideas of a 'native' food culture (Murcott 2019: 111). Indeed, the move to construct the category 'British food' in the hospitality industry was partly in response to the rise of 'ethnic' restaurants (Panayi 2008; Warde 2009).

As I have shown, many celebrity chefs' travelogues around the UK marginalize multiculturalism and attempt to fix an identifiable British tradition. This contrasts with 'the messy set of continuities and discontinuities that follow in the wake of our collective (but not common) colonial and imperial pasts' (Highmore 2009: 188). *Jamie's Great Britain* (2011) set out to reflect a more 'multicultural' nation in 'a road trip, scouring this gorgeous, crazy island called Britain' to 'show how centuries of foreign influences on our island have changed the whole landscape of what we eat and how we eat it'. This ambition is illustrated in a logo featuring a Union Jack made up of many different national flags. The series built on Oliver's developing portfolio of culinary travelogues such as *Jamie's Great Escape* to Italy (2005) and *Jamie's American Road Trip* (2009). It also built on his ethnically hybrid brand identity, from the elective Italian culinary identity established in *The Naked Chef* to his 2009 revelation to the *Radio Times* magazine that he was 'sixth-generation Sudanese' (Singh 2009). While the series still featured conventional elements of British culinary travelogues (pork pie makers, fish smokehouses) in familiar rural and coastal locations, it also privileged modernity, urban landscapes, histories of urban popular culture and, most crucially, Britain's 'ethnic communities' and their food practices. This was an image of Britishness very much of its time in the run up to the 2012 London Olympics whose bid and branding was based on an articulation of a 'heritage', rural and traditional Britain with an image of 'modern, international, progressive, youthful, cosmopolitan and harmonious multicultural London and post-colonial (and New Labour) Britain' (Winter 2013: [1]; see also Silk 2011).

Jamie's Great Britain initially appears progressive in its ambition to show how 'quintessentially British' dishes have been shaped by waves of immigration from the Romans onwards. Britishness is represented as inherently 'multicultural' in contrast to the largely 'monocultural' Britishness found in many other culinary travelogues around the UK (Leer 2019). This approach had particular purchase in a political climate in which the new Tory-led Coalition government was partly positioned against the advance of multiculturalism: as then Education Secretary Michael Gove put it in 2010, 'One of the under-appreciated tragedies of our time has been the sundering of our society from its past ... Children are growing up ignorant of one of the most inspiring stories I know – the history of our United Kingdom' (cited in Winter 2013: [4]). In contrast, *Jamie's Great Britain* sets out to construct a history of Britain as always already multicultural: for example, Jamie shows how Scottish fish smoking and haggis were both shaped by Viking settlement, how dried fruit for a traditional Clootie dumpling came from the

Middle East, how the Romans brought pie making to Britain and how fish and chips – often represented as the national dish – was introduced by immigrant Jewish cooks into London's East End. While many of these stories are familiar, his portrait of Britain is in striking contrast to most culinary travelogues and the government's political direction at the time.

While this emphasis on the positive contributions of immigrant cuisines to 'our' food was consistent with Jamie's brand image, his attempt to discuss food in ways that might suggest 'political correctness' was not. From the outset, his celebrity image was always partly informed by a 'new lad' identity associated with an ironic rejection of the politically correct (Hunt 1998; Jackson et al. 2001; Whelehan 2000; for more on Jamie Oliver as new lad see Hollows 2003a). Jamie's (often failed) attempts to take racial politics seriously in the series are countered by significant amounts of laddish sexism. This ranges from condescending flirtation with older (white) women and denigrating their 'mother-in-law … nuclear power station' scrambled eggs through to the punning pub-style name of the sexualized and feminized mobile ex-army truck he uses for his travels. 'I call her The Cock in Cider. And like any decent pub, she's got room for a party', he repeats at the start of each episode.

In contrast to his laddish sexism, Jamie takes a more serious approach to immigration. He adopts an educational tone in his explanations of how and when different waves of migrants settled in the UK, but glosses over the forms of economic, political and colonial power that sustained Empire and the slave trade. 'One of the biggest trades were people', says Jamie seriously in Bristol before quickly moving on to a happier tale of how trade brought 'sugar, molasses, rum, spices – spices galore'. Indeed, the term 'trade' frequently covers a multitude of British sins that are at odds with his celebration of British openness to 'others' and the resulting vibrant food culture. Nonetheless – across visits to homes, restaurants, places of worship and community centres – the series demonstrates the role of food as 'an important marker in migrant and diasporic culture', as 'a portable practice that can materially (and sensually) remake a "home" culture that has been left behind' (Highmore 2009: 184). As Jamie puts it in a Bristol Caribbean restaurant, 'When new immigrants arrive in this country they want to eat food that reminds them of home'.

However, by emphasizing how 'immigrant' cuisines maintain a sense of tradition, the series frequently represents these food cultures as fixed and unchanging. This reproduces elements of other culinary travelogues around Britain in which rural food cultures are associated with an unchanging British tradition. In 'one of the oldest mosques in Britain', Jamie finds Samira is trying to 'keep traditional Yemeni cooking alive' while three Jewish 'girls' in Leeds 'cook some of the best traditional Jewish food in town'. However, although some of the 'communities' he visits do create hybrid dishes drawing on both British and 'home' traditions – a Chinese man cooks trifle with lychee, a Guyanan woman serves pepperpot stew with Yorkshire pudding – it is Jamie and the white British who are represented as dynamic and modern in their embrace of 'foreign' cuisines.

A modern, adventurous and multicultural 'us' – the (white) British – are repeatedly distinguished from a traditional, exotic and monocultural 'them' (immigrants and their descendants) (Leer 2019). Near the start of the series, Jamie says, 'We're like magpies, we love to sort of get little ideas, get given or steal things and then, what the British are brilliant at, is making it our own'. In what could also be read as a justification for centuries of colonial exploitation – and an excellent example of cultural appropriation – Jamie demonstrates how 'we' have taken ownership of immigrant foods through a process of enculturation: 'It's ours now'. This creates an image of 'us' as inclusive bricoleurs: 'us Brits have embraced spices and tucked them under our magpie little wings'. This eclecticism, he suggests, makes British food superior: it's 'us Brits' willingness to take on new ingredients that makes our food so diverse and exciting'.

Not only is immigrant food represented as singular and traditional in contrast, it can only be legitimated through British acceptance. In relation to a discussion of the Jewish roots of fish and chips, Jamie comments: 'I love the fact that *we* think of fish and chips as *ours* but it's *theirs* but the most important thing is that *we* consider it *ours* which, at the end of the day, is a compliment to *them*' (my italics). This constant interplay between 'us' and 'them' means the series celebrates Britain as a vibrant, modern and multicultural country while also drawing distinctions between 'native' and 'immigrant' populations (and many of the 'immigrants' he meets are British born). As Leer (2019: 831) observes, in *Jamie's Great Britain*, 'the white majority has the capacity to adopt, mix and domesticate the world's cuisine' while the 'others' living in the UK are just there to add 'spice'. In this way, the series draws on the wider fetishization of 'culinary exoticism' in Western foodie discourses that 'essentialize and stereotype ethnic cultures' (Johnston and Baumann 2015: 90; see also Heldke 2003). Indeed, Jamie has an uneasy moment on a Bristol allotment in an encounter with an elderly man of Caribbean heritage who is growing borlotti beans, commonly associated with Italian cuisine. Jamie praises 'beautiful' borlotti beans and asks, 'Do you cook them yourself?' with a mildly surprised tone. 'Of course I do', replies the man deadpan, 'That's why I plant them'. As Jamie acknowledges, 'it was a stupid question' but it is a question that is shaped by many of the assumptions of the series which suggest that it's only the white British who have cosmopolitan tastes. The fetishization of the 'other's' authenticity comes unstuck, demonstrating how Jamie's celebration of British bricoleurs 'is itself premised on a false notion of the authenticity that it departs from' (Highmore 2009: 187).

Jamie's Great Britain fuses together more pastoral images of a traditional British food culture that is '*silently* marked as "white"' (Murcott 2019: 118) with largely urban manifestations of a multicultural British food culture which is (more noisily) marked as 'other'. Some aspects of national culture are represented as naturally British: the pork pies and Eccles cakes; a pie, adorned with RAF wings and a heart, dedicated to Prince William's marriage to Kate Middleton; and 'the asparagus season [that] is as British as Wimbledon'. In other places, this celebration of tradition is less easily incorporated into ideas of Britain as a welcoming and hybrid nation. In an uncritical representation of

Empire, Jamie explains that 'our passion for flavour motivated an incredible period' in which:

> Britain colonized countries across the globe in search of spices and commodities. At one point we ruled over a quarter of the world's population as the British Empire. One of our strongest bonds was with South Asia where the British Raj ruled for nearly 100 years. The bit I'm interested in is when these Brits returned from overseas, they craved the foods they'd left behind. This signalled a time when spices were available to all and our menus were revolutionized like you'd never believe.

Not only does this narrative simply accept Britain's right to colonize, rule and exploit other lands and peoples, it also focuses on how mobile white British subjects shaped the British taste for spice and marginalizes the huge impact of South Asian migrants on British food culture (Panayi 2008). Therefore, although the series celebrates the 'authentic' regional Indian cuisine of migrants to Leicester, it also highlights the ability of the white British people to hybridize and fuse languages and flavours as part of our 'Anglo-Indian romance'. This is evident in a trip to an international vegetable stall on Leicester market where the owners, who 'look as Anglo-Saxon as I've ever seen', have learned some Gujarati. It is also evident in his decision to make a celebratory 'mash up' of roast chicken dinner and curry, his 'Empire Roast Chicken'. Drawing on tropes used by foodies seeking out 'exotic' and 'simple' flavours, as he tucks into the finished dish, he declares 'this is Empire food – you can use your hands' – before inviting the crew to join him in a meal and a toast 'To The Empire'. This underscores the ways the series works 'imperially nostalgic recipes ... and retro-royalist dishes ... into a unionist narrative that endorsed the "magpie nation" and its imperial-derived ability to absorb all it encounters' (Potter and Westall 2013: 158).

These forms of Britishness in *Jamie's Great Britain* echo the way Britain was branded in preparation for the 2012 London Olympics. Drawing on Anne-Marie Fortier's work, Michael Silk (2011: 742) observes how the preparations for London 2012 used a 'multicultural nationalism' in which non-white British athletes were not only allowed into the image of the nation 'but redefined as integral to the self-image of the nation as "tolerant" and "inclusive"'. *Jamie's Great Britain* may revel in a colonial past but it also wants to represent Britain as inclusive and open (Leer 2019). As Jamie concludes at the end of episode three, 'We are very open-minded, we are incredibly embracing of other cultures and there's a real array of communities and understanding and food and I'm just incredibly proud to be British.' In this way 'ethnic' food – and the communities who cook it – do not just add 'spice' and interest to 'British food' but also work to brand Britain and Jamie Oliver as modern, hybrid and inclusive. This is underscored at a culinary level by the range of new hybrid British classics cooked up by Jamie throughout the series, from 'Empire chicken' and 'Apple pepperpot pudding' to 'McMoule mariniere', contributing to 'a new myth' of a British food culture 'based on curiosity, innovativeness and openness to other cultures' (Leer 2019: 830).

Jamie's Great Britain creates an image of Britain as a 'globalized and dynamic nation constantly in motion' in contrast to 'others' who are fixed in place (Leer 2019: 829). As I explore in more detail in the next section, these positions of mobility and fixity are not only 'racialized' and gendered but the qualities of the nation – as mobile, modern, tolerant, hybrid – are also mapped on to Jamie's food and his wider brand image. As the chef makes clear in the opening episode, his heritage is also one of migration and is shaped by urban culture, as his ancestors moved from running pubs in a working-class East End of London out to Essex. Jamie's positioning of himself as a fellow migrant – and his pick 'n' mix approach to elements of Britain's multicultural food landscape – has not been without criticism. In 2018, his 'Punchy Jerk Rice' ready meal gained considerable media attention after Labour MP Dawn Butler questioned whether Jamie knew what jerk is: 'It's not just a word you put before stuff to sell products. Your jerk rice is not OK. This appropriation from Jamaica needs to stop' (cited in Forrest 2018). Part of the ensuing debate focused on the inaccuracy of the designation 'jerk' to a product that lacked many of its key ingredients, with British-Caribbean celebrity chefs Rustie Lee and Levi Roots appearing on morning TV to explain why you can't simply use jerk as an imprecise marketing term. Oliver's promiscuous use of the term was also evident in *Jamie's Great Britain* where he 'explains' to two (noticeably surprised) people of Caribbean heritage that jerk is 'the same spices, give or take' as mulled wine. If Jamie's use of the term jerk as a synonym for 'spicy' has been seen as disrespectful to Britain's Jamaican community and their culinary traditions, then so was the way in which he used his privileged position to profit from other people's cuisine who lack his significant amounts of capital. Television culinary travelogues raise the question of who has the power and the right to define culinary traditions and cultures.

'Too Bengali to Eat Fish Fingers': Nadiya's British Food Adventure

Nadiya's British Food Adventure imagined multicultural British food culture very differently to *Jamie's Great Britain*. Hosted by *Great British Bake Off* winner Nadiya Hussain as she established herself as one of Britain's key celebrity chefs, the series is, in part, a highly conventional culinary travelogue around Britain: she tours primarily rural and coastal locations to meet the people 'who go the extra mile to make British food some of the best in the world'. However, by putting a Bangladeshi-British Muslim woman at the centre of the type of 'adventure' usually associated with white, male celebrity chefs, the series enables the relationships between food, nation, gender, race and travel to be imagined in different ways. In order to understand the significance of the series, it is first necessary to understand Nadiya's history on *Bake Off*, her developing celebrity image and how she was positioned in wider media debates about British politics and culture.

The largest UK TV audience of the year watched Nadiya win the 2015 *Great British Bake Off* final. Even Prime Minister David Cameron backed her win.

Her appearances on the show won Nadiya a huge fan base to become a 'national obsession': as Remona Aly (2015) commented in the *Guardian*,

> Nadiya's appeal is quite simple. She is the quietly brilliant girl next door, and someone you want to be mates with. As wholesome as GBBO [Great British Bake Off] itself, she is what we might define as 'quintessentially British'. Deeply humble – tick. Self-deprecating – tick. Unintentionally funny – tick. Good at Victoria Sponge – mega tick. Or as one fan simply tweeted, 'She's just so flipping lovely'.

Nadiya's identification as 'quintessentially British' was strengthened through her association with *Bake Off*, a show styled 'to resemble a British country fete' which 'capitalises upon imperially-rooted presentation of Britain's saleable version of pastoral Englishness … [and] the nostalgic "charms" of British bunting with English tea-parties and countrified kitchen aesthetics' (Casey 2019: 587; Potter and Westall 2013: 161).

However, at the same time, Nadiya also enabled audiences to identify with a diverse and inclusive image of Britishness (Aly 2015) during a period of rising Islamophobia in which the Muslim Council of Britain reported that anti-Muslim attacks in London had risen by 70 per cent in a year (Sherwood and Nardelli 2015). If the popularity of *Bake Off* offered a sense of unity in a divided nation (Casey 2019), Nadiya's apparent openness, charm and lack of artifice caused one journalist to describe her as 'a young Muslim woman in the public eye, [who] has also functioned as probably the single greatest antidote to the various accumulating toxicities of our age' (Mangan 2018b). As Jorie Lagerwey (2018: 447) argues, 'Nadiya's South Asian British hybrid identities' helped to sustain a fantasy of a collective national identity 'in a time when racial, ethnic and national divisions are once again hypervisible'. However, Nadiya's success was not universally embraced. Right-wing commentator Amanda Platell (2015) provoked controversy when she commented in the *Daily Mail* that the 2015 *Bake Off* final was 'a PC triumph', complaining that 'far too middle class' contestant Flora might have 'stood a chance […] if she'd made a chocolate mosque'. In the *Sun* newspaper, Ally Ross claimed that BBC executives 'no doubt did a multi-cultural jig of politically-correct joy' on Nadiya's win, calling her success a form of 'ideological warfare' (Allegretti 2015).

Since her *Bake Off* win, Nadiya has been transformed into a celebrity chef and a spokesperson for British Muslim women (who are frequently marginalized in public debate). This role was heightened as she became the target of sustained racial abuse on Twitter. In response, she tweeted: 'I get abused for merely existing. Too Brown to be English. Too Muslim to be British. Too Bengali to eat fish fingers' (cited in Powell 2017). If these comments show how mundane mass market foodstuffs can be politicized and racialized as symbols of national identity, her responses also highlight both her own experiences of racism and the more widespread racial abuse faced by British Muslims. As she tweeted in 2018,

Have you not realised by now, that saying 'go home' is just not working any more. Go home to where? I am home. If you want to spew hatred at least come up with something original. I'm getting fed up of being told to go home! For the millionth time, I AM HOME!

(cited in Shammas 2018)

In this way, Nadiya's generic associations with 'quintessential' Britishness, her Bengali-British background, her visible Muslim identity in a time of rampant anti-Muslim sentiment and her increasing use of her role as a celebrity chef to counter racism make her positioning within a culinary travelogue around Britain a significant departure from earlier examples.[11]

Nadiya's British Food Adventure is a conventional culinary travelogue in many ways. Although one episode is based in London and she visits some towns in Northern England, most of the producers she visits on her culinary tour are located in lush, green rolling landscapes or by the sea. Many of the ingredients that feature are entirely familiar signifiers of Britishness (Welsh lamb, Cromer crab, asparagus) as are many dishes that inspire her own recipes (scones, Bakewell tart, ploughman's lunch). Like many celebrity chefs, Nadiya subjects these dishes and ingredients to her own 'twists' that mark both her intervention and her brand identity. Some are a 'mash up' of familiar British dishes such as Eton Mess cheesecake and Yorkshire pudding with jam and custard. Others combine traditional British and Bangladeshi ingredients or dishes such as 'Derbyshire oatcake, potato and dill samosas' and a Welsh lamb bhuna, reflecting her own positioning between two traditions. As she puts it, 'I grew up with a collision of flavours. Mum and dad's spicy curries at home and traditional British meals at school'. Like other celebrity chefs she also combines aspects of British food culture with global flavours in dishes such as a steak and kidney pie with North African spicing.

However, the series departs from others in its 'everyday multiculturalism' grounded in the '*everyday practice* and lived experience of diversity' among minority communities rather from the perspective of white cosmopolitans (Wise and Velayutham 2009: 3). The series represents British-Asian dishes as part of everyday family mealtimes rather than public, urban spaces of the Indian restaurant or the Caribbean takeaway. While the episodes are peppered with the term 'exotic', this is not associated with ethnic 'others' but is part of the British landscape, found in rosewater with an 'exotic' flavour made by two middle-class white women in Wales and 'exotic' wild plants foraged from the Scottish countryside. While the series includes immigrant stories – an Israeli man running a traditional Scottish flour mill, a female Syrian refugee manufacturing Halloumi enhanced by the richness of Yorkshire milk – the other British-Asians in the series are skilled chefs experimenting with scent as a flavour in a high-end London supper club rather than running a Bradford curry house.

Nadiya's British Food Adventure demonstrates how oppositions between traditional and modern, past and future, custom and innovation, can be articulated rather than being a source of conflict. For example, in urban space, she finds 'London's first commercial farm' creating a sustainable future for British agriculture: herbs and salad grow in a 'greenhouse style warehouse' out of fish waste rather than soil. Stories of Britain's past and present are closely intertwined with the history of her own British-Bangladeshi family so that the narrative unites the national and the personal. Nadiya connects British agriculture with her experiences of her grandfather's rice farming in Bangladesh. She uses asparagus from the Home Counties to make an 'Indian five-spice vegetable stir-fry'. She fries the garlic separately – 'that's quite traditional in Bangladeshi cooking' – and adds five-spice that has 'more aromas of home'. 'Home' does not only reside in her Bangladeshi family but in the 'nostalgic' flavour of old-fashioned British rhubarb and custard flavour sweets. Bangladeshi and British identities are represented as inherently intertwined rather than antithetical. As she cooks on the roof of a car park in London's East End, she says, 'I feel like I'm cooking in modern Bangladesh, I've got the smell of curry and the smell of fumes'. However, Nadiya's identity is also associated with independence and innovation. She refuses to be simply bound by tradition, rejecting both her mother's time-intensive way of preparing a bhuna and her mother's rule that couscous should never be served with curry.

In contrast to *Jamie's Great Britain* which demonstrates Britain's multicultural communities' contribution to 'our' cuisine, *Nadiya's British Food Adventure* represents British food and culture as inherently multicultural through the figure of Nadiya herself. Unlike Nadiya's wider celebrity persona, the series is silent on how the experiences of racism and Islamophobia impact on the experience of 'home' although this is perhaps unsurprising in a format celebrating the 'niceness' of British food. Although the series gives a British-Bangladeshi woman a role that isn't limited to representing 'ethnic' cuisines, like most other culinary travelogues, there are few Black and ethnic minority food producers in the show.[12] At the same time, as Nadiya commented in discussion with *Queer Eye*'s Tan France, the presence of 'brown' people in primetime mainstream formats that represent Britishness is itself some form of progress in changing representations of who is included in 'our' food culture (Cheltenham Festivals 2020). In a similar manner to Ghanaian-Australian celebrity chef Dorinda Hafner in her international culinary travelogues, Nadiya's positioning in terms of 'British' food rather than 'cuisines of colour' enables a woman of colour to mediate 'white cuisines back to white audiences' (de Solier 2019: 212–13). Furthermore, the constant movement in the series between personal, domestic and national senses of 'home' not only serves to brand Nadiya but also highlights the more diverse ways in which people are attached to and sewn into the fabric of nation. Nadiya's portrayal of the intense joy of cooking and eating, the transparency of her emotions as she registers delight and the sense of inclusive national community constructed by the series may appear to offer an escapist fantasy but they also offer a glimpse of the 'utopian possibilities' of living differently in Britain (Dyer 1998; Geraghty 1991).

In putting a woman at its centre, *Nadiya's British Food Adventure* creates very different relationships between home, nation and mobility to those conventionally found in culinary travelogues. Each episode opens and closes in Nadiya's kitchen, repositioning her as a figure in domestic space rather than one on the move. As the opening voiceover states, 'I'm a busy mum and I need to feed my family everyday'. While male culinary adventurers are associated with movement and various forms of transport, Nadiya frequently simply *appears* on foot, walking across a field or down a lane to meet a food producer. She jokes about her discomfort with sea travel in episodes at the coast – 'I've never been on a boat on the sea' she confesses before getting seasick and claiming 'I'm so glad it's all over' and 'I feel safe in a kitchen'. While male celebrity chefs are often represented as travelling adventurers, when faced with the sea again in Bridlington, Nadiya confesses to finding the ocean 'scary' and declares 'I am a wimp'.[13]

This demonstrates how celebrity chefs in culinary travelogues are positioned within wider gender relations. In many travelogues, men travel and women feature as their stopping off points en route, trapped in domestic spaces in rural locations that are often positioned as outside modernity (Felski 2000; Giles 2004). As Bev Skeggs (2004: 51–2) argues, 'mobility is itself gendered on a variety of scales … male subjectivity is discursively linked to narratives of travel, adventure and discovery whereas female subjectivity is mapped as fixed place on the itinerary of male journey' (see also Bell and Hollows 2007). An exception can be found in the mid-1990s series featuring *The Two Fat Ladies* Clarissa Dixon-Wright and Jennifer Patterson who made culinary journeys around Britain on a motorbike and sidecar but their eccentricity rendered their performance comic rather than simply adventurous (see also Leer 2018). In *Nadiya's British Food Adventure*, Nadiya visits places but rarely *travels* to them and is shown to be uncomfortable with mobility, literally hugging dry land after she disembarks from a boat. This reinforces the idea, replayed across many culinary travelogues, that 'femininity is fixed so others can travel' (Skeggs cited in Bell and Hollows 2007: 2; see also Leer and Kjær 2015).

Nadiya's British Food Adventure developed Nadiya's brand as an emerging celebrity chef. In the series, she makes frequent references to sweetness – at one point she commands the viewer 'to get sweetness everywhere' – and this works to cement her already established connection to baking and the well-established 'sweetness' of her personality, a conventionally feminine attribute. The series helped to brand Nadiya as a 'national treasure' while weaving stories of Bangladeshi heritage into the very ordinary and everyday experiences of being British. While 'her performance of happy, fully integrated postcolonial subject' (Lagerwey 2018: 448) was in sharp contrast to her well-documented experience of racism, the series nonetheless offered a fantasy of a happier, more harmonious Britain in which both diversity and hybridity are ordinary and in which everyday domestic meals can express a 'multiethnic, multicultural subjectivity' (Ahad 2016: 14). However, at the same time, the series ultimately reaffirmed the very different roles offered to male and female celebrity chefs. If Keith Floyd's travelogues were a calculated break from the feminized domesticity of cookery television, then Nadiya's ability to leave home is dependent upon her return.

'I Should Have Been Bloody Italian': Jamie's European Escapes

Culinary travelogues that explore other regions and nations have become a staple element of British television. While many celebrity chefs embark on travels abroad, some are strongly associated with the format – for example, Keith Floyd, Rick Stein and The Hairy Bikers. Research on these series frequently draws on postcolonial theorists such as Edward Said and Sarah Ahmed to analyse how they 'other' particular cuisines, cultures and people and fix them as exotic and 'authentic' (for example, Bell and Hollows 2007; Jones 2006; Kelly 2017; Kong 2019; Leer and Kjær 2015). However, this section explores how celebrity chefs' travels abroad are also used to reflect on the meaning of food and identities at home. As Said argues in his work on Orientalism, visitors' images of the Orient say 'far more about the fears and desires of the West which produced it than … about the reality of life in the near East' (cited in Rose 1995: 93). Focusing on Jamie Oliver's continental travels in *Jamie's Great Escape* (2005) and *Jamie Does …* (2011), my analysis builds on earlier work by myself and others to examine how the representation of 'European' food culture is used not only to create distinctions between British and continental Europeans but also to reproduce a series of classed and gendered distinctions between 'good' and 'bad' forms of British identity (Bell and Hollows 2007; Leer and Kjaer 2015; Rossato 2015). I explore how these representations of Europeanness were particularly meaningful in a period leading up to the 2016 EU Referendum in which, as cultural intermediaries, celebrity chefs played a role in shaping the ways in which Europe was imagined (see also Chapter 8).

Both *Jamie's Great Escape* and *Jamie Does …* were broadcast during a boom in British TV culinary travelogues which included a significant number of tours of Italy. Alongside Jamie's series, other primetime television tours included *Two Greedy Italians* (2011–12) with chefs Gennaro Contaldo and Antonio Carluccio,[14] *Italy Unpacked* (2013–15) with chef Giorgio Locatelli and art critic Andrew Graham-Dixon and a number of series featuring Gino D'ACampo (2013–20) (for more on D'Acampo, see Wall 2018).[15] All of these series featured chefs whose Italian heritage, to various degrees, conferred an 'authenticity' that 'granted authority to comment on (and on behalf of) Italy and Italians' while 'performing the cultural Other to British audiences' (Wall 2018: 4–5).[16] In contrast, Jamie Oliver is not Italian but instead adopts an elective Italian identity, evident from his Italian mod styling and Vespa in *The Naked Chef* through to his professional identification with Italian restaurants and his identification of Gennaro Contaldo as his 'London father'.

This elective identity, that suggests that being British need not preclude also being European, is of particular interest in the context of Brexit Britain and is emphasized in the introduction to the book *Jamie's Italy* that accompanied the TV series.

> Since I was a teenager I've been totally besotted by the love, passion and verve for food, family and life itself that just about all the Italian people have, no matter where they're from or how rich or poor they might be … And you know what? I

should have been bloody Italian – why, oh why, was I born in Southend-on-Sea? No disrespect to my roots, of course! The truth is, when I'm in Italy, I feel Italian … and you know why? Because, like all Italians, I love my family for better or for worse and because food is something I've grown up around.

(Oliver 2005: ix–x)

While Oliver champions Britain and Britishness in shows such as *Jamie's Great Britain*, his star image represents the desirability of a hybrid identity, a way of being British but feeling Italian. The narrative of *Jamie's Great Escape* is structured around the need to escape Britain as a modern, industrial and commercial country with 'the pressures of being Jamie Oliver Inc.' where he is constrained by his own celebrity so that he can feel once again *at home* by connecting with the 'authenticity' of Italy and Italian cookery (Bell and Hollows 2007). In this way, the series contributes to a long history in which Italy operated as an 'Arcadian backdrop against which the existential dilemmas off modernity could be illuminated and explored by subjects from elsewhere' (Parkins 2004: 258). As he puts it in the voiceover at the start of each episode, 'It's gonna make me a better cook, I think it's gonna make me a better husband, I think it's gonna make me a better boss, I think it's gonna make me happier.' In this way, Jamie reproduces a longstanding myth of Italy, popularized by nineteenth-century authors who visited as part of the Grand Tour, which uses a 'premodern and primitive Italy to critique the ambiguities and forms of alienation that accompanied modernity' (Luzzi 2002: 50).

The series allows Jamie to examine the culinary problems of modern Britain by contrasting them to the seemingly authentic culinary traditions of Italy. With a nod back to *Jamie's School Dinners* and forward to *Jamie's Ministry of Food*, he suggests that Britain, with its love of processed and convenience food, can learn from Italian food culture. Echoing the values of simplicity, artisanship and tradition that characterize much contemporary foodie discourse (Johnston and Baumann 2015), Jamie extols the virtues of 'poor people's cooking' which, he claims, 'is some of the best cooking *in* Spain and Italy; these sort of artisan things aren't artisan things, they're *normal*; it's tradition, it's everyday, it's normal'. The Italian working classes appear to offer magical solutions to the problems of modern life in Britain. In *Jamie Does …*, he pursues a similar theme on a visit to the French Pyrenees where he enthuses 'What I love about this area is that some of the poorest people …. have eaten like kings'. This reproduces a 'romanticization of poverty' also found in foodie discourses in which Jamie recommends 'the seeming advantages of impoverished environments, creating an idea of the deliciousness of poverty' and fetishizing the poor as the best cooks (Johnston and Baumann 2015: 158).

This romanticization of continental working-class and peasant food cultures is done at the expense of their urban British counterparts.[17] At the opening of *Jamie's Great Escape*, Oliver comments:

I also wanna find out why millions of Italian families eat so well while millions of British families eat such scrote … I'm gonna be learning from people that count, the working class, builders, or you know, cucina povera, the poor man's cooking.

Of course, these are not any British families. His comment gestures towards those eating turkey twizzlers and kebab and chips in shows such as *Jamie's School Dinners* and *Jamie's Ministry of Food* (Bell and Hollows 2007; see Chapter 6). Indeed, Jamie explicitly identified the difference between continental and British working-class culinary culture in a controversial interview in the *Radio Times* magazine while promoting *Jamie's Money Saving Meals* in 2013. 'I'm not judgmental', he says before judging people who spend money on takeaways eaten in front of the 'massive fucking TV'. He continued:

> I meet people who say, 'You don't understand what it's like'. I just want to hug them and teleport them to the Sicilian street cleaner who has 25 mussels, 10 cherry tomatoes and a packet of spaghetti for 60 pence, and knocks out the most amazing pasta. You go to Italy or Spain and they eat well on not much money. We've missed out on that in Britain, somehow.
>
> (cited in Sherwin and Morse 2013)

Jamie's embrace of working-class European food may appear democratic with its emphasis on (allegedly) cheap ingredients and simple cooking methods but it also works to 'simultaneously perpetuate distinction' and 'taste hierarchies', not least between the taste for freshly cooked mussels and the taste for takeaway kebabs (Johnston and Baumann 2015: 84). Viewers of Jamie's travelogues are invited to improve their cooking practices through an identification with European popular culinary traditions and a disidentification with the mass-produced foods associated with the British working class.[18]

As I have already shown, television culinary travelogues are often structured by an opposition between the celebrity chef who embodies movement and those on their itinerary who represent fixity and authenticity, positions which are central to Ulf Hannerz's antinomy between the cosmopolitan and the local. Jamie fetishizes 'authentic' local Italian dishes but his viewers are invited to identify with his position as a cosmopolitan subject with an omnivorous appetite who can move across boundaries (Bell and Hollows 2007). If, as Hannerz (1996: 111) observes, 'there can be no cosmopolitans without locals', then Jamie is distinguished from those whose appetites are bound by locality, tradition or custom. Therefore, while he celebrates the lack of choice that makes Italian 'cucina povera' more creative, he also complains about Italian insularity:

> I sometimes find it frustrating that Italians can be stubborn and not want to try a dish or a different combination of flavours because it's not from their village or region or it's not the way their mamma would do it.
>
> (Oliver 2005: xv)

In some ways, the Italian working class are represented as fixed in the culinary practices as are the UK's 'immigrant communities' who maintain their culinary traditions in *Jamie's Great Britain*. Both groups are turned into 'bearers of "authenticity"' while Jamie distinguishes what can be authentic (Leer and Kjær 2015: 324).

Furthermore, *Jamies Great* Escape appears to centre around what Meaghan Morris identifies as 'a very powerful cultural link ... dear to a masculinist tradition inscribing "home" as the site of both frustrating containment ... and of a truth to be discovered' (cited in Morley 2000: 68). While it is not only women who are represented as fixed in their tastes, the 'authentic' local Italian cooking that Jamie simultaneously celebrates and dismisses is feminized, kept alive by the figure Jean Duruz (2004: 61) dubs 'Cooking Woman' who 'feeds the nostalgic "cosmopolitan" – literally [and] figuratively'.[19] He frequently invokes 'the mamma' and 'the nonna' who reproduce both family and culinary tradition. Jamie, on the other hand, has the power to make creative choices. In *Jamie Does ...* he repeatedly celebrates – and then transforms – local dishes to mark out his difference and distinction by transgressing culinary boundaries. He adds olive oil to gravlax in Stockholm and makes his 'classic minestrone' in Venice with baby farfalle pasta which he says is 'completely wrong'. In contrast, Italians who deviate from tradition have to be restored to their place as upholders of Italianicity: in *Jamie's Great Escape*, the monks he discovers living on a diet of processed foods have to be taught to cook 'Italian' food by Jamie (see Bell and Hollows 2007; Leer and Kjaer 2015; Rossato 2015). As a cosmopolitan subject, Jamie is allowed choice, mobility and change while those who represent the local – in ways that are powerfully classed, raced and gendered – are fixed as 'authentic' guardians of tradition for him to enjoy (Bell and Hollows 2007).

Conclusion

Television culinary travelogues are a key format for producing ideas about the nation and national cuisines. Many culinary travelogues around the UK have reproduced limited and conservative ideas of Britishness rooted in a pre-modern past and commodified for a global market in 'heritage'. These images may seem both innocent and dated but they play a role in the politics of the present. For example, in May 2019 – when images of Britain as a 'world-beating' power were helping to sustain a fantasy of a glorious post-Brexit future – Tory MPs Michael Gove and Nigel Huddleston drew on this iconography when they occupied parliament with claims about Britain's 'world-beating asparagus' produced by 'British farmers' in 'beautiful part[s] of the country'.[20] Representations of Britishness in culinary travelogues help to sustain wider political fantasies of a self-sufficient nation with distinctive traditions, of an independent Britain based on agricultural production and a proud fishing heritage, that featured heavily in images of a post-Brexit promised land. I develop some of these ideas in the discussion of Brexit in the next chapter.

While culinary travelogues celebrate British food culture, not everyone is included in these constructions of nation. In series such as *Jamie's Great Britain*, the embrace of migrant dishes and culinary traditions in the UK is used to represent the nation as dynamic, modern and inclusive. However, while 'ethnic' foods are valued because they add 'spice' to a British food culture characterized by hybridity and diversity, their 'authentic' flavours are associated with a fixed and unchanging monoculture (Leer 2019). Furthermore, distinctions between 'us' and 'them' continue to structure these representations despite their seeming inclusivity. This also has an impact on the careers of television chefs from ethnic minority backgrounds who, like their restaurant counterparts (see Chapter 1), often end up as representatives of foods from their 'homeland'. This can be found in BBC series such as *Indian Food Made Easy* (2007) with Anjum Anand, *Caribbean Food Made Easy* (2009) with Levi Roots and *Chinese Food Made Easy* (2008) with Ching-He Huang. Nadiya Hussain has skilfully negotiated these oppositions by using the culinary travelogue format to represent Bangladeshi and British foods and identities as inherently entwined. While *Nadiya's British Food Adventure* includes many familiar and conventional British dishes, her series represents the UK's ethnic minorities as part of a dynamic, British food culture – rather than fixed and static – through forms of 'everyday multiculturalism'.

However, the parameters of the nation in representations of British food culture are structured by class as well as race and ethnicity. In 2018, Jamie Oliver used images of nation in comments about the difference between middle- and working-class approaches to healthy eating. Addressing an implied middle-class reader, he said, 'We can't judge *our* equivalent of logic on *their's* because *they're* in a different gear, *almost in a different country*' (cited in Snead 2018; my italics). The suggestion that working-class people 'are in a different gear' suggests they are less dynamic and slower to move than their middle-class counterparts who characterize modern British food culture. More generally, while traditional working-class dishes such as Lancashire hotpot are included in representations of the national cuisine, culinary travelogues take place in a Britain in which contemporary white working-class food practices are largely invisible. Furthermore, these classed depictions of different nations – in which parts of the working class were 'in a different country' – had a wider resonance in the context of Brexit, in which the typical anti-EU Leave voter was characterized as white, Northern (English) and working class and the typical pro-EU Remain voter as part of a white, cosmopolitan and metropolitan elite.

Chapter 8

CELEBRITY CHEFS AND BRITISH FOOD CULTURE IN
THE TIMES OF BREXIT AND COVID-19

Michaela de Soucey (2010: 433) argues that 'foods constitute cultural and political resources that affect and respond to political agendas'. It is, therefore, unsurprising that celebrity chefs, as figures of legitimacy and authority on food, shape the narrative and discursive frameworks through which we understand food and which impact on everyday food practices. This book has already demonstrated a wide range of ways in which celebrities mediate political issues and, in this final chapter, I turn to two themes that have dominated life in the UK in recent years: Brexit and the Covid-19 pandemic. As I go on to show, food has operated as a key mechanism for discussing aspects of Brexit and the pandemic and celebrity chefs have shaped how they have been narrated, imagined and experienced.

Brexit has been inescapable for anyone living in the UK during the 2010s. Currents of Euroscepticism, which are a longstanding feature of British national life, were prominent in the lead-up to the 1975 Referendum on the UK's membership of the European Community and continued to circulate throughout Britain's membership of the European Union (EU). As the Conservative Party became worried that they were losing right-wing voters to the UK Independence Party (UKIP) with its anti-EU rhetoric, Prime Minister David Cameron promised a referendum on the UK's continued membership of the EU if his Conservative Party won the 2015 General Election. The result was the 2016 referendum on the UK's membership of the EU which divided Britain: 52 per cent of votes supported leaving the EU, and 48 per cent of votes were in favour of remaining in the EU. The political landscape of the following years was dominated by political divisions over Europe, and the Brexit process. The UK's withdrawal from the EU was finally confirmed in January 2020. While the intricacies of Brexit were unique to the UK, it occurred in a wider global context in which there was a rise of right-wing nationalism and anti-immigration rhetoric in many nations.

As I go on to show in this chapter, the 'aesthetics of Brexit often have a distinctive alimentary expression' (Rahman 2020: 72), with 'questions of food trade, sovereignty and safety' bound up with 'the sentiments of gastronationalism' (Edwards 2019: 633). However, food has long played a central role in how the British imagine their relationships to Europe and the EU. In news reporting, food is a well-established vehicle for Eurosceptic sentiment that fosters identifications opposed to Europe (Anderson and Weymouth 1999). As Menno Spiering (2006: 47) puts it, 'Eurosceptic discourse is larded with references to food'. Indeed, this was a sufficiently significant part of British popular culture for the 1984 Christmas special of the popular BBC sitcom *Yes, Minister* to feature a narrative about a European plot to rename British sausages 'Emulsified High-Fat Offal Tubes'.[1]

The years preceding the EU Referendum exemplified how 'food and identity are becoming like the "Euro", a single common currency through which to debate Europeanness and the implications of economic globalization' (Leitch 2003: 442). For example, media coverage of the horsemeat scandal in 2013, in which unacknowledged horse DNA was discovered in supermarket burgers, raised wider questions about Britain's membership of the EU. The scandal was used to question the EU's legitimacy, to assert the importance of British sovereignty and to support 'Buy British' campaigns in an expression of everyday gastronationalism (Abbots and Coles 2013: 544). By 'Europeanizing' the horsemeat scandal, the press represented 'British identity as besieged by processes outside of its control as a nation' and identified the need to protect national boundaries from 'contamination' (Ibrahim and Howarth 2017: 222; see also Ibrahim and Howarth 2016). Elsewhere, Eurosceptic arguments invoked explicit forms of gastronationalism, representing supposed threats to British food practices as 'assaults on heritage and culture' (de Soucey 2010: 433). The Leave campaign championed Britain's right to consume custard cream biscuits, bendy bananas and prawn cocktail crisps in the face of alleged attacks on them from the EU, attempting to bolster national identity against supposed threats to the British way of life. These alleged attacks formed the basis of a series of 'Euromyths' which included the false claims that the EU had tried to ban prawn cocktail crisps and bendy bananas and eliminate Britain's beloved custard creams.

In the first part of this chapter, I explore how celebrity chefs shaped the ways in which the UK's relationship to the EU was imagined. I have already touched on these issues earlier in the book: for example, in my analysis of how *Hugh's Fish Fight* represented the EU as a threat to British fishing and national sovereignty (Chapter 5) and my discussion of how pro-European identifications were promoted in culinary tours of the Continent (Chapter 7). In this chapter, I look more closely at how celebrity chefs represented the terms of the Brexit debate. Using a case study of the contradictory figure of Jamie Oliver, I demonstrate how representations of a diverse range of issues – from pig welfare in Denmark to restaurant staffing in the UK – were caught up with wider anti- and pro-EU discourses. This is followed by a more focused analysis of the power of celebrity chefs to shape political agendas in a case study of the well-publicized campaign against US chlorinated chicken. I demonstrate how the campaign created a negative political consensus against the spectre of Americanization that problematized wider debates about British sovereignty and the UK's relationship with the EU.

Food also played a key role in how the Covid-19 pandemic was imagined and experienced in the UK. Indeed, food figured from the outset as racist imagery about Wuhan wet markets and the practice of eating bats cemented initial ideas of Coronavirus as a 'Chinese virus'.[2] As Elaine Swan (2020: 693) observes, during spring 2020, food was woven through many aspects of the pandemic,

From racist memes about Chinese eating habits, to middle class social media images of sourdough baking, youtube cook-alongs and zoom dinner parties, through to media coverage of food bank volunteers, food for nurses and the so-called panic food buying and stockpilers and new reports about the so-called resilience of the global food system.

The pandemic was also particularly tough for the hospitality industry with escalating job losses and falling profits; food outlets were forced to close resulting in increasing political activism by leading chefs to protect their businesses and workers. As 2020 progressed, 'pandemic events … intertwined with other phenomena', including Brexit narratives in the UK and EU, transnational Black Lives Matter activism, national elections, environmental politics and a whole series of other 'global economic and political strains and crises' (Bentley and Borkowsky 2020: 11).

Developing themes from Chapter 6, my analysis of celebrity chefs and the pandemic focuses on two very different meanings of austerity that emerged in representations of food during 2020. First, I examine the hastily produced cooking shows broadcast during spring 2020 in which celebrity chefs lifestyled the lockdown experience using nostalgic Second World War imagery and ideas of 'blitz spirit' (Martin 2020b; McCormick 2020). I highlight how these series used romanticized images of a virtuous 'austerity chic' in which austerity was represented in terms of the absence of consumer choice. Second, I explore very different images of austerity demonstrated by the absence of food. These emerged in celebrity campaigns about food poverty during the pandemic and, in particular, via images of hungry children. I examine how footballer Marcus Rashford and a range of celebrity chefs helped to reshape the public understanding of food poverty and to denaturalize the government's austerity agenda.

Jamie Does … *Brexit*

As the Referendum and subsequent Brexit process dominated British political life, many celebrities intervened in the debate and advocated their support for Remain or Leave positions. Celebrity chefs were no exception. Even Delia Smith, usually a relatively low-key figure, addressed a huge 2018 rally in London organized by Remain supporters who wanted a second referendum and she personally funded coaches to enable people to travel to the follow-up event (O'Connor 2019). However, this is not the only way in which celebrity chefs shaped public debate. Through media appearances, writing and wider public interventions, celebrity chefs played a wider role in shaping Brexit discourses.

Using Jamie Oliver as a case study, this section explores some of the range of ways in which celebrity chefs shaped both pro-European and Eurosceptic positions. With his strong identification with Italy (see Chapter 7), Jamie might initially appear as a natural supporter of EU membership. Although he certainly adopted this position in the post-Referendum period, he is a far more contradictory

Figure 8.1 Celebrity chefs are part of political life: Clive Lewis MP carries a Delia Smith – inspired placard at the march for a People's Vote on the Brexit deal, 23 March 2019 (Credit: Emma Hampton).

figure than this suggests. As I go on to demonstrate, Jamie's position on a range of issues over a sustained period helped to reproduce anti-EU sentiments. This demonstrates some of the complexity of British relationships with the EU and illustrates Michael Skey's (2012: 476) argument that people can 'move between more (or less) cosmopolitan attitudes and perspectives, so that showing solidarity for an individual or group at one moment does not preclude the utilization of cultural stereotypes or support for exclusionary practices at another'.

Some of Jamie's most common complaints about the EU focused on Europe as a site of regulation and bureaucracy. For example, in his culinary travelogue *Jamie Does ...*, he dismisses Sweden's statism. 'I'm trying to think about one downside to Sweden and the only one I can think of is 80% tax', he quips. This comment echoes a longstanding distinction within British Euroscepticism between a positive Europe associated with art and culture (and, in Jamie's case, culinary culture in particular) and a negative Europe associated with the 'wrong' kinds of political structures and forms of government (Spiering 2014: 49). However, the focus of Jamie's critique is more often the EU rather than Europe.[3] In throwaway lines, he reproduces Euromyths and 'truths' about the EU's threats to British national sovereignty, echoing well-established tropes of Eurosceptic sentiment in the British press (Anderson and Weymouth 1999; Wring 2016). For example, in *Jamie Does ... Andalucia*, he uses a sarcastic tone as he tells the audience that 'I'm using their local cucumbers' but people will have to use 'the regular perfect EU straight ones' at home.

However, Jamie went much further in portraying the EU as a threat to British sovereignty. In November 2008, he acted as a witness on the government's Health Committee inquiry into health inequalities. Much to the joy of Eurosceptics on the panel, he stated

> I've got nothing nice to say about the EU at all. I really haven't. It saps the life … out of our farmers. Remember when the cucumber came in – if it's over that much of a bend, they can't sell it. How dare they. How dare they.

He continued

> I wish it had never existed and labelling is a perfect example. Great Britain cannot choose what its minimum standards for labelling and clarity is cos it has to go through the EU and the EU has got a lot more to worry about than Great Britain. I can take you to a supermarket now and it will say 'sourced in the UK' and on the back it will say 'from Denmark'. How dare they.

The populist indignation of Jamie's escalating 'how dare theys' would become familiar in media contributions from 'ordinary people' who used 'emotional and expressive' language to convey 'resentment and frustration and anger' in debates about Brexit (Calhoun 2017: 62; see also Davies 2018). In this contribution, Jamie succinctly articulated many key strands of anti-EU discourse. The EU and its regulations are represented as a threat to the British economy, the British way of life and British sovereignty. Indeed, it is perhaps unsurprising that Vote Leave Media (2008) posted a video clip of Oliver's contribution to the Committee on YouTube called 'Celebrity Chef Jamie Oliver Hates the European Union', while the UKIP supporting RobbingHoodUK (2014) extracted it in another YouTube video called 'Could Jamie Oliver be UKIP's Secret Weapon?'

Anti-EU sentiments also featured in *Jamie Saves Our Bacon* (2009), aired as part of Channel 4's Food Fight season, in which Jamie campaigned for better animal welfare standards in the pork industry. The show examined the differences between minimum animal welfare standards in the UK and other EU nations and, in particular, highlighted the Danish use of 'shocking' and 'inhumane' sow stalls that were banned in the UK.[4] The show created an opposition between British pork production which privileges animal welfare issues and an EU-permitted system that privileges profit and is 'an accountant's dream' and 'quite efficient if you don't care about pig welfare'.[5] EU imports were represented as a threat to British farmers who could not compete economically with a system which enables such intensive pork production. Viewers were invited to act morally by buying British bacon in order to support both animal welfare and British farmers.

Jamie also claimed that EU legislation threatened British people's ability to consume ethically. Echoing longstanding news discourses that represent the EU as interfering with 'our' food, Jamie claimed that EU labelling within the single market prevented British consumers from knowing whether they are buying British pork. MPs were described as 'powerless' to assert British sovereignty. Jamie pleaded with the audience to act together to 'save our bacon', articulating ethical concerns about animal welfare with nationalist modes of political consumption. The show closed with a further affective appeal – 'If you've watched the show tonight and don't buy British, shame on you, shame on you'. This closed down questions about who can afford to buy British by casting those who do not as both unethical and unpatriotic (while also marginalizing wider questions about animal welfare and the ethics of eating meat).

Jamie's comments about the EU both contributed to and helped to reproduce wider Eurosceptic discourses within the UK in which food became a contested site in claims about national sovereignty, identity and economic power. Although some of his comments were hijacked by right wing anti-EU UKIP supporters to attach the power of the Jamie brand to their cause, his anti-EU sentiments cannot simply be identified with the right. Food imagery is also used in left Euroscepticism as Marxist historian E.P. Thompson's (1975) comments about going into Europe in the 1970s make clear. He portrayed Europhiles as rampant consumers 'digesting a pasta of Fiats, a washing-up machine meunière' and claimed the 'Eurostomach is the logical extension of the existing eating-out habits of Oxford and North London' (see Rahman (2020) for commentary on similar imagery in recent debates about Brexit). Indeed, left-leaning newspaper the *Daily Mirror* (2014) reported favourably on Oliver's criticism of the potential threat that a transatlantic trade deal between the United States and EU posed to food standards, reinforcing objections to the EU more commonly associated with a left-wing pro-Brexit position.

Oliver's contribution to all these debates may appear surprising in a post-Referendum context in which he has been continually portrayed, primarily in the right-wing press, as 'Remainer Jamie Oliver'. This identity was cemented a few days after the EU Referendum when he posted a video of an EU flag on Instagram and confessed to being 'very sad' with the result. In a comment that garnered considerable attention in the British press, he continued

> I BEG YOU ONE THING GREAT BRITAIN. Give me Boris Johnson as Prime Minister and I'm done. I'm out ... So speak up people – let's stop being spectators! We cannot let this happen – share the hell out of this #BuggerOffBoris

While his comments might seem a surprising change of position from his anti-EU position-taking discussed above, they are consistent with his longstanding European and cosmopolitan identifications (and, perhaps, with his business interests). In retrospect, his post might seem ill-advised – Johnson became Prime Minister and Oliver is still living in Britain. It also enabled Jamie to operate as a figure upon which the press (particularly the right-wing press) could project a series of 'Remainer' identities. These were far more consistent with his established celebrity identity than his earlier anti-EU statements, especially in a context in which the Leave vote was as much a vote against cosmopolitan London elites (which Jamie is identified with) as it was against the EU (Calhoun 2017). In the following years, Jamie's previously anti-EU sentiments were quickly forgotten and he made further strongly anti-Brexit statements, including a much reported interview with German media in which he said he was 'angry' and 'embarrassed' about Brexit which was a 'really, really bad idea' (cited in Withers 2018). In the pro-Brexit right-wing press, he operated as one of a number of public figures who was identified by the epithet 'Remainer', epitomizing both a European-identified elite and the regulatory nanny state.

While a celebrity chef's position on Brexit might seem both trivial and unimportant, celebrities such as Jamie Oliver provided appealing ways for news outlets to discuss the meaning of food and Brexit. This matters because news media remain 'the main source of information for the public on food Brexit issues' (Strong and Wells 2020: 2197). Jamie was linked to a range of stories about Brexit but one key theme was its impact on the restaurant industry. Amid wider stories about a shortage of trained chefs, Oliver highlighted the potential impact of Brexit on British restaurants soon after the Referendum – 'It's an impossibility that Britain can function without European staff', he told *Good Housekeeping* magazine (cited in Saul 2016).[6] However, these concerns quickly became linked to the fortunes of his own restaurants as he blamed an immanent Brexit as a factor that caused a series of business failures from 2017 onwards. This provoked considerable ridicule as a series of celebrity chefs, media commentators and political figures mocked Jamie for blaming Brexit for his own personal failure. For example, following the collapse of the struggling Jamie's Italian chain in August 2019, Marco Pierre White called Oliver 'delusional', adding that he should 'put his hand up and say "I f***** up"', adding that Brexit was 'the lamest excuse in the world' (cited in Perring 2019). These comments operated within a wider climate in which opposition to Brexit was portrayed as a failure of masculinity following a Referendum which gave 'a binary choice and a clear winner and loser [that] appeals to the competitive element of masculinity' (Millar 2018; see also Higgins 2020). Gordon Ramsay's response to the loss of EU labour in the restaurant industry was to castigate the 'lazy' British who refused to compete with migrant labour prepared to 'work twice as hard for less money', claiming this was an opportunity and just the 'big kick up the a—' that the restaurant industry needed (Singh 2017).

The other key theme in Jamie's post-Referendum commentary on Brexit focused on food standards and regulation. While he acknowledged that 'clearer labelling' might be one of the potential 'upsides of Brexit' (cited in Dirnhuber 2018), his rhetoric shifted from the EU as a site of unwanted regulation to the threats posed by a *lack* of EU regulation after Brexit. However, as I go on to show in the next section, Jamie used the question of regulation to build a far more wide-ranging negative consensus, not against EU regulation but against Americanized deregulation that also was seen to pose a threat to British sovereignty.

'Meat from Hell' and the spectre of Americanization

This section examines the power of celebrity chefs to shape British food policy and political agendas in Brexit Britain. In the post-Referendum period between 2017 and 2020, this was demonstrated by the fight to protect British food standards from US influences. The government promised a bright, post-Brexit economic future, free from EU restrictions and regulation, that would be secured through a US trade deal. At the same time, there were increasing fears that US goods, subject to lower degrees of regulation, would threaten consumer standards and protections that the British currently enjoyed, in part through its EU membership. US 'chlorinated chicken' emerged as a 'folk devil' which represented the threat of Americanization and upon which a series of fears about both food standards and the UK's position in the world could be projected. The discourses through which the meanings of chlorinated chicken were produced, as Abbots and Coles (2013: 257) have argued in a different context, 'variously assemble, dissemble and reassemble, and/or are otherwise appropriated, to make ideological claims about not only our food, but the contemporary systems through which we provision it'. The use of oppositions between the UK and the United States worked to 'territorialize morality by delineating spaces of good (food)'.

As the implications of Brexit continued to unravel in 2017, there were an increasing number of British newspaper articles about how a new trade deal with the United States could threaten UK food standards by enabling goods such as 'chlorinated' or 'chlorine-washed' chicken to be sold in the UK, practices banned under EU regulations. While chlorinated chicken was not the only issue, it emerged as the focal point for a range of social anxieties across a range of fields that 'circulate[d] in unpredictable ways' (Jackson 2015: 86; Jackson et al. 2013: 29). Some of the key concerns centred on intensive industrial farming practices in the United States, with 'inhumane and unsanitary standards', that produced bacteria-ridden poultry and necessitated a chlorine wash to make them safe for human consumption (Dawson 2017). Other causes of concern were raised about whether chlorine-washing was sufficiently effective to prevent health risks such as salmonella and whether the chlorination process introduced carcinogens into food. Because there was no need for chlorination to be declared in food labelling, it was argued that consumers would be unable to know if their chicken had been chlorine-washed and, therefore, unable to make informed choices about whether to consume it (Dawson 2017). Anti-Brexit politicians such as Liam Fox MP, then Secretary of State for International Trade, mocked the British media for being 'obsessed with chlorine-washed chicken', which he saw as part of a plot to 'thwart' Brexit (Sculthorpe and Ferguson 2017). As media commentary about the potential threat of chlorinated chicken continued to resurface into 2019, other pro-US trade Brexiteers claimed concerns about chicken were a red herring and used to mask value-based choices about animal welfare rather than food safety (Blanchard 2019).

Chlorinated chicken came to represent the spectre of Americanization in a Britain beset by anxieties about its power, sovereignty, autonomy and place in a post-Referendum world. Commentary revived tropes found in fears about Americanization between the 1930s and 1960s in which the United States was associated with a 'levelling down' of standards because it was based on forms of 'inhuman', 'industrial barbarism' which privileged profit (Hebdige 1988: 47, 52). For example, the *Mirror* newspaper ran a series of articles which portrayed a 'cruel'

US poultry industry run in 'secrecy' by large 'cartels' and chickens raised in a 'silent hall of hell' (Bucktin 2020a). In another *Mirror* article with the headline 'Horror of US "Meat From Hell" Pumped Full of Hormones That Could Flood Britain', Christopher Bucktin (2020b) not only linked the United States with drugged-up animals, violence and desensitization to cruelty but a levelling-down process associated with 'a race to the bottom'. Even Meghan Markle entered the debate in March 2019 when she claimed US agriculture had become too 'industrial' (Forsey and Jones 2019).

US Ambassador Robert Wood Johnson mocked the concerns about chlorine-washed chicken as a form of EU protectionism that wanted to maintain a 'museum of agriculture' and privilege 'tradition over innovation' (cited in Howell 2019). However, in the process, he 'nourished a counter-myth of embattled … traditionalism' based on romanticized, pastoral images of pre-industrial British farming (Poole 2020: 142; see Chapter 7). Like campaigns against Americanized fast food in France, the fight against chlorinated chicken did not simply include radical critiques of US neoliberal capitalism and environmental destruction but also could be tied to a defence of 'indigenous cultural heritage and sovereignty', a defence of traditional British foodways and agriculture (Poole 2020: 148; see also Taylor 2001). This helped to pave the way for a 'negative consensus' in which more conservative and radical views could unite to campaign on the terms of the US trade deal.

In the second half of 2020, the right-wing *Mail Online* newspaper identified a 'powerful alliance of chefs, celebrities and charities' who wanted to shape post-Brexit trade deals in order to maintain food standards (Owen and Carlin 2020a). Celebrity chefs such as Jamie Oliver, Hugh Fearnley-Whittingstall and Jimmy Doherty joined together with other celebrities – most notably, Joe Wicks, a high-profile fitness guru and bestselling cookbook author whose popular daily YouTube videos during the UK's first Covid-19 lockdown had earned him the title of 'the nation's P.E. teacher'. The National Farmers Union (NFU) had launched a petition to maintain food standards that called on the government to make it a legal requirement that all food imports were subject to the same 'high' welfare and environmental standards as those legally required on UK farms (Laville 2020). Backed by an unlikely alliance between the ambivalently Leave-identified right-wing *Mail on Sunday* and 'Remainer Jamie',[7] the petition gained increased momentum after Jamie published a letter throwing his support behind it in the newspaper in May 2020. His letter articulated the need for a safe food supply, the needs of British farmers and child health (Owen and Carlin 2020a).

The threat of America to British sovereignty over food standards succeeded in aligning both former Leave and Remain supporters around a 'negative consensus' in what was commonly seen as a divided country. Jamie's support for the campaign was consistent with his previous support for transparent labelling and the role of food in child health as well as his ambivalent support of welfare standards in British farming. The *Mail on Sunday* put a defence of Britishness at the heart of their campaign to 'save our family farms' which relied on images of the small, independent farmer popularized by culinary travelogues (see Chapter 7).

These images drew on well-established connections between pre-modern rural landscapes and the essence of Englishness, conveniently forgetting how the ownership of much of British agriculture is concentrated in relatively few hands and heavily industrialized. The quintessentially British nature of the campaign was enhanced when *Great British Bake Off* judge Prue Leith offered her support in October 2020, claiming 'Everybody who cares about British food standards should back our farmers' (cited in Owen and Carlin 2020b). Unlike Jamie and Hugh, Leith was an outspoken Brexit supporter and a very public member of the Conservative Party and her son (Danny Kruger) is a Tory MP. Yet by late October 2020, she had left the Tory party in protest against the government's failure to 'enshrine high food standards in law' (cited in Mikhailova and Aitchison 2020).

Despite the campaign's use of conservative images of Britishness against the threat of Americanized produce, Jamie took a much more careful approach with his class politics than in many of his earlier campaigns. Perhaps because the campaign took place outside the generic conventions of television – and the use of consumer education and makeovers in many campaigning culinary documentaries – and because the pandemic had escalated concerns about food poverty, Jamie was freed up to argue that low standard American food couldn't simply be regulated through consumer choice because food poverty impacted on the ability to choose.

> it's not as simple as saying consumers can simply choose to buy something else – we know that the reality for millions of Britons looks very different. More families than ever are worried about where their next meal is coming from, the reliance on food banks has gone through the roof and unemployment is set to reach new highs, so families will find it even more challenging to afford a nutritious meal. A recent poll from the consumer organization Which? showed that people from lower-income families feel even more strongly about the need to uphold our UK food standards – they shouldn't be a luxury reserved for the well-off.
>
> (Oliver 2020)

Unlike the earlier horsemeat scandal in which uninformed consumers seeking cheap deals were seen as 'complicit' with powerful industrialized big agriculture (Abbots and Coles 2013: 543), here consumers were portrayed as victims of government policy.

The anti-regulation and pro-Brexit right-wing of the Tory party ridiculed Jamie as a do-gooder who was out of his depth in the world of trade deals. They claimed that Jamie represented middle-class concerns rather than the rights of working-class consumers: 'what he is really doing is defending a transfer of wealth from the poor to the rich' asserted former Tory MEP Daniel Hannan in the right-wing *Sunday Telegraph*. The *Mail*'s key competitor, the *Express*, also tried to discredit Jamie and the campaign by dubbing him a 'former Remain campaigner' and his concerns as 'hysterical'. To back up the argument, the article included tweets that dismissed the chef's concerns as ridiculous: 'Are we using celebrity chefs as trade experts now?' (cited in Adedokun 2020). Yet the views Jamie sought to represent were less easily dismissed. Market research with former 'red wall' voters – largely working-class voters in areas that traditionally voted Labour but had switched to the Tories in the 2019 'Brexit election' – showed food standards were a key issue and not simply a middle-class Remainer concern (Harvey 2021).

As legislation went on a lengthy journey through parliament, the campaign appeared to have scored substantial successes in enshrining protection for British food standards in law. However, in January 2021, it became clear that these attempts had failed as the new Trade Bill was passed and gave ministers the power to allow food imports subject to lower legal standards than British produce (Harvey 2021). Although the folk devil of chlorinated chicken itself had been vanquished, many equivalent – and potentially much worse – practices had not.

The campaign against chlorine-washed chicken and other US industrial food practices might initially appear as yet another brand building exercise by celebrity chefs. However, the 'negative consensus' against US food was notable because it involved unlikely alliances that offered alternative ways of imagining British politics outside both the polarized Leave and Remain identities produced by Brexit and traditional party politics. This consensus was partly built on a deeply conservative notion of Britishness located in a pre-industrial rural idyll and a misrepresentation of British farming as simply comprised of small, family farmers. Yet 'buying British' and a championing of 'local' produce also suggested a search for a sense of security and integrity in a period when forms of 'trust' were sadly lacking in British politics (Abbots and Coles 2013: 540). It also enabled a coalition of alternative and conservative politics around a form of gastronationalism against the Conservative government. As I go on to show later in the chapter, these were not the only alliances forged around food politics during this period.

Lifestyling the pandemic

In media coverage of the pandemic, celebrity chefs emerged across many contexts. They acted as trusted sources of advice to help the public, as spokespeople for the hospitality industry, as community organizers feeding people in need and as campaigners against food poverty. While generally represented positively, some celebrity chefs were singled out for their bad practice: Gordon Ramsay was used to exemplify selfish behaviour when he flouted lockdown rules (Gallagher 2020). During a period in which celebrity excess and entitlement was viewed as unpatriotic,[8] the celebrities who became most 'resonant' were 'those who appeared to adjust their lifestyle' and demonstrated they shared in a common experience (Ellis Cashmore cited in Dunn 2020). In this section, I examine how celebrity chefs employed the conventions of cookery TV to lifestyle the pandemic. The analysis demonstrates how lockdown cookery shows used aestheticized and retro-inspired images of austerity and frugality in which the difficulties of foodwork in a pandemic were associated with the absence of the usual freedoms to choose food at whim enjoyed by many middle-class consumers.

While chefs' attempts to represent the concerns of their industry and keep their businesses afloat generated considerable publicity, celebrity chefs also played far more familiar roles in the pandemic's media landscape by providing guidance on what and how to eat. Many celebrity chefs took to YouTube and Instagram with videos about how to cook from store cupboard ingredients in short series such as Jason Atherton's Social Kitchen Isolation and Romy Gill's Quarantine Kitchen.[9] The prototype for these shows in a European context was Massimo Bottura's Kitchen Quarantine on Instagram, produced during Italy's early and widespread lockdown which started in March 2020. It featured his family's improvised dinner preparations from limited ingredients and leftovers, filmed by his daughter Alexa.[10] The series proved incredibly popular – the episode in which he made bechamel sauce drew in over half a million viewers – and enabled Bottura to also underscore his wider anti-food waste campaigning in an informal and friendly way (Cooke 2020). The style of these kinds of chefs' videos was distanced from both the pseudo-domestic sets of many mainstream cookery television shows and the slick, professionalism of some YouTubers (although some were filmed in empty restaurant kitchens). They reproduced the 'intimate' and 'idiosyncratic' conventions of some homemade food videos which are 'tied to the rhythms and rituals of individual households', partially dissolving the distance between chef and viewer and helping to create a sense of a shared experience (Lewis 2020: 62).

During the pandemic, television became a 'vital resource'. It offered a sense of 'ontological security', linked 'the intimate to the public' and operated as a 'master storyteller' in making sense of experience (Hermes and Hill 2020: 659). As lockdown reshaped or removed many weekly rhythms of routine activities, many people felt that 'time slowed down and became confused' (McCormick 2020: 349). New TV shows aimed to give structure to everyday life and, in spring 2020, Channel 4 and BBC1 introduced daily weekday cookery series to help people cope with the challenges of feeding work during lockdown. These TV shows were hastily put together – and, in the case of BBC's *Daily Kitchen*, plagued by technical problems that mirrored the experience of many people trying to work from home. Like many of the self-produced lockdown cooking shows on social media, these TV series took viewers into celebrity chefs' homes. As lockdown restrictions increased, Jamie Oliver's *Keep Cooking and Carry On* moved from a studio production to a homespun series filmed by his wife Jools. Viewers witnessed Jamie feeding a large family on a daily basis. By showing that celebrities are 'like us', the series emphasized the ways in which lockdown united people around common problems and practices, a message underscored by morale-boosting slogans such as 'we can do this' and 'we're in this together'.

However, as I go on to show, things were not so straightforward and these series generated controversy from the outset. When Jamie Oliver was chosen to present Channel 4's *Keep Cooking and Carry On* – with a call to 'big up those store cupboard and freezer faves and hero recipes you can use a lot of ways' (cited in Watson 2020) – there was a huge Twitter backlash, partly orchestrated by Jack Monroe (for the backstory on Monroe, see Chapter 6). In her (now deleted) tweets, Monroe claimed, 'That Man [is] to do a quick series on tinned/store cupboard meals and that sound you can hear is me ripping cans open with my bare hands and throwing all my work and years of experience IN MY OWN NICHE at the fucking wall'. With her claim that 'it's jollof rice all over again', Monroe suggested that Jamie was guilty of cultural appropriation of the under-appreciated skills and knowledge that come from being 'a starving suicidal single mum in a foodbank'. A large number of fans and supporters backed her and argued that she was uniquely suited to give culinary advice in times of hardship. This campaign was credited with Monroe's subsequent casting as the co-host on the BBC competitor series *Daily Kitchen*, paired with experienced BBC chef Matt Tebbutt who presented BBC1's *Saturday Kitchen*. In *Daily Kitchen*, the hosts were joined via video with a range of guests including cookery writers, gardening experts, doctors and nutritionists.[11] Meanwhile Monroe, to substantial acclaim, also used the hashtag #JackMonroesLockdownLarder to offer daily tips on Twitter on how to make best use of ingredients at hand (Watson 2020).

If this public disagreement about which celebrity 'owns' lockdown cooking demonstrates the continuing public investment in celebrity chefs, the pro-Monroe Twitter campaign was also instructive in two ways. First, it showed little recognition of TV chefs such as Oliver as skilled media professionals and presenters – knowledge of particular cooking techniques and life experience was privileged over television skills, reproducing the conception that TV presenting is unskilled work. Second, Jack's claims to 'ownership' of store cupboard ingredients through her identity as the 'tin can cook' who is 'cooking on a bootstrap' were based on well-established associations between tinned food, eating cheaply and the contents of foodbank parcels. These meanings of store cupboard ingredients were largely erased as food media represented lockdown cookery in terms of the romanticized austerity of a make do and mend wartime spirit rather than the enforced austerity imposed by food poverty.

In *Keep Cooking and Carry On*, Jamie appeared to be a reassuring and trusted voice – as he put it in episode one, these are 'challenging times guys but don't let food be one of the things that worry you'. Public and private spheres were blurred as filming moved into his home, strengthening the sense that, despite being a celebrity, Jamie was still very much 'like us'. As Jessica Martin (2020b: 2) points out in her analysis of another Channel 4 lockdown offering *Kirstie: Keep Crafting and Carry On*, viewers' ability to witness Jamie's family cooking and mealtimes in his own home also contributed to a wider 'glorification of the domestic as a space in which to shelter from an increasingly turbulent public sphere'. Offering a rather different mode of domestic masculinity than in *The Naked Chef*, Jamie demonstrated that caring for the family through feeding work was not just a feminine responsibility but a struggle that all family members in lockdown shared. Indeed, as a public figure on TV offering advice during the pandemic, his caring role also extended to the nation. Nonetheless, cheerful images of the Oliver family's food preparation and mealtimes were at odds with wider experiences of domestic life during the period. For many, home was an increasingly fraught space as people – particularly women – tried to juggle paid work, caring work and domestic labour in the same space (Martin 2020b; Swan 2020). Indeed, despite the glorification of the 'home as an apolitical retreat' from the virus (Martin 2020b: 3) and the happy scenes of a united Oliver family putting together a home-based TV show at a time of crisis, Jack Monroe's struggle to transform her kitchen into a public broadcast space on *Daily Kitchen* enabled a glimpse into more widespread experience of people working from home.

Keep Cooking and Carry On generated some favourable commentary. In the *Telegraph*, Michael Hogan (2020) portrayed Jamie as a 'national treasure' offering a 'public service' in a time of crisis. However, the early episodes of *Keep Cooking and Carry On* also attracted widespread criticism. Jamie's basic store cupboard ingredients – which included coriander stalks and capers – demonstrated he was not very much 'like us' at a time when there was difficulty securing ingredients, exhortations to restrict shopping trips to limit the spread of the virus, escalating food poverty and increased economic insecurity for many people. Jamie acknowledged people needed to be constantly 'flexible' and 'agile' by swapping ingredients but this use of management discourse also underscored that, even in a pandemic, people were still required to exhibit the qualities of the good neoliberal citizen. Despite some attempt to respond to criticisms in later episodes, Jamie – like many other brands – constructed a 'universal we' who are in it together that excluded many people who lacked the material and temporal resources to participate (Sobande 2020: 1035).

The sense that the nation shared a collective experience of the pandemic was reinforced in other ways in spring 2020. The British response to the coronavirus was often framed through 'battle metaphors' and 'military language' that evoked the Second World War (McCormick 2020: 325, 331). This infused how the virus was narrated and put into discourse: for example, in the numerous references to 'Blitz spirit', in calls to 'shield' the vulnerable and attempts to 'enlist' people to 'Keep Calm and Carry On' (McCormick 2020: 331–2). Indeed, this phrase was explicitly referenced in Jamie's lockdown series which also gestured to his established associations with Second World War imagery in *Jamie's Ministry of Food*. In *Daily Kitchen*, there were archive clips on rationing to reinforce advice that people should not hoard goods. The series also featured videos of 'tips from nans' who had 'first-hand experience' of making food go further. There was also old footage of 'the amazing Marguerite Patten', the cook most strongly associated with the wartime Ministry of Food, demonstrating wartime recipes for Woolton pie and summer pudding (for more on Patten, see Chapter 2).

While a wartime ethos of 'make do and mend' shaped representations of food in the period, these austerity practices were often transformed into aestheticized lifestyle activities. *Daily Kitchen* featured photos of banana bread made by children and the British media landscape was peppered with middle-class professionals engaged in complex experiments with sourdough while working from home. These 'appeals to a British "blitz spirit"', as Jessica Martin (2020b: 3) argues, also 'contribute[d] to an austerity discourse which encourages patriotic stoicism in the face of adversity and presents this stoicism as morally desirable'. However, 'making do' had a class dimension. The second episode of *Keep Cooking and Carry On* featured a 'thrifty' fish pie involving 600g of fish, a relatively expensive ingredient in the UK, in which austerity was signified through the absence of shellfish. Indeed, in *Keep Cooking and Carry On* and many other food texts during the period, austerity was not defined in terms of economic constraint but as the *absence of choice* – the inability for middle-class consumers to choose what to eat when they wanted it.

As I discuss later in this chapter, millions of households experienced intensifying food insecurity during the first UK lockdown (O'Connell and Brannen 2020). However, lifestyle media offered a 'performative thriftiness' (Martin 2020b: 3). Jamie's recommendations for 'humble ingredients' tapped into the virtue associated with thrift that had been established with 'austerity chic' (see Chapter 6) and allowed middle-class 'audiences to feel satisfied that the moral imperatives of frugality and modesty are being engaged' (Martin 2020b: 3). These trends were widespread: during the pandemic, evidence suggests there was a renewed interest in home pickling, a 600 per cent rise in 'UK social media mentions of pulses' and a more organized and attentive approach to meal planning and food waste (Guilbert 2020). Frugality was also a way of demonstrating creativity and culinary capital. On *Daily Kitchen*, Matt Tebbutt's recommendation that viewers should 'elevate' leftover Easter lamb was not presented as a response to necessity but as part of 'a personal project of self-improvement' through which the educated middle classes display their distinction (Wincott 2016: 38).

However, conflicts between different meanings of austerity emerged on *Daily Kitchen* as Jack Monroe punctured aestheticized middle-class notions of frugality. When Tebbutt suggested a broth using leftover lamb and (expensive) arborio rice, Monroe suggested that any long-grain rice could be substituted. This set the terms for an opposition between culinary legitimacy and economic constraint that resurfaced during the series: as Monroe put it, 'I'm sure yours is much nicer but mine would be cheaper'. Throughout the series, Monroe's budget suggestions made *Daily Kitchen* appear more inclusive but failed to displace the legitimacy of Tebbutt's culinary tastes. Despite showing admiration for some of her ideas, Tebbutt's screwed up face also demonstrated visceral rejection of some of her recipes and he proclaimed that her recipe for spinach and chickpea stew was 'pretty basic'. In the process, the celebrity chefs represented the tension between the labour of getting food on the table and the leisure-work associated with domestic cookery as a creative practice.

Monroe's established celebrity image as a campaigner against government austerity measures (see Chapter 6) could have disrupted middle-class forms of austerity chic that were central to *Daily Kitchen*. However, alternative meanings were overwhelmed by the conventions of the format and the culinary credentials of her co-host. Although there was some public outcry at Tebbutt's displays of 'snobbery' towards Monroe (Tweedy 2020b) and an ongoing struggle between what they saw as culinary priorities in a pandemic, Monroe was partly incorporated within romanticized and retro images of austerity. Her styling often drew on established elements of austerity culture with its nod towards 1940s and 1950s feminine styles (Bramall 2013). This was evident in her fondness for blue shirts that evoked the idealized US female war worker Rosie the Riveter and in her pompadour hairstyle associated with both wartime film stars such as Bette Davis and 1950s rockabilly style. In this way, Monroe's associations with food poverty campaigns and an anti-austerity message were temporarily neutralized as they were incorporated within forms of 'nostalgic domesticity' and retro femininity that evoked 'patriotic stoicism' and made frugality an 'aesthetic and moral choice' (Martin 2020b: 1, 3).

By representing food practices as creative, leisured lockdown activities, *Keep Cooking and Carry On* and *Daily Kitchen* not only ignored the pressures that lockdown created for many households but also added to the labour involved in feeding people. For parents (and, in particular, mothers) tasked with childcare and home schooling while working full time – or experiencing economic precarity exacerbated by the pandemic – getting the kids involved in the 'fun' of baking simply added to the normative expectations involved in feeding the family. While Jamie extolled the opportunities that lockdown offered for family mealtimes and teaching children to cook, lockdown was represented in terms of the abundance rather than absence of time. When new evidence emerged that suggested a link between obesity and increased risks of serious illness from Covid-19, this feeding work expanded. In order not to be a burden on the overstretched NHS, people were given further responsibility for their family's health by producing healthy meals and bodies. As Elaine Swan (2020: 698) comments, 'foodwork practices of doing good and eating right create new types of labour and inequalities'. While the middle class had the digital access and economic resources to pay for food deliveries, many people found that everyday practices such as shopping for food became more labour-intensive during the pandemic. This was particularly the case for people on low income, those juggling multiple forms and sites of labour, and people who were shielding or had disabilities (Swan 2020: 696). There is widespread evidence to suggest that women felt the negative economic impacts of the pandemic more strongly than men because they had more job insecurity, more unpaid work and greater risk of poverty – an experience very much at odds with retro images of the 'happy, thrifty housewife' (Martin 2020b: 3–4).

Celebrity chefs, therefore, played a role in the aestheticization and lifestylization of foodwork during the pandemic using romanticized images of austerity in which frugality was associated with morality. The meaning of austerity was also represented in terms of the absence of choice enjoyed by the middle classes in consumer culture. This was in stark contrast to increasing evidence of very real forms of economic hardship as the handling of the pandemic exacerbated inequalities and increased food poverty. However, as the pandemic progressed, some celebrity chefs shifted their emphasis from 'resilience' to 'resistance' (Martin 2020b: 5). This intervention would be led by an unanticipated food hero.

Celebrity politics and food poverty

As the UK lived through successive waves of Covid-19 that brought increasing levels of hardship and distress to many, attempts to lifestyle the pandemic diminished. It was reported that 10 per cent of adults had visited a food bank during June 2020

(Butler 2020). In September 2020 research by the Food Foundation demonstrated that people in 14 per cent of households were unable to eat properly in the previous six months because they could not afford or access food (O'Connell and Brannen 2021). In this context, a new 'food superhero' (Adams 2021) emerged in the unlikely form of 23-year-old Premier League footballer, Marcus Rashford. While this book has focused on celebrity chefs, different forms of 'food celebrity' can emerge who use their influence to shape the contemporary foodscape in powerful ways (Johnston and Goodman 2015: 206). During 2020, Rashford became 'a national hero, especially to schoolchildren' (Caplan 2021) and a leading food celebrity because of his interventions in public understandings of food poverty and government austerity policies. Working with third sector organizations and celebrity chefs, Rashford helped to reimagine public involvement in pandemic food culture, away from wartime-notions of community 'resilience' and towards community-based, small-scale acts of collective resistance.

Before proceeding, it is worth noting that the government's austerity agenda was losing public support in the late 2010s as an increasing number of people felt that cuts to benefits and the welfare safety-net had gone too far. This was exacerbated by the UN Report into widespread poverty in the UK (see Chapter 6). In the Victorian era, journalists and novelists punctured images of a Britain as a prosperous land of plenty. This eventually led to the 'denaturalizing and politicizing of hunger', the formation of the welfare state and 'an understanding of the nation as having a collective and moral responsibility for those less fortunate' (Howarth 2020: 5). As I demonstrated in Chapter 6, government austerity policies became increasingly naturalized after 2010 as the 'profligate' and 'workshy' were distinguished from the virtuous 'austerity citizen' (May et al. 2020: 211). Bloggers such as Jack Monroe attempted to denaturalize these austerity narratives with 'personal narratives of the everyday experience of precarity'. Increasing press reports about food banks also created a sense of 'national scandal' about the rise of 'callousness and cruelty' and the breakdown of a welfare system based on 'British values of compassion' (Howarth 2020: 7–8). Criticisms of the austerity agenda intensified as the pandemic progressed and romanticized ideas of collective interdependence associated with the welfare state were partially resuscitated in the response to Covid-19. As Will Davies (2020) observed, the pandemic was accompanied by 'a surge in voluntary civic activity': 'feelings of solidarity and empathy were unusually high and the ruthless competitive norms of neoliberalism have become taboo.'

It is in this context that Marcus Rashford gained an increasing public and campaigning role in relation to food poverty and, in particular, child food poverty. Although Rashford was a young superstar footballer for Manchester United, his own experiences of precarity – as a Black, working-class child growing up on a Manchester council estate – shaped his response. When schools closed during the first lockdown, he wondered how children who received free school meals (FSM) would get fed (Adams 2021). Initially he approached FareShare – a UK charity who redistribute surplus food to people vulnerable to food poverty – to make a donation and to motivate others to do the same (FareShare N.D). As an ambassador for FareShare, Rashford spoke publicly about his own experiences of poverty, his former reliance on FSM and his experiences of growing up as the government's austerity agenda was implemented. In the process he highlighted how austerity during the pandemic should not be understood in terms of the absence of choices over food but the absence of food itself.

After schools closed during the first lockdown, the government introduced a voucher scheme to help feed children from poorer families who would usually receive FSM. However, despite widespread food poverty and increased economic hardship as a result of the pandemic, the government decided that this scheme would not continue during the school summer holidays. In June 2020 Rashford wrote a politically skilful, emotional and widely publicized letter to MPs, asking the government to reverse this decision and to guarantee the extension of the food voucher scheme across the summer vacation (Rashford 2020). Speaking 'as a black man from a low-income family in Wythenshawe, Manchester' who has the opportunity to give children living in poverty a voice, Rashford highlighted how the nation wasn't simply dealing with one pandemic: 'Food poverty in England is a pandemic' (Rashford 2020). Speaking on behalf of children who do not have a voice, Rashford showed the power of collective interdependence and communities built on care: 'without the kindness and generosity of the community I had around me, there wouldn't be the Marcus Rashford you see today' (Rashford 2020). However, rather than simply championing a model of charity and the 'big society', he also highlighted how systemic failures produce class and racial inequality. 'There is a system failure', he wrote, that encourages 'the cycle of hardship to continue'. 'The system was not built for families like mine to succeed, regardless of how hard my mum worked' (Rashford 2020).

In his letter, Rashford frequently mobilized the figure of his mum, Melanie Maynard, to challenge the abject 'figures of dependency' (Tyler 2020) that populated discourses of austerity, poverty porn and series such as *Jamie's Ministry of Food* (see Chapter 6). He wrote 'my mum worked full-time, earning minimum wage to make sure we always had a good evening meal on the table. But it was not enough'. His mum would operate as a consistent figure in his campaigning around child hunger, seen clearly in the BBC documentary *Marcus Rashford – Feeding Britain's Children* broadcast later in the year. His letter portrayed people living in poverty and unable to feed their kids as precisely the type of hard-working people who took responsibility for their families that government policies called for:

> The man you see stood in front of you today is a product of her love and care. I have friends who are from middle-class backgrounds who have never experienced a small percentage of the love I have gotten from my mum: a single parent who would sacrifice everything she had for our happiness. THESE are the kind of parents we are talking about.
>
> (Rashford 2020)

He was also careful that the use of his mum didn't essentialize caring as a feminine disposition and female responsibility: 'Men, women, caregivers, are calling out for our help and we aren't listening' (Rashford 2020). In this way, his campaigning also addressed 'the political issues that most affect our daily lives' which can form the basis for 'subversion and resistance' (hooks 1991: 48). By criticizing the failures of the Universal Credit welfare system to adequately and effectively provide for families,[12] the letter also reminded the government of its responsibility to care for the people in the same way families and communities care for each other and to make 'our most vulnerable a top priority' (Rashford 2020). His request that the government put the same effort into 'protecting all vulnerable children' as they did to protecting the economy revived ideas of collective interdependence by showing that we should not simply relegate 'humane values to the home' (Johnson and Lloyd 2004: 160). While it is easy to get lost in hyperbole and overstate the lasting power of Rashford's campaign, its affective power to mobilize people around child hunger was part of a wider process to build 'public support for an ideological shift away from individualized, competitive and monetized frameworks that have tried to ease out responsibility and compassion' (Skeggs and Wood 2020: 645).

Rashford's campaign forced a government U-turn. Schoolchildren from low-income families received food vouchers during the summer holidays in 2020. Rashford was awarded an MBE for his campaigning work. If the government thought this was the end of this celebrity's campaigning, they were wrong. Rashford continued to press ahead with campaigning on child hunger during the summer and, in September 2020, formed the Child Food Poverty Task Force, a coalition of charities and major food retailers and producers (End Child Food Poverty 2020a).

In October 2020, with the Autumn half-term holidays looming, the Labour Party introduced a motion in parliament to extend the FSM holiday scheme until Easter 2021 (Caplan 2021). The motion was defeated. In the process, some Tory MPs took the opportunity to discredit Rashford: Brendon Clarke-Smith called for 'less celebrity virtue signalling on Twitter' (Adams 2021). Others such as Ben Bradley (2020) tried to revive negative representations of the poor:

> Gov has lots of responsibilities: supporting the vulnerable, helping people to help themselves, balancing the books. Not as simple as you make out Marcus. Extending FSM to sch[ool] hols passes responsibility for feeding kids away from parents, to the State. It increases dependency.
>
> (Tweet by Ben Bradley MP)

In a now deleted tweet he went on to link FSM with crime, degeneracy and unfit parenting in his own constituency: 'One kid lives in a crack den, another in a brothel. These are the kids that most need our help, extending FSM doesn't reach these kids' (cited in Walker 2020).

However, it was becoming increasing difficult for the government to secure consent for their austerity agenda. The defeat of the motion led Rashford to tweet 'A significant number of children are going to bed tonight not only hungry but feeling they do not matter because of the comments that have been made today' (cited in Caplan 2021). His campaign to overturn the decision not only gained widespread support – including a petition with over a million signatures – but also galvanized the public into action. A large number of individuals, charities, public organizations and businesses came forward with direct offers to feed hungry children at half term. As Rashford retweeted these offers of help to his ever-increasing number of followers, these small, grassroots acts increasingly appeared to be widespread, collective and national action.[13]

Although there was substantial political anger at the government's decision, many offers of help also used the Dickensian trope of 'the hungry child' where images of 'innocence disrupted dominant understandings of hunger as punishment for individual failure' and 'evoked … pity and outrage' (Howarth 2020: 5). Although some of these images of childhood innocence did little to disturb the more widespread discourse of poor parenting, Rashford's campaign carefully negotiated this territory by positioning children as a collective and government responsibility. He spoke as a former hungry child and enabled children to actively speak about their own position rather than being reduced to passive victims.

While government cuts to welfare had begun to lose their legitimacy prior to the pandemic, the Rashford campaign created more conditions of possibility for people 'to identify with the hungry and question what their suffering said about British values and how the nation wanted to imagine itself' (Howarth 2020: 4). As Rashford tweeted, 'Selflessness, kindness, togetherness, this is the England I know' (cited in Delahunty 2020). His celebrity activism prompted a (half-hearted) government U-turn. However, the politicization of hunger in his campaign also reshaped the national political imagination in ways that mainstream politicians had failed to do.

Furthermore, while many sympathetic depictions of the 'hungry child' in the 2010s glossed over racial inequalities (Howarth 2020: 12), Rashford's use of both his own and his mother's experience of poverty made the experience of low-income Black Britons visible. This happened within a wider context in which Rashford clearly demonstrated public support for the Black Lives Matter movement by taking the knee and tweeting his support.

Rashford was probably the most influential 'food celebrity' in the UK during 2020. In March 2021, he made it on to *Time* magazine's list of 'The NEXT 100 most influential people' and featured on one of their front covers. While hundreds of relatively unknown figures in the hospitality industry gained a moment of national recognition as Rashford retweeted their offers of help, his campaign also generated widespread celebrity backing. The End Child Food Poverty website features support from footballers, TV stars and musicians as well as celebrity chefs such as Nigella Lawson and Jamie Oliver. Although some celebrities went little further than clicktivism, their actions nonetheless legitimated and publicized the campaign to an ever-widening audience.

However, celebrity chefs such as Jamie Oliver, Jack Monroe, Tom Kerridge and Hugh Fearnley-Whittingstall played a key role in the campaigns around child food poverty during the pandemic.[14] Oliver's involvement was unsurprising given his longstanding campaigning about school dinners and the importance of healthy eating in childhood. He also had an established interest in holiday hunger. 'I've smelt it and seen it and felt it', he told a *Telegraph* journalist in 2016 and he acknowledged that his books were probably irrelevant to someone struggling to feed their children (Gordon 2016). By 2017, he was campaigning to keep school kitchens open during the summer vacation in order to feed hungry children and in April 2020, he backed a voucher scheme through which children in receipt of FSM could receive food during the Easter holidays. Furthermore, in 2019, Oliver founded Bite Back 2030, an organization that aimed to give young people a voice in shaping food policy with a mission 'to achieve a world where all young people have the opportunity to be healthy, no matter where they live'. Despite the organization's anti-obesity agenda, it played a key role in growing campaigns around FSM (Bite Back 2030 2019). Oliver threw his support behind Rashford's campaigns in June and October 2020, pledging to be '100 per cent on board' to help the footballer 'anyway he can' and sending his chefs to South London schools to feed children during the Autumn half-term holidays (Woolcock et al. 2020).

Debates about child poverty continued into early 2021 as the UK entered its third lockdown in response to a rapid escalation in Covid-19 cases. As schools closed, there were renewed questions about how best to feed children who would normally be in receipt of FSM. The government's decision to distribute food parcels – rather than food vouchers – to these children came in for widespread criticism. Images of the pitiful quantity and quality of the food in these parcels circulated on social media and the company providing them was accused of putting their profits before the rights and needs of hungry children. Across social media platforms, people mobilized the very discourses that had been used to construct the responsible neoliberal citizen in shows such as *Eat Well for Less* (see Chapter 6) – the need to budget wisely, eat appropriate quantities and take responsibility for nutritional quality – to criticize the companies that failed to live up to the demands place on ordinary citizens. Rashford and many celebrity chefs were among the many critics of the government scheme – as the footballer put it in a tweet, 'We MUST do better. This is 2021' (cited in Campbell and Weale 2021).

Meanwhile, temporarily freed from the narrative constraints of the campaigning culinary documentary, a cross-channel coalition of celebrity chefs – Jamie Oliver, Hugh Fearnley-Whittingstall, Tom Kerridge and Jack Monroe – united with Rashford and actor Emma Thompson on a new campaign to tackle child hunger. Alongside a wide range of key figures from civil society, professional bodies, the food industry, health and education, the celebrities wrote to the prime minister calling for a widespread review of FSM policy (Rashford et al. 2021). They asked the government to widen eligibility for FSM, to examine levels of funding and how contracts were awarded and to learn from experience during the pandemic. While Jamie and Hugh's campaigning culinary documentaries often responsibilized individuals to solve their own problems, the campaigns around FSM policy demanded the government fulfil its duty to care for its citizens.

Cookery shows during the UK's first lockdown in spring 2020 offered one image of the austerity larder that drew on lifestyled reworkings of Second World War in which appropriate consumption resulted in a planned, plentiful yet constrained austerity larder. As Bramall (2015: 195) observes, 'a full cupboard is used to picture austerity in a way that an empty cupboard cannot'. Under the government's austerity agenda, an empty cupboard was a sign of irresponsible consumption and failed citizenship and, through the lifestylization of pandemic food practices, celebrity chefs reproduced these discourses in their representations of well-prepared yet unselfish consumption practices. These images were punctured by celebrity-led campaigns around child food poverty during 2020 in which a powerful image of 'the empty larder' was shown to be a result of the government's austerity policies rather than inappropriate consumption (May et al. 2020). In the process, this celebrity activism helped to question the legitimacy of the government's policies and decisions, forcing a series of U-turns in policy as commentators claimed that Rashford was running an 'alternative government' that had achieved sufficient political and moral leadership to overcome many entrenched political divisions (Caplan 2021). While celebrity interventions in debates about food poverty may not create long-term radical shifts in political consciousness on their own, their affective power can act as part of an '*accumulation, reverberation* and *reshaping*' of 'affective responses' that can help to reshape the political landscape (Pedwell 2017: 165).

Conclusion

Celebrity chefs play a key role in shaping how people think about what and how to eat. They are high-profile public figures who shape ideas about 'good' and 'bad' ways of cooking and eating. They intervene in public debates about health, poverty, climate change, animal welfare and the meaning of a national diet. They raise questions about how food is – and should be – produced and distributed as well as consumed.

This book has demonstrated how celebrity chefs use the symbolic capital they acquire in the culinary and entertainment fields to move beyond them and to become more significant public and political actors (Hollows and Jones 2010b). Their influence extends beyond food as they shape wider political debate about political structures, citizenship, the nation and responses to the pandemic, about not only how to eat but how we should live. The nature of their interventions cannot be thought of simply as either progressive or reactionary and they are often shot through with contradictions. Culinary travelogues may present images of an inclusive multicultural nation while also reinforcing the 'whiteness' of national culinary cultures. Calls for increased action to combat climate change and to protect the environment may highlight the need for interventions by industry and government but they rarely demand systemic or structural change and privilege individual responsibility. The promotion of 'kinder' and more ethical modes of consumption frequently reinforce classed, gendered and racial hierarchies and distinctions.

The formats and genres used by celebrity chefs also shape how they represent the politics of food. Celebrity chefs' campaigns are shaped by narrative structures and discursive frameworks that are frequently reproduced across campaigning culinary documentaries. This not only informs how 'problems' and 'crises' are identified but also the solutions proposed by celebrity chefs. In the campaigns led by Jamie Oliver and High Fearnley-Whittingstall, the demands of a comprehensible and entertaining narrative in which the celebrity chef appears as an embattled and passionate hero frequently come at the expense of an engagement with the complex politics of food production, distribution, retailing and consumption and their relationship to wider forms of governance and inequalities. The heroic resistance exemplified by television chefs in campaigning culinary documentaries often mirrors wider ways in which celebrity resistance can work to 'reinforce capitalism, consumerism and neoliberalism' (Duvall and Heckemeyer 2018: 394). As a result, many celebrity chefs' campaigns are often deeply contradictory and chefs can often be polarizing figures.

However, as recent campaigns around food poverty demonstrate, there is also the potential for food celebrities to take forms of moral and political leadership that not only reshape political and national imaginations but also act as an affective force to mobilize people into new forms of collective action. While the generic conventions of food media might constrain how they engage with politics as they also battle to attract audiences, their public profile means that mediated accounts of celebrity chefs' activism have the potential to reshape food politics in new ways.

Despite the devastating consequences of both the pandemic and poverty, these campaigns demonstrate how celebrities can mobilize people, create collective action, hold government to account and effect change within the contemporary foodscape. That the politics of food became such a touchstone within national politics during both Brexit and the pandemic is perhaps unsurprising given its centrality and necessity to everyday lives. While much celebrity philanthropy uses 'technocratic, de-politicized, individualized responses to inequality, injustice and problematic governance' (Johnston and Goodman 2015: 211), food celebrities led campaigns around child poverty during the pandemic that reshaped discourses around austerity and poverty and enabled the nation to be imagined in more collective, compassionate and caring ways. Compared to the lifestyled responses to the pandemic in television cookery series, these campaigns shifted the emphasis from the choice of virtuous frugality to imposed austerity, from 'resilience' to 'resistance' (Martin 2020b).

NOTES

Chapter 1

1. For studies of Gordon Ramsay, see, for example, Higgens et al. (2012), Leer and Kjær (2015) and Leer (2016a).
2. There are some exceptions. For example, *The Final Table* featured chef Charles Michel who is employed in research, teaching and art fields, and partly supported through Patreon, rather than in restaurants (Michel n.d.).
3. Thanks to Lorenzo Domaneschi for alerting me to this and helping with translation.
4. Chefs can't technically hand back their stars but the claim that they can operates as an 'urban myth' that continues to receive press coverage (Canavan 2017).
5. For more on competition formats for professional chefs, see Ray (2007), Naccarato and Lebesco (2012), Gallagher (2004), Curnutt (2015) and Oren (2013, 2016).
6. *Iron Chef UK* only ran for one season in 2010 on Channel 4.
7. This was the second British iteration of *Masterchef*. An earlier series with a different format ran from 1990 to 2001.
8. *Masterchef* and *Great British Bake Off*, both competition formats for amateurs, spawned spin-offs for professionals – *Masterchef: The Professionals* and *Bake Off: The Professionals* – that enabled some contestants to build their media profile.
9. In each episode, the contestants were asked to reinvent a central dish within a particular national cuisine. As Stuart Heritage (2018) commented in the *Guardian*, this seemed a strange choice 'given the debate about the place of cultural appropriation in food'.
10. For more on the Slow Food Movement, see, for example, Parkins and Craig (2006), Petrini (2003) and Simonetti (2012).
11. These stories often have much in common with wider media representations of great (male) chefs and how the narrative of their careers is structured around a 'turning point' in which they break with tradition (Harris and Giuffre 2015: 58–9).
12. For work on how some similar strategies are used in media representations of small-scale food production, see Phillipov (2017).
13. Black Lives Matter not only provoked significant media commentary on the position of chefs of colour in both the restaurant industry and food media, but also generated a wide range of criticisms of practices within food media and responses that attempted to remedy discrimination. One example in the UK is the online food newsletter *Vittles* which aims to publish voices excluded by traditional food media. In the United States, the established food magazine *Bon Appetit* was exposed for having a racist culture and extensive forms of racial discrimination (Young 2020).

Chapter 2

1. Elizabeth David had a significant impact on middle-class cooking practices in the UK and she profited from the interest in her writing with her own kitchen shop. Her adventurous life has generated two biographies and a BBC TV drama *A Life in Recipes* (Chaney 1998; Cooper 1999; Jones and Taylor 2001).
2. For a more on post-war British television cookery, see, for example, Strange (1998), Moseley (2009), Bonner (2005, 2009, 2011), Geddes (2018, 2022) and Charlesworth (2022).
3. Julia Child, one of the most popular US television chefs of the 1960s and 1970s, is often credited with merging education and spectacle in innovative ways. However, when the BBC finally broadcast her show *The French Chef* in an afternoon slot in the late 1970s, it received little promotion and was a ratings flop (Polan 2011).
4. This is based on a search of *Radio Times* TV programme descriptions using the digitized copies available via the BBC's Genome Project (https://genome.ch.bbc.co.uk/). While terms such as 'television chef' and 'top chef' occur earlier, the first use of the term celebrity chef appears in a description of the comedy series *Chef!* starring Lenny Henry in 1993. Its first use in relation to television food programming appears in June and July 1996 in descriptions for the cookery competition series *Ready, Steady, Cook* and the culinary magazine series *The Good Food Show*.
5. For more on the history of the Food Network, see Collins (2009), Naccarato and Lebesco (2012) and Salkin (2014).
6. The 1990 Broadcasting Act required the BBC to outsource 25 per cent of production to independents.
7. However, this was not an entirely new phenomenon. Philip Harben's series *The Man in the Kitchen* was broadcast at night by the BBC in 1952 (Geddes 2022).
8. This shift built on longer-term trends. See for example Hollows (2002) on the representation of masculinity and cooking in *Playboy* magazine in the post-war period.
9. See Leer (2016a) and Johnston et al. (2014) for more on celebrity chefs' identities and masculinity.
10. For more on the production techniques in *The Naked Chef* and producer Pat Llewelyn, see G. Smith (2020).
11. Garson appeared in a 2009 episode of BBC2's *The Money Programme* on 'The Rise of the Superchef' which explored how leading chefs were transformed into multi-million pound brands.
12. For more on D'Acampo, see Wall (2018).
13. Figures correct in June 2020.

Chapter 3

1. Two new articles on clean eating and Deliciously Ella were published between the first and final drafts of this chapter by Rachel O'Neill (2020) and Karen Wilkes (2021) and I've incorporated their ideas where possible. O'Neill offers a detailed and compelling argument about the significance of Ella's entrepreneurial femininity. Wilkes offers a much-needed analysis of how the images and discourses associated with clean eating are racialized.
2. Deborah Lupton (2018a: 73) also notes the popularity of 'best foods for' and superfood searches on Google.

Chapter 4

1. A flexitarian diet is primarily vegetarian but allows for some consumption of meat.
2. Veg* is commonly used as a term that incorporates both vegans and vegetarians (see, for example, Mycek 2018).
3. BBC Wales is the Welsh nation's division of the BBC and produces some of its own programming. While *Dirty Vegan* was produced for broadcast in Wales, it was available across the UK through the BBC's streaming platform i-player.
4. Adams' radical feminist position has numerous problems, not least its gender essentialism, that has made it subject to extensive critique. See, for example, Hamilton (2016) and Koletnik (2017).
5. There are also popular female vegan YouTubers with an emphasis on body building such as Naturally Stefanie, albeit promoting a distinctly feminine aesthetic.
6. There is a well-established tradition of wild, aggressive and rebellious vegan food personalities on YouTube such as Vegan Black Metal Chef Brian Manowitz located in a 'kitchen dungeon' (see Lewis 2020: 89–90).
7. Indeed, beyond the obvious differences, there are some interesting points of comparison between the style of *Dirty Vegan* and the macho world of YouTube channels such as Epic Meal Time which combine high calorie and meaty dishes with '*Jackass* style meta irony' and 'hypermasculine kitchen adventures' (Lewis 2020: 89).
8. Vegan meat substitutes using ingredients such as tofu and gluten have a much longer history in Chinese culinary traditions influenced by Buddhist monks (see, for example, Lott-Lavigna 2019).
9. One notable exception in a British context is YouTube star and cookery writer Rachel Ama who blends influences from her African, Caribbean and British heritage on her channel.

Chapter 5

1. For more on *Jamie's Kitchen* and *Jamie's Kitchen Australia*, see Kelly and Harrison (2009) and Pike and Kelly (2014).
2. Although broadcast on Channel 4, *Jamie's Kitchen* was produced by Talkback Productions. As well as spawning international versions, Channel 4 broadcast a follow-up British series *Jamie's Chef* in 2007.
3. For more on *Jamie's School Dinners* see, for example, Fox and Smith (2011), Hollows (2016), Naik (2008) and Pike and Kelly (2014).
4. However, not all celebrity chef campaigns conform to this. In *Jamie's Dream School* (2011), Oliver – who frequently comments on his lack of success at school – set out to transform education, drawing more on his credentials as an agent for social change than as a celebrity chef. It is notable that this was one of his less successful campaigning documentaries.
5. The channel also adapted the format to enable some of its other lifestyle stars to embark on non-culinary campaigns. Examples include the Mary Portas vehicles *Mary's Bottom Line* and *Mary Queen of the High Street*.
6. This discussion draws heavily on earlier work with David Bell (Bell and Hollows 2011).
7. For more on how poshness works as part of Fearnley-Whittingstall's ethical consumption, see Phillipov (2017).

8   Green lifestyle programming is often used to refer to a sub-genre of lifestyle television that focuses on ethical issues, frequently with an environmental dimension (Bonner 2010; Lewis 2008b; Parkins and Craig 2011).
9   These issues generally became less prominent as the series progressed.
10 For more on community digging projects, see the website accompanying the AHRC-funded 'Cultural Values of Digging' project (Cultural Values of Digging 2013).
11 For more details, see https://www.rivercottage.net/. See also Phillipov (2017: 60).
12 The discussion that follows draws heavily on Bell and Hollows (2011) and, to a lesser extent, Bell et al. (2017) and Hollows (2016).
13 This was not Fearnley-Whittingstall's first attempt to makeover people's eating habits – he had already tackled convenience food 'addicts' in *River Cottage Treatment* (2006) – but it was the first to employ the CCD format.
14 These tensions are played out in other CCDs. For example, *The People's Supermarket* shows the conflicts between ethical performances of middle-class consumers who want the supermarket to be stocked with locally sourced and organic fresh produce and working-class women who request 'plain, basic stuff' to feed their families for a reasonable price.
15 This section partly draws on earlier work with David Bell and Steve Jones (Bell et al. 2017).
16 Freedom Food is a food assurance scheme monitored by the RSPCA, an animal welfare charity. Standards exceed the legal minimum but do not require production to be free range. In contrast, the 'standard system' does not require chickens to be provided with natural light and it maintains cramped conditions.
17 For more on both these series, see Bell et al. (2017).
18 As Hopkinson and Cronin (2015) note, this campaign had a limited impact. While sales of less known fish increased, sales of established favourites did not significantly decrease.

Chapter 6

1   There is, of course, a longer history of lifestyle guides and cookbooks advocating frugal practices and forms of austere living (Wincott 2016).
2   Nonetheless, a significant number of recipes in the accompanying cookbook fail to conform to mainstream health recommendations (Hollows and Jones 2010b).
3   For more on the opposition between care and convenience see, for example, Warde (1997), Halkier (2017), Jackson and Viehoff (2016); and Meah and Jackson (2017).
4   For a useful critique of the concept of obesogenic environment, see Colls and Evans (2014).
5   In more recent series, some episodes feature households who underspend compared to the average but these people must also be reformed because they need to be educated to spend wisely on the 'right' kinds of food.
6   A good illustration of this can be found in the photos accompanying her series of recipes in the *Guardian* newspaper in 2012–14.

Chapter 7

1   See, for example, individual episodes of shows such as Anthony Bourdain's *No Reservations* (2005–12) or series such as *Luke Nguyen's United Kingdom* (2015) for

the Australian channel SBS. De Solier's (2019) analysis of Dorinda Hafner's *Tastes of Britain* (1998) offers a useful starting point.
2   Not all locations are as easily commodifiable – Sat Bains' two Michelin star Nottingham restaurant is located under an urban motorway flyover! Culinary travelogues often return to already established locations, shaping how national culinary cultures are represented.
3   *A Farewell to Floyd*, BBC2, 26 September 2009.
4   *Radio Times* accessed through BBC Genome Project.
5   There were earlier attempts to produce a 'canon' of British food: Philip Harben's 1953 cookbook *Traditional Dishes of Britain* contains similar dishes to later culinary travelogues (Panayi 2008: 16).
6   Rhodes also reinvented mass-produced British 'traditions' such as the Jaffa Cake, a trend still evident today in the popularity of Snickers-inspired desserts in British restaurants.
7   This search for 'folk' traditions in British cookery was not entirely new – see, for example, Florence White (1932/1999) in the interwar period.
8   Johnston and Baumann use the term foodie discourse to refer to a specific 'culinary *discourse*' which organizes 'how food is talked about, discussed and understood in the public realm' (2015: 37). Foodie discourse is produced by cultural intermediaries such as food writers and celebrity chefs – and reproduced by foodies – and Johnston and Baumann demonstrate how it operates to demarcate 'what foods and food trends are interesting, relevant and high status for foodies' (2015: 38).
9   For more on how ideas of traditional British food can be understood within the wider 'heritage industry', see Ashley et al. (2004).
10 For more on globalization, food and homogenization see, for example, Ritzer (1993) and Schlosser (2001). For work on the relationships between global, the local and culinary diversity, see for example Cook and Crang (1996) and Maxwell and DeSoucey (2016). For work on migration and 'ethnic' foods in Britain, see Panayi (2008), Highmore (2008, 2009) and Cook and Harrison (2003).
11 Nadiya is not the first woman of colour to do a culinary travelogue round Britain, although she is the first to star in one in a British production for primetime TV. Dorinda Hafner's *Tastes of Britain* directed 'a postcolonial black anthropological gaze back at the white colonizers' (de Solier 2019: 213).
12 Nisha Katona's 2018 BBC series *Recipes That Made Me* offered a thoughtful address to these issues.
13 However, Nadiya is represented on the move in *Nadiya's American Adventure* (2020).
14 A restaurant chef, Contaldo gained television exposure through his association with Jamie Oliver. Antonio Carluccio had a chain of mid-market restaurants and a range of eponymous branded produce. He is also a well-known TV chef and cookery writer.
15 The fictional comedy series *The Trip to Italy* (2014) was also based on a culinary journey.
16 In the same period, Rick Stein visited Italy in *Rick Stein's Taste of Italian Opera* (2010), and in his series *Mediterranean Escapes* (2007), *Rick Stein: From Venice to Istanbul* (2015) and *Rick Stein's Long Weekend* (2016).
17 For more on the representation of working-class food in *Jamie's Great Escape*, see Bell and Hollows (2007) and Rossato (2015).
18 Jamie's Italian TV travelogue and accompanying book were not only translated into Italian but were a commercial success there (Rossato 2015). Some of Gino D'Acampo's books on Italian food have been translated into Italian (Wall 2018). These acts of

Notes

translation can also involve significant transformations in meaning (Rossato 2015, see also Tominc 2017).
19 See Bell and Hollows (2007) for more on how femininity is fixed in place in *Jamie's Great Escape* and other food media.
20 Hansard: Topical Questions: Volume 659: Thursday 9 May 2019: column 650.

Chapter 8

1 An extract from the episode can be found on YouTube on a channel celebrating the Brexit process (Channel Brexit 2017). I am grateful to Jonatan Leer who told me about this episode. As I do the final edit of this book in June 2021, the phrase 'sausage war' features in many UK newspaper headlines as part of ongoing Brexit negotiations between the UK and the EU.
2 These issues are incisively and humorously analysed in Berlin-based Chinese filmmaker Pop Fan's spoof YouTube cooking and language-learning video *Lerne Deutsch in meiner Küche* (Fan 2020), analysed by Bao (2021).
3 A rather different combative relationship to Europe can be found in his 2012 Channel 4 series *Jamie and Jimmy's Food Fight Club*. The show included a series of highly performative and jingoistic food battles which aimed to 'take on our continental cousins' in a 'winner takes all battle of national pride'.
4 The UK is highly dependent on imported pork and Denmark is the biggest supplier. An estimated 25 per cent of UK pork came from Denmark in 2017.
5 This reproduces longstanding associations between Englishness and 'sentimentality about animals' observed by George Orwell in his 1947 *The English People* (Clarke 2006: 94).
6 As I revise this book for submission in May 2021, Oliver's predictions have proved correct with news reports of serious staff shortages in the hospitality industry.
7 Despite the *Mail* and *Mail on Sunday* playing a key role in promoting Brexit, changing editorships add complexity to this picture.
8 There are some parallels here with the representation of film stars during the Second World War.
9 Jason Atherton is a Michelin-starred chef with an established TV career. Romy Gill is best known as a chef and cookery writer with a developing TV profile.
10 Obviously Massimo Bottura's leftovers and limited supplies were significantly different to many other people's.
11 In *Daily Kitchen*, Tebbutt was studio-based and guests 'visited' online. Monroe co-hosted from her home in the earlier episodes but joined Tebbutt in the studio later in the series. The show modelled social distancing for viewers at home, sometimes with difficulty.
12 Universal Credit was introduced by the Government in 2013 as an attempt to integrate and simplify the welfare system. Its implementation was accompanied by successive problems and it has been widely criticized for being slow moving, needlessly harsh and causing significant hardship.
13 The results of this campaign live on via the End Child Food Poverty website, supported by charities and the food industry, which provides a map of emergency food support around the UK so people can find help.
14 During the revision process of this book, Tom Kerridge joined forces with Rashford in a new initiative Full Time. Kerridge is a Michelin-starred chef who is also part

of the BBC stable of TV chefs and, like Rashford, received FSM when he was growing up. The campaign centres around fifty-two simple and economical recipes – distributed weekly on Instagram – that aim to help families on small budgets to produce healthy meals (Higginbotham 2021). The campaign shows rather more sympathy with people experiencing food poverty than many other schemes to get people feeding the family in healthy ways on restricted budgets. Nonetheless, it risks shifting responsibility for dealing with food poverty back on to individuals with its emphasis on developing cooking skills and techniques.

BIBLIOGRAPHY

Abbots, E.-J. (2015) The Intimacies of Industry: Consumer Interactions with the 'Stuff' of Celebrity Chefs. *Food, Culture and Society* 18(2): 223–43.

Abbots, E.-J. and B. Coles (2013) Horsemeat-gate: The Discursive Production of a Neoliberal Food Scandal. *Food, Culture and Society* 16(4): 535–50.

Abidin, C., D. Brockington, M. Goodman, M. Mostafanezhad and L.A. Richey (2020) The Tropes of Celebrity Environmentalism. *Annual Review of Environment and Resources* 45 (1). Available at: http://centaur.reading.ac.uk/88800/ (accessed 20 October 2020).

Adams, C. (1990) *The Sexual Politics of Meat: A Feminist-Vegetarian Critical Theory*. Cambridge: Polity.

Adams, T. (2021) Marcus Rashford: The Making of a Food Superhero. *Observer*, 17 January. Available at: https://www.theguardian.com/football/2021/jan/17/marcus-rashford-the-making-of-a-food-superhero-child-hunger-free-school-meals (accessed 13 February 2021).

Adedokun, N. (2020) Remainer Jamie Oliver Sparks Backlash over 'Ridiculous' Brexit Food Warning. *Express*, 9 October. Available at: https://www.express.co.uk/news/uk/1345945/brexit-news-jamie-oliver-latest-post-brexit-food-standards-uk-vn (accessed 12 January 2021).

Adema, P. (2000) Vicarious Consumption: Food, Television and the Ambiguity of Modernity. *Journal of American and Comparative Cultures* 23(3): 113–23.

Aftab, K. (2018) The Final Table: Has Netflix Reinvented the Recipe for Food Programmes. *Independent*, 16 November. Available at: https://www.independent.co.uk/life-style/food-and-drink/netflix-the-final-table-show-cooking-competition-clare-smyth-programme-a8635256.html (accessed 23 October 2019).

Ahad, B. (2016) Post-Blackness and Culinary Nostalgia in Marcus Samuelsson's *Yes, Chef*. *American Studies* 54(4): 5–26.

Ahmed, S. (2004) Affective Economies. *Social Text* 22(2): 117–39.

Allegretti, A. (2015) Tabloid Columnist Slammed for Claiming 'GBBO' Winner's Success Is 'Ideological Warfare'. *Huffington Post*, 8 October. Available at: https://www.huffingtonpost.co.uk/2015/10/08/the-sun-nadiya-hussain-gbbo-winner_n_8261848.html (accessed 14 May 2021).

Allinson, K. and K. Featherstone (2019a) Around the World with Pinch of Nom. *Mail Online*, 1 May. Available at: https://www.dailymail.co.uk/femail/food/article-6978069/Suppers-spice-life-authors-Britains-fastest-selling-cookbook-ever.html (accessed 20 April 2020).

Allinson, K. and K. Featherstone (2019b) 'Fakeaway' Dishes So Tasty You'll Pinch Yourself. *Mail Online*, 30 April. Available at: https://www.dailymail.co.uk/femail/article-6970501/Fakeaway-diet-dishes-tasty-youll-pinch-yourself.html (accessed 20 April 2020).

Allinson, K. and K. Featherstone (2019c) *Pinch of Nom: 100 Slimming Home-style Recipes*. London: Bluebird.

Allinson, K. and K. Featherstone (2020a) Family Feasts from Pinch of Nom. *Mail Online*, 17 January. Available at: https://www.dailymail.co.uk/femail/food/article-7887293/New-Pinch-Nom-book-deliciously-food-400-calories-fewer-meal.html (accessed 20 April 2020).

Allinson, K. and K. Featherson (2020b) How to Make Your Own Takeaways. *Mail Online*, 22 January. Available at: https://www.dailymail.co.uk/femail/food/article-7914191/How-make-takeaways.html (accessed 20 April 2020).

Allinson, K. and K. Featherstone (2020c) Devilish Desserts without the Guilt. *Mail Online*, 21 January. Available at: https://www.dailymail.co.uk/femail/food/article-7909897/Try-guide-delicious-treats-wont-pile-pounds.html (accessed 20 April 2020).

Allinson, K. and K. Featherstone (2020d) The Hot 400! *Mail Online*, 20 January. Available at: https://www.dailymail.co.uk/femail/food/article-7906137/The-hot-400-everyday-light-meals-400-calories.html (accessed 20 April 2020).

Allinson, K. and K. Featherstone (2020e) *Pinch of Nom Everyday Light*. London: Bluebird.

Aly, R. (2015) Nadiya Hussain Has Won So Much More Than the Great British Bake Off. *Guardian*, 8 October. Available at: https://www.theguardian.com/commentisfree/2015/oct/08/nadiya-hussain-has-won-so-much-more-than-the-great-british-bake-off (accessed 17 May 2021).

Anderson, P.J. and A. Weymouth (1999) *Insulting the Public: The British Press and the European Union*. London: Routledge.

Angry Chef (2019) I Never Gave a Shit about Your Poxy Fucking Diet. *The Angry Chef*, 17 May. Available at: https://angry-chef.com/blog/i-never-gave-a-shit-about-your-poxy-fucking-diet (accessed 23 April 2020).

Appadurai, A. (1988) How to Make a National Cuisine: Cookbooks in Contemporary India. *Comparative Studies in Society and History* 30(1): 3–24.

Ashley, B., J. Hollows, S. Jones and B. Taylor (2004) *Food and Cultural Studies*. London: Routledge.

Ashton, J.R., J. Middleton and T. Lang (2014) Open Letter to Prime Minister David Cameron on Food Poverty in the UK. *The Lancet* 283: 1631.

Aspinall, G. (2020) Idolising the Aldi 22p Breakfast Isn't Helping Anyone. *Grazia*, 26 October. Available at: https://graziadaily.co.uk/life/in-the-news/aldi-whole-chicken-food-poverty/ (accessed 12 February 2021).

Avant-Garde Vegan (2017a) High Protein Vegan Meal Prep. YouTube, 15 October. Available at: https://www.youtube.com/watch?v=P_wD2zydD_g (accessed 23 April 2020).

Avant-Garde Vegan (2017b) Vegan Steak, Chips and Peppercorn Sauce. YouTube, 17 September. Available at: https://www.youtube.com/watch?v=Ad4kA8e51g4 (accessed 23 April 2020).

Avant-Garde Vegan (2018) Vegan Streaky Bacon *Must See*. YouTube, 25 March. Available at: https://www.youtube.com/watch?v=vEF0-sjeWmw (accessed 24 April 2020).

Avant-Garde Vegan (2019a) Protein Pancakes Recipe and Home Work Out! YouTube, 10 February. Available at: https://www.youtube.com/watch?v=8TLxHSk_0DM (accessed 23 April 2020).

Avant-Garde Vegan (2019b) This Made Me Go Vegan Overnight. YouTube, 30 January. Available at: https://www.youtube.com/watch?v=WI13QaCWBx0&t=98s (accessed 23 April 2020).
Baker, S. and C. Rojek (2020) *Lifestyle Gurus: Constructing Authority and Influence Online*. Cambridge: Polity.
Baker, S. and M. Walsh (2020) You Are What You Instagram: Clean Eating and the Symbolic Representation of Food, in D. Lupton and Z. Feldman, eds, *Digital Food Cultures*. London: Routledge, pp. 53–67.
Banet-Weiser, S. (2012) *Authentic: The Politics of Ambivalence in a Brand Culture*. New York: NYU Press.
Banet-Weiser, S. (2017) 'I'm Beautiful the Way I am': Empowerment, Beauty and Aesthetic Labour, in A.S. Elias, R. Gill and C. Scharff, eds, *Aesthetic Labour: Rethinking Beauty Politics in Neoliberalism*. London: Palgrave Macmillan, pp. 265–82.
Bao, H. (2021) Queer Disidentification: Or How to Cook Chinese Noodles in a Global Pandemic? *Portal Journal of Multidisciplinary International Studies* 17(1/2): 85–90.
Baraclough, L. (2014) Jamie Oliver's Fresh One Extends Output Deal with Freemantle Media. *Variety*, 5 March. Available at: https://variety.com/2014/tv/global/jamie-olivers-fresh-one-extends-output-deal-with-fremantlemedia-1201125698/ (accessed 12 March 2021).
Barnes, C. (2017) Mediating Good Food and Moments of Possibility with Jamie Oliver: Problematizing Celebrity Chefs as Talking Labels. *Geoforum* 84: 169–78.
Barnett, C., P. Cloke, N. Clarke and A. Malpass (2005) Consuming Ethics: Articulating the Subjects and Spaces of Ethical Consumption. *Antipode* 37(1): 23–45.
Barrie, C. (1999) BBC Brands New Global Strategy. *The Guardian*, 19 February. https://www.theguardian.com/media/1999/feb/19/bbc (accessed 19 June 2020).
Barrie, J. (2019) Wagamama's New Vegan Egg Will Look Great on Instagram, but It's Definitely Not an Egg. *I*, 14 May. Available at: https://inews.co.uk/inews-lifestyle/food-and-drink/wagamamas-vegan-egg-instagram-gaz-oakley-502001 (accessed 5 March 2020).
BBC News (2001) Gordon Ramsay: Chef Terrible. *BBC News*, 20 July. Available at: http://news.bbc.co.uk/1/hi/uk/1448742.stm (accessed 14 October 2019).
BBC News (2018) Vegetarian and Vegan: A Quarter of UK Dinners Have No Meat or Fish. *BBC News*, 7 February. Available at: https://www.bbc.co.uk/news/uk-42973870 (accessed 2 March 2020).
BBC Food (2019) 'I Once Lived Almost Entirely on Tins of Food'. Available at: https://www.bbc.co.uk/food/articles/cooking_with_tins (accessed 12 February 2021).
BBC News (2019) Pinch of Nom. *BBC News*, 27 March. Available at: https://www.bbc.co.uk/news/entertainment-arts-47718289 (accessed 28 May 2021).
Beardsworth, A. and T. Keil (1997) *Sociology on the Menu: An Invitation to the Study of Food and Society*. London: Routledge.
Bell, D. (2002) From Writing at the Kitchen Table to TV Dinners: Food Media, Lifestylization and European Eating, paper presented at Eat, Drink and Be Merry? Cultural Meanings of Food in the 21st Century conference, Amsterdam, June 2002.
Bell, D. and J. Hollows (2005) Making Sense of Ordinary Lifestyles, in D. Bell and J. Hollows, eds, *Ordinary Lifestyles: Popular Media, Consumption and Taste*. Maidenhead: Open University Press, pp. 1–18.
Bell, D. and J. Hollows (2007) Mobile Homes. *Space and Culture* 10(1): 22–39.

Bell, D. and J. Hollows (2011) From River Cottage to Chicken Run: Hugh Fearnley-Whittingstall and the Class Politics of Ethical Consumption. *Celebrity Studies* 2(2): 179–91.

Bell, D., J. Hollows and S. Jones (2017) Campaigning Culinary Documentarties and the Responsibilization of Food Crises. *Geoforum* 84: 179–87.

Bell, D. and G. Valentine (1997) *Consuming Geographies: We Are Where We Eat*. London: Routledge.

Bennett, J. (2008) The Television Personality System: Televisual Stardom Revisited after Film Theory. *Screen* 49(1): 32–50.

Bennett, J., (2010) *Television Personalities: Stardom and the Small Screen*. Abingdon: Routledge.

Bentley, A. and S. Borkowsky (2020) The Food and COVID-19 NYC Archive: Mapping the Pandemic's Effect on Food in Real Time. *Gastronomica* 20(4): 8–11.

Berg, M. (2016) How Gordon Ramsay Earned as Much as Beyoncé in 2016. *Forbes*, 13 July. Available at: https://www.forbes.com/sites/maddieberg/2016/07/13/how-gordon-ramsay-earned-as-much-as-beyonce-in-2016/#6187dbaf2798 (accessed 14 October 2019).

Bhattacharyya, G. (2016) Trying to Discern the Impact of Austerity in Lived Experience, in P. Bennett and J. McDougall, eds, *Popular Culture and the Austerity Myth: Hard Times Today*. Abingdon: Routledge, pp. 17–27.

Bianchi, L. (2011) Massimo Bottura's Culinary Avant-garde. *The World's Best 50 Restaurants*, 23 May. Available at: https://www.theworlds50best.com/blog/Events/massimo-bottura%E2%80%99s-culinary-avant-garde.html (accessed 16 October 2019).

Billig, M. (1995) *Banal Nationalism*. London: Sage.

Biltekoff, V. (2013) *Eating Right in America: The Cultural Politics of Food and Health*. Durham, NC: Duke University Press.

Binkley, S. and J. Littler (2008) Cultural Studies and Anti-Consumerism: A Critical Encounter. *Cultural Studies* 22(5): 519–30.

Binns, D. (2018) The Netflix Documentary House Style. *Fusion* 14: 60–71.

Biressi, A. and H. Nunn (2013) *Class and Contemporary British Culture*. Basingstoke: Palgrave Macmillan.

Bite Back 2030 (2019) We Are Bite Back. Available at: https://biteback2030.com (accessed 21 May 2021).

Blanchard, S. (2019) Chlorinated Chicken Poses 'No Health Problems' and the UK Should Consider Importing It after Brexit, Claims Senior Government Scientist. *MailOnline*, 30 August. Available at: https://www.dailymail.co.uk/health/article-7410539/Chlorinated-chicken-poses-no-health-problems-claims-senior-Government-scientist.html (accessed 12 January 2021).

Bod Edit (2018) The Celebrity Chef Featuring Michel Roux Jr. *The Bod Edit*, 19 January. Available at: https://thebodedit.com/food/celebrity-chef-michel-roux-jr/ (accessed 16 October 2019).

Bonner, F. (2003) *Ordinary Television: Analyzing Popular TV*. London: Sage.

Bonner, F. (2005) Whose Lifestyle Is It Anyway? in D. Bell and J. Hollows, eds, *Ordinary Lifestyles: Popular Media, Consumption and Taste*. Maidenhead: Open University Press, pp. 35–46.

Bonner, F. (2009) Early Multi-Platforming: Television Food Programmes, Cookbooks and Other Print Spin-Offs. *Media History* 15(3): 345–8.

Bonner, F. (2010) Lifestyle Television: Gardening and the Good Life, in T. Lewis and E. Potter, eds, *Ethical Consumption*. London: Routledge, pp. 231–43.

Bonner, F. (2011) *Personality Presenters: Television's Intermediaries with Viewers*. Farnham: Ashgate.

Booth, R. (2013) Nigella Lawson, Charles Saatchi and the 'Case With no Winners'. *Guardian*, 20 December. Available at: https://www.theguardian.com/uk-news/2013/dec/20/nigella-lawson-charles-saatchi-trial-case-no-winners (accessed 7 July 2020).

Booth, R and P. Butler (2018) UK Austerity Has Inflicted 'Great Misery' on Citizens, UN Says. *Guardian*, 16 November. Available at: https://www.theguardian.com/society/2018/nov/16/uk-austerity-has-inflicted-great-misery-on-citizens-un-says (accessed 11 February 2021).

Bordo, S. (2003) *Unbearable Weight: Feminism, Western Culture, and the Body*. 2nd edition. Berkeley and Los Angeles: University of California Press.

Boshoff, A., (1997) BBC's £9m Epic Is Outdone by Cookery Shows. *Daily Telegraph*, 6 February.

Bourdain, A. (2000) *Kitchen Confidential: Adventures in the Culinary Underbelly*. London: Bloomsbury.

Bourdieu, P. (1971) Intellectual Field and Creative Project, in M.F.D. Young, ed., *Knowledge and Control: New Directions for the Sociology of Education*. London: Collier-Macmillan, pp. 89–119.

Bourdieu, P. (1984) *Distinction: A Social Critique of the Judgement of Taste*. London: Routledge.

Bourdieu, P. (1993) *The Field of Cultural Production*. Cambridge: Polity.

Bowlby, R. (1992) *Still Crazy after All These Years: Women, Writing and Psychoanalysis*. London: Routledge.

Boyce Kay, J. and H. Wood (2020) Cultural Commons: Critical Responses to COVID-19, part 2. *European Journal of Cultural Studies* 23(6): 1019–24.

Boykoff, M., M. Goodman and J. Littler (2010) 'Charismatic Megafauna': The Growing Power of Celebrities and Pop Culture in Climate Change Campaigns. Environment Politics and Development Working Paper Series: WP28. Department of Geography, King's College London.

Boyle, R. and L. Kelly (2010) The Celebrity Entrepreneur on Television. *Celebrity Studies* 1(3): 334–50.

Bradley, B. (2020) 21 October. Available at: https://twitter.com/BBradley_Mans/status/1318860839437406209 (accessed 12 February 2021).

Bramall, R. (2013) *The Cultural Politics of Austerity: Past and Present in Austere Times*. Basingstoke: Palgrave Macmillan.

Bramall, R. (2015) The Austerity Larder: Mapping Food Systems in a New Age of Austerity. *Journal of Consumer Culture* 15(2): 183–201.

Braun, V. and S. Carruthers (2020) Working at Self and Wellness: A Critical Analysis of Vegan Vlogs, in D. Lupton and Z. Feldman, eds, *Digital Food Cultures*. Abingdon: Routledge, pp. 82–96.

Brockington, D. (2013) *Celebrity and the Environment: Fame, Wealth and Power in Conservation*. London: Zed Books, e-book edition.

Brunsdon, C. (2003) Lifestyling Britain: The 8–9 Slot on British Television. *International Journal of Cultural Studies* 6(1): 5–23.

Brunsdon, C. (2006) The Feminist in the Kitchen: Martha, Martha and Nigella, in J. Hollows and R. Moseley, eds, *Feminism in Popular Culture*. Oxford: Berg, pp. 41–56.

Brunsdon, C., C. Johnson, R. Moseley and H. Wheatley (2001) The Midlands Television Group '8–9' Project. *European Journal of Cultural Studies* 4(1): 29–31.
Bucktin, C. (2020a) Inside Grim US Megasheds of Chlorine-Washed Chickens That Brits May Soon Be Eating. *Mirror*, 23 February. Available at: https://www.mirror.co.uk/news/us-news/inside-grim-megasheds-chlorine-wash-21561931 (accessed 12 January 2021).
Bucktin, C. (2020b) Horror of US 'Meat From Hell' Pumped Full of Hormones That Could Flood Britain. *Mirror*, 27 September. Available at: https://www.mirror.co.uk/news/us-news/horror-meat-hell-pumped-full-22751305 (accessed 12 January 2021).
Bugge, A. Bahr and R. Almås (2006) Domestic Dinner: Representations and Practices of a Proper Meal among Young Suburban Mothers. *Journal of Consumer Culture* 6(2): 203–28.
Busby, G., R. Huang and R. Jarman (2013) The Stein Effect: An Alternative Film-induced Tourism Perspective. *International Journal of Tourism Research* 15(6): 570–82.
Buscemi, F. (2022) Mario Soldati and His *Viaggio nella Valle del Po*: A Culinary Journey between Early Television and Italian Culinary Identity, in A. Tominc, ed., *Food and Cooking on Early Television in Europe*. London: Routledge.
Butler, P. (2014) Tory Peer Says Poor People Go Hungry because They Do Not Know How to Cook. *Guardian*, 8 December. Available at: https://www.theguardian.com/society/2014/dec/08/tory-peer-apologises-poor-hungry-do-not-know-cook (accessed 11 February 2021).
Butler, P. (2020) UK's Poorest 'Skip Meals and Go Hungry' during Coronavirus Crisis. *Guardian*, 13 August. Available at: https://www.theguardian.com/uk-news/2020/aug/12/coronavirus-lockdown-hits-nutritional-health-of-uks-poorest (accessed 11 March 2021).
Bryant, A. (2018) 'Bacon' Bites and KFC ('kruelty-free chicken'). *Telegraph*, 11 January. Available at: https://www.telegraph.co.uk/recipes/0/bacon-bites-kfc-kruelty-free-chicken-meet-gaz-oakley-youtube/ (accessed 27 February 2020).
Caines, M. (2020) No Young Chef Should Be Judged by Their Skin Colour before They Walk through the Door. *Telegraph*, 22 June. Available at: https://www.telegraph.co.uk/food-and-drink/features/no-young-chef-should-judged-skin-colour-walk-door/ (accessed 13 March 2021).
Cairns, K. and J. Johnston (2015) *Food and Femininity*. London: Bloomsbury.
Cairns, K., J. Johnston and N. MacKendrick (2013) Feeding the 'Organic Child': Mothering through Ethical Consumption. *Journal of Consumer Culture* 13(2): 97–118.
Calhoun, C. (2017) Populism, Nationalism and Brexit, in W. Outhwaite, ed., *Brexit: Sociological Responses*. London: Anthem, pp. 57–66.
Campbell, L. and S. Weale (2021) Rashford: Something 'Going Wrong' with Free School Meal Deliveries. *Guardian*, 12 January. Available at: https://www.theguardian.com/education/2021/jan/12/not-good-enough-marcus-rashford-condemns-free-school-meal-packages (accessed 21 May 2021).
Canavan, H. Dixler (2017) Why Chefs 'Give Back' Their Michelin Stars. *Eater*, 21 September. Available at: https://www.eater.com/2017/9/21/16345242/chefs-give-back-michelin-stars (accessed 21 October 2019).
Caplan, P. (2021) The Footballer and the Prime Minister. Food Poverty UK Blog. Available at: https://sites.gold.ac.uk/food-poverty/ (accessed 3 March 2021).
Cappellini, B. and E. Parsons (2013) Practising Thrift at Dinnertime: Mealtime Leftovers, Sacrifice and Family Membership. *Sociological Review* 60(S2): 121–34.

Casey, E. (2019) From *Cookery in Colour to the Great British Bake Off*: Shifting Gendered Accounts of Home-Baking and Domesticity. *European Journal of Cultural Studies* 22(5–6): 579–94.

Cashmore, E. (2006) *Celebrity Culture*. London: Routledge.

Chaney, L. (1998) *Elizabeth David: A Biography. A Mediterranean Passion*. London: Macmillan.

Channel 4 (2008) Channel 4 Food Season Extended Trailer. YouTube, 8 January. Available at: https://www.youtube.com/watch?v=ObkmppcqG6E (accessed 19 August 2020).

Channel 4 (2009) The Great British Food Fight. YouTube, 4 January. Available at: https://www.youtube.com/watch?v=-lL-_3OEjDY (accessed 19 August 2020).

Channel Brexit (2017) Yes Minister on the Euro Sausage. Available at: https://www.youtube.com/watch?v=KZZvLVhhjJs (accessed 21 May 2021).

Charles, N. and M. Kerr (1988) *Women, Food and Families: Power, Status, Love, Anger*. Manchester: Manchester University Press.

Charlesworth, D. (2022) Negotiating and Validating the 'Housewife' Identity, in A. Tominc, ed., *Food and Cooking on Early Television in Europe*. London: Routledge.

Chef's Pencil (2020) Top Most Popular Countries and Cities for Vegans in 2020. *Chef's Pencil*, 2 September. Available at: https://www.chefspencil.com/top-most-popular-countries-and-cities-for-vegans-in-2020/ (accessed 20 October 2021).

Cheltenham Festivals (2020) Nadiya Hussain and Tan France. YouTube, 24 January. Available at: https://www.youtube.com/watch?v=o_kOmuxhfuU (accessed 14 May 2021).

Chibelushi, W. (2018) The Complexities of Being Black, British and Vegan. *Vice*, 22 March. Available at: https://www.vice.com/en_uk/article/ne9v8b/the-complexities-of-being-black-british-and-vegan (accessed 27 February 2020).

Chiorando, M. (2021) Number of Vegans Skyrocketed by 40% in 2020, Claims Survey. *Plant Based News*, 8 January. Available at: https://plantbasednews.org/culture/ethics/vegans-in-britain-skyrocketed/ (accessed 29 April 2021).

Clarke, B. (2006) Orwell and Englishness. *The Review of English Studies* 57(228): 83–105.

Clarke, S. (2017) Gordon Ramsay Talks Working around the World and Why He Hates 'TV Chef'. *Variety*, 14 October. Available at: https://variety.com/2017/tv/features/gordon-ramsay-studio-ramsay-interview-mipcom-1202584359/ (accessed 18 October 2019).

Cochran, J. (2020) Cooking at a High Level Still Feels Like a Very, White Privileged Vocation. *Big Hospitality*, 6 July. Available at: https://www.bighospitality.co.uk/Article/2020/07/06/James-Cochran-chef-1251-Around-The-Cluck (accessed 13 March 2021).

Cole, M. and K. Morgan (2011) Vegaphobia: Derogatory Discourses of Veganism and the Reproduction of Speciesism in UK National Newspapers. *British Journal of Sociology* 62(1): 134–53.

Collins, D. (2019) We Were Bullied at School. Now We're Outselling Jamie. *Sunday Times*, 2 June. Available at: https://www.thetimes.co.uk/article/pinch-of-nom-chefs-were-bullied-at-school-now-theyre-outselling-jamie-oliver-g2qvp0fmk (accessed 20 April 2020)

Collins, K. (2009) *Watching What We Eat: The Evolution of Television Cooking Shows*. London: Continuum.

Colls, R. and P. Dodd (1985) Representing the Nation: British Documentary Film, 1930–45. *Screen* 26(1): 21–33.

Colls, R. and B. Evans (2014) Making Space for Fat Bodies? A Critical Account of 'the Obesogenic Environment'. *Progress in Human Geography* 38(6): 733–53.

Contois, E. (2015) Guilt-free and Sinfully Delicious: A Contemporary Theology of Weight Loss Dieting. *Fat Studies* 4(2): 112–26.

Contois, E. (2017) 'Lose Like a Man': Gender and the Constraints of Self-Making in Weight Watchers Online. *Gastronomica* 17(1): 33–43.

Contois, E. (2020) *Diners, Dudes and Diets: How Gender and Power Collide in Food Media and Culture*. Chapel Hill, NC: University of North Carolina Press.

Cook, I. and P. Crang (1996) The World on a Plate: Culinary Culture, Displacement and Geographical Knowledges. *Journal of Material Culture* 1(2): 131–53.

Cook, I. and M. Harrison (2003) Cross over Food: Re-materializing Postcolonial Geographies. *Transactions of the Institute of British Geographers* 28(3): 296–317.

Cooke, R. (2020) Keep it Simple: What I've Learned from Cooking with Chefs Online. *Observer*, 21 June. Available at: https://www.theguardian.com/food/2020/jun/21/what-ive-learned-from-cooking-with-chefs-online (accessed 12 February 2021).

Cooper, A. (1999) *Writing at the Kitchen Table: The Authorized Biography of Elizabeth David*. London: Michael Joseph.

Couldry, N. (2010) *Why Voice Matters: Culture and Politics after Neoliberalism*. London: Sage.

Couldry, N. (2015) Celebrity, Convergence, and the Fate of Media Institutions, in P. David Marshall and S. Redmond, eds, *A Companion to Celebrity*. London: John Wiley. https://doi.org/10.1002/9781118475089.ch6

Courtenay, W. (2000) Constructions of Masculinity and Their Influence on Men's Well-Being: A Theory of Gender and Health. *Social Science and Medicine* 50(10): 1385–401.

Coveney, J., A. Begley and D. Gallegos (2012) 'Savoir Faire': Are Cooking Skills a New Morality? *Australian Journal of Adult Learning* 52(3): 617–42.

Craig, G. (2019) Sustinable Everyday Life and Celebrity Environmental Advocacy in *Hugh's War on Waste*. *Environmental Communication* 13(6): 775–89.

Crawford, R. (2006) Health as a Meaningful Social Practice. *Health* 10(4): 401–20.

Cultural Values of Digging (2013) Cultural Values of Digging: A Project about Digging. Available at: https://culturalvaluesofdigging.wordpress.com (accessed 21 August 2020).

Curnutt, H. (2015) Cooking on Reality TV: Chef-Participants and Culinary Television, in P. Bradley, ed., *Food, Media and Contemporary Culture: The Edible Image*. Basingstoke: Palgrave Macmillan, pp. 144–63.

Czikszentmihalyi, M. and E. Rochberg-Halton (1981) *The Meaning of Things: Domestic Symbols and the Self*. Cambridge: Cambridge University Press.

Daily Mail Reporter (2008) Chef Jamie Oliver Slams the 'Uncivilized' British Who Would 'Rather Get Drunk than Eat Well'. *MailOnline*, 25 August. Available at: http://www.dailymail.co.uk/news/article-1048752/Chef-Jamie-Oliver-slams-uncivilised-British-drunk-eat-well.html (accessed 2 February 2009).

Daily Telegraph (2015) 'New Nigella' Sends Sales of Obscure Ingredients Skyward. *Daily Telegraph*, 15 February: 10.

Davenport, K., W. Solomons, S. Puchalska and J. McDowell (2018) Size Acceptance: A Discursive Analysis of Online Blogs. *Fat Studies* 7(3): 278–293.

Davies, W. (2018) *Nervous States: How Feeling Took over the World*. London: Vintage.

Davies, W. (2019) Why Can't We Agree on What's True Any More? *Guardian*, 19 September. Available at: https://www.theguardian.com/media/2019/sep/19/why-cant-we-agree-on-whats-true-anymore (accessed 27 August 2021).

Davies, W. (2020) Coronavirus and Progressive Taxation. Discover Society. Available at: https://research.gold.ac.uk/id/eprint/28397/1/William%20Davies,%20W.%20(2020)%2Coronavirus%20and%20Progressive%20Taxation_AAM.pdf (accessed 12 March 2021).

Davis, A. (2013) *Promotional Cultures: The Rise and Spread of Advertising, Public Relations, Marketing and Branding*. Cambridge: Polity.

Dawson, S. (2017) Chlorine-Washed Chicken Q&A. *The Conversation*, 2 August. Available at: https://theconversation.com/chlorine-washed-chicken-qanda-food-safety-expert-explains-why-us-poultry-is-banned-in-the-eu-81921 (accessed 12 January 2021).

Day, E. (2013) Nigella Lawson: 'I'm Not a Chef: I'm Not Even Trained'. *Guardian*, 19 October. Available at: https://www.theguardian.com/lifeandstyle/2013/oct/19/nigella-lawson-chef-feminism-interview (accessed 27 May 2021).

de Solier, I. (2005) TV Dinners: Culinary Television, Education and Distinction. *Continuum* 19(4): 465–81.

de Solier (2018) Tasting the Digital: New Food Media, in K. Lebesco and P. Naccarato, eds, *The Handbook of Food and Popular Culture*. London: Bloomsbury, pp. 54–65.

de Solier, I. (2019) *Ethnodelicious*: Mediatized Culinary Anthropology and the Mediation of Global Food Cultures, in J. Dürrschmidt and Y. Kautt, eds, *Globalized Eating Cultures: Mediation and Mediatization*. Basingstoke: Palgrave Macmillan, pp. 203–19.

Deans, J. (2013) Jamie Oliver Bemoans Chips, Cheese and Giant TVs of Modern-Day Poverty. *Guardian*, 27 August. Available at: https://www.theguardian.com/lifeandstyle/2013/aug/27/jamie-oliver-chips-cheese-modern-day-poverty (accessed 11 February 2021).

Dejmanee, T. (2016) 'Food Porn' as Postfeminist Play. *Television and New Media* 17(5): 429–48.

Delahunty, S. (2020) FareShare Receives Record Number of Donations in Response to Marcus Rashford's Campaign. *Third Sector*, 23 October. Available at: https://www.thirdsector.co.uk/fareshare-receives-record-number-donations-response-marcus-rashfords-campaign/fundraising/article/1698181 (accessed 24 April 2021).

Deller, R.A. and K. Murphy (2019) 'Zoella Hasn't Written a Book, She's Written a Cheque': Mainstream Media Representations of YouTube Celebrities. *European Journal of Cultural Studies*. Advanced online publication: https://doi.org/10.1177/1367549419861638

DeSoucey, M. (2010) Gastronationalism: Food Traditions and Authenticity Politics in the European Union. *American Sociological Review* 75(3): 432–55.

DeVault, M. (1991) *Feeding the Family: The Social Organization of Caring as Gendered Work*. Chicago: University of Chicago Press.

Dickinson, R. (1998) Modernity, Consumption and Anxiety: Television Audiences and Food Choice, in R. Dickinson, R. Haraindranath and O. Linnes, eds, *Approaches to Audiences: A Reader*. London: Arnold, pp. 257–71.

Dinner by Heston (n.d.) Chef's Table. Available at: https://www.dinnerbyheston.co.uk/chefs-table (accessed 15 October 2019).

Diridin, V. (2019) Massimo Bottura: 'Non Vado in TV, lì la Cucina è Urla e Schiamazzi'. *Dissapore*, 2 May. Available at: https://www.dissapore.com/notizie/massimo-bottura-non-vado-in-tv-li-la-cucina-e-urla-e-schiamazzi/ (accessed 17 October 2019).

Dirnhuber, J. (2018) Taxing Issue: Jamie Oliver Claims Brexit Could Make Kids HEALTHIER after Calling for Milkshake Tax. *Sun*, 2 May. Available at: https://www.thesun.co.uk/news/6189921/jamie-oliver-welcome-brexit-red-tape-food/ (accessed 12 December 2020).

DML (2021) Our Clients: Ben Ebbrell. Available at: http://www.dml-uk.com/our-clients/ben-ebbrell/ (accessed 1 June 2021).

Douglas, M. (1966) *Purity and Danger: An Analysis of the Concepts of Pollution and Taboo*. London: Routledge and Kegan Paul.

Doyle, J. (2016) Celebrity Vegans and the Lifestyling of Ethical Consumption. *Environmental Communication*, 10(6): 777–90.

Draper, J. (2020) Interview with Matt Pritchard from Dirty Vegan. *Penarth Times*, 23 January. Available at: https://www.penarthtimes.co.uk/news/18180386.interview-matt-pritchard-dirty-vegan/ (accessed 27 Feburary 2020).

Driessens, O. (2012) The Celebritization of Society and Culture: Understanding the Structural Dynamics of Celebrity Culture. *International Journal of Cultural Studies* 16(6): 641–57.

Driessens, O. (2013) Celebrity Capital: Redefining Celebrity Using Field Theory. *Theory and Society* 42: 543–60.

Dropbox (2019) Co-founders and Friends Behind Sorted Food Reveal How a Life-Changing Business Idea Came from a Catch up at the Pub. *Metro*, 2 June. Available at: https://metro.co.uk/2019/06/02/co-founders-and-friends-behind-sorted-food-reveal-how-a-life-changing-business-idea-came-from-a-catch-up-at-the-pub-9528351/ (accessed 1 June 2021).

Dubisch, J. (2017) You Are What You Eat: Religious Aspects of the Health Food Movement, in C. Delaney, ed., *Investigating Culture: An Experiential Introduction to Anthropology*, 3rd edition. Oxford: Wiley Blackwell, pp. 279–87.

Duffy, B.E. and E. Hund (2015) 'Having It All' on Social Media: Entrepreneurial Femininity and Self-Branding among Fashion Bloggers. *Social Media and Society* 1(2): 1–11.

Dunn, D. (2005) Playing the Tourist: Ideology and Aspiration in British Television Holiday Programmes, in D. Bell and J. Hollows, eds, *Ordinary Lifestyles: Popular Media, Consumption and Taste*. Maidenhead: Open University Press, pp. 128–42.

Dunn, L. (2020) The Feel Good Power List. *Daily Telegraph*, 16 May. Available at: https://www.telegraph.co.uk/news/0/feel-good-power-list-people-making-real-difference-corona-crisis/ (accessed 12 January 2020).

Duruz, J. (2004) Haunted Kitchens: Cooking and Remembering. *Gastronomica* 4: 57–68.

Duvall, S.-S. and N. Heckemeyer (2018) #BlackLivesMatter: Black Celebrity Hashtag Activism and the Discursive Formation of a Social Movement. *Celebrity Studies* 9(3): 391–408.

Dyer, R. (1987) *Heavenly Bodies: Film Stars and Society*. London: BFI.

Dyer, R. (1998) *Stars*. London: BFI.

Edwards, J. (2019) *O, The Roast Beef of Old England!* Brexit and Gastronationalism. *Political Quarterly* 90(4): 629–36.

Elgot, J. (2014) Feeding Britain 'Poor People Don't Know How to Cook' Says Tory Baroness Jenkin. *Huffington Post*, 8 December. Available at: https://www.huffingtonpost.co.uk/2014/12/08/feeding-britain-tory-cook_n_6287454.html (accessed 12 February 2021).

Elias, A.S., R. Gill and C. Scharff (2017) Aesthetic Labour: Beauty Politics in Neoliberalism, in A.S. Elias, R. Gill and C. Scharff, eds, *Aesthetic Labour: Rethinking Beauty Politics in Neoliberalism*. London: Palgrave Macmillan, pp. 3–29.

End Child Food Poverty (2020a). End Child Food Poverty Home Page. Available at: https://endchildfoodpoverty.org (accessed 20 May 2021).

End Child Food Poverty (2020b) Find Help. Available at: https://endchildfoodpoverty.org/help (accessed 21 May 2021).

English, P. and D. Fleischman (2019) Food for Thought in Restaurant Reviews. *Journalism Practice* 13(1): 90–104.

Eriksson, G. and D. Machin (2020) Discourses of 'Good Food': The Commercialization of Healthy and Ethical Eating. *Discourse, Context and Media* 33: doi.org/10.1016/j.dcm.2019.100365

Evans, D. (2011) Thrifty, Green or Frugal: Reflections on Sustainable Consumption in a Changing Economic Climate. *Geoforum* 42(5): 550–7.

Evans, D. (2018) Rethinking Material Cultures of Sustainability: Commodity Consumption, Cultural Biographies and Following the Thing. *Transactions of the Institute of British Geographers* 43(1): 110–21.

Evening Standard (2010) Jamie Oliver's School Dinners Drive Boosts School Exam Results. *Evening Standard*, 29 March. Available at: https://www.standard.co.uk/hp/front/jamie-oliver-s-school-dinners-drive-boosts-school-exam-results-6719647.html (accessed 18 October 2020).

Evening Standard (2012) TV Cook Delia Smith Lambasts 'Celebrity Chefs and Their Arrogant Attitudes'. *Evening Standard*, 11 April. Available at: https://www.standard.co.uk/showbiz/tv-cook-delia-smith-lambasts-celebrity-chefs-and-their-arrogant-attitudes-6645018.html (accessed 27 May 2021).

Famuwera, J. (2020) What It's Like to Be the Only Black Restaurant Critic in Town. *GQ*, 4 October. Available at: https://www.gq-magazine.co.uk/lifestyle/article/the-only-black-food-critic (accessed 25 March 2021).

Fan, P. (2020) Lerne Deutsch in Meiner Küche. Radio Eins/RBB, 10 April. Available at: https://www.radioeins.de/themen/kunst_kultur/4-waende-berlin/lerne-deutsch-in-meiner-kueche.html (accessed 11 June 2021).

Fareshare (n.d.) Marcus Rashford's Work with Fareshare. Available at: https://fareshare.org.uk/marcus-rashford/ (accessed 20 May 2021).

Farrell, A. Erdman (2011) *Fat Shame: Stigma and the Fat Body in American Culture*. New York: New York University Press.

Farrer, J. (2020) From Cooks to Chefs: Skilled Migrants in a Globalizing Culinary Field. *Journal of Ethnic and Migration Studies*. Online first: https://doi.org/10.1080/1369183X.2020.1731990.

Featherstone, M. (1991) *Consumer Culture and Postmodernism*. London: Sage.

Fegitz, E. and D. Pirani (2018) The Sexual Politics of Veggies: Beyoncé's 'Commodity Veganism'. *Feminist Media Studies* 18(2): 294–308.

Felski, R. (2000) *Doing Time: Feminist Theory and Postmodern Culture*. New York: New York University Press.

Ferguson, P. Parkhurst (2001) A Cultural Field in the Making, in L. Schehr and A. Weiss, eds, *French Food on the Table, on the Page and in French Culture*. London: Routledge, pp. 5–50.

Ferguson, P. Parkhurst (2003) Writing Out of the Kitchen: Carême and the Invention of French Cuisine. *Gastronomica* 3(3): 40–51.

Ferguson, P. Parkhurst (2004) *Accounting for Taste: The Triumph of French Cuisine*. Chicago: University of Chicago Press.

Ferguson, P. Parkhurst and S. Zukin (1998) The Careers of Chefs, in R. Scapp and B. Seitz, eds, *Eating Culture*. Albany: SUNY Press, pp. 93–111.

Finkelstein, J. (1999) Rich Food: McDonald's and Modern Life, in B. Smart, ed., *Resisting McDonaldization*. London: Sage, pp. 70–82.

Finney, C. (2020) 'We Are the End Result of a Flow Chart That Is Designed to Preserve the Status Quo'. *Independent*, 5 September: magazine, p. 52.

Firth, H. and I. Theasby (2019) *BOSH! How to Live Vegan*. London: HarperCollins, E-book.

Fischler, C. (1980) Food Habits, Social Change and the Nature/Culture Dilemma. *Social Science Information* 19(6): 937–53.

Flood, A. (2019) Slimming Cookbook Becomes Bestselling Non-Fiction Book since Records Began. *Guardian*, 27 March. Available at: https://www.theguardian.com/books/2019/mar/27/slimming-cookbook-becomes-fastest-selling-non-fiction-book-since-records-began (accessed 21 April 2020).

Flowers, R. and E. Swan (2011) 'Eating at Us': Representations of Knowledge in the Activist Documentary Film Food Inc. *Studies in the Education of Adults* 43: 234–50.

Food For Soul (n.d.) About Us. Available at: https://www.foodforsoul.it/about-us/ (accessed 17 October 2019).

Forrest, A. (2018) Jamie Oliver Accused of Cultural Appropriation over 'Punchy Jerk Rice'. *Independent*, 20 August. Available at: https://www.telegraph.co.uk/news/celebritynews/6083245/Jamie-Oliver-Im-sixth-generation-Sudanese.html (accessed 14 May 2021).

Forsey, Z. and T. Jones (2019) Meghan Markle Voices Concern about American Food Production during Party for Charles. *Mirror*, 5 March. Available at: https://www.mirror.co.uk/news/uk-news/meghan-markle-voices-concern-american-14091729 (accessed 12 Jan 2021).

Fort, M., (1999) A Question of Taste. *Guardian*, 21 December. Available at: https://www.theguardian.com/media/1999/dec/21/tvandradio.television1 (accessed 19 June 2020).

Foster, D. (2018) It's Now Clear: Austerity Is Bad for Your Health. *Guardian*, 10 July. Available at: https://www.theguardian.com/commentisfree/2018/jul/10/austerity-health-cuts-healthcare-poorest-tories (accessed 11 Feb 2021).

Foucault, M. (1990) *The History of Sexuality Volume 3: The Care of the Self*. London: Penguin.

Fox, R. and G. Smith (2011) Sinner Ladies and the Gospel of Good Taste: Geographies of Food, Class and Care. *Health and Place* 17: 403–12.

Francis, J.B. (2018) The Mighty Bosh. Why Going Vegan Can Make You Feel Great and Last Longer in Bed. *Sun*, 18 April. Available at: https://www.thesun.co.uk/fabulous/food/6086777/vegan-dishes-that-make-you-last-longer-in-bed/ (accessed 27 February 2020).

Francis, J.B. (2020) Pamela Anderson Slid into Our DMs to Suggest an Aphrodisiac Vegan Recipe. It's So Surreal. *Sun*, 13 January: 26, 27.

Freidberg, S. (2004) The Ethical Complex of Corporate Food Power. *Environment and Planning D: Society and Space* 22: 513–31.

Friedlander, J. and C. Riedy (2018) Celebrities, Credibility, and Complementary Frames: Raising the Agenda of Sustainable and Other 'Inconvenient' Food Issues in Social Media Campaigning. *Communication Research and Practice* 4(3): 229–45.

Gallagher, M. (2004) What's So Funny about Iron Chef? *Journal of Popular Film and Televion* 31(4): 176–84.

Gallagher, M. (2020) Tail Turn. *Sun*, 29 May. Available at: https://www.thesun.co.uk/tvandshowbiz/11737672/gordon-ramsay-cornwall-neighbours-home/ (accessed 19 May 2021).

Geddes, K. (2018) It's All in the Booklet! Fanny Cradock's Power as a Pioneer TV Celebrity Chef and How She Used It to Transform Cooking Shows on the BBC. Paper delivered at the Dublin Gastronomy Symposium, 29–30 May.

Geddes, K. (2022) 'The Man in the Kitchen'. Boulestin and Harben – Representation, Gender, Celebrity and Business in the Early Development of Television Cooking Programmes in Britain, in A. Tominc, ed., *Food and Cooking on Early Television in Europe*, London: Routledge.

Geraghty, C. (1991) *Women and Soap Opera: A Study of Prime-Time Soap Operas*. Cambridge: Polity.

Giard, L. (1998) Doing Cooking, in M. De Certeau, L Giard and P. Mayol, eds, *The Practice of Everyday Life. Vol. 2: Living and Cooking*. Minneapolis: University of Minnesota Press, pp. 149–247.

Gibson, K.E. and S.E. Dempsey (2013) Make Good Choices, Kid: Biopolitics of Children's Bodies and School Lunch Reform in Jamie Oliver's. *Food Revolution: Children's Geographies* 33(1): 44–58.

Giddens, A. (1991) *Modernity and Self-Identity: Self and Society in the Late Modern Age*. Cambridge: Polity.

Giles, J. (2004) *The Parlour and the Suburb: Domestic Identities, Class, Femininity and Modernity*. Oxford: Berg.

Gill, R. (2003) Power and the Production of Subjects: A Genealogy of the New Man and the New Lad. *Sociological Review* 51(1): 34–56.

Gill, R. (2017) The Affective, Cultural and Psychic Life of Postfeminism. *European Journal of Cultural Studies* 20(6): 606–26.

Gill, R., K. Henwood and C. McLean (2005) Body Projects and the Regulation of Normative Masculinity. *Body and Society* 11(1): 37–62.

Gillespie, C. (1994) Gastrosophy and Nouvelle Cuisine. *British Food Journal* 96(10): 19–23.

Giousmpasoglou, C., L. Brown and J. Cooper (2019) The Role of the Celebrity Chef. *International Journal of Hospitality Management*. https://doi.org/10.1016/j.ijhm.2019.102358 (accessed 10 October 2019).

Goodman, M. (2013) Celebritus Politicus, Neo-liberal Sustainabilities and the Terrains of Care, in G. Fridell and M. Konings, eds, *Age of Icons: Exploring Philanthrocapitalism in the Contemporary World*. Toronto: University of Toronto Press. Available at: https://www.researchgate.net/profile/Michael-Goodman-14/publication/236219570_Celebritus_Politicus_Neo-liberal_Sustainabilities_and_the_Terrains_of_Care/links/00b4951c80c94c06ff000000/Celebritus-Politicus-Neo-liberal-Sustainabilities-and-the-Terrains-of-Care.pdf (accessed 14 June 2021)

Goodman, M. and J. Littler (2013) Celebrity Ecologies: Introduction. *Celebrity Studies* 4(3): 269–75.

Goodman, M., J. Littler, D. Brockington and M. Boykoff (2016) Spectacular Environmentalisms: Media, Knowledge and the Framing of Ecological Politics. *Environmental Communication* 10(6): 677–88.

Goodman, M.K. and S. Jaworska (2020) Mapping Digital Foodscapes: Digital Food Influencers and the Grammars of Good Food. *Geoforum* 117 (December): 183–93.

Gordon, B. (2016) My Kids Would Love Me to Do Bake Off. *Daily Telegraph*, 17 September, features: 27–8.

Gray, C. (2001) Delia Is Defined in New Edition of Dictionary. *Independent*, 3 December. Available at: https://www.independent.co.uk/news/uk/home-news/delia-is-defined-in-new-edition-of-dictionary-9148267.html (accessed 19 May 2020).

Greenebaum, J. (2017) Questioning the Concept of Vegan Privilege: A Commentary. *Humanity and Society* 41(3): 355–72.

Greenebaum, J. (2018) Vegans of Color: Managing Visible and Invisible Stigmas. *Food, Culture and Society* 21(5): 680–97.

Greenebaum, J. and B. Dexter (2018) Vegan Men and Hybrid Masculinity. *Journal of Gender Studies* 27(6): 637–48.

Grice, E. (2016) Deliciously Ella: 'There's a Pressure to Be Sparkly and Shiny All the Time'. *Daily Telegraph*, 23 January. Available at: https://www.telegraph.co.uk/food-and-drink/features/deliciously-ella-interview-new-book-Deliciously-Ella-Every-Day/ (accessed 10 March 2020).

Gualtieri, G. (2021) Discriminating Palates: Evaluation and Ethnoracial Inequality in American Fine Dining. *Social Problems*. Online first: https://doi.org/10.1093/socpro/spaa075 (accessed 12 March 2021).

Guilbert, S. (2020) A New Consumer World View? Available at: http://sites.exeter.ac.uk/foodsystemimpactscv19/blog/2020/12/16/a-new-consumer-world-view/ (accessed 20 May 2021).

Gullestad, M. (1995) Home Decoration as Popular Culture: Constructing Homes, Genders and Classes in Norway, in S. Jackson and S. Moores, eds, *The Politics of Domestic Consumption: Critical Readings*. Hemel Hempstead: Harvester Wheatsheaf, pp. 321–35.

Gunders, J. (2008) Professionalism, Place and Authenticity in The Cook and the Chef. *Emotion, Space and Society* 1(2): 119–26.

Hale, B. (2019a) How Diet Book Pinch of Nom Beat a Jamie Oliver Classic to Top the Bestseller Charts. *Daily Mail*, 26 April. Available at: https://www.dailymail.co.uk/femail/food/article-6963395/How-Pinch-Nom-read-slimming-recipes-including-English-breakfast.html (accessed 20 April 2020).

Hale, B. (2019b) Have YOU Discovered Britain's Slimming Food PheNOMenon? *MailOnline*, 26 April. Available at: https://www.dailymail.co.uk/femail/article-6961261/Meet-food-lovers-freely-admit-not-skinny-minnies.html (accessed 20 April 2020).

Halkier, B. (2010) *Consumption Challenged: Food in Medialised Everyday Lives*. Farnham: Ashgate.

Halkier, B. (2017) Normalizing Convenience Food? *Food, Culture and Society* 20(1): 133–51.

Hamilton, C. (2016) Sex, Work, Meat: The Feminist Politics of Veganism. *Feminist Review* 114(1): 112–29.

Hannerz, U. (1996) *Transnational Connections: Culture, People, Places*. London: Routledge.

Harjunen, H. (2016) *Neoliberal Bodies and the Fat Gendered Body*. London: Routledge.

Harper, A. Breeze (2010) Introduction: The Birth of the Sistah Vegan Project, in A. Breeze Harper, ed., *Sistah Vegan: Black Female Vegans Speak on Food, Identity, Health, and Society*. New York: Lantern, pp. xiii–xix.

Harris, J. (2020) 26 October. Available at: https://twitter.com/Joannechocolat/status/1320663874488668160 (accessed 12 February 2021).

Harris, D.A. and P. Giuffre (2015) *Taking the Heat: Women Chefs and Gender Inequality in the Professional Kitchen*. New Brunswick, NJ: Rutgers University Press.

Harvey, F. (2021) UK Ministers Gain Power to Allow Lower-Standard Food Imports. *Guardian*, 19 January. Available at: https://www.theguardian.com/environment/2021/jan/19/uk-ministers-gain-power-to-allow-lower-standard-food-imports (accessed 19 May 2021).

Haywood, K. and M. Yar (2006) The 'Chav' Phenomenon: Consumption, Media and the Construction of a New Underclass. *Crime Media Culture* 2: 9–28.

Hearn, A. and S. Schoenhoff (2015) From Celebrity to Influencer: Tracing the Diffusion of Celebrity Value across the Data Stream, in P. David Marshall and S. Redmond, eds, *A Companion to Celebrity*. London: John Wiley. https://doi.org/10.1002/9781118475089.ch11

Heathcote Amory, E. (2005) Why We Should All Back the Naked Chef's Crusade to Stop Feeding Our Children Junk Food. *Daily Mail*, 11 March: 14.

Hebdige, D. (1988) *Hiding in the Light*. London: Routledge.

Heldke, L. (2003) *Exotic Appetites: Ruminations of a Food Adventurer*. New York: Routledge.

Henderson, E. (2017) The Women Proving Male and Female Chefs Are Equal. *Independent*, 7 April. Available at: https://www.independent.co.uk/life-style/food-and-drink/women-proving-male-and-female-chefs-are-equal-monica-galetti-a7660666.html (accessed 25 March 2019).

Hermes, J. and A. Hill (2020) Television's Undoing of Social Distancing. *European Journal of Cultural Studies* 23(4): 655–61.

Heritage, S. (2018) Is Netflix's the Final Table Culinary TV's Last Supper? *Guardian*, 19 November. Available at: https://www.theguardian.com/tv-and-radio/2018/nov/19/is-netflixs-the-final-table-culinary-tvs-last-supper (accessed 23 October 2019).

Hickman, M. (2008) The Campaign that Changed the Eating Habits of a Nation. *Independent*, 28 February. Available at: https://www.independent.co.uk/life-style/food-and-drink/news/the-campaign-that-changed-the-eating-habits-of-a-nation-788557.html (accessed 7 June 2021).

Higgens, M., M. Montgomery, A. Smith and A. Tolsen (2012) Belligerent Broadcasting and Makeover Television: Professional Incivility in *Ramsay's Kitchen Nightmares*. *International Journal of Cultural Studies* 15(5): 501–18.

Higginbotham, E. (2021) Footballer and Chef Team Up to Call Full Time on Hunger. *Waitrose Weekend*, April 22: 2–3.

Higgins, M. (2020) Political Masculinities and Brexit: Men of War. *Journal of Language and Politics* 19(1): 89–106.

Highmore, B. (2008) Alimentary Agents: Food, Cultural Theory and Multiculturalism. *Journal of Intercultural Studies* 29(4): 381–98.

Highmore, B. (2009) The Taj Mahal in the High Street: The Indian Restaurant as Diasporic Popular Culture. *Food, Culture and Society* 12(2): 173–90.

Hill, J. (1986) *Sex, Class and Realism: British Cinema, 1956–63*. London: BFI.

Hochschild, A. R. (2000) *The Time Bind: When Work Becomes Home and Home Becomes Work*. New York: Owl Books.

Hochschild, A. Russell. (2003) *The Second Shift*, with A. Machung. London: Penguin.

Hogan, M. (2020) In Times of Crisis, Jamie Oliver Is the National Treasure We Need. *Telegraph*, 24 March. Available at: https://www.telegraph.co.uk/tv/2020/03/24/times-crisis-jamie-oliver-national-treasure-need/ (accessed 12 June 2021).

Holland, M. (2018) Clare Smyth's Best Female Chef Award Raises Questions about Sexism. *Guardian*, 20 June. Available at: https://www.theguardian.com/lifeandstyle/2018/jun/20/clare-smyth-best-female-chef-award-raises-questions-about-sexism (accessed 25 March 2021).

Hollows, J. (2002) The Bachelor Dinner: Masculinity, Class and Cooking in *Playboy*, 1953–61. *Continuum* 16(2): 143–55.

Hollows, J. (2003a) Oliver's Twist: Leisure, Labour and Domestic Masculinity in *The Naked Chef*. *International Journal of Cultural Studies* 6(2): 229–48.

Hollows, J. (2003b) Feeling Like a Domestic Goddess: Postfeminism and Cooking. *European Journal of Cultural Studies* 6(2): 179–202.

Hollows, J. (2016) 'The Worst Mum in Britain': Class, Gender and Caring in the Campaigning Culinary Documentary, in J. Leer and K. Klitgard Povlsen, eds, *Food and Media: Practices, Distinctions and Heterotopias*. London: Routledge, pp. 78–94.

Hollows, J. (2021) Enthusing about Green Peppers: The Europeanisation of British Food Culture in Post-war Britain, 1960–75. *Contemporary British History*. Online first available at: https://doi.org/10.1080/13619462.2021.1925549.

Hollows, J. and S. Jones (2010a) *Please* Don't Try This at Home: Heston Blumenthal, Cookery TV and the Culinary Field. *Food, Culture and Society* 13(4): 521–37.

Hollows, J. and S. Jones (2010b) 'At Least He's Doing Something': Moral Entrepreneurship and Individual Responsibility in Jamie's Ministry of Food. *European Journal of Cultural Studies* 13(3): 307–22.

Holmes, S. and S. Redmond (2006) Introduction: Understanding Celebrity Culture, in S. Holmes and S. Redmond, eds, *Framing Celebrity: New Directions in Celebrity Culture*. London: Routledge, pp. 1–15.

hooks, b. (1991) *Yearning: Race, Gender and Cultural Politics*. Boston: Turnaround.

Hopkinson, G. and J. Cronin (2015) 'When People Take Action …': Mainstreaming Malcontent and the Role of the Celebrity Institutional Entrepreneur. *Journal of Marketing Management* 31(13–14): 1383–402.

Howarth, A. (2015) Hunger Hurts: The Politics of an Austerity Food Blog. *International Journal of E-Politics* 6(3): http://dx.doi.org/10.4018/ijep.2015070102 (accessed 29 October 2020).

Howarth, A. (2017) Challenging the De-Politicization of Food Poverty: Austerity Food Blogs, in Y. Ibrahim, ed., *Politics, Protest and Empowerment in Digital Spaces*. Pennsylvania: IGI Global, pp. 124–42.

Howarth, A. (2020) A British National Scandal: Hunger, Foodbanks and the Deployment of a Dickensian Trope. *Journal of Contemporary European Studies*. Online first: https://doi.org/10.1080/14782804.2020.1839395.

Howell, M. (2019) Why Top Chefs Love Their Chicken to Be on a Grow-Slow. *Telegraph*, 17 March. Available at: https://www.telegraph.co.uk/food-and-drink/features/top-chefs-love-chicken-beon-grow-slow/ (accessed 12 January 2021).

Humble, N. (2005) *Culinary Pleasures: Cook Books and the Transformation of British Food*. London: Faber.

Hunt, E. (2020) From Tofu Lamb Chops to Vegan Steak Bakes. *Guardian*, 12 January. Available at: https://www.theguardian.com/lifeandstyle/2020/jan/12/mock-lamb-chops-vegan-steak-bakes-history-fake-meat (accessed 2 March 2020).

Hunt, L. (1998) *British Low Culture: From Safari Suits to Sexploitation*. London: Routledge.

Hurst, P. (2019) The Unexpected Rise of the Vegan Lad. *Vice*, 22 May. Available at: https://www.vice.com/en_uk/article/xwnama/vegan-men-influencers-lads-recipes-bosh-interview (accessed 27 February 2020).

Hyman, G., (2008) The Taste of Fame: Chefs, Diners, Celebrity, Class. *Gastonomica* 8(3): 43–52.

Ibrahim, Y. (2018) The Re-aestheticization of Poverty: Blogging Hunger in the Age of Austerity. *Social Identities* 24(3): 364–79.

Ibrahim, Y. and A. Howarth (2016) Constructing the Eastern European Other: The Horsemeat Scandal and the Migrant Other. *Journal of Contemporary European Studies* 24(3): 397–413.

Ibrahim, Y. and A. Howarth (2017) Contamination, Deception and 'Othering': The Media Framing of the Horsemeat Scandal. *Social Identities* 23(2): 212–23.

Ichijo, A. (2020) Food and Nationalism: Gastronationalism Revisited. *Nationalities Papers* 48(2): 215–23.
Ichijo, A. and R. Ranta (2016) *Food, National Identity and Nationalism: From Everyday to Global Politics.* Basingstoke: Palgrave Macmillan.
Inglis, D. and A-M Almila (2019) Creating and Routinising Style and Immediacy: Keith Floyd and South-West English Roots of New Cookery Mediatizations, in J. Dürrschmidt and Y. Kautt, eds, *Globalized Eating Cultures: Mediation and Mediatization.* Basingstoke: Palgrave Macmillan, pp. 221–44.
Iqbal, N. (2020) Asma Khan: 'Restaurants Should Be Ranked on How They Treat Their People'. *Observer*, 20 September. Available at: https://www.theguardian.com/food/2020/sep/20/asma-khan-restaurants-ranked-on-how-they-treat-people-chefs-table-netflix-darjeeling-express (accessed 13 March 2021).
Jackson, P. (2015) *Anxious Appetites: Food and Consumer Culture.* London: Bloomsbury.
Jackson, P. (2016) Go Home Jamie: Reframing Consumer Choice. *Social and Cultural Geography* 17(6): 753–7.
Jackson, P. and V. Viehoff (2016) Reframing Convenience Food. *Appetite* 98: 1–11.
Jackson, P., N. Stevenson and K. Brooks (2001) *Making Sense of Men's Magazines.* Cambridge: Polity.
Jackson, P., M. Watson and N. Piper (2013) Locating Anxiety in the Social: The Cultural Mediation of Food Fears. *European Journal of Cultural Studies* 16(1): 24–42.
Jallinoja, P., M. Vinnari and M. Niva (2019) Veganism and Plant-Based Eating: Analysis of Interplay between Discursive Strategies and Lifestyle Political Consumerism, in M. Boström, M. Micheletti and P. Oosterveer, eds, *The Oxford Handbook of Political Consumerism.* Pre-publication accepted version available at https://helda.helsinki.fi//bitstream/handle/10138/309766/Veganism_and_plant_based_eating.pdf?sequence=4 (accessed 29 July 2020).
James, A. (1997) How British Is British Food, in P. Caplan, ed., *Food, Health and Identity.* London: Routledge, pp. 71–86.
Jensen, T. and I. Tyler (2015) 'Benefit Broods': The Cultural and Political Crafting of Anti-Welfare Commonsense. *Critical Social Policy* 35(4): 470–91.
Johnson, J.A. (2011) Hegans: An Examination of the Emerging Male Vegan. *Theses, Dissertations and Other Capstone Projects*: Paper 124. Available at: https://cornerstone.lib.mnsu.edu/cgi/viewcontent.cgi?referer=https://scholar.google.com/scholar?hl=en≈sdt=0%2C5&q=justine+johnson+hegans&btnG=&httpsredir=1&article=1123&context=etds (accessed 2 March 2020).
Johnson, L. and J. Lloyd (2004) *Sentenced to Everyday Life: Feminism and the Housewife.* Oxford: Berg.
Johnston, J. and S. Baumann (2007) Democracy versus Distinction: A Study of Omnivorousness in Food Writing. *American Journal of Sociology* 113(1): 165–204.
Johnston, J. and S. Baumann (2015) *Foodies: Democracy and Distinction in the Gourmet Landsscape*, 2nd edition. New York: Routledge.
Johnston, J. and M. Goodman (2015) Spectacular Foodscapes: Food Celebrities and the Politics of Lifestyle Mediation in an Age of Inequality. *Food, Culture and Society* 18(2): 205–22.
Johnston, J., A. Rodney and P. Chong (2014) Making Change in the Kitchen? A Study of Celebrity Cookbooks, Culinary Personas, and Inequality. *Poetics* 47 (December): 1–22.
Johnston, J., K. Cairns and M. Oleschuk (2018) A Kind Diet: Cultivating Consumer Politics, Status and Femininity through Ethical Eating, in K. Lebesco and P. Naccarato, eds, *The Bloomsbury Handbook of Food and Popular Culture.* London: Bloomsbury, pp. 286–300.

Jones, L. (2020) Veganism: Why Are Vegan Diets on the Rise? *BBC News*, 2 January. Available at: https://www.bbc.co.uk/news/business-44488051 (accessed 2 March 2020).

Jones, S. (2006) Where the Boys Are/Where the Girls Are: Masculinity, Food Writing and Travel. MeCCSA Annual Conference, Leeds Metropolitan University.

Jones, S. and B. Taylor (2001) Food Writing and Food Cultures: The Case of Elizabeth David. *European Journal of Cultural Studies* 4(2): 171–88.

Kelly, C.R. (2017) *Food Television and Otherness in the Age of Globalization*. Lanham, MA: Lexington Books.

Kelly, I. (2003) *Cooking for Kings: The Life of Antoine Carême the First Celebrity Chef*. London: Short Books.

Kelly, P. and L. Harrison (2009) *Working in Jamie's Kitchen: Salvation, Passion and Young Workers*. Basingstoke: Palgrave Macmillan.

Ketchum, C. (2005) The Essence of Cooking Shows: How the Food Network Constructs Consumer Fantasies. *Journal of Communication Inquiry* 29(3): 217–34.

Ketchum, C., (2007) Tunnel Vision and Food: A Political-Economic Analysis of the Food Network, in S. Banet-Weiser, C. Chris and A. Freitas, eds, *Cable Visions: Television beyond Broadcasting*. New York: New York University Press, pp. 158–76.

Khamis, S., L. Ang and R. Welling (2017) Self-branding, 'Micro-celebrity' and the Rise of Social Media Influencers. *Celebrity Studies* 8(2): 191–208.

Kjaer, K. Meldgaard (2019) Detoxing Feels Good: Dieting and Affect in 22 Days Nutrition and GOOP Detoxes. *Feminist Media Studies* 19(5): 702–16.

Knapman, J. (2018) The Power of Plants: How Veganism Conquered the Mainstream. *Wales Online*, 2 March. Available at: https://www.walesonline.co.uk/whats-on/food-drink-news/power-plants-how-veganism-conquered-14339553 (accessed 27 February 2020).

Koletnik, A. (2017) Ethical Transfeminism: Transgender Individuals' Narratives as Contributions to Ethics of Vegetarian Ecofeminisms, in D.A. Vakoch and S. Mickey, eds, *Women and Nature? Beyond Dualism in Gender, Body and Environment*. London: Routledge, pp. 57–74.

Kong, J. (2019) Feasting on 'the Other': Performing Authenticity and Commodifying Difference in Celebrity Chefs' Food and Travel Television Programmes, in C. Leong-Salobir, ed., *Routledge Handbook of Food in Asia*. Abingdon: Routledge, pp. 207–21.

Lagerwey, J. (2018) The Great British Bake Off, Joy and the Affect of Nadiya Hussain's Amateur Celebrity. *Celebrity Studies* 9(4): 442–54.

Lambie-Mumford, H. and M.A. Green (2017) Austerity, Welfare Reform and the Rising Use of Food Banks by Children in England and Wales. *Area* 49(3): 273–79.

Lane, C. (2010) The Michelin-Starred Restaurant Sector as a Cultural Industry: A Cross-National Comparison of Restaurants in the UK and Germany. *Food, Culture and Society* 13(4): 493–519.

Lane, C. (2013) Taste Makers in the 'Fine-Dining' Restaurant Industry: The Attribution of Aesthetic and Economic Value by Gastronomic Guides. *Poetics* 41(4): 342–65.

Lane, H., (1999) Twenty Years on, We're Still in Love with Delia. *Observer*, 12 December. Available at: https://www.theguardian.com/theobserver/1999/dec/12/focus.news (accessed 19 June 2020).

Laville, S. (2020) Petition Calls for Ban on Low-Quality Food Imports in Post-Brexit Deals. *Guardian*, 3 June. Available at: https://www.theguardian.com/politics/2020/jun/03/petition-calls-ban-low-quality-food-imports-post-brexit-deals (accessed 19 May 2021).

Lawson, N. (1998) Can't Cook, Don't Want To. *Guardian*, 13 October. Available at: https://www.theguardian.com/books/1998/oct/13/houseandgarden (accessed 19 June 2020).

LeBesco, K. (2011) Neoliberalism, Public Health and the Moral Perils of Fatness. *Critical Public Health* 21(2): 153–64.

Lee, N. (2014) Celebrity Chefs: Class Mobility, Media, Masculinity. Unpublished PhD thesis, University of Sydney.

Leer, J. (2016a) What's Cooking Man? Masculinity in European Cooking Shows after *The Naked Chef*. *Feminist Review* 114: 72–90.

Leer, J. (2016b) Homosocial Heterotopias and Masculine Escapism in TV Cooking Shows, in J. Leer and K. Klitgard Povlsen, eds, *Food and Media: Practices, Distinctions and Heterotopias*. London: Routledge, pp. 110–26.

Leer, J. (2017) 'If You Want to, You Can Do It!': Home Cooking and Masculinity Makeover in *Le Chef Contre-Attaque*, in M. Szabo and S.L. Koch, eds, *Food, Masculinities and Home: Interdisciplinary Perspectives*. London: Routledge, pp. 182–96.

Leer, J. (2018) Gender and Food Television: A Transnational Perspective on the Gendered Identities of Televised Celebrity Chefs, in K. Lebesco and P. Naccarato, eds, *The Handbook of Food and Popular Culture*. London: Bloomsbury, pp. 13–26.

Leer, J. (2019) Monocultural and Multicultural Gastronationalism. *European Journal of Cultural Studies* 22(5–6): 817–34.

Leer, J. and K. Meldgaard Kjær (2015) Strange Culinary Encounters: Stranger Fetishism in *Jamie's Italian Escape* and *Gordon's Great Escape*. *Food, Culture and Society* 18(2): 309–27.

Leer, J. and S.G. Strøm Krogager, eds (2021) *Research Methods in Digital Food Studies*. London: Routledge.

Leitch, A. (2003) Slow Food and the Politics of Pork Fat: Italian Food and European Identity. *Ethnos* 68(4): 437–62.

Lewis, T. (2008a) *Smart Living: Lifestyle Media and Popular Expertise*. New York: Peter Lang.

Lewis, T. (2008b) Transforming Citizens? Green Politics and Ethical Consumption on Lifestyle Television. *Continuum* 22(2): 227–40.

Lewis, T. (2010) Branding, Celebritization and the Lifestyle Expert. *Cultural Studies* 24(4): 580–98.

Lewis, T. (2020) *Digital Food: From Paddock to Platform*. London: Bloomsbury.

Lewis T. and A. Huber (2015) A Revolution in an Eggcup? Supermarket Wars, Celebrity Chefs and Ethical Consumption. *Food, Culture and Society* 18(2): 289–307.

Littler, J. (2007) Celebrity CEOs and the Cultural Economy of Tabloid Intimacy, in S. Redmond and S. Holmes, eds, *Stardom and Celebrity: A Reader*. London: Sage, pp. 230–43.

Littler, J. (2008) 'I Feel Your Pain': Cosmopolitan Charity and the Public Fashioning of the Celebrity Soul. *Social Semiotics* 18(2): 237–51.

Littler, J. (2009) *Radical Consumption: Shopping for Change in Contemporary Culture*. Maidenhead: Open University Press.

Littler, J. (2011) What's Wrong with Ethical Consumption, in T. Lewis and E. Potter, eds, *Ethical Consumption: A Critical Introduction*. London: Routledge, pp. 27–39.

Lott-Lavigna, R. (2019) The Origins of Fake Meat Are Rooted in Chinese Cooking. *Vice*, 2 May. Available at: https://www.vice.com/en/article/8xyqqz/the-origins-of-fake-meat-are-rooted-in-chinese-cooking (accessed 29 April 2021).

Lupton, D. (1996) *Food, the Body and the Self*. London: Sage.

Lupton, D. (2017) Digital Media and Body Weight, Shape, and Size: An Introduction and Review. *Fat Studies* 6(2): 119–34.

Lupton, D. (2018a) Cooking, Eating, Uploading: Digital Food Cultures, in K. Lebesco and P. Naccarato, eds, *The Handbook of Food and Popular Culture*. London: Bloomsbury, pp. 66–79.

Lupton, D. (2018b) Vitalities and Visceralities: Alternative Body/Food Politics in New Digital Media, in M. Phillipov and K. Kirkwood, eds, *Alternative Food Politics: From the Margins to the Mainstream*. Abingdon: Routledge, pp. 151–68.
Lupton, D. (2018c) *Fat*, 2nd edition. Abingdon: Routledge.
Lupton, D. and Z. Feldman, eds (2020) *Digital Food Cultures*. London: Routledge.
Lury, C. (1996) *Consumer Culture*. Cambridge: Polity.
Lutrario, J. (2017) TV Dinners – the Problems with Great British Menu Dishes. *Big Hospitality*, 17 October. Available at: https://www.bighospitality.co.uk/Article/2017/10/17/Great-British-Menu-chef-dishes (accessed 22 October 2019).
Luzzi, J. (2002) Italy without Italians: Literary Origins of a Romantic Myth. *MLN* 117(1): 48–83.
Lytton, C. (2020) Pinch of Nom. *Daily Telegraph*, 24 January. Available at: https://www.telegraph.co.uk/health-fitness/nutrition/pinch-nom-telling-us-fat-going-do-harm-good/ (accessed 20 April 2020).
McCahill, E. (2017) Jamie Oliver Reveals He Wants to End His Eight Year Feud with Rival Gordon Ramsay after Miscarriage Row. *Sun*, 6 December. Available at: https://www.thesun.co.uk/tvandshowbiz/5082303/jamie-oliver-wants-end-eight-year-feud-gordon-ramsay-miscarriage-row/ (accessed 18 October 2019).
McCormick, L. (2020) Marking Time in Lockdown: Heroization and Ritualization in the UK during the Coronavirus Pandemic. *American Journal of Cultural Sociology* 8: 324–51.
McKenzie, L. (2015) *Getting By: Estates, Class and Culture in Austerity Britain*. Bristol: Policy Press.
McPhail, D., B. Beagan and G.E. Chapman (2012) 'I Don't Want to Be Sexist but …': Denying and Reinscribing Gender through Food. *Food, Culture and Society* 15(3): 473–89.
McRobbie, A. (2009) *The Aftermath of Feminism: Gender, Culture and Social Change*. London: Sage.
McShane, B. (2017) What Will Brexit Mean for Our Bacon? *BBC News*, 31 October. Available at: https://www.bbc.co.uk/news/business-41804993 (accessed 18 May 2021).
Makalintal, B. (2020) A Case for a More Regional Understanding of Food. *Vice*, 20 November. Available at: https://www.vice.com/en/article/93wb7e/a-case-for-a-more-regional-understanding-of-food (accessed 14 May 2021).
Mangan, L. (2018a) How Brexit, Donald Trump and the New Cold War Have Killed Off Clean Eating. *Daily Telegraph*, 16 March. Available at: https://www.telegraph.co.uk/women/life/brexit-donald-trump-new-cold-war-have-killed-clean-eating/ (accessed 11 Mar 2020).
Mangan, L. (2018b) Nadiya's Asian Odyssey Review. *Guardian*, 3 December. Available at: https://www.theguardian.com/tv-and-radio/2018/dec/03/nadiya-hussain-asian-odyssey-review (accessed 17 May 2021).
Marshall, P. D. (1997) *Celebrity and Power: Fame in Contemporary Culture*. Minneapolis: University of Minnesota Press.
Martin, B. (2018) What *The Final Table* Says about the Power Structures of Fine Dining. *Los Angeles Magazine*, 28 November. Available at: https://www.lamag.com/digestblog/final-table-netflix/ (accessed 23 October 2019).
Martin, J. (2020a) *Voices from the Kitchen Table: (Post)Feminism and Domestic Cultures During Austerity*. PhD Thesis, University of Leicester.
Martin, J. (2020b) Keep Crafting and Carry On: Nostalgia and Domestic Cultures in the Crisis. *European Journal of Cultural Studies*. Online first: https://doi.org/10.1177/1367549420958718 (accessed 1 February 2021).

Marwick, A. (2015) You May Know Me from YouTube: (Micro-)Celebrity in Social Media, in P. David Marshall and S. Redmond, eds, *A Companion to Celebrity*. London: John Wiley. https://doi.org/10.1002/9781118475089.ch18

Matta, R. (2019) Celebrity Chefs and the Limits of Playing Politics from the Kitchen, in J. Dürrschmidt and Y. Kautt, eds, *Globalized Eating Cultures: Mediation and Mediatization*. Basingstoke: Palgrave Macmillan, pp. 183–201.

Matwick, K. and K. Matwick (2019) *Food Discourse of Celebrity Chefs of Food Network*. Basingstoke: Palgrave Macmillan.

Maxwell, R. and M. DeSoucey (2016) Gastronomic Cosmopolitanism: Supermarket Products in France and the United Kingdom. *Poetics* 56 (June): 85–97.

May, J., A. Williams, P. Cloke and L. Cherry (2020) Food Banks and the Production of Scarcity. *Transactions of the Institute of British Geographers* 45(1): 208–22.

Mayoh, J. (2019) Perfect Pregnancy? Pregnant Bodies, Digital Leisure and the Presentation of Self. *Leisure Studies* 38(2): 204–217.

Meah, A. and P. Jackson (2017) Convenience as Care: Culinary Antinomies in Practice. *Environment and Planning A* 49(9): 2065–81.

Meddings, S. (2019) Pinch of Nom: The Cookbook That's Selling Like Hot Cakes. *Sunday Times*, 31 March. Available at: https://www.thetimes.co.uk/article/pinch-of-nom-the-cookbook-thats-selling-like-hot-cakes-9zslrn2h7 (accessed 20 April 2020).

Mennell, S. (1996) *All Manners of Food: Eating and Taste in England and France from the Middle Ages to the Present*. 2nd edition. Chicago: University of Illinois Press.

Michel, C.X. (n.d.) My Work. Available at: https://charlesxmichel.com/ (accessed 17 October 2019).

Michelin (2019) 5 Questions with Chef Gary Rhodes on Modernising British Cuisine. Available at: https://guide.michelin.com/en/article/people/5-questions-with-chef-gary-rhodes-on-modernising-british-cuisine (accessed 14 May 2021).

Mikhailova, A. and M. Aitchison (2020) Prue Leith Quits Conservative Party in Protest at Government's Stance over Food Standards. *Mail on Sunday*, 24 October. Available at: https://www.dailymail.co.uk/news/article-8875887/Prue-Leith-quits-Conservative-Party-protest-Governments-stance-foods-standards.html (accessed 12 January 2020).

Millar, J. (2018) The Brexiteers Represent the Four Faces of Toxic Masculinity. *New Statesman*, 5 July. Available at: https://www.newstatesman.com/politics/staggers/2018/07/brexiteers-represent-four-faces-toxic-masculinity (accessed 18 May 2021).

Miller, D. (1998) *A Theory of Shopping*. Cambridge: Polity.

Mintel (2019) Veganuary: UK Overtakes Germany as World's Leader for Vegan Food Launches. Mintel Press Office, 10 January. Available at: https://www.mintel.com/press-centre/food-and-drink/veganuary-uk-overtakes-germany-as-worlds-leader-for-vegan-food-launches (accessed 2 March 2020).

Mohdin, A. (2018) Only Two Black Head Chefs in UK's Michelin-starred Restaurants. *Guardian*, 5 December. Available at: https://www.theguardian.com/food/2018/dec/06/only-two-black-head-chefs-in-uks-michelin-starred-restaurants (accessed 12 March 2021).

Monaghan, L.F., E. Rich and A.E. Bombak (2019) Media, 'Fat Panic' and Public Pedagogy: Mapping Contested Terrain. *Sociology Compass* 31(1): https://doi.org/10.1111/soc4.12651

Monroe, J. (2014) *A Girl Called Jack*. [e-book] London: Penguin.

Monroe, J. (2019) *Tin Can Cook*. London: Bluebird.

Monroe, J. (2020a) 24 October. Available at: https://twitter.com/BootstrapCook/status/1320104342293184515 (accessed 29 October 2020; tweet no longer available).

Monroe, J. (2020b) 28 October. Available at: https://twitter.com/BootstrapCook/status/1320104342293184515(accessed 30 November 2020; tweet no longer available)

Moores, S. (1993) *Interpreting Audiences: The Ethnography of Media Consumption*. London: Sage.

Moores, S. (2000) *Media and Everyday Life in Modern Society*. Edinburgh: Edinburgh University Press.

Morabito, G. (2018) Netflix Rewrites the Recipe for Cooking Shows on 'The Final Table'. *Eater*, 8 November. Available at: https://www.eater.com/2018/11/8/18072524/final-table-netflix-show-chefs-judges-premiere-date (accessed 23 October 2019).

Moran, J. (2000) *Star-Authors: Literary Celebrity in America*. London: Pluto.

Morgan, Z. (2018) Why Are Our Professional Kitchens Still Male Dominated?, *BBC News*, 16 September. Available at: https://www.bbc.co.uk/news/uk-wales-45486646 (accessed 25 March 2021).

Morley, D. (2000) *Home Territories: Media, Mobility and Identity*. London: Routledge.

Morris, C. (2017) 'Taking the Politics out of Broccoli': Debating (De)meatification in UK National and Regional Newspaper Coverage of the Meat Free Mondays Campaign. *Sociologia Ruralis* 58(2): 433–52.

Moseley, R. (2000) Makeover Takeover on British TV. *Screen* 41(3): 299–314.

Moseley, R. (2001) 'Real Lads *Do* Cook … but Some Things Are Still Hard to Talk about: the Gendering of 8–9'. *European Journal of Cultural Studies* 4(1): 32–40.

Moseley, R. (2009) Marguerite Patten, Television Cookery and Post War British Femininity, in S. Gillis and J. Hollows, eds, *Feminism, Domesticity and Popular Culture*. New York: Routledge, pp. 17–32.

Mudry, J. (2018) Nutrition, Health, and Food: 'What Should I Eat?' in K. Lebesco and P. Naccarato, eds, *The Handbook of Food and Popular Culture*. London: Bloomsbury, pp. 274–85.

Murcott, A. (1995) 'It's a Pleasure to Cook for Him': Food, Gender and Mealtimes in Some South Wales Households, in S. Jackson and S. Moores, eds, *The Politics of Domestic Consumption: Critical Readings*. Hemel Hempstead: Harvester Wheatsheaf, pp. 89–99.

Murcott, A. (2019) *Introducing the Sociology of Food and Eating*. London: Bloomsbury.

Murray, S. (2013) Food and Television, in K. Albala, ed., *Routledge International Handbook of Food Studies*. New York: Routledge, pp. 187–97.

Myall, S. (2014) Former MasterChef Star Michel Roux Jnr Prefers British Chefs because French Are 'too lazy'. *Mirror*, 12 November. Available at: https://www.mirror.co.uk/tv/tv-news/former-masterchef-star-michel-roux-4608553 (accessed 14 October 2019).

Myall, S. (2018) Vegan Cooking Sensations BOSH! Reveal How Two Meat-eating School Friends Changed Their Lives to Become the Newest Diet Gurus. *Mirror*, 30 January. Available at: https://www.mirror.co.uk/news/real-life-stories/vegan-cooking-sensations-bosh-reveal-11934814 (accessed 27 Feburary 2020).

Mycek, M.K. (2018) Meatless Meals and Masculinity: How Veg* Men Explain Their Plant-based Diets. *Food and Foodways* 26(3): 223–45.

Naccarato, P. and K. Lebesco (2012) *Culinary Capital*. London: Berg.

Naik, A. (2008) Did Jamie Oliver Really Put School Dinners on the Agenda? An Examination of the Role of the Media in Policy Making. *Political Quarterly* 79(3): 426–33.

Nava, M. (1987) Consumerism and Its Contradictions. *Cultural Studies* 1(2): 204–10.

Negus, K. (1992) *Producing Pop: Culture and Conflict in the Popular Music Industry*. London: Arnold.

Nemeschansky, B., L. Neill. S. Wright and M. Brocx (2017) His Own Kind of Honour: Reluctant Celebrity Chef Michael Van de Elzen. *Celebrity Studies* 8(3): 378–92.

Neuhaus, J. (2012) *Manly Meals and Mom's Home Cooking: Cookbooks and Gender in Modern America*. Baltimore: Johns Hopkins University Press.

Neuman, N., L. Gottzén and C. Fjellström (2019) Distinctions and Boundaries in Men's Talk about Food Celebrities. *British Food Journal* 121(2): 520–32.

Nguyen, V. (n.d.) At the 'Chef's Table': Interview with Creator David Gelb. *Cinemathread*. Available at: https://cinemathread.com/tv-film/at-the-chefs-table-interview-with-creator-david-gelb/ (accessed 24 October 2019).

Onwuemezi, N. (2017) Emma Mills Wins Nielsen Award for Selling 250K Copies. *The Bookseller*, 25 July. Available at: https://www.thebookseller.com/news/ella-mills-wins-specsavers-bestseller-award-597156 (accessed 26 March 2020).

O'Connell, R. and J. Brannen (2020) We're Not 'All in This Together': COVID-19 Exposes Stark Realities of Food Insecurity. *UCL Europe Blog*, 12 May. Available at: https://ucleuropeblog.com/2020/05/12/were-not-all-in-this-together-covid-19-exposes-stark-realities-of-food-insecurity/ (accessed 28 January 2021).

O'Connell and J. Brannen (2021) Young People in Food Poverty: A Lost Generation? *BMJ Blogs*, 29 January. Available at: https://blogs.bmj.com/bmj/2021/01/29/young-people-in-food-poverty-a-lost-generation/ (accessed 12 February 2021).

O'Connell, R. and L. Hamilton (2017) Hunger and Food Poverty, in V. Cooper and D. Whyte, eds, *The Violence of Austerity*. London: Pluto Press, pp. 94–100.

O'Connell, R., A. Knight and J. Brannen (2019) *Living Hand to Mouth: Children and Food in Low-Income Families*. London: CPAG.

O'Connor, R. (2019) People's Vote. *Independent*, 23 March. Available at: https://www.independent.co.uk/arts-entertainment/films/news/brexit-march-london-people-s-vote-celebrity-supporters-steve-coogan-latest-a8836516.html (accessed 18 May 2021).

Oliver, J. (2005) *Jamie's Italy*. London: Michael Joseph.

Oliver, J. (2008) *Jamie's Ministry of Food*. London: Michael Joseph.

Oliver, J. (2020) Chlorinated Chicken? I Wouldn't Want My Children to Eat It. *Times*, 7 October. Available at: https://www.thetimes.co.uk/article/jamie-oliver-chlorinated-chicken-i-wouldnt-want-my-kids-to-eat-it-mzllpsst5 (accessed 12 January 2020).

Ommundsen, W. (2007) From the Altar to the Market-Place and Back Again: Understanding Literary Celebrity, in S. Redmond and S. Holmes, eds, *Stardom and Celebrity: A Reader*. London: Sage, pp. 244–55.

O'Neill, R. (2020) 'Glow from the Inside Out': Deliciously Ella and the Politics of 'Healthy Eating'. *European Journal of Cultural Studies*. Online first: https://doi.org/10.1177/1367549420921868 (accessed 12 February 2021).

Onwuemezi, N. (2017) Ella Mills Wins Nielsen Award for Selling 250K Copies. *Bookseller*, 25 July. Available at: https://www.thebookseller.com/news/ella-mills-wins-specsavers-bestseller-award-597156 (accessed 30 April 2020).

Oren, T. (2013) On the Line: Format, Cooking and Competition as Television Values. *Critical Studies in Television* 10(8): 20–35.

Oren, T. (2016) The Blood Sport of Cooking: On Asian-American Chefs and Television, in S. Davé, L. Nishime and T. Oren, eds, *Global Asian American Popular Cultures*. New York: New York University Press, pp. 244–60.

Ouellette, L. and J. Hay (2008) Makeover Television, Governmentality and the Good Citizen. *Continuum* 24: 471–84.

Owen, G. and B. Carlin (2020a) Don't Betray Our Farmers. *Mail on Sunday*, 31 May. Available at: https://www.dailymail.co.uk/news/article-8373145/Most-Britons-oppose-ditching-animal-welfare-environmental-rules-trade-deal-says-MoS-poll.html (accessed 19 May 2021).

Owen, G. and B. Carlin (2020b) Back UK Farmers, Says Great British Bake Off's Prue Leith. *Mail on Sunday*, 10 October. Available at: https://www.dailymail.co.uk/news/article-8826879/Back-UK-farmers-says-Great-British-Bake-Offs-Prue-Leith.html (accessed 12 January 2021).

Panayi, P. (2008) *Spicing Up Britain: The Multicultural History of British Food*. London: Reaktion.

Parasecoli, F. (2016) Starred Cosmopolitanism: Celebrity Chefs, Documentaries, and the Circulation of Global Desire. *Semiotica* 211: 315–39.

Parker, O. (2015) Deliciously Ella: I Want People to Get Excited about Veg. *Daily Telegraph*, 24 January. Available at: https://www.telegraph.co.uk/foodanddrink/11362275/Deliciously-Ella-I-want-to-get-people-excited-about-veg.html (accessed 10 March 2020).

Parkins, W. (2004) At Home in Tuscany: Slow Living and the Cosmopolitan Subject. *Home Cultures* 1: 257–74.

Parkins, W. and G. Craig (2006) *Slow Living*. Oxford: Berg.

Parkins, W. and G. Craig (2011) Slow Living and the Temporalities of Sustainable Consumption, in T. Lewis and E. Potter, eds, *Ethical Consumption: A Critical Introduction*. London: Routledge, pp. 189–201.

Parsons, J.M. (2015) *Gender, Class and Food: Families, Bodies and Health*. Basingstoke: Palgrave Macmillan.

Pedwell, C. (2017) Mediated Habits: Images, Networked Affect and Social Change. *Subjectivity* 10: 147–69.

Perrier, M. and E. Swan (2020) 'Crazy for Carcass': Sarah Wilson, Foodie-Waste Femininity and Digital Whiteness, in D. Lupton and Z. Feldman, eds, *Digital Food Cultures*. Abingdon: Routledge, pp.129–44.

Perring, R. (2019) Marco Pierre White Blasts Remoaner Jamie Oliver for Brexit Blame. *Express*, 21 August. Available at: https://www.express.co.uk/news/uk/1168473/jamie-oliver-brexit-Marco-Pierre-White-comment-brexit-news (accessed 12 December 2020).

Petrini, C. (2003) *Slow Food: The Case for Taste*. New York: Columbia University Press.

Phillipov, M. (2017) *Media and Food Industries: The New Politics of Food*. London: Palgrave Macmillan.

Phillipov, M. and F. Gale (2020) Celebrity Chefs, Consumption, Politics and Food Labelling: Exploring the Contradictions. *Journal of Consumer Culture* 20(4): 400–18

Pike, J. and P. Kelly (2014) *The Moral Geographies of Children, Young People and Food: Beyond Jamie's School Dinners*. Basingstoke: Palgrave Macmillan.

Piper, N. (2013) Audiencing Jamie Oliver: Embarrassment, Voyeurism and Reflexive Positioning. *Geoforum* 45: 346–55.

Piper, N. (2015) Jamie Oliver and Cultural Intermediation. *Food, Culture and Society* 18(2): 245–64.

Platell, A. (2015) Poor Flora Wasn't PC Enough for BBC. *Daily Mail*, 3 October. https://www.dailymail.co.uk/femail/article-3258338/AMANDA-PLATELL-womb-transplants-make-shudder.html (accessed 14 May 2021).

Polan, D. (2011) *Julia Child's The French Chef*. Durham, NC: Duke University Press.

Poole, B. (2020) French Fast Food and the Myth of Americanisation. *Modern and Contemporary France* 28(2): 141–56.

Potter, L. and C. Westall (2013) Neoliberal Britain's Austerity Foodscape: Home Economics, Veg Patch Capitalism and Culinary Temporality. *New Formations* 80: 156–78.

Powell, E. (2017) GBBO Star Nadiya Hussain Hits Back at Racist Twitter Trolls Telling Her to Leave the UK. *Evening Standard*, 31 October. Available at: https://www.standard.co.uk/showbiz/celebrity-news/gbbo-star-nadiya-hussain-hits-back-at-racist-twitter-trolls-telling-her-to-leave-the-uk-a3672596.html (accessed 17 May 2021).

Powell, H. and S. Prasad (2010) 'As Seen on TV'. The Celebrity Expert: How Taste Is Shaped by Lifestyle Media. *Cultural Politics* 6(1): 111–24.

Presswood, A. (2020) *Food Blogs, Postfeminism and the Communication of Expertise: Digital Domestics*. Lanham: Lexington.

Probyn, E. (2019) Mediating Fish: Mediatization, Consumer Choice and Media Morality, in J. Dürrschmidt and Y. Kautt, eds, *Globalized Eating Cultures: Mediation and Mediatization*. Basingstoke: Palgrave Macmillan, pp. 247–65.

Rahman, M. (2020) Consuming Brexit: Alimentary Discourses and the Racial Politics of Brexit. *Open Arts Journal* 8. Available at: https://openartsjournal.files.wordpress.com/2020/08/oaj_issue8_rahman-1.pdf (accessed 16 January 2021).

Raisborough, J. (2016) *Fat Bodies, Health and the Media*. London: Palgrave Macmillan.

Ramsay, G. (n.d.) About Gordon. Available at: https://www.gordonramsay.com/gr/about-gordon/ (accessed 14 October 2019).

Randall, S. (1999) Television Representations of Food: A Case Study. *International Journal of Tourism and Hospitality Research* 1(1): 41–54.

Randall, S. (2000) Mediated Meanings of Hospitality: Television Personality Food Programmes, in C. Lashley and A. Morrison, eds, *In Search of Hospitality: Theoretical Perspectives and Debates*. London: Routledge, pp. 118–33.

Rao, H., P. Monin and R. Durand (2003) Institutional Change in Toque Ville: Nouvelle Cuisine as an Identity Movement in French Gastronomy. *American Journal of Sociology* 108(4): 795–843.

Rashford, M. (2020) Protect the Vulnerable. *Guardian*, 15 June. Available at: https://www.theguardian.com/football/2020/jun/15/protect-the-vulnerable-marcus-rashfords-emotional-letter-to-mps (accessed 20 May 2021).

Rashford, M. et al. (2021) Government Needs to Urgently Fix Free School Meal Policy Long-Term (letter to the Prime Minister). Available at: https://foodfoundation.org.uk/wp-content/uploads/2021/01/FAO-PM-Boris-Johnson-21.01.21-update.pdf (accessed 21 May 2021).

Ray, K. (2007) Domesticating Cuisine: Food and Aesthetics on American Television. *Gastronomica* 7(1): 50–63.

Redmond, S. and S. Holmes, eds (2007) *Stardom and Celebrity: A Reader*. London: Sage.

Reiner, A. (2020) The Age of the Politically Agnostic Chef Is Over. *Restaurant Manifesto*, 1 November. Available at: https://www.restaurantmanifesto.com/food-and-politics-the-agnostic-chef/ (accessed 28 May 2021).

Rich, E. (2011) 'I See Her Being Obesed': Public Pedagogy, Reality Media and the Obesity Crisis. *Health* 15: 3–21.

Ritzer, G. (1993) *The McDonaldization of Society*. London: Sage.

RobbingHoodUK (2014) Could Jamie Oliver Be UKIPs Secret Weapon? Available at: https://www.youtube.com/watch?v=sVGOvaoCq-w (accessed 18 May 2021).

Rodney, A. (2019) The Rise of the Blogspert: Biopedagogy, Self-knowledge, and Lay Expertise on Women's Healthy Living Blogs. *Social Theory and Health*: https://doi.org/10.1057/s41285-019-00095-z.

Rodney, A. (2020) The Authentic 'Healthy Everywoman'? Readers' Evaluation of Healthy Living Bloggers' Identities, in J.P. Williams and K.C. Scharz, eds, *Studies on the Social Construction of Identity and Authenticity*. London: Routledge, pp. 43–57.

Rodney, A., S. Cappeliez, M. Oleschuk and J. Johnston (2017) The Online Domestic Goddess: An Analysis of Food Blog Femininities. *Food, Culture and Society* 20(4): 685–707.

Rogers, R.A. (2008) Beasts, Burgers and Hummers: Meat and the Crisis of Masculinity in Contemporary Television Advertisements. *Environmental Communication* 2(3): 281–301.

Rojek, C. (2001) *Celebrity*. London: Reaktion.

Rose, G. (1995) Place and Identity: A Sense of Place, in D. Massey and P. Jess, eds, *A Place in the World*. Oxford: Oxford University Press, pp. 87–132.

Rose, H. (2018) The Bosh! Boys: The Vegan Jamie Olivers. *Times*, 31 March. Available at: https://www.thetimes.co.uk/article/the-bosh-boys-the-vegan-jamie-olivers-30xl7ttq9 (accessed 4 June 2021).

Rossato, L. (2015) Le Grand Culinary Tour: Adaptation and Retranslation of Gastronomic Journeys across Languages and Food Cultures. *The Translator* 21(3): 271–95.

Rousseau, S. (2012a) *Food and Social Media: You Are What You Tweet*. Plymouth: Alta Mira Press.

Rousseau, S. (2012b) *Food Media: Celebrity Chefs and the Politics of Everyday Interference*. Oxford: Berg.

Rowe, P and E. Grady (2020) I See Your Expertise and Raise You Mine: Social Media Foodscapes and the Rise of the Celebrity Chef, in D. Lupton and Z. Feldman, eds, *Digital Food Cultures*. Abingdon: Routledge, pp. 114–28.

Ruby, M.B. and S.J. Heine (2011) Meat, Morals, and Masculinity. *Appetite* 56(2): 447–50.

Rybczynski, W. (1987) *Home: A Short History of an Idea*. Harmondsworth: Penguin.

Sanders, L. Shapiro (2008) Consuming Nigella, in S. Gillis and J. Hollows, eds, *Feminism, Domesticity and Popular Culture*. London: Routledge, pp. 151–63.

Salkin, A. (2014) *From Scratch: The Uncensored History of the Food Network*. New York: Berkley.

Salter, J. (2014) Deliciously Ella: The Blogger Inspiring Healthy Eating. *Daily Telegraph*, 20 February. Available at: https://www.telegraph.co.uk/foodanddrink/healthyeating/10648654/Deliciously-Ella-the-blogger-inspiring-healthy-eating.html (accessed 10 Mar 2020).

Sarkar, A. (2020) Cooking Up a Storm. *Telegraph India*, 29 August. Available at: https://www.telegraphindia.com/culture/people/cooking-up-a-storm-calcutta-bred-london-based-chef-asma-khan-on-her-quest-for-change-through-the-kitchen/cid/1790377 (accessed 13 March 2021).

Saul, H. (2016) Jamie Oliver Dismisses Controversy over Having Children Watch Wife Give Birth. *Independent*, 2 December. Available at: https://www.independent.co.uk/news/people/jamie-oliver-wife-jools-birth-brexit-a7451556.html (accessed 10 December 2020).

Savage, M., G. Bagnall and B. Longhurst (2001) Ordinary, Ambivalent and Defensive: Class Identities in the Northwest of England. *Sociology* 35(4): 875–92.

Schlosser, E. (2001) *Fast Food Nation*. Harmondsworth: Penguin.

Scott, E. (2020) Healthism and Veganism: Discursive Constructions of Food and Health in Online Vegan Communities, in D. Lupton and Z. Feldman, eds, *Digital Food Cultures*. Abingdon: Routledge, pp. 66–81.

Sculthorpe, T. and K. Ferguson (2017) Liam Fox Tells Remoaners Plotting to Thwart Brexit They Are DREAMING if They Think They Can Undo Last Year's Historic Referendum Result. *MailOnline*, 24 July. Available at: https://www.dailymail.co.uk/news/article-4724130/First-round-Brexit-trade-talks-kicks-off.html (accessed 12 Jan 2020).

Sender, K. and M. Sullivan (2008) Epidemics of Will, Failures of Self-Esteem: Responding to Fat Bodies in *The Biggest Loser* and *What Not to Wear*. *Continuum* 22: 573–84.

Shammas, J. (2018) 'I am Home'. *Sun*, 23 January. Available at: https://www.thesun.co.uk/news/5410398/great-british-bake-off-star-nadiya-hussain-blasts-vile-twitter-trolls-who-told-her-to-go-home/ (accessed 17 May 2021).

Sherwin, A. and F. Morse (2013) Jamie Oliver: Let Them Eat Stale Bread. *Independent*, 28 August. Available at: https://www.independent.co.uk/life-style/food-and-drink/news/jamie-oliver-let-them-eat-stale-bread-8785062.html (accessed 14 May 2021).

Sherwood, H. and A. Nardelli (2015) Muslim Leaders in UK Warn of 'Worrying' Levels of Islamophobia. *Guardian*, 26 October. Available at: https://www.theguardian.com/world/2015/oct/26/muslim-leaders-in-uk-warn-of-worrying-levels-of-islamophobia (accessed 14 May 2021).

Shilling, J. (2005) Can Our Hero Slay the Beast of the Turkey Twizzler? *Times*, 25 March: Section 2: 2.

Sikka, T. (2019) The Contradictions of Superfood Consumerism in a Postfeminist, Neoliberal World. *Food, Culture and Society* 22(3): 354–75.

Silk, M. (2011) Towards a Sociological Analysis of London 2012. *Sociology* 45(5): 733–48.

Silk, M., J. Francombe and F. Bachelor (2011) The Biggest Loser: The Discursive Constitution of Fatness. *Interactions: Studies in Communication & Culture* 1(3): 369–89.

Silva, E. (2007) Gender, Class, Emotional Capital and Consumption in Everyday Life, in E. Casey and L. Martens, eds, *Gender and Domestic Consumption: Domestic Consumption and the Commercialization of Everyday Life*. Aldershot: Ashgate, pp. 141–59.

Simonetti, L. (2012) The Ideology of Slow Food. *Journal of European Studies* 42(2): 168–89.

Singh, A. (2017) Gordon Ramsay: Why Brexit Will Be a Good Thing for Lazy Britain. *Telegraph*, 11 October. Available at: https://www.telegraph.co.uk/news/2017/10/10/gordon-ramsay-brexit-will-good-thing-lazy-britain/ (accessed 12 December 2020).

Singh, A. (2009) Jamie Oliver: I'm Six-Generation Sudanese. *Daily Telegraph*, 29 August. Available at: https://www.telegraph.co.uk/news/celebritynews/6083245/Jamie-Oliver-Im-sixth-generation-Sudanese.html (accessed 14 May 2021).

Sitwell, W. (2019) At Home with the Bosh! Boys. *Telegraph*, 24 September. Available at: https://www.telegraph.co.uk/food-and-drink/features/home-bosh-boys-much-sense-does-new-vegan-manifesto-make/ (accessed 27 February 2020).

Skeggs, B. (2004) *Class, Self, Culture*. London: Routledge.

Skeggs, B. (2005) The Making of Class and Gender through Visualizing Moral Subject Formation. *Sociology* 39: 965–82.

Skeggs, B. and H. Wood (2020) Clap for Carers? From Care Gratitude to Care Justice. *European Journal of Cultural Studies* 23(4): 641–47.

Skey, M. (2012) We Need to Talk about Cosmopolitanism: The Challenge of Studying Openness towards Other People. *Cultural Sociology* 6(4): 471–87.

Slocum, S., J. Shannon, K. Cadieux and M. Beckman (2011) 'Properly, with Love, from Scratch': Jamie Oliver's Food Revolution. *Radical History Review* 110: 178–91.

Smith, A. (2020) Clean Eating's Surprising Normalisation: The Case of Nigella Lawson. *Discourse, Context and Media* 35. Online first: https://doi.org/10.1016/j.dcm.2020.100376

Smith, G. (2020) *Taste and the TV Chef*. Bristol: Intellect.

Smithers, R. (2020) Veganuary Signed Up Record 400,000 People, Campaign Reveals. *Guardian*, 3 February. Available at: https://www.theguardian.com/food/2020/feb/03/veganuary-signed-up-record-400000-people-campaign-reveals (accessed 29 July 2020).

Snead, F. (2018) Jamie Oliver: 'Middle-class Logic' Does Not Work for Obese People from Poorer Backgrounds. *Independent*, 4 July. Available at: https://inews.co.uk/news/health/jamie-oliver-middle-class-logic-not-work-obese-people-poorer-backgrounds-132021 (accessed 17 May 2021).

Sobal, J. (2005) Men, Meat and Marriage: Models of Masculinity. *Food and Foodways* 13(1–2): 135–58.

Sobande, F. (2020) 'We're All in This Together': Commodified Notions of Connection, Care and Community in Brand Response to COVID-19. *European Journal of Cultural Studies* 23(6): 1033–7.

Soper, K. (2008) Alternative Hedonism, Cultural Theory and the Role of Aesthetic Revisioning. *Cultural Studies* 22(5): 567–87.

Sotherby's (2019) Massimo Bottura at the Intersection of Art and Artisan. Available at: https://www.youtube.com/watch?v=dnHwSyKfeFU (accessed 17 October 2019).

Spiering, M. (2006) Food, Phagophobia and English National Identity. *European Studies* 22 (January): 31–48.

Spiering, M. (2014) *A Cultural History of British Euroscepticism*. Basingstoke: Palgrave Macmillan.

Steafel, E. (2019) Pinch of Nom. *Daily Telegraph*, 29 March. Available at: https://www.telegraph.co.uk/health-fitness/nutrition/women-behind-pinch-nom-diet-cookbook-healthyish-home-cooks/ (accessed 20 April 2020).

Stiritup (2019) Leading Lights: Adam Reid. 26 April. Available at: https://stiritupmagazine.co.uk/leading-lights-adam-reid/ (accessed 22 October 2019).

Strange, N., (1998) Perform, Educate, Entertain: Ingredients of the Cookery Programme Genre, in C. Geraghty and D. Lusted, eds, *The Television Studies Book*. London: Arnold, pp. 301–12.

Strong, H. and R. Wells (2020) Brexit-Related Food Issues in the UK Print Media: Setting the Agenda for Post-Brexit Food Policy. *British Food Journal* 122(7): 2187–201.

Sun, The (2020a) THE VEG of Glory. *Sun*, 11 January: 7.

Sunday Times (2019) The Sunday Times Influencer List 2019. *Sunday Times*, 7 September. Available at: https://www.thetimes.co.uk/article/the-sunday-times-influencer-list-2019-meet-the-uks-top-100-hsmhv8dlp. (accessed 27 February 2020).

Svejenova, S., C. Mazza and M. Planellas (2007) Cooking Up Change in Haute Cuisine: Ferran Adrìa as Institutional Entrepreneur. *Journal of Organizational Behaviour* 28(5): 539–61.

Swan, E. (2020) COVID-19 Foodwork, Race, Gender, Class and Food Justice: An Intersectional Feminist Analysis. *Gender in Management* 35(7/8): 693–703.

Swanson, C. (2015) The U.K.'s Top Selling Cookbook Comes Stateside. *Publishers Weekly*, 27 February. Available at: https://www.publishersweekly.com/pw/by-topic/industry-news/cooking/article/65731-the-u-k-s-top-selling-cookbook-comes-stateside.html (accessed 26 Mar 2020).

Sweeney, T. (2019) Dirty Vegan. *Irish Times*, 26 January. Available at: https://www.irishtimes.com/life-and-style/food-and-drink/dirty-vegan-my-hangover-food-is-linda-mccartney-sausages-and-chips-1.3759001 (accessed 27 February 2020).

Sweney, M. (2017) Jamie Oliver to Launch New Show as Part of Deal with Channel 4. *Guardian*, 20 March. Available at: https://www.theguardian.com/media/2017/mar/20/jamie-oliver-new-show-deal-channel-4-tv (accessed 26 May 2020).

Tandoh, R. (2017) Bad Fad. *Guardian*, 23 January. Available at: https://www.theguardian.com/lifeandstyle/2017/jan/23/bad-fad-ruby-tandoh-on-how-clean-eating-turned-toxic (accessed 30 April 2020).

Tandoh, R. (2019) Pinch of Nom Suddenly Makes Delia and Heston Look at Little Stale. *Guardian*, 29 March. Available at: https://www.theguardian.com/commentisfree/2019/mar/29/pinch-of-nom-delia-heston-cookbook-weight-loss (accessed 20 April 2020).

Taylor, B. (2001) Food in France: From la Nouvelle Cuisine to la Malbouffe, in E. McCaffrey and J. Marks, eds, *French Cultural Debates*. Newark: University of Delaware Press, pp. 52–64.

Thompson, E.P. (1975) Going into Europe. *Sunday Times*, 27 April.

Thompson, M. (2020) So What Now? Black Erasure in the British Food Industry. *Vittles*, 5 June. Available at: https://vittles.substack.com/p/vittles-612-black-erasure-in-the (accessed 8 March 2021).

Thompson, T. (2016) 'I'm a Chef Not a Celebrity. I'm Not Interested in Fame.' *Friday*, 26 February. Available at: https://fridaymagazine.ae/life-culture/people-profiles/i-m-a-chef-not-a-celebrity-i-m-not-interested-in-fame-1.1678614 (accessed 14 October 2019).

Throsby, K. (2020) Pure, White and Deadly: Sugar Addiction and the Cultivation of Urgency. *Food, Culture and Society* 23(1): 11–29.

Turner, G. (2004) *Understanding Celebrity*. London: Sage.

Tominc, A. (2017) *The Discursive Construction of Class and Lifestyle: Celebrity Chef Cookbooks in Post-Socialist Slovenia*. Amsterdam: John Benjamins Publishing.

Tominc, A. ed. (2022a) *Food and Cooking on Early Television in Europe*. London: Routledge.

Tominc, A. (2022b) Food and Cooking on Early Television in Europe: An Introduction, in A. Tominc, ed., *Food and Cooking on Early Television in Europe*, London: Routledge.

Tronto, J. (1989) Women and Caring: What Can Feminists Learn about Morality from Caring?, in A.M. Jaggar and S. Bordo, eds, *Gender/Body/Knowledge*. New Brunswick, NJ: Rutgers University Press, pp. 172–97.

Trussell Trust (2019) End of Year Stats. Available at: https://www.trusselltrust.org/news-and-blog/latest-stats/end-year-stats/ (accessed 11 February 2021).

Tweedy, J. (2020a) Couple Behind Pinch of Nom. *MailOnline*, 7 January. Available at: https://www.dailymail.co.uk/femail/article-7860477/Pinch-Nom-couple-say-called-two-fat-chefs-makes-angry.html (accessed 20 April 2020).

Tweedy, J. (2020b) Bitter Lemons! *MailOnline*, 14 April. Available at: https://www.dailymail.co.uk/femail/article-8217635/Bake-star-Ruby-Tandoh-slams-host-BBCs-new-Daily-Kitchen-Live-Matt-Tebbutt.html (accessed 27 January 2021).

Tyler, I. (2008) Chav Mum, Chav Scum: Class Disgust in Contemporary Britain. *Feminist Media Studies* 8: 17–34.

Tyler, I. (2011) Pramface Girls: The Class Politics of Maternal TV, in H. Wood and B. Skeggs, eds, *Reality Television and Class*. London: BFI, pp. 210–24.

Tyler, I. (2020) *Stigma: The Machinery of Inequality*. London: Zed Books.

Ulver, S. and M. Klasson (2018) Social Magic for Dinner? The Taste Script and Shaping of Foodieness in Netflix's *Chef's Table*, in Z. Arsel and J. Bean, eds, *Taste, Consumption, and Markets: An Interdisciplinary Volume*. New York: Routledge, pp. 38–56.

Usher, B. (2020) Rethinking Microcelebrity: Key Points in Practice, Performance and Purpose. *Celebrity Studies* 11(2): 171–88.

van Ryn, L. (2018) Confronting Food Waste in *Masterchef Australia*: Media Production and Recalcitrant Matter, in M. Phillipov and K. Kirkwood, eds, *Alternative Food Politics: From the Margins to the Mainstream*. Abingdon: Routledge, pp. 216–33.

Vegan Society (n.d.) Statistics. The Vegan Society. Available at: https://www.vegansociety.com/news/media/statistics (accessed 2 March 2020).

Vote Leave Media (2008) Celebrity Chef Jamie Oliver Hates the European Union (EU). Available at: https://www.youtube.com/watch?v=f3qcgAQGbEI&t=1s (accessed 18 May 2021).

Walker, A. (2020) Ben Bradley Urged to Apologise over Free School Meals Tweets. *Guardian*. 24 October. Available at: https://www.theguardian.com/education/2020/oct/24/ben-bradley-under-pressure-to-apologise-over-free-school-meals-tweets (accessed 20 May 2021).

Wall, G. (2018) Putting the Accent on Authenticity: A Case Study of Celebrity Chef Gennaro 'Gino' D'Acampo. *Modern Languages Open* 1: http://doi.org/10.3828/mlo.v0i0.161

Walsh, M.J. and S.A. Baker (2020) Clean Eating and Instagram: Purity, Defilement and the Idealization of Food. *Food, Culture and Society* 23(5): 570–88.

Ward, V. (2018) Try a Man's Kitchen, Top Chef Told Me. *Sunday Telegraph*, 12 August. Available at: https://www.telegraph.co.uk/news/2018/08/11/female-chef-left-seething-michelin-starred-rival-told-take-risk/ (accessed 25 March 2021).

Warde, A. (1997) *Consumption, Food and Taste: Culinary Antinomies and Commodity Culture*. London: Sage.

Warde, A. (2009) Imagining British Cuisine: Representations of Culinary Identity in the Good Food Guide, 1951–2007. *Food, Culture and Society* 12(2): 151–71.

Warin, M. (2011) Foucault's Progeny: Jamie Oliver and the Art of Governing Obesity. *Social Theory and Health* 9: 22–40.

Watson, F. (2020) Jamie Oliver vs Jack Monroe: Why Is Bootstrap Cook Not on Keep Cooking and Carry On? *Express*, 24 March. Available at: https://www.express.co.uk/showbiz/tv-radio/1259177/Jamie-Oliver-Jack-Monroe-Bootstrap-Cook-Keep-Cooking-And-Carry-On-controversy-Channel-4 (accessed 28 January 2021).

Wells, R. and M. Caraher (2014) UK Print Media Coverage of the Food Bank Phenomenon: From Food Welfare to Food Charity? *British Food Journal* 116(9): 1426–45.

Western Mail (2020) 'I'm Proof Vegan Food Doesn't Make You Weak'. *Western Mail*, 11 January: 33.

Whelehan, I. (2000) *Overloaded: Popular Culture and the Future of Feminism*. London: Pluto.

White, F. (1932/1999) *Good Things in England: A Practical Cookery Book for Everyday Use*. London: Persephone.

White, M.P. (1990) *White Heat*. London: Mitchell Beazley.

Wilkes, K. (2021) Eating, Looking and Living Clean: Techniques of White Femininity in Contemporary Neoliberal Food Culture. *Gender, Work and Organization*. Online First: https://doi.org/10.1111/gwao.12620 (accessed 9 February 2021).

Wilkinson, S. (2019) The Oral History of Jamie Oliver's 'The Naked Chef'. *Vice*, 17 April. Available at: https://www.vice.com/en_uk/article/7xgpyb/the-oral-history-of-jamie-olivers-the-naked-chef (accessed 7 July 2020).

Wilson, B. (2017) Why We Fell for Clean Eating. *Guardian*, 11 August. Available at: https://www.theguardian.com/lifeandstyle/2017/aug/11/why-we-fell-for-clean-eating (accessed 30 April 2020).

Wilson, J. (1999) Delia's Omelette in the Dock Again. *The Guardian*, 4 February. Available at: https://www.theguardian.com/uk/1999/feb/04/jamiewilson (accessed 19 June 2020).

Wincott, A. (2016) The Allotment in the Restaurant: The Paradox of Foodie Austerity and Changing Food Values, in P. Bennett and J. McDougall, eds, *Popular Culture and the Austerity Myth: Hard Times Today*. Abingdon: Routledge, pp. 28–41.

Winter, A. (2013) Race, Multiculturalism and the 'Progressive' Politics of London 2012: Passing the 'Boyle Test'. *Sociological Research Online* 18(2): 137–43.

Wise, A. and S. Velayutham (2009) Introduction: Multiculturalism and Everyday Life, in A. Wise and S. Velayutham, eds, *Everyday Multiculturalism*. Basingstoke: Palgrave Macmillan, pp. 1–17.

Withers, P. (2018) 'I'm Angry and Embarrassed!': Jamie Oliver Blasts Brexit amid Fears for Trade Relations. *Express*, 26 November. Available at: https://www.express.co.uk/news/uk/1050709/brexit-news-latest-jamie-oliver-uk-european-union-trade-relations (accessed 12 December 2020).

Woods, J. (2018) The Mighty Bosh! Meet the YouTube Superstars Revolutionizing Our Eating Habits. *Daily Mail*, 25 March. Available at: https://www.dailymail.co.uk/home/you/article-5518231/The-mighty-Bosh-YouTube-stars-revolutionising-eating-habits.html (accessed 27 February 2020).

Woodward, E. (n.d.) About Me. *Deliciously Ella blog* (archived version). Available at: https://web.archive.org/web/20120722060649/http://deliciouslyella.com/about/ (accessed 19 March 2020).

Woodward, E. (2012a) Triple Stuffed Butternut Squash: Vegan, Gluten & Dairy Free. *Deliciously Ella archived blog*. Available at: http://deliciouslyella.com/2012/04/26/stuffed-squash-with-a-rocket-quinoa-pine-nut-and-pomegranate-salad/ (accessed 20 March 2020).

Woodward, E. (2012b) Strawberry, Banana and Cinnamon Muffins. *Deliciously Ella archived blog*. Available at: http://deliciouslyella.com/2012/04/26/strawberry-banana-and-cinnamon-muffins/ (accessed 20 March 2020).

Woodward, E. (2012c) Fresh Vegan Pesto Pasta with Spring Greens: Gluten and Dairy Free. *Deliciously Ella archived blog*. Available at: http://deliciouslyella.com/2012/05/06/fresh-vegan-pesto-pasta/ (accessed 20 Mar 2020).

Woodward, E. (2012d) Raw Brownies: Gluten, Dairy & Sugar Free. *Deliciously Ella archive blog*. Available at: http://deliciouslyella.com/2012/04/29/raw-brownies/ (accessed 20 March 2020).

Woodward, E. (2012e) Wild Rice with Avocado, Cherry Tomatoes, Broccoli and Pomegranates: Vegan. *Deliciously Ella archived blog*. Available at: https://web.archive.org/web/20120918041822/http://deliciouslyella.com/2012/04/29/wild-rice-with-avocado-cherry-tomatoes-broccoli-and-pomegranates/ (accessed 20 March 2020).

Woodward, E. (2012f) Baked Sweet Potato Wedges with Rosemary, Cinnamon and Paprika. *Deliciously Ella archived blog*. Available at: http://deliciouslyella.com/2012/04/27/baked-sweet-potato-wedges-with-guacomole/ (accessed 20 Mar 2020).

Woodward, E. (2012g) Kale Chips. *Deliciously Ella archived blog*. Available at: http://deliciouslyella.com/2012/05/11/kale-chips/ (accessed 20 March 2020).

Woodward, E. (2012h) Avocado Cream. Deliciously Ella archived blog. Available at: http://deliciouslyella.com/2012/05/08/avocado-cream-mayonnaise/ (accessed 20 March 2020).

Woodward, E. (2015a) Deliciously Ella's Healthy Sweet Treats Recipes. *Daily Telegraph*, 2 May. Available at: https://www.telegraph.co.uk/foodanddrink/11574373/Deliciously-Ellas-healthy-sweet-treat-recipes.html (accessed 10 Mar 2020).

Woodward, E. (2015b) Healthy Dinner Party Recipes. *Daily Telegraph*, 3 April. Available at: https://www.telegraph.co.uk/foodanddrink/healthy-recipes/11513903/Deliciously-Ella-healthy-dinner-party-recipes.html (accessed10 Mar 2020).

Woodward, E. (2015c) Afternoon Delight. *Daily Telegraph*. 1 August: 10–11.

Woodward, E. (2016) Deliciously Ella: My New Year's Resolution Every Year? To Ignore Fad Diets. *Daily Telegraph*, 18 January. Available at: https://www.telegraph.co.uk/food-and-drink/features/deliciously-ella-my-resolution-every-year-to-ignore-fad-diets/ (accessed 10 Mar 2020).

Woolcock, N., E. Yeomans, F. Elliott and S. Griffiths (2020) Tory Councils Turn against PM in Battle for Free School Meals. *Times*, 24 October. Available at: https://www.thetimes.co.uk/article/tory-councils-turn-against-pm-in-battle-for-free-school-meals-fnmc9ndsm (accessed 24 January 2021).

Wrenn, C.L. (2019) The Vegan Society and Social Movement Professionalization, 1944–2017. *Food and Foodways* 27(3): 190–210.

Wright, L. (2015) *The Vegan Project: Food, Animals and Gender in the Age of Terror*. Athens, GA: University of Georgia Press.

Wring, D. (2016) From Super-Market to Orwellian Super-State: The Origins and Growth of Newspaper Scepticism, in D. Jackson, E. Thorsen and D. Wring, eds, *EU Referendum Analysis 2016: Media, Voters and the Campaign*. Bournemouth, UK: The Centre for the Study of Journalism, Culture and Community. Available at: http://eprints.bournemouth.ac.uk/24337/1/EU%20Referendum%20Analysis%202016%20-%20Jackson%20Thorsen%20and%20Wring%20v1.pdf (accessed 12 December 2020)

Yeo, G. (2017) Why Clean Eating Is Now a Dirty Word. *Daily Telegraph*, 14 January: 23–4.

Young, S. (2020) Bon Appétit Magazine Issues 'Long-overdue Apology' amid Accusations of Racism. *Independent*, 11 June. Available at: https://www.independent.co.uk/life-style/bon-appetit-racism-apology-adam-rapoport-brownface-photo-a9560266.html (accessed 25 March 2021).

Zagzoule, S. (2019) Back to Basics. *Sun*, 16 June. Available at: https://www.thesun.co.uk/fabulous/food/9275315/ian-theasby-henry-firth-veganism/ (accessed 27 February 2020).

INDEX

Abbots, E.-J. 17, 148, 154
Adams, C. 71
Adrià, F. 15, 19, 20
advertising 34, 41, 72, 112
Allinson, K. (*see* Pinch of Nom)
Allsopp, K. 122
Almila, A.-M. 7, 128
Alston, P. 119–20
Ama, R. 46, 172n9
Americanization 153–6
Anand, A. 145
animal rights 71, 75
animal welfare 77, 92–4, 96, 151–2, 154
Atherton, J. 3, 158
audience research 7, 40–1
austerity 105–24, 149, 157, 159–65, 167–8
    anti-austerity campaigns 120–3, 161
    austerity bloggers 120, 122
    austerity chic 105–6, 110, 120, 122, 123, 124, 149, 161
authenticity 20, 30, 42, 46, 47, 56, 59, 63, 120
Avant-Garde Vegan 45, 70, 73–84

Bainbridge, R. 23
Baker, S. 45, 55
Banet-Weiser, S. 45, 47
Bangladeshi food 138–40
Banks, T. 23
barbeque 82
Barber, D. 26, 27
Barnes, C. 7, 40–1
Barnett, C. 93
Baumann, S. 24, 26, 27, 38, 130, 142
Bavin, C. 115–19
BBC 34–6, 37, 38
beauty 60–1
Bell, D. 85, 87–9, 99, 103, 141–4
Bennett, J. 3, 34, 42, 45, 90
Bentley, A. 149
Bertinelli, V. 43

Big Family Cooking Showdown 23
Billig, M. 125–6
Binns, D. 25
Black Lives Matter 11, 28, 29, 43, 166, 170 n.13
bloggers 47, 48, 51, 54, 55, 56, 57, 59–60, 120, 122
Blumenthal, H. 6, 16, 17, 21, 33, 89
body, the
    body positivity 66–7
    fatness 53, 63–4, 66–7, 112, 114–15
    fatphobia 63, 66–7
    feminine 54, 58, 60–2, 72
    masculine 73, 74–7, 81
    obesity 66–7, 111–15
    slimming diets 52, 58, 60–7, 114
    slimness 53, 61–2, 66
Boiling Point 14
Bombak, A.E. 66
Bonner, F. 36, 41, 42
Borowsky, S. 149
BOSH! 45, 70, 73–4, 76–84
Bosi, C. 28
Bottura, M. 19–20, 22, 26, 27, 158
Boulestin, M. 34
Bourdain, A. 27, 37, 126
Bourdieu, P. 2, 6, 18, 20, 40, 44, 48, 121
Boykoff, M. 5, 86, 93
Bradley, B. 165
Bramall, R. 91, 105, 107, 110, 167
brand-extensions 17–18, 20–1, 34, 41, 86, 91
branding 14–18, 20–1, 24, 34, 41, 44–7, 60, 62–4, 73, 89, 90–2
Braun, V. 56, 78
Brexit 98, 103, 126, 144, 145, 147, 147–57
Britain's Fat Fight 88, 111–15, 123–4
British food 125–6, 128–36, 138–9, 143, 144–5
Britishness 129–32, 135, 137–9, 142, 144, 148, 156, 157

Brockington, D. 86, 93
Brown, L. 16
Brunsdon, C. 38
Butler, D. 136
Burgess, J. 48

Caines, M. 21, 23, 29–30
Cairns, K. 53, 54, 58, 67, 94, 117
Calhoun, C. 151
Cameron, D. 106, 111, 147
Campbell, G. 24
Can't Cook, Won't Cook 38
Cappeliez, M. 54
Carême, M.-A. 5, 14
Caribbean Food Made Easy 145
caring 6, 54, 65, 86, 93–4, 103, 107, 116, 159, 164
    self-care 54, 57, 65, 72, 76
Carlton Food Network 37
Carruthers, S. 56, 78
Casey, E. 137
celebrity 3–4, 14, 19–21, 24, 41–4, 157
    anti-celebrity 62–4, 68
    celebrity capital 44
    celebrity field 44
    celebritization 43–4
    environment celebrities 86, 97, 99
    microcelebrity 45, 47
Channel 4 41, 87–9
chefs 2–3, 21–2 (*see also* culinary field; restaurant industries)
    as artisans 15, 18
    as artists 15, 18–21, 25–7
    chef-proprietors 15
    as cultural entrepreneurs 15
    gender 27–8
    race 27, 28–31
    self-branding 14–15, 44
    social media use 16–17, 44
    visual style 15–16
Chef's Table 14, 24–8, 30
Cherry, L. 124, 163
chicken
    chlorinated 148, 154–7
    production 92–6
    welfare 92–6
Chickens, Hugh … and Tesco too 92, 95–6
Child, J. 171n3
Chinese Food Made Easy 145

Chong, P. 15, 30, 31
Clarke, N. 93
class 40, 55, 65, 67, 93–4, 100–1, 142–4, 156–7 (*see also* austerity)
    new middle classes 6, 40, 91
    working class 93–4, 100–1, 107–11, 114, 142
clean eating 51, 53, 54–64, 65, 67, 70–1, 74, 81
Cloke, P. 93, 124, 163
Cole, M. 72
Coles, B. 148
colonialism 126, 132–5, 141
comfort food 65–6, 78–82
consumer activism 78, 97, 99
Contaldo, G. 141
Contois, E. 52, 56, 71
convenience food 107–8, 117–18, 142
Cook on the Wild Side, A 90
cookbooks 9, 51, 55–6, 62–3
Cooper, J. 16
cosmopolitanism 134, 143, 144, 150, 152
Covid-19 1, 148–9, 157–68
Cowspiracy 77
Cradock, F. 34, 35–6
Craig, G. 91–2, 100
Crawford, R. 53, 57, 58
Cronin, J. 97, 99
culinary capital 4, 6, 19, 161
culinary field 3, 12, 15, 18–22, 24, 25–6, 28–31, 44
cultural appropriation 134, 136, 159
cultural intermediaries 2, 6, 8, 37, 39, 41, 48, 55, 59, 86
Curnutt, H. 23, 24

D'Acampo, G. 43, 141
Daily Kitchen 158–62
Daily Mail 108
David, E. 171n1
Davies, W. 163
Davis, A. 15
De Solier, I. 139
Dejmanee, T. 54
Delia Smith's Cookery Course 35
Deliciously Ella (*see* E. Woodward)
Deller, R.A. 45, 49, 59
democratization 6, 39, 40, 49, 52
Dempsey, S.E. 109, 112

DeSoucey, M. 125, 147, 148
DeVault, M. 116
Dexter, B. 72, 73, 74
Dickinson, R. 5
Dickson-Wright, C. 140
digital food media 7, 44–8, 51, 54, 73–4 (*see also* social media)
   clicktivism 99, 102, 114
   communities 59, 63
   participatory culture 59
dirty foods 51, 64, 65–6, 71, 81–2
Dirty Vegan 70, 73–5, 77, 79–80, 83
Dirty Vegan, The 70, 75, 79–80, 83
Doherty, J. 88, 96, 155
domestic cookery 6, 35, 38–40, 65, 107–8, 110, 129, 144, 159
   'proper meal' 61, 80
domestic labour 6, 35, 38, 54, 65, 93, 101, 116, 118, 159, 161–2
domestic space 6–7, 38, 140, 159
Doyle, J. 72–3
Driessens, O. 43, 44
Drummond, R. 42, 45
dude food 79–80, 81–2
Duffy, B.E. 48, 56
Dufresne, W. 17
Duruz, J. 144

Eat Well for Less 106, 115–19, 123, 167
Ebbrell, B. 46 (*see also* SORTEDfood)
Edwards, J. 147
emotion 86, 93, 103, 151–2, 165, 168
environmental politics 71, 77, 83, 86, 91, 97–103, 118, 155, 168
   sustainability 86, 97–8, 100
ethical consumption 85–6, 90–7, 100, 102, 151–2
'ethnic' cuisines 29–30, 131–6, 138–9, 144–5
Europeanness 141, 143, 153
European Union (EU) 97–9, 147–8, 149–53 (*see also* Brexit)
   anti-EU positions 97–8, 145, 147–8, 150–2
   Euromyths 148, 150
   Euroscepticism, 147–8, 149, 150–2
   Referendum (2016) 141, 145, 147–8, 152
   regulation 97–9, 150–1, 153, 154

Evans, D. 100, 118
Evans, J. 3, 43
Evans, M. 6
experts 39, 48–9, 77, 87
   amateur 46, 49, 59–60
   blogspert 55
   and Brexit 98
   expert patient 56
   lifestyle 5, 87, 89, 90
   ordinary 47, 48, 49, 52, 55

Facebook 62–4
Famuwera, J. 30
farming 92–6, 102, 103, 139, 144, 151, 154–7
Farrer, J. 18, 21
fast food 65, 79, 80, 81, 83, 107–10, 114, 143
Fassnidge, C. 17, 21
Fearnley-Whittingshall, H. 70, 86, 88–103, 105, 121, 127, 130–1, 155, 166–7
   animal welfare 85, 92–6
   environmentalism 97–102
   fish and fishing 96–9
   lifestyle 6, 90–4
   moral entrepreneur 91, 94, 96, 112
   obesity 111–15
Featherstone, K. (*see* Pinch of Nom)
Featherstone, M. 39
feeding work 52, 54, 65, 93, 110, 116–18, 159, 162
Ferguson, P. Parkhurst 5, 14, 15–16
Final Table, The 24
Firth, H. (*see* BOSH!)
fish and fishing 96–9, 148
Flavours of India 35
Floyd, K. 127–8, 131, 140
Floyd on Britain and Ireland 127
food banks 119, 122, 159, 162–3
food celebrities 3–4, 163, 169
Food and Drink 127
Food for Soul 19
foodies 38, 79, 130, 135, 174 n.8
food labelling 95, 97, 112, 151–5
Food Network 37–8
food personalities 3–4
food production 85–6, 89, 91–9, 101–3, 113, 130, 151–2, 154–7
foodscapes 1–2, 44, 163

food standards 148, 153–7
food television 87–9, 156
    campaigning culinary documentaries (CCDs) 85–103, 106–15
    competition formats 12–13, 22–4
    Covid-19 157–62
    documentaries 24–8
    game show formats 38
    global markets 9, 38, 89, 127
    history 5, 34–41
    lifestyle television 4, 5–6, 36–41, 45, 48, 87, 89, 94, 115–19
    and 'ordinary people' 88, 90, 92–4, 115–19
    production 7, 36, 38, 39, 158, 160
    scheduling 34–5, 38
    travelogues 125–45
    vegan 70, 73–8, 80, 83
food waste 99–102
Fort, M. 37
Fox, L. 154
'free from' foods 57, 58, 69
free school meals 163–5, 167
French food 24, 125, 129, 142

Galloping Gourmet, The 36
Garson, B. 43, 46
Garten, I. 42
Gaultier, A. 80
Gelb, D. 25, 26
Geddes, K. 34, 36
gender 27–30, 52, 56, 65, 107–8, 116–17, 139–40, 144, 153
    body 54, 58, 59–62, 74–8, 81
    and class 93–4, 100–1, 107–11
    domestic masculinity 38, 159
    and food television 26–8, 34–6, 38–40, 139–40
    and lifestyle 6–7, 38–40
    mothering 65, 93–4, 108, 110, 116–17, 162
    and veganism 70–84
Gibson, K.E. 109, 112
Giddens, A. 39
Gilbert, J. 110
Gill, Ros 54, 56, 74
Gill, Romy 158
Gillespie, C. 15
Giousmpasoglou, C. 16

Giuffre, P. 28–9
globalization 9, 125, 126, 130, 131, 148
Good Food 38
Good Food Guide 129
Goodman, M. 2, 3, 5, 7, 42, 44, 45, 47, 48, 86, 93, 123, 169
Gordon, Gino and Fred: Road Trip 128
Gordon Ramsay: Shark Bait 97
Gove, M. 144
Great British Bake Off 23, 136–7
Great British Menu 23–4, 127
Green, J. 48
Greenebaum, J. 72, 73, 74, 82
Gualtieri, G. 29–30
Guthman, J. 91

Hafner, D. 139
Hairy Bikers 43, 130–1
Hairy Bikers Food Tour of Britain, The 130–1
Hague, W. 105
Hamilton, L. 119, 121
Hannerz, U. 143
Harben, P. 34, 35
Harjunen, H. 53, 66
Harriott, A. 29, 38, 43
Harris, D. 28–9
Hartnett, A. 22, 23
Hay, J. 101, 109
health 52–62, 64–8, 75–8, 82–3, 107–16, 162
    body 53–4, 60–2, 66, 74–8
    detoxing 57
    eating disorders 58, 61
    fitness 73, 74–5
    healthy eating 52, 53–4, 58–62, 107, 109, 112, 114, 117, 145
    and indulgence 58, 65–6, 78, 81
    lifestyle 53, 55, 58–62, 67, 76–8, 116–17
    mental health 56–7, 65
    NHS 110, 114–15, 124, 162
    nutrition 52, 75–7, 81, 117
    obesity 66, 107–8, 110, 111–15, 162
    wellness 53, 54, 59, 67
healthism 53–4, 57, 66–7, 78, 82, 114
Hearn, A. 45
Hemsley + Hemsley 55
Henderson, F. 105

Hermes, J. 158
Heston's Fishy Feast 97
Highmore, B. 132, 133, 134
Hill, A. 158
Holmes, S. 24
Holst, A. 35
Hopkinson, G. 97, 99
Howarth, A. 148, 163, 166
How to Cook 35
Huang, Ching-He 145
Hugh's Chicken Run 88, 92–5, 100, 101
Hugh's Fish Fight 96–9, 148
Hugh's War on Waste 88, 99–102
Hund, E. 48, 56
Hunt, J. 113
Hussain, N. 1, 42, 47, 70, 136–40

Ibrahim, Y. 119, 148
Ichijo, A. 126, 129
Indian Food Made Easy 145
Inglis, D. 7, 128
Instagram 60, 66–7
Iron Chef 22
Iron Chef America 22
Islamophobia 137–9
Italian food 141–4, 174n18
Italy Unpacked 141

Jackson, P. 110
Jaffrey, M. 35
Jallinoja, P. 70, 83
James Martin's Great British Adventure 130
Jamie's American Road Trip 132
Jamie Does … 141, 142, 144, 150
Jamie Oliver's Food Revolution 9, 89, 109, 110
Jamie Saves our Bacon 151–2
Jamie's Fish Supper 97
Jamie's Fowl Dinners 92
Jamie's Great Britain 131–6, 143
Jamie's Great Escape 132, 141–4
Jamie's Kitchen 87
Jamie's Ministry of Food 88, 98, 106, 107–11, 123, 143, 160
Jamie's Money Saving Meals 143
Jamie's Return to School Dinners 108
Jamie's School Dinners 44, 85, 87–8, 111, 112, 143
Jamie's Sugar Rush 111–15, 123–4

Jaworska, S. 7, 44, 45, 47, 48
Jimmy and the Giant Supermarket 96
Jiro Dreams of Sushi 25
Johnson, B. 111, 152
Johnson, J. 73
Johnston, J. 2, 3, 15, 24, 26, 27, 30, 31, 38, 42, 53, 54, 58, 67, 94, 117, 123, 130, 142, 169
Jones, S. 21, 85, 87–9, 98, 99, 103, 107–11, 168

Keep Cooking and Carry On 158–62
Ken Hom's Chinese Cookery 127
Kerr, G. 36
Kerridge, T. 22, 23, 43, 166, 167, 175 n.14
Ketchum, C. 37
Khan, A. 22, 28, 30–1
Kim, E. 45
King, S. (*see* Hairy Bikers)
Kjaer, K. Meldgaard 53, 57, 143
Klasson, M. 26

Lagerwey, J. 137
Lane, C. 16, 21
Lawson, N. 2, 5, 6, 9, 37, 38, 40, 42–3, 55, 116, 166
Lebesco, K. 6, 53, 113
Lee, N. 16, 27
Lee, R. 136
Leer, J. 130, 132, 134, 135, 143
Leitch, A. 148
Leith, P. 156
Lewis, T. 5, 40, 46, 47, 48, 52, 79, 90–1, 158
lifestyle 5–6, 47, 67, 82–3, 105–6, 121
    calculated hedonism 78, 81
    Covid-19 157, 160–2
    green 86, 90–2
    health 53, 55, 59–62, 66, 76–8, 82–3, 115
    and labour 40
    and leisure 38, 39, 40, 116
    magazines 76
    makeovers 39, 66, 68, 72, 76, 87–8, 92–3, 109, 114, 115–19
Littler, J. 5, 86, 93, 94, 95, 99, 103
Living on the Veg 70, 74, 76–8, 80, 83
Llewellyn, P. 9
Lupton, D. 53, 65
Lygnac, C. 130

MacKendrick, N. 94
McCormick, L. 158, 160
McKenzie, L. 106
McRobbie, A. 60
MAD Symposium 2
Mallmann, F. 27
Malpass, A. 93
Markle, M. 155
Martin, Jessica 120, 122, 159–60, 162
Martin, James 43, 89, 131
Marwick, A. 45
Masterchef 22–3
Masterchef Australia 9, 22–3, 27
Matta, R. 2
May, Jon 124, 163
May, James 43
meat 69, 71–2, 78–82, 151–2
mediatization 43
methodology 7
Michelin Guide 16, 21, 25, 28, 29, 30
migration 132–6, 143
Mills, E. (*see* E. Woodward)
Ministry of Food 110, 160
mobility 128, 136, 140
Monaghan, L.F. 66
Monroe, J. 46
　austerity 107, 120–3, 124, 162–3
　Covid-19 1, 158–62
　poverty 107, 120–3, 124, 162, 166–7
Moran, J. 19, 20, 26
Morgan, K. 72
Morris, M. 144
Moseley, R. 5–6, 35, 38, 39
multi-platforming 34, 36
Murcott, A. 54, 134
Murphy, K. 45, 49, 59
Mycek, M. 73
Myers, D. (*see* Hairy Bikers)
My Kitchen Rules 17

Naccarato, P. 6
Nadiya's British Food Adventure 136–40, 145
Nakayama, N. 27
Naked Chef, The 5, 6, 38–40, 132, 141
nation 125–45, 147–8, 150
　and multiculturalism 126, 130–2,
　　134–6, 138–40, 145
　national identity 125–6, 129–32, 135,
　　137–9, 141–2, 144–5
　nationalism 125–6, 135, 147, 152

national food cultures 125–45
　gastronationalism 125, 148, 155, 157
　and multiculturalism 126, 130–2,
　　134–6, 138–40, 145
　and regional foods 125, 129–31, 143
neoliberalism 53, 54, 57–8, 77, 78, 94, 96,
　102, 109, 111–13, 115, 124, 160, 167
Netflix 9, 24, 26
neophobia 80–1, 118
Nigella Bites 5, 38, 40
Nilsson, M. 26–7
Niva, M. 70, 83
nouvelle cuisine 15

Oakley, G. (*see* Avant-Garde Vegan)
O'Connell, R. 119, 121
Oleshuck, M. 54
Oliver, J. 8–9, 40, 70, 74, 123, 145
　animal welfare 85, 92
　austerity 106, 121, 166–7
　branding 20–1, 43
　Brexit 145, 148–53, 155–6
　British food 131–6
　campaigning 85, 86, 87–9, 98, 107–15,
　　148–53, 155–6
　celebrity 42, 88
　Channel 4 41, 87–9
　Covid-19 1, 158–62
　food poverty 142–3, 166–7
　lifestyle 5–6, 38–41
　masculinity 6, 38
　moral entrepreneur 87, 111–12
　obesity 107–8, 110, 111–13, 115
　social media 44–5, 47
　school meals 85, 87–8, 107–8, 143,
　　166–7
　travelogues 141–4
Oliver's Twist 9
Ommundsen, W. 20
O'Neill, R. 56, 59, 60, 62, 65, 67, 171n1
Operation Hospital Food 89
Optomen 38
ordinariness 39, 42, 67, 68
Oren, T. 22
Ottolenghi, Y. 9
Ouellette, L. 101, 109

Paltrow, G. 43
Parasecoli, F. 25
Parkins, W. 91–2, 142

Patten, M. 34, 35, 110, 160
Patterson, J. 140
People's Supermarket, The 88, 96
Phillipov, M. 17, 90, 96, 127, 130
Pinch of Nom 51, 62–8
Piper, N. 7, 40–1, 109
post-feminism 54, 56, 60–1
Potter, L. 121
Potts-Dawson, A. 88, 96
poverty 109, 111, 119–23, 142–3
    cultural poverty 109, 120–1
    food poverty 100, 106, 114, 118, 119–23, 149, 156, 159, 162–8
pregnancy 60
Presswood, A.L. 47
Preston, M. 26
Pritchard, M. (*see* Dirty Vegan)
Probyn, E. 99
public relations 15, 17, 43, 46
public service broadcasting 34–6, 38–9, 41, 87, 160
publishing 36
Puck, W. 16

race 28–31, 65, 84, 126, 131–8, 145
    and culinary field 28–31
    digital media 47
    racism 31, 84, 131, 137–9, 140, 148–9
    and restaurant industry 28–31
    whiteness 27, 29, 55, 60, 84, 91, 134
racial discrimination 29
racial inequality 30, 164, 166
Rahman, M. 147
Raisborough, H. 113
Ramsay, G. 3, 14, 17, 20–1, 43, 44, 89, 153, 157
Randall, S. 131
Ranta, R. 126, 129
Rashford, M. 1, 149, 163–8, 175 n.14
Rea, A. 45
Ready, Steady, Cook 38
reality TV 22, 43, 66, 87, 91, 106, 109, 122
recycling 100–1
Redzepi, R. 19, 22
Reiner, A. 2
restaurant industries 12–16 (*see also* culinary field)
    Brexit 153
    changes in 15–16
    and Covid-19 1, 149

    economics 16, 19, 21, 22, 23
    gender 28–31
    race 28–31
    work 22
restaurant reviewing 16, 30
Reid, A. 23
Redmond, S. 24
Rhodes, G. 35, 39, 43, 128, 129
Rhodes Around Britain 35, 128, 129
Rick Stein's Food Heroes 128–9, 130
River Cottage 6, 90–2, 100, 121, 130–1
Rodney, A. 15, 30, 31, 53, 54, 55, 57
Rogers, R.A. 72
Roots, L. 136, 145
Rossato, L. 127
Rousseau, S. 5
Roux Jr, M. 3, 18
rural 6, 90–1, 127, 130–1, 134, 157

Said, E. 141
Sarno, D. 83
Scannell, P. 42
Schoenhoff, S. 45
Scott, E. 78, 82
Second World War 105, 110, 149, 160, 167
sexual harassment 28
Shewry, B. 26
Sikka, T. 57, 59, 61, 78, 81
Silk, M. 135
Silverstone, A. 72–3
Simply Nigella 55
Skeggs, B. 140, 165
Skey, M. 150
Skinner, Z. 128
Slater, N. 105, 121
slow food 25
Smith, A. 55, 56
Smith, D. 2, 3, 35, 36, 39, 128, 149, 150
Smith, G. 7
Smyth, C. 24
social media 24, 44–8, 51, 56, 62–4, 70, 99, 137–8, 158 9
    marketing techniques 63–4
    influencers 51–2, 54–5, 59, 62
SORTEDfood 46–7
Stein, R. 127, 128–9, 130, 131
Stone, C. 17
Strange, N. 36, 127
sugar 56–7, 58, 61, 112–13, 115

superfoods 55, 57, 76
supermarkets 17, 83, 94–6, 101, 112
Swan, E. 148–9, 162
sweetness 58, 61, 140

Tandoh, R. 55, 62, 63–4
Tebbutt, M. 1, 159–61
television personalities 37, 41, 42, 90
terroir 26, 130
Theasby, I. (*see* BOSH!)
Thompson, E.P. 152
Thompson, M. 30
thrift 93, 101, 105–6, 100, 118–19, 121, 122, 161–22
Throsby, K. 112, 115
Thunberg, G. 86
Tominc, A. 9
Top Chef 22, 23
Turner, G. 42
TV Dinners 90
Two Fat Ladies 128, 140
Two Greedy Italians 141
Tyler, I. 100, 101, 106, 109

UK Food 37
Ulver, S. 26
Usher, B. 47

Van Ryn, L. 7
veganism 10, 46, 57, 58, 69–84
veganuary 69, 70
Velayutham, S. 138
Vinnari, M. 70, 83
vloggers 45–7

Wall, G. 141
Wallace, G. 115–19
Walsh, M. 45, 55
Warde, A. 78, 81, 129
Warin, M. 113
Westall, C. 121
White, M.-P. 27, 153
Wicks, J. 155
Wilkes, K. 55, 60, 171 n.1
Williams, A. 124, 163
Winch, A. 60
Wincott, A. 105, 121, 123
Wise, A. 138
Wood, H. 165
Woodward, E. 45, 46, 51, 55–62, 63, 64–5, 66, 67, 70, 72
Worrall Thompson, A. 43, 129
Wrenn, C.L. 71

YouTube 9, 44–7

Milton Keynes UK
Ingram Content Group UK Ltd.
UKHW021304060324
439036UK00006B/95